Mathematics for Christian Living Series

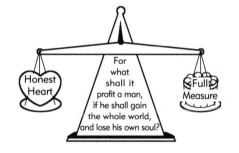

Mathematics for Christian Living Series

Gaining Skill With Arithmetic

Grade 5

Rod and Staff Publishers, Inc.

Hwy. 172, Crockett, Kentucky 41413

Telephone: (606) 522-4348

Acknowledgments

We are indebted to God for the vision of the need for a *Mathematics for Christian Living Series* and for His enabling grace. Charitable contributions from many churches have helped to cover the expenses for research and development.

This revision was written by Sister Sandra Bauman. The brethren Marvin Eicher, Jerry Kreider, and Luke Sensenig served as editors. Brother Lester Miller, Brother Timothy Conley, and Sister Twila Hostetter drew the illustrations. The work was evaluated by a panel of reviewers and tested by teachers in the classroom. Much effort was devoted to the production of the book. We are grateful for all who helped to make this book possible.

–The Publishers

Table of Contents

Chapter 8 Adding and Subtracting Unlike Fractions

Chapter 9 More Division by Two-Digit Divisors

Chapter 10 Decimals

Chapter 11 Ratios

Chapter 12 Multiplication and Division of Fractions

Chapter 13 Bible Measure and Metric Measure

Chapter 14 Multiplication and Division of Decimals

Chapter 15 Geometry and Square Measure

Chapter 16 Graphs and Scale Drawings

Chapter 17 Reinforcement and Enrichment

Chapter 1

Survey of the Four Number Processes

Study to shew thyself approved unto God, a workman that needeth not to be ashamed, rightly dividing the word of truth.
(2 Timothy 2:15)

1. Reviewing Addition

Addition is one of the four basic processes of arithmetic. A thorough knowledge of addition is necessary to understand the other three processes: subtraction, multiplication, and division. This page will show how much you remember about addition.

A. *You may use folded paper to write the answers for rows 1–3. Ask your teacher how to do it. If there are any addition facts you do not know immediately, study them and write them 5 times.*

1.

8	5	9	7	8	6	8	9	4
+ 6	+ 7	+ 8	+ 9	+ 7	+ 7	+ 8	+ 5	+ 7

2.

5	8	4	9	7	5	3	8	9
+ 6	+ 5	+ 8	+ 9	+ 3	+ 8	+ 9	+ 9	+ 6

3.

5	8	4	2	9	3	6	1
7	3	5	6	4	3	4	6
6	4	3	5	4	5	3	3
+ 4	+ 3	+ 8	+ 7	+ 5	+ 7	+ 7	+ 9

B. *Copy and add carefully.*

4.

45	93	27	56	88	19
78	22	53	34	28	45
+ 43	+ 77	+ 16	+ 85	+ 53	+ 54

5.

9,456	4,328	5,019	7,653	6,845
+ 5,923	+ 7,519	+ 6,596	+ 8,748	+ 2,885

6.

856	340	928	476	582
453	895	466	466	945
+ 549	+ 467	+ 375	+ 525	+ 536

Telling Time

When God first made the earth, He also created time. "And the <u>evening</u> and the <u>morning</u> were the first <u>day</u>." The three underlined words are units of time.

Every day we use numbers to tell time. The clock shows the time for classes, recess, and dismissal time at school.

Times can be written in two ways, as shown in the box.

6 o'clock 6:00	half past 7 . . . . .7:30
quarter after 10 . . . .10:15	twenty (minutes) after 4 . . . .4:20
quarter till 10 . . . . . .9:45	twenty (minutes) till 4 . . . . . .3:40

A.M. or P.M. is often included with time.
   A.M. time is from 12:00 midnight until 12:00 noon.
   P.M. time is from noon until midnight.

C. *Do these exercises with time.*

7. Write these times with numbers and A.M. or P.M.
   a. 3 o'clock in the morning
   b. 10 minutes after 7 in the evening
   c. quarter till 11 at night
   d. 25 minutes after 1 o'clock in the afternoon
   e. 5 minutes till 9 in the morning

8. What times are shown on these clocks?

a.   b.   c.   d.   e.

D. *Solve these reading problems.*

9. There are 13 fifth graders at Felton Christian School. On the first day of school, each pupil received 7 textbooks to use that year. How many books in all did the fifth graders receive?

10. Grades 4 to 6 are in Room 2. There are 8 pupils in Grade 4, 13 pupils in Grade 5, and 9 in Grade 6. Altogether, how many pupils are in Room 2?

2. More Work With Addition

Study this box to review facts you should know about addition.

---

1. In an addition problem, the numbers added are **addends.** The answer is the **sum.**

2. Addends can be grouped in any order, and the sum will be the same.

   $$17 + 24 = 24 + 17 \qquad 8 + 6 + 5 + 4 = 4 + 5 + 6 + 8$$

3. Regrouping addends is a good way to check addition problems.

4. Regrouping addends makes addition easier, especially if we can make groups of 10. To add $7 + 8 + 3 + 7$, think:

   $$7 + 8 \text{ is } 15; \qquad 3 + 7 \text{ is } 10; \qquad 15 + 10 \text{ is } 25.$$

The problems in Part A are not basic facts, but they are based on addition facts. You should be able to do the adding mentally. When you add columns of numbers, you use this kind of mental addition often.

$13 + 5 = ?$	$16 + 4 = ?$
Think: $3 + 5 = 8$	Think: $6 + 4 = 10$
$\qquad 13 + 5 = 18$	I must carry 1, $16 + 4 = 20$

A. Write the answers only. You may use folded paper.

1.	$4 + 5$	$14 + 5$	$24 + 5$	$44 + 5$	$74 + 5$
2.	$7 + 3$	$17 + 3$	$37 + 3$	$47 + 3$	$67 + 3$
3.	$17 + 4$	$18 + 8$	$15 + 5$	$19 + 7$	$16 + 8$
4.	$14 + 9$	$27 + 7$	$29 + 5$	$17 + 8$	$24 + 6$
5.	$10 + 5$	$10 + 15$	$17 + 10$	$14 + 12$	$13 + 11$

B. Add these columns, starting at the top. Write the answers on folded paper. Then check your work by adding from the bottom.

6.	8	4	9	7	5	2	6
	6	7	8	5	8	4	3
	5	6	3	7	4	7	9
	+ 4	+ 9	+ 4	+ 8	+ 6	+ 9	+ 4

C. Group the addends in any order. Write the answers on folded paper.

7.	8	7	4	9	3	6	5
	6	3	8	5	8	9	7
	3	9	9	4	6	5	5
	+ 7	+ 4	+ 6	+ 9	+ 4	+ 6	+ 9

D. *Copy and add. Regroup addends when you can.*

8.

		84	✕ 68			
∧56	73	25	72	329	475	∧613
77	89	57	46	450	368	523
+ 94	+ 31	+ 65	+ 37	+ 254	+ 732	+ 865

9.

∧6,849	4,938	9,023	∧ 4,187	✕ 3,265
3,265	3,186	4,583	346	5,123
+ 1,455	+ 7,142	+ 3,644	+ 2,586	+ 499

E. *Fill in the blanks.*

10. The answer to an addition problem is called the _____ .

11. The addends in 7 + 8 = 15 are _____ and _____ .

12. 43 + 8 is 51, so 8 + 43 = _____ .

13. 6 + 5 + 4 = 4 + 5 + _____ .

General Review

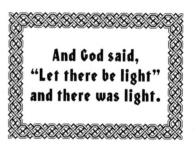

And God said,
"Let there be light"
and there was light.

F. *Do these exercises with time.*

14. Would you probably be in school at 2:00 A.M.?

15. Write **half past 12** with numbers.

16. How many minutes are in a quarter hour?

17. How long does the minute hand take to travel from 2 to 4?

18. Tell what times are shown on the clocks below.

a. b. c. d. e.

G. *Solve these reading problems.*

19. A small box of cereal costs $1.49 and a large box costs $2.65. What is the cost of 3 small boxes?

20. How much more do two small boxes of cereal cost than one large box? (See number 19.)

3. Review of Subtraction

Subtraction, the second of the four processes of arithmetic, is the opposite of addition. If you know the addition facts well, subtraction facts will be rather easy.

You cannot subtract a large number from a smaller one. Always use borrowing if the digit in any place is larger than the digit from which you are subtracting.

Study the problems in the box to review the borrowing process. Remember that when you cross out a digit to the left and write 1 beside the right-hand digit, you are adding 10 to the right-hand digit.

5 13	7 9	8 6	6 9 9
$\cancel{6}\cancel{4}^1 0$	$\cancel{8}\cancel{0}^1 2$	$\cancel{9},\cancel{2}\,\cancel{7}^1 4$	$\cancel{7},\cancel{0}\cancel{0}^1 0$
- 2 5 9	- 3 8 5	- 8,6 3 8	- 4,3 6 1
3 8 1	4 1 7	6 3 6	2,6 3 9

A. *Using folded paper, write answers only for these subtraction facts. Study them until you know them well.*

1.
9	8	7	10	9	13	12	11	18
-7	-5	-3	-6	-4	-8	-4	-7	-9

2.
11	13	15	12	10	14	17	16	14
-9	-6	-8	-7	-8	-7	-9	-7	-5

B. *Copy and subtract, borrowing where necessary.*

3.
84	118	450	721	800	902
- 55	- 37	- 257	- 681	- 394	- 267

4.
683	719	136	900	785	532
- 547	- 566	- 88	- 228	- 384	- 246

5.
640	501	400	739	964	823
- 265	- 489	- 234	- 144	- 627	- 475

Addition and Subtraction in Reading Problems

C. *Write* add *or* subtract **to tell how you would solve these problems if you had all the information you needed.**

6. How much farther does Harry live from school than Jacob does?

7. What is the total cost for the items Father bought?

8. How much change did Father receive from $20.00?

9. How much money did Father have left?

10. How much more did the lamp cost after the sale was over?

11. How many people were in all three rooms?

12. What is the sum?

13. What is the difference between their weights?

14. How much do both boys weigh together?

D. *Solve the problems below. Show your work on your paper.*

15. Water freezes at 32° F. and boils at 212° F. What is the difference between the freezing point and the boiling point of water?

16. One morning the temperature was 47°. By afternoon the temperature had risen 24°. What was the temperature in the afternoon?

17. God created chickens to maintain a body temperature of 105°. If the air temperature is 39°, how many degrees warmer is a chicken than the surrounding air?

18. Eugene gathers the eggs in the chicken house each day. On Monday he found 4 eggs in one nest, 8 in another nest, 5 eggs in a third nest, 3 eggs in the fourth, and 6 in the last nest. How many eggs did Eugene gather on Monday?

19. On Tuesday Eugene found 33 eggs in the chicken house, and on Wednesday he found 39. How many eggs did he gather on both days?

20. Altogether Eugene's family has 40 chickens. Twelve of them are old hens and the rest are young hens. How many young hens are there?

*21. Eugene's father estimates that the cost of chicken feed each day is about $1.75. How much is spent for feed in a week?

4. More Work With Subtraction

This box reviews several facts you should know about subtraction.

1. In a subtraction problem, the top number is the **minuend**, and the number taken from it is the **subtrahend**. The answer is called the **difference** or the **remainder**.	72 (minuend) $-$ 18 (subtrahend) 54 (difference)
2. Subtraction can be expressed in different ways. The problem above could be read *72 minus 18* or *72 take away 18* or *18 from 72* or *18 subtracted from 72* or *72 decreased by 18*.	
3. Addition can be used to check subtraction. Add the difference and the subtrahend, and the sum should equal the minuend.	54 $+$ 18 72

A. *Write the answers only, using folded paper.*

1.
12	10	15	17	11	16	13	14	12
$-$ 8	$-$ 6	$-$ 9	$-$ 8	$-$ 5	$-$ 8	$-$ 7	$-$ 5	$-$ 3

B. *Copy in straight columns and subtract.*

2.
600	713	905	162	460
$-$ 288	$-$ 347	$-$ 789	$-$ 85	$-$ 155

3.
8,000	4,631	7,020	8,509	6,250
$-$ 2,815	$-$ 3,267	$-$ 4,575	$-$ 2,836	$-$ 3,447

C. *Do these subtractions.*

4. a. Subtract 345 from 792.   **b.** From 258 subtract 149.

5. a. Take 77 from 395.   **b.** 182 decreased by 96.

6. a. 164 minus 49.   **b.** 480 from 700.

D. *Copy, subtract, and check by addition, following the pattern in the sample problem.*

7.
6 13 9 7,40 1 1 $-$ 2,684 ⎣4,717⎦ 7,401	6,430 $-$ 1,359	7,000 $-$ 5,998	9,012 $-$ 3,849	8,396 $-$ 5,748

General Review

E. *Follow the directions.*

8. Write answers only. Regroup where you can.

6	7	4	3	2	0	9
8	4	9	5	8	5	3
3	8	5	8	7	8	9
+ 4	+ 7	+ 6	+ 9	+ 9	+ 6	+ 1

9. Copy and add.

57	84	297	328	4,653	3,582
64	95	562	643	7,855	8,417
+ 89	+ 27	+ 448	+ 325	+ 1,674	+ 4,689

10. Write numerals for these words.

  a. two thousand, twenty-five
  b. nine thousand, six hundred
  c. eleven thousand, four hundred fifty
  d. seven thousand, eight

F. *Write the correct answers.*

11. The answer to a subtraction problem is called the _____ .

12. The answer to an addition problem is the _____ .

13. Look at this problem: 78 – 16 = 62.
The subtrahend is _____ , and the minuend is _____ .

14. True or false: The problem in number 13 could be read "78 from 16 is 62."

15. Which digit in this number is in thousands' place? 56,409

16. What number is 100 more than 7,213?

17. Is 6:00 A.M. in the morning or in the evening?

18. A quarter till 9 is written with numerals as _____ .

19. Write the times shown these clocks.

a.   b.   c.   d.   e.

5. Reviewing Place Value to Hundred Millions

Study the grid below to review the number places to hundred millions. Each place is ten times greater than the place to its right.

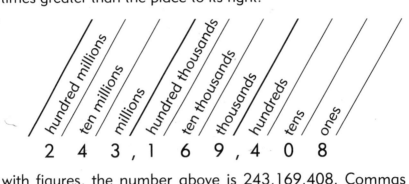

Written with figures, the number above is 243,169,408. Commas divide the number into groups of three places, called **periods,** beginning at the right. Commas make the number easier to read because the periods can be easily seen at a glance.

The number above is read "Two hundred forty-three million, one hundred sixty-nine thousand, four hundred eight." Notice that when the number is written with words, commas are again used to separate the periods. Hyphens are used for numbers like "forty-three."

A. *Read these numbers.*

1. a. 14,000,000   b. 34,602   c. 101,800,716

2. a. 26,635,401   b. 440,632,323   c. 880,444,921

3. a. 700,000,000   b. 508,060,010   c. 650,000,013

B. *Copy these numbers, placing commas correctly. Read the numbers.*

4. a. 736452   b. 300300   c. 40004000   d. 2020202

5. a. 2345678   b. 11111111   c. 637046189   d. 100001100

C. *Do these exercises.*

6. Tell what the 6 stands for in each number. (The first answer is 6,000.)

    a. 36,710   b. 843,627   c. 132,605,829   d. 346,578,021

7. Tell what the 3 stands for in each number of exercise 6.

8. Write the number that is one more than each of these. (If you have trouble, write the number on your paper and add 1.)

    a. 999   b. 9,999   c. 99,999   d. 999,999   e. 2,000,000

9. Write numerals for these number words.

    a. one hundred eighteen thousand, fifteen

    b. nine hundred million, two hundred two

    c. thirty-one million, five hundred thirty-six thousand

    d. eighty-four million, three hundred sixty thousand, twelve

    e. one hundred ten million, ten thousand, one hundred one

Reviewing Multiplication

D. *Write the answers only, using folded paper.*

10.
7	9	5	8	4	6	6	9	5
× 2	× 6	× 6	× 4	× 4	× 4	× 6	× 3	× 5

11.
7	9	6	9	7	7	8	8	7
× 6	× 5	× 3	× 4	× 3	× 4	× 5	× 6	× 5

*Study the 0's to 6's facts until you can answer them in 2 minutes.

Refresh your memory of the multiplication process by studying the box below.

$$
\begin{array}{r}
426 \\
\times\ 6 \\
\hline
2{,}556
\end{array}
$$

    1. Multiply 6 × 6. Write 6 in ones' place and carry 3.

    2. Multiply 6 × 2. Add 3. Write 5 in tens' place and carry 1.

    3. Multiply 6 × 4. Add 1. Write 25.

E. *Copy and multiply. Multiply the ones first, then the tens, . . .*

12.
32	58	43	47	73	15
× 9	× 2	× 3	× 5	× 6	× 6

13.
74	87	58	96	60	85
× 4	× 3	× 6	× 4	× 9	× 5

14.
146	679	825	963	796
× 5	× 2	× 3	× 6	× 4

15. Mr. Sims' car can travel 325 miles on one tank of gasoline. At that rate, how far can the Sims family travel on 4 tanks of gasoline?

6. More Work With Multiplication

Study the box below to review some facts about multiplication.

> **1.** The numbers multiplied are called **factors.** The answer is the **product.**   factor × factor = product
>
> **2.** **Multiplier** and **multiplicand** are other names for the factors.
> multiplier × multiplicand = product
>
> multiplicand
> × multiplier
> product
>
> **3.** Multiplication is a fast way of adding the same number again and again.   6 + 6 + 6 + 6 + 6 + 6 + 6 = 7 × 6 = 42
>
> **4.** Exchanging the factors in a multiplication problem does not change the answer.   11 × 42 = 42 × 11
> Exchanging factors can be used to check multiplication.

A. *Do this exercise.*

1. What is 8 in each problem? Write **multiplier, multiplicand,** or **product.**

   a. 3 × 8 = 24   b. 4 × 2 = 8   c.   7   d.   8
                                            × 8   × 9
                                            56   72

B. *Write the answers only.*

2. 7   5   3   9   6   4   7   8   6
       × 6   × 9   × 8   × 3   × 6   × 7   × 5   × 4   × 4

3. 8   7   9   6   8   9   7   4   6
       × 8   × 7   × 8   × 9   × 7   × 9   × 9   × 9   × 8

*Study the 6's to 9's facts until you can answer them in 2 minutes.

C. *Copy and multiply.*

4.   465   320   953   712   842
        × 7   × 6   × 5   × 8   × 4

5.   920   385   718   948   753
        × 7   × 4   × 8   × 6   × 7

6. 7,859   1,345   6,820   9,413   1,478
        × 3   × 6   × 6   × 8   × 5

General Review

D. *Follow the directions.*

7. Copy and subtract. Box your answer, and check by addition.

8,000	4,720	7,106	8,329	6,052
− 7,254	− 2,589	− 3,858	− 6,254	− 1,947

8. Write the answers only.

8	6	7	4	1	9	3	5
6	3	4	6	7	5	7	7
4	9	7	8	6	5	9	8
+ 5	+ 4	+ 8	+ 9	+ 7	+ 5	+ 6	+ 4

9. Write numerals for these number words.
   a. one hundred eleven million, ten thousand
   b. twelve million, one hundred twelve thousand, twelve
   c. one million, one thousand, one
   d. three hundred million, four hundred ninety-eight
   e. seventy-five thousand, seventy-five

10. Answer **yes** or **no**.
   a. Would people eat breakfast at 7:00 P.M.?
   b. Are there 60 hours in a day?
   c. Does the 3 in 643,210 stand for 3,000?
   d. Are 17 and 8 addends in 17 − 8 = 9?
   e. Could someone have a birthday on February 29?

E. *Solve these problems.*

11. In 1912 the 882-foot-long *Titanic* made its first voyage across the Atlantic Ocean. It hit an iceberg that made a 300-foot-long gash in the ship's side. How many feet on the side of the ship were not gashed by the iceberg?

12. Some people escaped from the sinking *Titanic* on lifeboats. Twelve people were on one boat, 28 people on another, and 40 people in a third boat. In all, how many people, were on the three lifeboats?

13. One of the 3 boats was made to hold 40 people, and the other two boats could each have held 65 people. How many people could have been on the 3 boats if the boats had been full?

7. Multiplication With Two-Digit Multipliers

Study the problem in the box to review multiplication with a two-digit multiplier.

Example 74 x 58 ——— 592 370 ——— 4,292	**1.** Multiply 8 x 74. You get 592. 592 is the first **partial product.** **2.** Multiply 5 x 74. You get 370. 370 is the second **partial product.** Because 5 is in the tens' place, write the 0 of 370 in the tens' column. **3.** Add the two partial products to find the **product.**

A. *Copy and multiply, following the example above. Be sure to keep the columns straight.*

1. $\quad$ 30 $\qquad$ 52 $\qquad$ 17 $\qquad$ 65 $\qquad$ 81
    $\quad$ x 45 $\qquad$ x 78 $\qquad$ x 46 $\qquad$ x 11 $\qquad$ x 84

2. $\quad$ 44 $\qquad$ 72 $\qquad$ 36 $\qquad$ 90 $\qquad$ 25
    $\quad$ x 49 $\qquad$ x 37 $\qquad$ x 85 $\qquad$ x 57 $\qquad$ x 70

3. $\quad$ 32 $\qquad$ 84 $\qquad$ 79 $\qquad$ 18 $\qquad$ 60
    $\quad$ x 19 $\qquad$ x 52 $\qquad$ x 20 $\qquad$ x 55 $\qquad$ x 39

B. *Write the answers only.*

4. $\quad$ 8 $\quad$ 7 $\quad$ 6 $\quad$ 4 $\quad$ 9 $\quad$ 7 $\quad$ 9 $\quad$ 8 $\quad$ 6
    $\quad$ x 8 $\quad$ x 7 $\quad$ x 9 $\quad$ x 7 $\quad$ x 8 $\quad$ x 9 $\quad$ x 9 $\quad$ x 7 $\quad$ x 8

5. $\quad$ 10 $\quad$ 11 $\quad$ 10 $\quad$ 10 $\quad$ 7 $\quad$ 9 $\quad$ 11 $\quad$ 10 $\quad$ 11
    $\quad$ x 7 $\quad$ x 4 $\quad$ x 10 $\quad$ x 11 $\quad$ x 6 $\quad$ x 4 $\quad$ x 9 $\quad$ x 8 $\quad$ x 11

6. $\quad$ 12 $\quad$ 12 $\quad$ 11 $\quad$ 12 $\quad$ 12 $\quad$ 12 $\quad$ 12 $\quad$ 12 $\quad$ 12
    $\quad$ x 7 $\quad$ x 4 $\quad$ x 12 $\quad$ x 10 $\quad$ x 12 $\quad$ x 8 $\quad$ x 6 $\quad$ x 5 $\quad$ x 9

If you do not know the answers to some of the multiplication facts in rows 4–6, look at the page of facts at the back of the book. Then write those facts 5 times on another paper.

General Review

C. *Do these exercises.*

7. Write this number, using words: 13,130,003.

8. Is 3:00 at night 3:00 A.M. or 3:00 P.M.?

9. Add 8 to each number.

    a. 9   **b.** 6   **c.** 17   **d.** 11   **e.** 15   **f.** 22   **g.** 28

10. Write the letters of the words in the columns at the left. After each letter, write the number or numbers from the problems that fit with the word.

a. minuend	**f.** partial product		
b. sum	**g.** multiplier		
c. subtrahend	**h.** difference		
d. product	**i.** multiplicand		
e. addend			

$$
\begin{array}{r} 41 \\ \times\,32 \\ \hline 82 \\ 123 \\ \hline 1{,}312 \end{array}
\qquad
\begin{array}{r} 63 \\ -\,49 \\ \hline 14 \end{array}
\qquad
\begin{array}{r} 95 \\ +\,88 \\ \hline 183 \end{array}
$$

D. *Solve these reading problems.*

11. How much do 6 bags of feed weigh if each bag weighs 50 pounds?

12. If one bag of feed costs $7.69, what is the cost of 3 bags?

13. In science the fifth graders learned that God made all the planets to travel around the sun. The length of time required to travel once around the sun is a year. On the planet Earth, one year is 365 days. On the planet Mercury, one year is only 88 Earth days. How much longer is our year than a year on Mercury?

14. If a baby is as old as 4 Mercury years, how many days old is the baby?

15. The planet Venus has a year of about 225 Earth days. How much shorter is that than a year on Earth?

16. A year on the planet Mars is 687 Earth days. Which is longer: one year on Mars or two years on Earth?

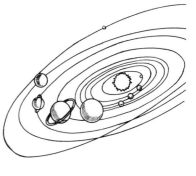

17. At the same time that God keeps the planets traveling around the sun, He also causes the sun to move through space at a speed of about 170 miles per second. At that rate, how far does the sun travel in 5 seconds?

8. Reviewing Division Facts

Study the box to review some facts you should know about division.

1. In a division problem, the number being divided is the **dividend**, the number it is divided by is the **divisor,** and the answer is the **quotient.**

$$dividend \div divisor = quotient \qquad divisor \overline{)dividend}^{\,quotient}$$

2. Division is a fast way of subtracting the same number again and again. $12 \div 3 = 12 - 3 - 3 - 3 - 3$

3. Division is the opposite of multiplication. To check division, multiply the quotient by the divisor. The product should equal the dividend.

$$42 \div 7 = 6$$
and
$$6 \times 7 = 42$$

A. *Write the answers only to these division facts.*

1. $4\overline{)8}$ $5\overline{)30}$ $2\overline{)18}$ $6\overline{)6}$ $3\overline{)27}$ $5\overline{)25}$

2. $5\overline{)0}$ $2\overline{)10}$ $3\overline{)24}$ $4\overline{)24}$ $6\overline{)24}$ $6\overline{)42}$

3. $5\overline{)40}$ $6\overline{)54}$ $3\overline{)18}$ $3\overline{)12}$ $5\overline{)45}$ $6\overline{)48}$

4. $16 \div 4$ $8 \div 2$ $30 \div 6$ $35 \div 5$

5. $28 \div 4$ $5 \div 1$ $21 \div 3$ $36 \div 6$

*Study the 1's to 6's facts until you can answer them in 2 minutes.

B. *Copy and multiply.*

6.
$$\begin{array}{r} 579 \\ \times\ 6 \\ \hline \end{array} \qquad \begin{array}{r} 426 \\ \times\ 8 \\ \hline \end{array} \qquad \begin{array}{r} 7{,}315 \\ \times\ 9 \\ \hline \end{array} \qquad \begin{array}{r} 2{,}980 \\ \times\ 5 \\ \hline \end{array} \qquad \begin{array}{r} 8{,}743 \\ \times\ 8 \\ \hline \end{array}$$

7.
$$\begin{array}{r} 19 \\ \times 14 \\ \hline \end{array} \qquad \begin{array}{r} 44 \\ \times 58 \\ \hline \end{array} \qquad \begin{array}{r} 37 \\ \times 76 \\ \hline \end{array} \qquad \begin{array}{r} 95 \\ \times 52 \\ \hline \end{array} \qquad \begin{array}{r} 86 \\ \times 31 \\ \hline \end{array}$$

8.
$$\begin{array}{r} 90 \\ \times 99 \\ \hline \end{array} \qquad \begin{array}{r} 56 \\ \times 15 \\ \hline \end{array} \qquad \begin{array}{r} 91 \\ \times 83 \\ \hline \end{array} \qquad \begin{array}{r} 29 \\ \times 50 \\ \hline \end{array} \qquad \begin{array}{r} 42 \\ \times 76 \\ \hline \end{array}$$

Reviewing Roman Numerals

In Grade 4 you studied the following five digits for writing Roman numerals. (The numerals we use most are called Arabic numerals.)

| I = 1 | V = 5 | X = 10 | L = 50 | C = 100 |

Review these facts and rules about Roman numerals.

1. Roman numerals do not have place value.

2. If a digit is **followed** by an equal or smaller digit, **add** the values. CC = 200 CLX = 160

3. If a smaller digit comes **before** a larger one, **subtract** the smaller value from the larger.   XC = 100 – 10, or 90

4. If a smaller digit is **between** two larger ones, **subtract** the smaller digit from the one that follows it.   CXC = 190

5. Do not repeat a digit more than three times.   40 is written XL, not XXXX.

6. Never repeat or subtract V or L.   VV and VX are not correct.

7. Never subtract more than one digit.   8 is VIII not IIX

8. Use I before V or X, the next two higher digits.   Do not use I before L or C.

C. *Change these Arabic numerals to Roman numerals.*

9. a. 18   b. 81   c. 37   d. 73   e. 11   f. 99

10. a. 40   b. 58   c. 65   d. 26   e. 14   f. 42

D. *Change these Roman numerals to Arabic numerals.*

11. a. XC   b. LXXXI   c. XXXVIII   d. LXX   e. XLVI

12. a. VIII   b. XXV   c. LXIV   d. XIII   e. XXXIX

13. a. LI   b. XLIX   c. XCII   d. LXXXIV   e. LVII

14. What times do these clocks show?

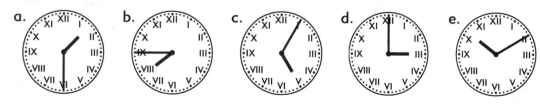

9. Reviewing Long Division

Review the steps of the long division process in the box below.

The Six Steps of Long Division

1. **Divide.** Think: There are no 3's in 1. How many 3's are in 14? Write 4 above the 4 in 14.

2. **Multiply.** Think: What is 4 times 3? Write 12 below the 14 of the dividend.

3. **Compare.** Think: Is 12 less than 14? Yes.

4. **Subtract.** 14 minus 12 is 2. Write 2 below the 12.

5. **Compare.** Think: Is 2 less than the divisor? Yes.

6. **Bring down.** Bring down the 4 from the dividend and write it beside the remainder.

$$
\begin{array}{r} 4 \\ 3\overline{)144} \end{array}
\qquad
\begin{array}{r} 4 \\ 3\overline{)144} \\ \underline{12} \\ 2 \end{array}
$$

$$
\begin{array}{r} 4 \\ 3\overline{)144} \\ 12 \\ 24 \end{array}
\qquad
\begin{array}{r} 48 \\ 3\overline{)144} \\ 12 \\ 24 \\ \underline{24} \\ 0 \end{array}
$$

Now go through the steps again, using 24 as the dividend. 24 minus 24 is 0, so there is no remainder. There are no more digits in the dividend to bring down. The answer to 144 ÷ 3 is 48.

A large division problem may have more digits in the dividend. Bring down one digit at a time, and go through all the steps. If there is a remainder after you have brought down the last digit, write the remainder with the quotient.

A. *Copy and divide, following the first five steps. Write the remainders with the quotient. The first one is started for you.*

1. 3 R $3\overline{)10}$ $\underline{9}$ $6\overline{)15}$ $5\overline{)24}$ $3\overline{)20}$ $4\overline{)29}$ $2\overline{)11}$

2. $5\overline{)47}$ $2\overline{)17}$ $4\overline{)19}$ $6\overline{)33}$ $3\overline{)26}$ $6\overline{)50}$

B. *Copy and divide, following all six steps. There are no remainders.*

3. $5\overline{)380}$ $4\overline{)116}$ $3\overline{)108}$ $2\overline{)84}$ $6\overline{)372}$

4. $2\overline{)138}$ $5\overline{)215}$ $6\overline{)468}$ $4\overline{)320}$ $3\overline{)225}$

General Review

C. *Write the answers only.*

5. $6\overline{)54}$ $7\overline{)49}$ $8\overline{)48}$ $5\overline{)35}$ $8\overline{)64}$ $9\overline{)63}$

6. $4\overline{)32}$ $8\overline{)56}$ $9\overline{)81}$ $9\overline{)36}$ $7\overline{)63}$ $6\overline{)42}$

7. $9\overline{)72}$ $8\overline{)24}$ $7\overline{)7}$ $7\overline{)56}$ $8\overline{)72}$ $6\overline{)72}$

8.

11	12	10	12	12	11	12	12	12
× 11	× 12	× 10	× 11	× 8	× 10	× 9	× 7	× 10

9.

9	12	8	7	9	8	6	8	9
× 8	× 6	× 8	× 9	× 6	× 7	× 7	× 6	× 9

10. $\boxed{7}$ — $\boxed{× 6}$ — $\bigcirc{+ 3}$ — $\langle ÷ 9 \rangle$ — $\boxed{× 7}$ — $\diamondsuit{- 3}$ — $\langle ÷ 4 \rangle$ = $\bigcirc{8 ?}$

Practice With Roman Numerals

This sample shows how to think when changing a large Roman numeral to an Arabic numeral.

> Sample: CCXLVII = ?
>
> CC = 100 + 100 = 200; XL = 50 – 10 = 40; VII = 5 + 1 + 1 = 7
>
> CCXLVII = 200 + 40 + 7 = 247

The numerals in the exercises below are larger than those in Lesson 8, but they are not larger than any you had in Grade 4.

D. *Change these Roman numerals to Arabic numerals.*

11. a. CXLVI   b. CCCV   c. CCLXXX   d. CXIV   e. CCCLI

12. a. CXC   b. CXXXIII   c. CCCXXVII   d. CCXCII   e. CIX

E. *Change these Arabic numerals to Roman numerals.*

13. a. 144   b. 389   c. 253   d. 218   e. 167

F. *Write the numbers in these sentences as Roman numerals.*

14. Enoch was 365 when God took him to heaven.

15. Adam lived 130 years before his son Seth was born.

16. Have you memorized verse 97 of Psalm 119?

17. Psalm 46 has 11 verses.

10. More Practice With Long Division

You will be able to divide more accurately if you always decide first how many digits will be in the quotient. Find the first **partial dividend**. The first partial dividend is the smallest part of the dividend that is **as large as** or **larger than** the divisor.

When you know the first partial dividend, write the first quotient figure directly above it. Count the digits left in the dividend to decide how many quotient figures altogether.

Example: How many digits will be in the quotient of this problem? $6\overline{)234}$

Think: The first partial dividend is 23. The first quotient figure is written above the 3. One digit is left in the dividend, so the quotient will have **two** digits.

A. *Do these exercises.*

1. Write the first partial dividend of each problem below. The first one is 11.

$3\overline{)119}$ $5\overline{)718}$ $4\overline{)234}$ $6\overline{)645}$ $5\overline{)460}$ $3\overline{)717}$

2. Tell how many digits will be in each quotient. Do not solve.

$7\overline{)789}$ $4\overline{)317}$ $6\overline{)92}$ $5\overline{)280}$ $8\overline{)59}$ $3\overline{)526}$

B. *Copy and divide. The problems in row 3 do not have remainders.*

3. $4\overline{)96}$ $6\overline{)726}$ $5\overline{)235}$ $4\overline{)352}$ $3\overline{)534}$

4. $6\overline{)325}$ $5\overline{)88}$ $3\overline{)29}$ $4\overline{)723}$ $7\overline{)395}$

5. $8\overline{)60}$ $4\overline{)333}$ $6\overline{)728}$ $2\overline{)351}$ $5\overline{)72}$

C. *Divide. Check by multiplication. The first one is done for you.*

6.
$$
\begin{array}{r}
67\text{R}3 \\
6\overline{)405} \\
36 \\
\hline
45 \\
42 \\
\hline
3
\end{array}
\qquad
\begin{array}{r}
67 \\
\times\ 6 \\
\hline
402 \\
+\ \ 3 \\
\hline
405
\end{array}
$$

$7\overline{)30}$ $5\overline{)92}$ $4\overline{)304}$ $3\overline{)732}$

D. *Write answers only to these division facts. Study any facts that you do not know well.*

7.   9⟌99   9⟌63   8⟌56   6⟌42   7⟌70   8⟌96

8.   11⟌11   12⟌144   12⟌84   11⟌132   12⟌60   11⟌121

9.   10⟌50   10⟌100   12⟌108   9⟌81   12⟌132   11⟌110

10. 12⟌48   12⟌36   10⟌120   12⟌72   10⟌80   11⟌66

E. *Examine these division problems. Then answer the questions.*

Example A: $\dfrac{12\,\text{R}\,2}{7⟌86}$ Example B: 72 ÷ 6 = 12

11. What number is the **dividend** in example A? in example B?
12. What is the **divisor** in example A? in example B?
13. What is the **quotient** in example A? in example B?
14. What is the first **partial dividend** in example A?

General Review

F. *Do these exercises.*

15. Copy and multiply.

2,473	9,136	95	64	80
× 6	× 8	× 42	× 39	× 17

16. Write these Arabic numerals as Roman numerals.
     a. 79   b. 140   c. 368   d. 293   e. 57   f. 314

17. Write these Roman numerals as Arabic numerals.
     a. CCLV   b. CXVIII   c. CCCIV   d. CXCVI   e. CCXLIX

G. *Solve these reading problems.*

18. Mr. Stevens has 10 beehives. When he extracted honey, he poured 70 pounds of honey into 5-pound jars. How many jars did he fill?

19. Mr. Stevens poured 96 pounds of honey into 12-pound jars. How many 12-pound jars did he fill?

20. Mr. Stevens filled 48 two-pound jars. How many pounds of honey did it take to fill the jars?

21. Mr. Stevens also filled 80 one-pound jars. He filled how many more one-pound jars than two-pound jars? (See number 20.)

*22. How many pounds of honey did Mr. Stevens have altogether?

11. Chapter 1 Review

A. *Write the answers only.*

1.
7	6	4	3	9	8	4	7	8
+ 9	+ 8	+ 9	+ 8	+ 6	+ 7	+ 8	+ 6	+ 9

2.
12	16	14	11	10	9	12	11	13
- 7	- 8	- 5	- 4	- 8	- 6	- 9	- 6	- 8

3.
6	8	9	7	11	12	12	11	8
× 8	× 9	× 7	× 8	× 11	× 8	× 9	× 12	× 8

4.   8)24   3)18   4)32   7)21   4)8   7)7

5.   7)42   8)56   9)81   9)36   6)54   8)72

6.
8	6	9	3	9	7	2
1	7	8	5	4	8	9
7	5	3	7	6	5	6
+ 5	+ 8	+ 9	+ 7	+ 5	+ 3	+ 8

B. *Do these exercices.*

7. Write the names of the lettered parts of the problems at the right. For example, write: a. addends

37	890	53	65
+ 45	- 457	× 8	3)195
82	433	424	

a. 37and 45   d. 457   g. 8   j. 3

b. 82   e. 433   h. 53 and 8 k. 65

c. 890   f. 53   i. 424   l. 195

8. Write numerals for these number words.

a. sixty-nine million, two hundred seventy-five thousand

b. eight million, fifteen

c. three hundred million, forty-two thousand, nine

d. seven hundred twenty-eight million, nine hundred fifty-one thousand, two hundred eleven

9. Copy these numbers, and place commas correctly.

a. 7940327   b. 49376   c. 109832764   d. 751325

10. Copy this number: 44,444,444. Circle the 4 that means 40,000.

11. Write Roman numerals for these Arabic numerals.

a. 29   b. 147   c. 390   d. 254   e. 86

12. Write Arabic numerals for these Roman numerals.

a. XLVIII   b. CCVI   c. CLXXIX   d. CCCLIII   e. XCIV

13. Write the times shown on these clocks.

a.    b.   c.   d.

Review of Computation

C. *Follow the signs. Work carefully.*

14.

```
           88              392
  45       95     754      478                     7,653
  73       47     265      543      4,997          5,419
+ 98     + 63   + 729    + 175    + 6,899        + 8,762
```

15.

```
   703      827     6,000     7,123      9,152
 - 257    - 692   - 1,947   - 3,624    - 8,545
```

16.

```
   80      325      769     6,514      8,679
  x 8      x 7      x 4     x    6     x    3
```

17.

```
   29       54       98       70         63
 x 15     x 58     x 66     x 79       x 63
```

18.   3)28   5)75   6)166   4)732   7)399

19. Subtract. Show the check by addition.   5,040
                                                     - 3,582

20. Divide. Show the check by multiplication.   4)375

(continued on next page)

Reading Problem Review

D. *How would you find the answer to the following questions? Write* add, subtract, multiply, **or** divide.

21. You have some candy pieces to be shared equally by 3 girls. How would you find the number of pieces each girl should have?

22. You know the price for one can of paint. How would you find what Father would pay for 4 cans of paint?

23. You know how long Methuselah and Abraham each lived. How can you find how much older Methuselah was?

24. How do you find the change from a 20-dollar bill?

25. You know how many people are in each Sunday school class. How can you find how many people attended Sunday school altogether?

26. You know how far a car travels in one hour. How can you find the distance the car will travel in 6 hours?

27. You know how many rabbits were in your hutches and how many you sold. How can you find how many rabbits are left?

28. How many 8's are in 112?

E. *Solve these reading problems.*

29. One room at Allentown Christian Day School has 3 rows of desks with 6 in each row. How many desks are in the room?

30. How long will it take to cut down 135 trees at the rate of 9 trees per hour?

31. What is the total weight of sixteen 11-pound bags of nuts?

32. Noah lived six hundred years before the Flood. After the Flood he lived three hundred fifty years. How many more years did he live before the Flood than after the Flood?

33. Of Brother Mason's 5,340 laying hens, 734 died one hot summer. At the end of the summer Brother Mason sold the remaining hens. How many hens did he sell?

34. Job had 3,000 camels, 7,000 sheep, 1,000 oxen, and 500 asses. What was the total number of animals Job had?

35. Job lost all those animals, but later God gave him twice as many as he had before. How many oxen and asses did he have then?

12. Chapter 1 Test

Chapter 2

Working With Larger Numbers

World Population: 5,660,000,000

After this I beheld, and, lo, a great multitude, which no man could
number, of all nations, and kindreds, and people, and tongues,
stood before the throne, and before the Lamb.
(Revelation 7:9)

13. Problems With Missing Information

You cannot solve reading problems unless you have all the necessary information. The problems on this page have some information missing. For each problem write
a. what is missing.
b. how you would solve the problem if you had the missing information. (Write **add**, **subtract**, **multiply**, or **divide**.)

Example: Mother bought 3 bags of sugar for $1.59 each.
How much money did she have left?

Answer: **a.** how much money Mother had before she bought the sugar
b. multiply, then subtract

A. *For each problem, follow the pattern above, and write answers a and b.*

1. The present livestock auction sale barn was built after the old one burned down. How many years ago was that?

2. The sale barn is 120 feet long. How many livestock pens fit in one row along that side?

3. At a livestock sale, hogs sold for $0.47 a pound live weight. How much did Mr. Cox get for four hogs?

4. The Coxes bought a 950-pound steer to butcher. How much did they pay for the steer?

5. Mr. Cox wrote a check for $522.58. How much money was left in his checking account?

6. Mr. Cox sold 4 hogs for $0.47 a pound and one cow for $648.70. How much money did he receive altogether?

7. Great-grandpa Cox said, "I remember the days when we bought weaned pigs for 50¢ apiece." How much more does a weaned pig cost now?

8. A farmer living in Great-grandpa Cox's younger days would have expected to receive _____ for a litter of pigs.

Working With Large Numbers

A number like 540,923 can be broken down as shown below. This is called **writing the number in expanded form.**

$$540,923 = 500,000 + 40,000 + 0 + 900 + 20 + 3$$

The expanded form can be put together again by adding the parts.

The sum of the problem on the right is 540,923.

```
  500,000
   40,000
        0
      900
       20
 +      3
_____
```

B. *Do these exercises.*

9. Write answers about this number: 851,347.

   a. The 8 stands for _____ hundred thousands, or 800,000.

   b. The 5 stands for 5 ten thousands, or _____ .

   c. The 1 stands for 1 _____ , or _____ .

   d. The 3 stands for 3 _____ , or _____ .

   e. The 4 stands for 4 _____ , or _____ .

   f. The 7 stands for 7 _____ , or 7.

   g. Write 851,347 in expanded form.

10. Write in expanded form: a. 7,290   b. 65,148

11. In 19,352
   a. what does the 9 stand for?   c. what is the value of the 1?
   b. what does the 5 stand for?   d. what is the value of the 3?

12. Be ready to read these numbers aloud in class.
   a. 785,003,210   b. 4,587,000   c. 19,025,003   d. 606,600,060

Remember that > means "is greater than" and < means "is less than."

C. *Do these exercises.*

13. Copy each pair of numbers, and write > or < between them.
   a. 99,999 ___ 990,000   b. 12,999 ___ 12,099   c. 51,099 ___ 51,100

14. Count by 1's from 995 to 1,005. Write the numbers.

15. Count by 10's from 3,000 to 3,100. Write the numbers.

16. Count by 100's from 4,000 to 5,000. Write the numbers.

17. Count by 1,000's from 10,000 to 20,000. Write the numbers.

18. Write the next three numbers that would come after these if you were counting by 1's. If you are not sure, add 1 each time. The first one is done for you.
   a. 13,098 <u>13,099</u> <u>13,100</u> <u>13,101</u>   c. 45,997 _____ _____ _____
   b. 7,899 _____ _____ _____   d. 9,998 _____ _____ _____

14. Learning About Billions

You have studied numbers up to hundred millions. The things you learned so far can be extended to the next period of numerals, called **billions**. Study and learn the place values in the following grid.

The number on the grid is written 238,086,103,759 as a numeral. It is read "238 billion, 86 million, 103 thousand, 759."

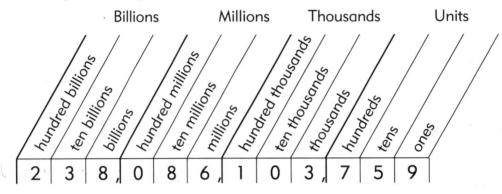

A million is 1,000 thousand, and a billion is 1,000 million. Can you imagine how large a billion is? If you started counting now and said one number every second, day and night, it would take you more than 31 years 8 months to count to a billion!

One billion is almost too large for us to understand, yet our great God created billions and billions of stars. Scientists estimate that the Milky Way galaxy alone contains one hundred billion stars (100,000,000,000).

A. *Copy the following numbers, placing commas correctly.*

1. a. 428701   b. 16005   c. 1655035
2. a. 7192000018   b. 21000000   c. 999999999999
3. a. 48016327195   b. 756009023   c. 19809742350
4. a. 756230   b. 654320109756   c. 5500000000

B. *Do these exercises.*

5. Make a grid like the one at the top of the page, and place the numbers from rows 1 to 4 on the grid. Put each number on a separate line.

6. Be ready to read the numbers in class.

7. Write numerals for these number words. Use zeroes where needed.

    a. one hundred forty billion

    b. two hundred eighty-six million, three hundred one thousand, sixteen

    c. seventy-six billion, five hundred twenty-three million, two hundred fifty-seven

    d. six hundred billion, five hundred fifty million

8. Copy each pair of numbers, and write < or > between them.

    a. 87,000,000 _____ 87,000,000,000

    b. 3,980,000,000 _____ 3,899,999,999

General Review

C. *Write the answers only.*

9.

11	12	10	12	11	12	12	12	10	11
× 9	× 12	× 10	× 9	× 11	× 7	× 11	× 8	× 6	× 10

10.

7	6	4	1	9	4	5	2
8	5	4	7	4	3	5	9
5	8	9	6	7	7	8	5
+ 3	+ 9	+ 5	+ 8	+ 9	+ 6	+ 8	+ 6

D. *Do these exercises.*

11. Write Roman numerals for these Arabic numerals.

    a. 48   **b.** 360   **c.** 193   **d.** 89   **e.** 216   **f.** 154

12. Copy and multiply.

86	44	27	63	60
× 18	× 59	× 78	× 83	× 97

13. Copy and divide. Show your check by multiplication.

    5)85   4)33   7)320   3)804   6)99

14. What number belongs at the end of the trail?

Start 12 → × 7 → + 68 → ÷ 2 → − 49 → ÷ 3 → × 9 → = ?

15. Rounding Numbers to the Nearest Ten, Hundred, or Thousand

Rounded numbers are not exact. Whenever we measure a line, we round the measurement to the nearest inch or quarter inch, or perhaps to the nearest sixteenth inch. Depending on what is being measured, we measure to the nearest foot or the nearest yard.

Larger numbers are often rounded to the nearest ten, hundred, or thousand. For example, the distance around the earth is 25,000 miles to the nearest thousand miles. A more exact measurement is 24,902 miles, but it is much easier to remember 25,000.

Numbers rounded to the nearest ten end with 0, numbers rounded to the nearest hundred end with 00, and numbers rounded to the nearest thousand end 000.

In order to round numbers properly, you must know the "halfway numbers." Half of 10 is 5; half of 100 is 50; half of 1,000 is 500. Because the "halfway numbers" involve 5, the following steps can be used to round off numbers.

Example: Round 5,482 to the nearest hundred.

1. Find the digit in the place to which you are rounding.	In 5,482, 4 is in the hundreds' place.
2. If the digit to the right of that place (step 1) is less than 5, **round down** by changing all digits to the right of that place to 0.	In 5,482, 8 is to the right of 4. 8 is more than 5. Do not round down.
3. If the digit to the right of that place (step 1) is 5 or more, **round up** by adding 1 to that place and changing all digits to the right of that place to 0.	8 is more than 5. Change 4 to 5. Change 82 to 00. 5,482 rounded to the nearest hundred is 5,500.

A. *Write the numbers that belong in the blanks.*

1. Half of 10 is 5, so halfway between 40 and 50 is _____ .

2. Half of 100 is 50, so halfway between 600 and 700 is _____ .

3. Half of 1,000 is 500, so halfway from 2,000 to 3,000 is _____ .

B. *Write the number that is halfway between each pair of numbers.*

4. **a.** 30 and 40   **b.** 60 and 70   **c.** 80 and 90   **d.** 320 and 330

5. **a.** 300 and 400   **b.** 700 and 800   **c.** 1,100 and 1,200

6. **a.** 5,000 and 6,000   **b.** 1,000 and 2,000   **c.** 17,000 and 18,000

C. *Follow the directions.*

7. Round these numbers to the nearest ten: **a.** 53   **b.** 76   **c.** 285   **d.** 6,412

8. Round to the nearest hundred: **a.** 357   **b.** 4,213   **c.** 14,041   **d.** 9,376

9. Round to the nearest thousand: **a.** 7,099   **b.** 28,905   **c.** 235,155

10. Round these prices to the nearest dollar. Remember that half a dollar is $0.50 (50¢).
   a. $3.59   **b.** $8.12   **c.** $15.70   **d.** $37.28

Review of Large Numbers

D. *Do these exercises.*

11. Write these numbers with all figures.
   a. 11 billion, 6 million, 420 thousand   **c.** 2 billion, 578 thousand, 50
   b. 350 billion   **d.** 57 billion, 250 million, 75 thousand, 8

12. Write these numbers in expanded form. (See Lesson 13.)
   a. 5,873   **b.** 16,045   **c.** 986,412

13. Write whether < or > belongs in each blank.
   a. 8,999,999 _____ 9,111,000   **b.** 10,999,988 _____ 10,998,999

General Review

E. *Write the answers.*

14. $10\overline{)90}$ $11\overline{)77}$ $12\overline{)84}$ $12\overline{)36}$ $10\overline{)110}$ $10\overline{)30}$

15. $12\overline{)132}$ $12\overline{)96}$ $11\overline{)121}$ $10\overline{)100}$ $12\overline{)144}$ $12\overline{)120}$

16. Write each price in two ways: **a.** sixteen cents   **b.** eight dollars

17. Write with a dollar sign and a decimal point: thirty-six dollars and nine cents.

18. Copy the subtrahend in this fact: $17 - 8 = 9$.

19. Copy the dividend in this fact: $56 \div 7 = 8$.

20. Copy the multiplier in this fact: $12 \times 11 = 132$.

21. Write these Roman numerals as Arabic numerals.
   a. LXXXIV   **b.** CCLIX   **c.** CXLIII   **d.** CCCXXI   **e.** XCVII

F. *Do these problems.*

22.
1,857	3,259	60	84	97
× 7	× 5	× 48	× 83	× 36

16. Rounding to the Nearest Ten Thousand or Hundred Thousand

The steps given in Lesson 15 can be used to round numbers to the nearest ten thousand or hundred thousand. A number rounded to ten thousands ends with four zeroes. A number rounded to hundred thousands ends with five zeroes.

> Example A: Round 36,419 to the nearest ten thousand.
>   Think: 3 is in ten thousands' place.
>   6 is to the right of 3; round up.
>   36,419 to the nearest ten thousand is 40,000.
>
> Example B: Round 5,549,800 to the nearest 100,000.
>   Think: 5 is in hundred thousands' place.
>   4 comes after the 5; round down.
>   5,549,800 to the nearest hundred thousand is 5,500,000.

A. Do these exercises.

1. Round these numbers to the nearest hundred.
   a. 580   b. 7,285   c. 15,473   d. 925

2. Round these numbers to the nearest thousand.
   a. 7,285   b. 15,473   c. 91,580   d. 605,099

3. Round these numbers to the nearest ten thousand.
   a. 15,473   b. 359,999   c. 91,580   d. 605,099

4. Round these numbers to the nearest hundred thousand.
   a. 359,999   b. 862,740   c. 4,239,727   d. 17,145,800

B. The chart in number 5 shows the populations of the five largest cities in United States one year. Round each number on the chart first to the nearest thousand and then to the nearest hundred thousand. An example is done for you.

	City	Population		
5. Example:	San Diego, CA	1,070,310	1,070,000	1,100,000
a.	New York, NY	7,352,700		
b.	Los Angeles, CA	3,411,610		
c.	Chicago, IL	2,977,520		
d.	Houston, TX	1,698,090		
e.	Philadelphia, PA	1,688,210		

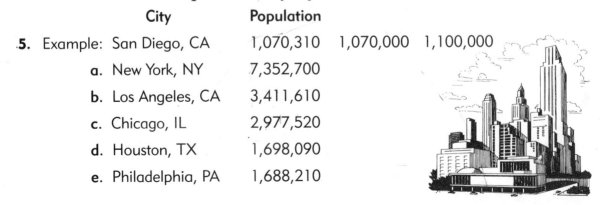

Review of Counting Money

C. *Write the answers.*

6. Count the money in the picture.

7. Write the value of the following sets of coins.

  a. 6 dimes

  b. 9 nickels

  c. 7 quarters

  d. 3 dimes, 18 pennies

  e. 2 quarters, 5 nickels

  f. 4 dimes, 3 nickels, 11 pennies

  g. 3 quarters, 3 dimes

  h. 4 quarters, 2 dimes, 4 nickels

  i. 1 half dollar, 3 quarters

  j. 2 half dollars, 1 dime, 7 nickels

8. Write the value of the following sets of bills.

  a. one 20-dollar bill, three 10-dollar bills

  b. five 10-dollar bills, five 5-dollar bills

  c. three 10-dollar bills, four 5-dollar bills, six 1-dollar bills

  d. two 20-dollar bills, one 10-dollar bill, three 5-dollar bills

General Review

D. *Do these exercises.*

9. Copy and multiply.

28	93	45	77	18
× 36	× 95	× 52	× 43	× 70

10. Copy and divide. Check by multiplication.

$7\overline{)38}$ $3\overline{)57}$ $4\overline{)144}$ $5\overline{)600}$ $6\overline{)490}$

11. Change to Roman numerals.

  a. 98   **b.** 56   **c.** 127   **d.** 209   **e.** 340   **f.** 164

E. *Solve these reading problems.*

12. Jonas bought 4 flats of broccoli plants at a greenhouse. The flats had 8 rows of plants with 12 plants in each row. How many plants were on one flat?

13. A flat of lettuce has 72 plants. How many plants are in 4 flats of lettuce?

14. Jonas bought 240 cauliflower plants, and he prepared 5 rows in the field for planting them. If Jonas plants the same number in each row, how many cauliflower plants will be in each row?

17. Larger Roman Numerals

You already know five 1-digit Roman numerals. Only two more are commonly used. When you know them, you will know all the Roman numerals you are ever likely to need.

> The last two digits in the row below are the new ones.
>
> L = 50   C = 100   D = 500   M = 1,000

The first row below is Roman numerals counting by tens. The second row is Roman numerals counting by hundreds. You should be able to see a similarity between the two rows.

X   XX   XXX   XL   L   LX   LXX   LXXX   XC   C   CX   CXX

C   CC   CCC   CD   D   DC   DCC   DCCC   CM   M   MC   MCC

> The rules in Lesson 8 also apply to larger Roman numerals.
>
> MC = 1,000 + 100   CM = 1,000 – 100   MCM = 1,000 + 900
>
> Another hint to help you with larger numbers is that only C can be placed before D or M. For example, the Roman numeral for 999 is written CMXCIX, not IM.

A. *Change these Arabic numerals to Roman numerals.*

1. a. 385   b. 529   c. 814   d. 952   e. 436   f. 647

B. *Change these Roman numerals to Arabic numerals.*

2. a. DCLXXIV   b. CDXXXV   c. DCCCXI   d. CMLXXXIX   e. MM

3. a. CCLXVIII   b. DCCXIV   c. MDCLXI   d. CCCXLVII   e. MXCVIII

C. *Do these exercises with numbers.*

4. Write these numbers with Arabic numerals.
   a. two hundred forty-nine billion
   b. three billion, eight hundred fifty million
   c. twelve billion, four hundred twenty-five million, sixty thousand, five hundred thirty-seven
   d. six hundred eighty-four million, nineteen
   e. ninety-five billion, seven hundred thousand

5. Read these numbers to yourself. Then write the value of each 4. The first one is done for you.
   a. 45,693,821 (40,000,000)   b. 879,405,217   c. 358,976,392,140

6. Now write the value of each 5 in row 5.

7. Write the value of each 8 in row 5.

8. Round these numbers to the nearest thousand.
   a. 78,126   b. 123,567   c. 90,783   d. 3,456,489

9. Round the numbers in row 8 to the nearest ten thousand.

10. Round to the nearest hundred thousand.
   a. 123,567   b. 3,456,489   c. 21,037,486

11. Count the money.

a.

b.

D. *Solve these reading problems.*

12. When Gideon gathered the men of Israel to fight the Midianites, God said, "You have too many men." The 22,000 men who were afraid were told to leave. That left 10,000 men to fight. How many men had Gideon gathered together at first?

13. God said that 10,000 men were still too many for His purposes. Only 300 men out of the 10,000 were chosen to help fight. How many men were sent back home?

14. Each of the 300 men in Gideon's army used three tools: a trumpet, a pitcher, and a lamp. How many tools did Gideon's army need altogether?

15. Mother bought a set of flannel sheets on sale for $22.99. The regular price was $26.95. How much did Mother save by buying the sheets on sale?

16. Gerald is 4 years old and Seth is 12. Seth said, "In 9 years I will be 21 years old." How old will Gerald be when Seth is 21?

17. One week Kathy and Karen weeded the beans and the corn in the garden. It took them 2 hours to weed the beans, and it took twice as long to weed the corn. Altogether, how much time did the girls spend weeding?

18. Karen and Kathy weeded 3 rows of beans and 12 rows of corn. Each row was 42 feet long. How many feet of vegetables did Karen and Kathy weed?

18. Finding Change by Subtraction

To find the amount of change by subtraction, subtract the amount of the purchase from the amount given to the clerk. This is the method you learned in Grade 4.

A. *Find the amount of change by subtraction.*

42¢ a pound

	Amount of Purchase	Amount Given
1.	$5.82	$6.00
2.	$3.98	$5.00
3.	$4.37	$10.00
4.	$7.14	$10.00
5.	$12.95	$15.00
6.	$13.65	$20.00

B. *Copy and fill in the chart below to tell the correct pieces of money to use for the given amounts of change. Use the smallest number of pieces possible. A sample is done for you.*

	Amount of Change	$10.00 Bills	$5.00 Bills	$1.00 Bills	Quarters	Dimes	Nickels	Pennies
S.	$3.37			3	1	1		2
7.	$0.16							
8.	$12.60							
9.	$7.43							
10.	$0.79							
11.	$8.28							
12.	$17.22							
13.	$2.55							
14.	$6.81							
15.	$11.09							

C. *Find the answers to these two-step reading problems.*

16. Mother bought bananas for $1.75 and peaches for $5.50. What was her change from a 10-dollar bill?

17. Aunt Rose bought a dozen oranges for $1.99 and 3 lemons for $0.15 each. What was her total bill?

18. Uncle Philip bought 10 pounds of apples for $0.42 a pound. How much change should he receive from $5.00?

Multiplication Practice

You already know that the factors in multiplication problems can be exchanged, and the answer is the same. In this lesson you will check multiplications by exchanging the factors. Study the sample in the box. Note that the partial products for the two problems are different, but the products are the same.

```
    48          37
  x 37        x 48
   336         296
   144         148
 1,776       1,776
```

D. *Copy and multiply. Check your work by exchanging the factors and multiplying again. If the two answers are not the same, find your mistake.*

19. a.   85   b.   90   c.   47
       x 17   x 68   x 73

20. a.   28   b.   53   c.   69
       x 58   x 39   x 45

21. a.   84   b.   18   c.   61
       x 94   x 36   x 67

E. *Copy and multiply. Check by going over your work.*

22.   342   764   853   977   619
      x 34   x 56   x 73   x 46   x 93

General Review

F. *Do these exercises.*

23. Change these Arabic numerals to Roman numerals.
    a. 1,074   b. 958   c. 2,340   d. 689   e. 1,700

24. Change these Roman numerals to Arabic numbers.
    a. CCLXXXVI   b. MDVII   c. DCCCXL   d. MMCDLV

25. Round to the nearest thousand.
    a. 35,602   b. 92,498   c. 109,845   d. 328,350

26. Round to the nearest hundred thousand.
    a. 409,627   b. 572,980   c. 3,450,287   d. 15,643,000

27. Answer the following questions about this problem: 8 x 32 = 256
    a. What is the product?   b. What is the multiplier?

19. Counting Change

Remember to use subtraction to find the amount of change.

A. *Draw a chart as you did in Lesson 18. Subtract to find the amount of change. Then fill in the correct pieces of money to use for those amounts of change.*

	Amount of Purchase	Amount Given	Amount of Change	$5.00 Bills	$1.00 Bills	25¢	10¢	5¢	1¢
S.	$5.52	$10.00	$4.48		4	1	2		3
1.	$0.38	$1.00							
2.	$2.89	$5.00							
3.	$13.88	$15.00							
4.	$2.44	$10.00							
5.	$1.60	$5.00							
6.	$2.30	$3.00							
7.	$7.75	$10.00							
8.	$14.23	$20.00							
9.	$3.56	$10.00							
10.	$12.95	$20.00							

When **counting out change** to a customer, start with the amount of the purchase. Give the smallest denominations of money first. Continue counting until you reach the amount given.

Example: Count out the change when $5.00 is given for a purchase of $3.68.

Say: $3.68, $3.69, $3.70, $3.75, $4.00, $5.00

Give: 2 pennies, 1 nickel, 1 quarter, 1 dollar

Check: $5.00 – $3.68 = $1.32   1 dollar, 1 quarter, 1 nickel, and 2 pennies = $1.32

B. *Was the change counted back in the best way? Answer* yes *or* no.

11. Amount of purchase: $2.70   Amount given: $5.00

Say: $2.70, $2.80, $2.90, $3.00, $4.00, $5.00   Give: 3 dimes, 2 dollars

12. Amount of purchase: $4.33   Amount given: $10.00

Say: $4.33, $4.34, $4.35, $4.40, $4.50, $4.75, $5.00, $10.00.

Give: 2 pennies, 1 nickel, 1 dime, 2 quarters, 1 five-dollar bill.

Multiplication and Division Practice

C. *Answer the following questions. Do not solve the problems.*

13. What is the first partial dividend in each problem? (See Lesson 10.)

$$5\overline{)940} \qquad 3\overline{)4,673} \qquad 2\overline{)1,682} \qquad 6\overline{)3,480} \qquad 4\overline{)7,126}$$

14. How many digits will be in each quotient?

$$6\overline{)709} \qquad 5\overline{)460} \qquad 7\overline{)8,000} \qquad 4\overline{)3,864} \qquad 3\overline{)8,213}$$

D. *Copy and divide.*

15. $\quad 4\overline{)500} \qquad 3\overline{)783} \qquad 6\overline{)417} \qquad 5\overline{)710} \qquad 7\overline{)118}$

16. $\quad 5\overline{)1,320} \qquad 4\overline{)7,548} \qquad 8\overline{)9,152} \qquad 3\overline{)2,343} \qquad 6\overline{)3,810}$

E. *Copy, divide, and check by multiplication.*

17. $\quad 3\overline{)441} \qquad\qquad 5\overline{)7,000} \qquad\qquad 9\overline{)4,815}$

18. $\quad 4\overline{)2,500} \qquad\qquad 7\overline{)5,125} \qquad\qquad 6\overline{)7,164}$

F. *Copy, multiply, and check by exchanging the factors.*

19. a. $\begin{array}{r} 68 \\ \times\ 17 \\ \hline \end{array}$ b. $\begin{array}{r} 25 \\ \times\ 96 \\ \hline \end{array}$ c. $\begin{array}{r} 70 \\ \times\ 74 \\ \hline \end{array}$

20. a. $\begin{array}{r} 73 \\ \times\ 95 \\ \hline \end{array}$ b. $\begin{array}{r} 44 \\ \times\ 58 \\ \hline \end{array}$ c. $\begin{array}{r} 89 \\ \times\ 23 \\ \hline \end{array}$

G. *Copy and follow the signs. Be sure to place the dollar sign and decimal point in each answer.*

21.

$\begin{array}{r} \$12.53 \\ \times\quad 8 \\ \hline \end{array} \qquad \begin{array}{r} \$43.26 \\ \times\quad 6 \\ \hline \end{array} \qquad \begin{array}{r} \$50.00 \\ -\ 27.84 \\ \hline \end{array} \qquad \begin{array}{r} \$3.86 \\ 6.43 \\ +\ 9.78 \\ \hline \end{array} \qquad 4\overline{)\$5.12}$

20. Chapter 2 Review

A. *Write the answers only.*

1.
8	4	9	6	7	3	8	5	9	7
x 7	x 8	x 9	x 7	x 9	x 9	x 8	x 7	x 8	x 7

2.
12	12	11	10	12	11	12	10	11	12
x 6	x 8	x 10	x 10	x 12	x 11	x 9	x 12	x 12	x 7

3. $6\overline{)48}$ $7\overline{)42}$ $9\overline{)63}$ $11\overline{)55}$ $10\overline{)80}$ $12\overline{)60}$

4. $8\overline{)72}$ $9\overline{)54}$ $5\overline{)30}$ $12\overline{)48}$ $11\overline{)132}$ $12\overline{)108}$

B. *Do these exercises.*

5. Copy and place commas correctly. Then circle the digit indicated.
   a. 8409321   Circle the digit in hundred thousands' place.
   b. 9032760015   Circle the digit in ten millions' place.
   c. 751023480620   Circle the digit in billions' place.

6. Copy each pair of numbers, and write < or > between them.
   a. 6,701,000 _____ 6,701,099   b. 45,000,000 _____ 44,999,998

7. Write numerals for these number words.
   a. sixty-seven billion, one hundred fifty million
   b. eight hundred twenty-five billion
   c. fourteen billion, eighty thousand
   d. 9 billion, 470 million, 15 thousand, eight

8. Round to the nearest ten thousand.
   a. 670,348   b. 28,496   c. 3,844,725

9. Round to the nearest thousand.
   a. 16,520   b. 451,389   c. 722,564

10. Round to the nearest hundred thousand.
    a. 451,389   b. 722,564   c. 7,360,128

11. Change to Roman numerals.
    a. 84   b. 395   c. 538   d. 769   e. 950   f. 1,047

12. Change to Arabic numerals.
    a. LXXVII   b. CXLVIII   c. DCLIII   d. CDXXIX   e. MDXIV

13. Count the money.

a.   b.

C. *Count out the correct change. Tell what coins and bills should be used. Then subtract to find the total amount of change. Study the sample.*

	Amount of Purchase	Amount Given	
S.	$3.35	$5.00	Answer: 1 nickel, 1 dime, 2 quarters, 1 dollar
14.	$2.87	$10.00	
15.	$1.43	$5.00	
16.	$13.59	$20.00	

$$\begin{array}{r} \$5.00 \\ -\ 3.35 \\ \hline \$1.65 \end{array}$$

Computation Review

D. *Copy and follow the signs. Check as indicated.*

17. Check by exchanging the factors.

84	36	19	70	85	27
× 24	× 85	× 96	× 38	× 59	× 67

18. Check by going over your work.

4,318	5,827	9,360	7,695
× 6	× 4	× 7	× 5

19. Check by addition. Draw boxes around answers as in Lesson 4.

$5.00	$10.00	$12.00	$20.00
− 3.69	− 6.42	− 10.85	− 13.78

20. Check by multiplication.

5)380   7)593   4)712   3)801

21. Check by multiplication.

4)2,000   6)7,632   8)2,650   5)7,825

(continued on next page)

Reading Problem Review

E. *How can you find the answers? Write* add, subtract, multiply, *or* divide.

22. How much older is Janice than Leroy?

23. What is the total cost of the items Father bought?

24. How much change will Father receive from $40.00?

25. How many can each boy have if they share the candy?

26. How much for 6 cans if you know the price of one can?

27. What is the difference between two numbers?

28. What is the product of two numbers?

29. How many 5-pound bags can be filled from a barrel of flour?

F. *Solve the problems. Show your work on your paper.*

30. If 76 chickens are placed in cages with 4 chickens in a cage, how many cages will be filled?

31. If the price of one grapefruit is $0.29, how much will you pay for a dozen grapefruits?

32. Martha bought 5 pounds of bananas at $0.33 a pound, a dozen oranges at $1.89 a dozen, and a pound of grapes for $0.75. What was Martha's total bill?

33. One week Martha paid for purchases of $8.79 with a 10-dollar bill. What was her change?

34. Several sisters from church baked 156 cookies. They divided the cookies into 6 boxes and gave a box to each of the widows in the community. How many cookies were in each box?

35. In 1990 Father and the boys remodeled the living room. When they tore down a wall, they found a newspaper dated 1916. How old was the newspaper?

---

21. Chapter 2 Test

Chapter 3

Fractions

Molasses Crinkles

Cream together:
- ¾ cup shortening
- 1 cup brown sugar
- 1 egg
- ¼ cup dark molasses

Sift together and add:
- 2¼ cup flour
- ½ t. salt
- 2 t. soda
- 1 t. cinnamon
- 1 t. ginger
- ½ t. ground cloves

Mix thoroughly. Chill dough several hours. Shape dough into balls 1" in diameter. Roll in granulated sugar and place 2" apart on greased baking sheet. Bake at 350° for 12-15 minutes.

And that ye . . . work with your own hands.
(1 Thessalonians 4:11)

22. Introduction to Fractions

Study these facts about fractions. You learned most of them before.

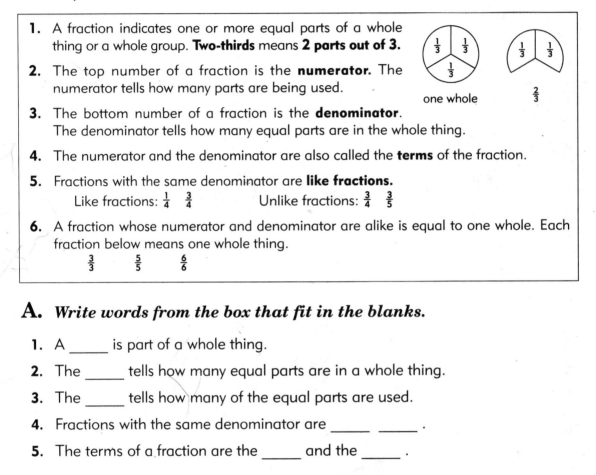

1. A fraction indicates one or more equal parts of a whole thing or a whole group. **Two-thirds** means **2 parts out of 3.**

2. The top number of a fraction is the **numerator.** The numerator tells how many parts are being used.

one whole $\frac{2}{3}$

3. The bottom number of a fraction is the **denominator.** The denominator tells how many equal parts are in the whole thing.

4. The numerator and the denominator are also called the **terms** of the fraction.

5. Fractions with the same denominator are **like fractions.**
    Like fractions: $\frac{1}{4}$ $\frac{3}{4}$ Unlike fractions: $\frac{3}{4}$ $\frac{3}{5}$

6. A fraction whose numerator and denominator are alike is equal to one whole. Each fraction below means one whole thing.
    $\frac{3}{3}$ $\frac{5}{5}$ $\frac{6}{6}$

A. *Write words from the box that fit in the blanks.*

1. A _____ is part of a whole thing.

2. The _____ tells how many equal parts are in a whole thing.

3. The _____ tells how many of the equal parts are used.

4. Fractions with the same denominator are _____ _____ .

5. The terms of a fraction are the _____ and the _____ .

B. *Write these fractions with numbers.*

6. a. one-fourth   c. three-sixths   e. one-twelfth
    b. seven-tenths   d. five-eighths   f. four-fifths

C. *Do these exercises.*

7. Write a fraction for the shaded part of each thing or group.

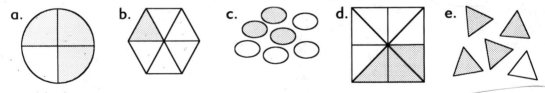

a.   b.   c.   d.   e.

8. Now write the fractions for the unshaded parts above.

9. Write the fractions described below.
   a. The numerator is 4 and the denominator is 7.
   b. The denominator is 6 and the numerator is 5.
   c. It means 3 parts out of 5.
   d. It means one part out of three parts.

10. Copy the pairs of like fractions.
   a. $\frac{1}{5}$ $\frac{3}{5}$ b. $\frac{3}{8}$ $\frac{4}{3}$ c. $\frac{2}{10}$ $\frac{3}{10}$ d. $\frac{5}{8}$ $\frac{5}{10}$

11. Copy the fractions that are equal to one whole.

   $\frac{4}{4}$ $\frac{7}{7}$ $\frac{4}{7}$ $\frac{1}{2}$ $\frac{3}{3}$ $\frac{6}{7}$ $\frac{8}{8}$

General Review

D. *Follow the directions.*

12. Write the answers only.

5	8	4	3	9	2	6
5	5	7	3	5	6	8
4	3	8	5	4	9	6
2	5	6	7	7	8	4
+ 6	+ 9	+ 3	+ 8	+ 4	+ 7	+ 2

13. Copy and multiply. Check by exchanging the factors.

   a.   57   b.   84   c.   19   d.   28
       × 26   × 78   × 69   × 46

14. Copy and multiply. Check by going over your work.

   360   876   418   925
   × 36   × 54   × 37   × 15

15. Copy and subtract. Check by addition.

   6,000   5,012   7,364   9,135
   - 1,596   - 2,754   - 3,457   - 4,655

E. *Solve these reading problems.*

16. Mother likes to send greeting cards to sick or elderly people. She bought a package of 6 cards for $1.98. What was the price per card?

17. If Mother buys single greeting cards for $0.75 each, how much does she pay for 6 cards?

23. Mixed Numbers, Proper Fractions, and Improper Fractions

Study the box to refresh your memory of the terms **mixed number, proper fraction,** and **improper fraction.**

---

1. A **mixed number** includes a whole number and a fraction.

2. Fractions with the numerator smaller than the denominator are **proper fractions.** They are less than one whole.
    $\frac{3}{8}$ and $\frac{4}{5}$ are proper fractions.

3. Fractions with the numerator the same as or larger than the denominator are **improper fractions.** They are equal to or larger than one whole.
    $\frac{8}{8}$ and $\frac{7}{5}$ are improper fractions.

4. To change an improper fraction to a whole number or mixed number, divide the numerator by the denominator.
    $\frac{6}{3} = ?$ $6 \div 3 = 2$, so $\frac{6}{3} = 2$

A. *Do these exercises.*

1. Write **P** for proper fraction, **I** for improper fraction, and **M** for mixed number.

    a. $\frac{3}{7}$ b. $3\frac{1}{2}$ c. $\frac{8}{12}$ d. $\frac{12}{8}$ e. $1\frac{5}{6}$ f. $\frac{4}{4}$ g. $\frac{7}{8}$

2. Write **L** for like fractions and **U** for unlike fractions.

    a. $\frac{3}{8}$ $\frac{5}{8}$ b. $\frac{1}{2}$ $\frac{1}{12}$ c. $\frac{4}{5}$ $\frac{3}{4}$ d. $\frac{1}{4}$ $\frac{3}{4}$ e. $\frac{3}{6}$ $\frac{5}{6}$

3. Write these as mixed numbers or proper fractions.

    a. two and three-sevenths   d. three-eighths

    b. eight and five-sixths   e. five and two-thirds

    c. four and one-half   f. six-tenths

4. Write a mixed number for the shaded part of each picture.

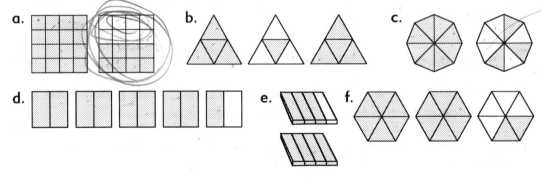

5. Now write an improper fraction for each picture in number 4.

6. Copy and fill in the missing numbers as you count by thirds. You will write improper fractions.

$$\frac{1}{3}, \quad \frac{2}{3}, \quad \frac{?}{3}, \quad \frac{4}{3}, \quad \frac{?}{3}, \quad \frac{?}{?}, \quad \frac{?}{?}, \quad \frac{?}{?}, \quad \frac{9}{3}$$

7. Count by thirds again. This time fill in the blanks with whole numbers or mixed numbers.

$$\frac{1}{3}, \quad \frac{2}{3}, \quad 1, \quad 1\frac{1}{3}, \quad \underline{\quad}, \quad \underline{\quad}, \quad 2\frac{1}{3}, \quad \underline{\quad}, \quad 3, \quad \underline{\quad}$$

8. Count by halves to 5 without using improper fractions.
   Begin: $\frac{1}{2}$, 1, $1\frac{1}{2}$ ...

9. Tell how may of these parts are in one whole thing.

   a. thirds   c. tenths   e. halves
   b. fifths   d. eighths   f. fourths

General Review

B. *Follow the directions.*

10. Write numerals for these number words.

    a. two billion, eighty-five million, three hundred thousand
    b. four hundred seventy-two billion
    c. 42 billion, 867 million, 18 thousand, 50
    d. 970 billion, 5 million, 76 thousand, 340

11. Change to Roman numerals.

    a. 78   b. 326   c. 559   d. 784   e. 917   f. 1,440

12. Copy and multiply. Check by going over your work.

726	895	650	238	914
× 47	× 34	× 89	× 53	× 48

C. *Copy and divide. Check by multiplication.*

13. 6)7,312   5)4,430   3)8,562   8)9,312

14. 4)6,531   2)3,654   7)5,368   6)5,724

24. Equivalent Fractions

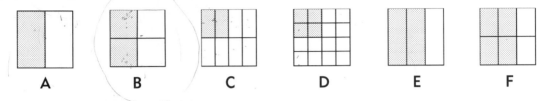

| A | B | C | D | E | F |

Samuel said that one-half of Square B was shaded. Lavern said that two-fourths of Square B was shaded. Both of them were right because one-half and two-fourths are equal. Fractions that are the same size, like $\frac{1}{2}$ and $\frac{2}{4}$, are **equivalent fractions.**

One way to find equivalent fractions is to **multiply** both the numerator and the denominator by the same number.

Examples: $\dfrac{2 \times 2 = 4}{3 \times 2 = 6}$ $\dfrac{2 \times 3 = 6}{3 \times 3 = 9}$ $\dfrac{2 \times 4 = 8}{3 \times 4 = 12}$

$\frac{2}{3}$, $\frac{4}{6}$, $\frac{6}{9}$, and $\frac{8}{12}$ are equivalent fractions.

Another way to find equivalent fractions is to **divide** both terms of a fraction by the same number.

Examples: $\dfrac{4 \div 2 = 2}{12 \div 2 = 6}$ $\dfrac{4 \div 4 = 1}{12 \div 4 = 3}$

$\frac{4}{12}$, $\frac{2}{6}$, and $\frac{1}{3}$ are equivalent fractions.

A. *Do these exercises.*

1. Write the fraction for **one part** of each square at the top of the page.

2. Write a fraction for the shaded part of each square above.

3. Write the letter of each pair of fractions below that is equivalent. For the first pair think: Were 1 and 3 multiplied by the **same number** to equal 3 and 9? The boxes at the top of the page may help you with some of these.

    a. $\frac{1}{3}$ $\frac{3}{9}$ b. $\frac{3}{4}$ $\frac{8}{12}$ c. $\frac{1}{2}$ $\frac{3}{6}$ d. $\frac{3}{4}$ $\frac{6}{8}$ e. $\frac{2}{5}$ $\frac{4}{15}$

4. Find equivalent fractions by multiplying both terms of each fraction by 2.

    a. $\frac{1}{3}$ b. $\frac{1}{2}$ c. $\frac{2}{5}$ d. $\frac{3}{4}$ e. $\frac{3}{8}$

5. Find equivalent fractions by multiplying both terms of each fraction by 3.

    a. $\frac{1}{2}$ b. $\frac{1}{4}$ c. $\frac{5}{6}$ d. $\frac{2}{3}$ e. $\frac{4}{5}$

B. *Fill in the missing numbers to make pairs of equivalent fractions. Think: By what number should I multiply?*

6. a. $\frac{1}{4} = \frac{4}{?}$ b. $\frac{2}{3} = \frac{4}{?}$ c. $\frac{2}{5} = \frac{6}{?}$ d. $\frac{1}{2} = \frac{4}{?}$ e. $\frac{3}{4} = \frac{9}{?}$

7. a. $\frac{1}{2} = \frac{?}{16}$ b. $\frac{3}{4} = \frac{?}{8}$ c. $\frac{1}{3} = \frac{?}{12}$ d. $\frac{2}{3} = \frac{?}{9}$ e. $\frac{4}{5} = \frac{?}{10}$

C. *Write the answers.*

8. One whole equals _____ thirds, _____ sixths, or _____ eighths.

9. Count by fourths to 4. Begin: $\frac{1}{4}$, $\frac{1}{2}$, $\frac{3}{4}$, 1, $1\frac{1}{4}$, $1\frac{1}{2}$ . . .

10. Write **P** for proper fraction, **I** for improper fraction, and **M** for mixed number.

    a. $4\frac{1}{2}$ b. $\frac{4}{10}$ c. $\frac{3}{2}$ d. $2\frac{7}{8}$ e. $\frac{5}{5}$ f. $\frac{11}{16}$

D. *Solve these reading problems.*

> **Hint:** To find the number of years between two dates, subtract the earlier date from the later one.

11. Menno Simons was born in 1496. He died a natural death in 1561. How many years did he live?

12. Menno Simons was ordained to the ministry in 1537 and was a minister until he died in 1561. How many years did Menno serve in the ministry?

13. The first Swiss Brethren congregation was organized in 1525. That was _____ years after Menno Simons was born in 1496.

14. The Waldensian Church was started by Peter Waldo around 1170. How many years after the founding of the Waldensian Church was the first Swiss Brethren congregation formed? (See number 13.)

15. The first Mennonites migrated to America from Europe in 1683. They moved to America _____ years after the founding of the first Swiss Brethren congregation. (See number 13.)

16. Columbus discovered America in 1492. How many years later did the first Mennonites move to America? (See number 15.)

17. How many years ago did the first Mennonites come to America? (You need to know the present year.)

25. Reducing Fractions to Lowest Terms

In Lesson 24 you multiplied both terms of a fraction to make an equivalent fraction. If both terms of a fraction are **divided** by the same number, the result is also an equivalent fraction. This operation is called **reducing the fraction**. The fraction is in **lowest terms** if both terms cannot be divided by any number other than 1.

Examples: Reduce $\frac{6}{12}$. $\frac{6 \div 2 = 3}{12 \div 2 = 6}$ $\frac{6 \div 3 = 2}{12 \div 3 = 4}$ $\frac{6 \div 6 = 1}{12 \div 6 = 2}$

$\frac{6}{12}$, $\frac{3}{6}$, $\frac{2}{4}$, and $\frac{1}{2}$ are equivalent fractions.

Only $\frac{1}{2}$ is in **lowest terms**.

A. *Reduce these fractions to lowest terms.*

1. a. $\frac{3}{9}$ b. $\frac{2}{8}$ c. $\frac{6}{10}$ d. $\frac{8}{16}$ e. $\frac{4}{12}$ f. $\frac{9}{12}$

2. a. $\frac{4}{8}$ b. $\frac{5}{10}$ c. $\frac{2}{16}$ d. $\frac{6}{15}$ e. $\frac{8}{12}$ f. $\frac{16}{24}$

3. a. $\frac{6}{9}$ b. $\frac{2}{12}$ c. $\frac{10}{20}$ d. $\frac{12}{30}$ e. $\frac{6}{24}$ f. $\frac{9}{15}$

B. *Do these exercises.*

4. Count by eighths to 2, beginning like this: $\frac{1}{8}$, $\frac{2}{8}$, $\frac{3}{8}$ . . . Write the numbers.

5. Write the numbers by eighths again. This time reduce any fractions that can be reduced. Begin: $\frac{1}{8}$, $\frac{1}{4}$, $\frac{3}{8}$, $\frac{1}{2}$ . . .

6. Write the letter of each set that is a pair of like fractions.

   a. $\frac{3}{4}$ $\frac{4}{5}$ b. $\frac{1}{3}$ $\frac{4}{3}$ c. $\frac{3}{8}$ $\frac{5}{8}$ d. $\frac{7}{8}$ $\frac{7}{10}$

7. Write the missing terms to make equivalent fractions.

   a. $\frac{3}{4} = \frac{?}{8}$ b. $\frac{1}{2} = \frac{?}{12}$ c. $\frac{4}{5} = \frac{12}{?}$ d. $\frac{2}{3} = \frac{6}{?}$ e. $\frac{2}{5} = \frac{?}{20}$

Adding Like Fractions

Only like fractions can be added or subtracted. Add the numerators only. The denominator is the label.

$$\begin{array}{r} 5 \text{ ninths} \\ + 2 \text{ ninths} \\ \hline 7 \text{ ninths} \end{array} \qquad \begin{array}{r} \frac{5}{9} \\ + \frac{2}{9} \\ \hline \frac{7}{9} \end{array}$$

To add mixed numbers, add the fractions first. Then add the whole numbers.

$$\begin{array}{r} 3\frac{1}{5} \\ + 4\frac{2}{5} \\ \hline 7\frac{3}{5} \end{array} \qquad \begin{array}{r} 8\frac{7}{11} \\ - 5\frac{3}{11} \\ \hline 3\frac{4}{11} \end{array}$$

When fractions are added or subtracted, the answer should always be reduced to lowest terms.

Sample: $\frac{3}{8} + \frac{1}{8} = \frac{4}{8} = \frac{1}{2}$

C. *Add these fractions. They are like fractions, so you can add without changing denominators.*

8.
$$\begin{array}{r} \frac{1}{3} \\ + \frac{1}{3} \end{array} \qquad \begin{array}{r} \frac{4}{7} \\ + \frac{2}{7} \end{array} \qquad \begin{array}{r} \frac{1}{5} \\ + \frac{3}{5} \end{array} \qquad \begin{array}{r} \frac{1}{8} \\ + \frac{4}{8} \end{array} \qquad \begin{array}{r} \frac{3}{11} \\ + \frac{2}{11} \end{array}$$

D. *Add these fractions and mixed numbers. Reduce the answers to lowest terms.*

9.
$$\begin{array}{r} \frac{2}{9} \\ + \frac{4}{9} \end{array} \qquad \begin{array}{r} \frac{1}{6} \\ + \frac{3}{6} \end{array} \qquad \begin{array}{r} \frac{1}{12} \\ + \frac{1}{12} \end{array} \qquad \begin{array}{r} \frac{7}{12} \\ + \frac{1}{12} \end{array} \qquad \begin{array}{r} \frac{3}{16} \\ + \frac{5}{16} \end{array}$$

10.
$$\begin{array}{r} \frac{3}{10} \\ + \frac{5}{10} \end{array} \qquad \begin{array}{r} \frac{2}{9} \\ + \frac{1}{9} \end{array} \qquad \begin{array}{r} \frac{1}{16} \\ + \frac{3}{16} \end{array} \qquad \begin{array}{r} \frac{5}{8} \\ + \frac{1}{8} \end{array} \qquad \begin{array}{r} \frac{1}{12} \\ + \frac{5}{12} \end{array}$$

11.
$$\begin{array}{r} 2\frac{3}{7} \\ + 4\frac{2}{7} \end{array} \qquad \begin{array}{r} 1\frac{1}{8} \\ + 1\frac{3}{8} \end{array} \qquad \begin{array}{r} 3\frac{2}{9} \\ + 1\frac{1}{9} \end{array} \qquad \begin{array}{r} 4\frac{3}{10} \\ + 5\frac{1}{10} \end{array} \qquad \begin{array}{r} 2\frac{5}{16} \\ + 6\frac{7}{16} \end{array}$$

E. *Write the answers only to these column additions.*

12.
$$\begin{array}{r} 6 \\ 8 \\ 4 \\ + 5 \end{array} \qquad \begin{array}{r} 8 \\ 9 \\ 3 \\ + 8 \end{array} \qquad \begin{array}{r} 4 \\ 7 \\ 8 \\ + 5 \end{array} \qquad \begin{array}{r} 7 \\ 6 \\ 7 \\ + 8 \end{array} \qquad \begin{array}{r} 5 \\ 8 \\ 9 \\ + 4 \end{array} \qquad \begin{array}{r} 3 \\ 9 \\ 8 \\ + 5 \end{array}$$

26. Finding a Part of a Number

Fractions and division are closely related. The fraction $\frac{1}{2}$ actually means $1 \div 2$. The fraction $\frac{3}{4}$ means $3 \div 4$.

> **To find one part of a number, divide by the denominator of the fraction.**
>
> Example: To find $\frac{1}{2}$ of a number, divide by 2. $\frac{1}{2}$ of 10 = 5
>
> To find $\frac{1}{5}$ of a number, divide by 5. $\frac{1}{5}$ of 30 = 6
>
> To find $\frac{1}{7}$ of a number, divide by 7. $\frac{1}{7}$ of 21 = 3

A. *Find the following parts. Write the answers only.*

1. $\frac{1}{2}$ of 24 $\frac{1}{4}$ of 24 $\frac{1}{8}$ of 24 $\frac{1}{6}$ of 24

2. $\frac{1}{7}$ of 42 $\frac{1}{9}$ of 81 $\frac{1}{5}$ of 40 $\frac{1}{3}$ of 36

3. $\frac{1}{4}$ of 36 $\frac{1}{8}$ of 56 $\frac{1}{2}$ of 18 $\frac{1}{7}$ of 63

Sometimes we need to find more than one part of a number. We may need to find $\frac{3}{8}$ of 24, instead of only $\frac{1}{8}$. First divide by 8 to find $\frac{1}{8}$ of 24. Then multiply the answer by 3 to find $\frac{3}{8}$ of 24.

> **To find a part of a number, first divide by the denominator of the fraction, and then multiply by the numerator.**
>
> Example: Find $\frac{3}{8}$ of 24.
>
> First divide by 8: $24 \div 8 = 3$.
>
> Then multiply by 3: $3 \times 3 = 9$.
>
> Answer: $\frac{3}{8}$ of 24 = 9

B. *Find the following parts. Write the answers only.*

4. $\frac{1}{3}$ of 30 $\frac{2}{3}$ of 30 $\frac{1}{5}$ of 25 $\frac{3}{5}$ of 25

5. $\frac{1}{8}$ of 56 $\frac{5}{8}$ of 56 $\frac{1}{9}$ of 36 $\frac{7}{9}$ of 36

6. $\frac{2}{5}$ of 40 $\frac{3}{4}$ of 16 $\frac{4}{7}$ of 49 $\frac{3}{8}$ of 32

7. $\frac{7}{8}$ of 48 $\frac{5}{6}$ of 30 $\frac{4}{9}$ of 27 $\frac{2}{3}$ of 18

C. *Do these exercises.*

8. Reduce these fractions to lowest terms.

    a. $\frac{4}{12}$ b. $\frac{2}{8}$ c. $\frac{8}{20}$ d. $\frac{9}{30}$ e. $\frac{12}{18}$ f. $\frac{6}{30}$

9. Follow the signs. Reduce answers to lowest terms.

$$\begin{array}{r} \frac{5}{8} \\ + \frac{1}{8} \end{array} \qquad \begin{array}{r} \frac{11}{12} \\ - \frac{1}{12} \end{array} \qquad \begin{array}{r} \frac{1}{16} \\ + \frac{9}{16} \end{array} \qquad \begin{array}{r} 2\frac{1}{9} \\ + 3\frac{5}{9} \end{array} \qquad \begin{array}{r} 7\frac{5}{6} \\ - 1\frac{1}{6} \end{array}$$

10. Copy and multiply.

$$\begin{array}{r} 564 \\ \times 48 \end{array} \qquad \begin{array}{r} 839 \\ \times 76 \end{array} \qquad \begin{array}{r} 176 \\ \times 36 \end{array} \qquad \begin{array}{r} 447 \\ \times 79 \end{array} \qquad \begin{array}{r} 930 \\ \times 98 \end{array}$$

11. Write what pieces of money should be given as change. Start at the amount of purchase, and name the smallest pieces first.

	Amount of Purchase	Amount Given	
S.	$9.61	$20.00	Answer: 4 pennies, 1 dime, 1 quarter, 1 ten-dollar bill
a.	$8.47	$10.00	
b.	$2.65	$5.00	
c.	$12.78	$20.00	
d.	$7.40	$20.00	

D. *Solve these reading problems.*

12. Esther and Ruby are making a quilt to use up scraps of fabric. When the quilt is finished, it will have 7 rows of large patches with 6 in each row. How many large patches will the girls make for their quilt?

13. Esther and Ruby are using 9 small 3-inch patches to make each large patch. How many small patches do they need to make 6 large patches?

14. If the girls have 30 large patches yet to make, how many small patches do they need to make them? (See number 13.)

15. Esther and Ruby plan to make a border of small patches around the edge of the quilt. If the quilt is 90 inches long, how many 3-inch patches will fit on that side?

16. Esther and Ruby need 5 yards of fabric for the back of the quilt. At $3.59 a yard, how much will they pay for the fabric?

17. Mother found some fabric on sale for $2.75 a yard. At that price they will save _____ per yard. (See number 16.)

27. Multiplying Whole Numbers by Mixed Numbers

Many whole numbers can be multiplied mentally by mixed numbers. Use the following steps.

	Example: $3\frac{1}{2} \times 6 = ?$
1. Multiply by the whole number.	$3 \times 6 = 18$
2. Multiply by the fraction.	$\frac{1}{2} \times 6 = 3$
3. Add the two products together.	$18 + 3 = 21$
	Answer: $3\frac{1}{2} \times 6 = 21$

Remember: $\frac{1}{2}$ **of** 6 is the same as $\frac{1}{2}$ **times** 6.

A. Write the numbers that belong in the blanks.

1. $2 \times 10 = $ ____ $\frac{1}{2}$ of $10 = $ ____ $2\frac{1}{2} \times 10 = $ ____

2. $4 \times 4 = $ ____ $\frac{1}{2}$ of $4 = $ ____ $4\frac{1}{2} \times 4 = $ ____

3. $3 \times 8 = $ ____ $\frac{1}{4}$ of $8 = $ ____ $3\frac{1}{4} \times 8 = $ ____

B. Write the answers only.

4. $3\frac{1}{2} \times 4$ $5\frac{1}{3} \times 6$ $1\frac{1}{6} \times 12$

5. $2\frac{1}{4} \times 8$ $1\frac{1}{2} \times 18$ $2\frac{1}{3} \times 9$

6. $1\frac{1}{8} \times 24$ $1\frac{1}{4} \times 12$ $3\frac{1}{4} \times 4$

7. $5\frac{1}{2} \times 4$ $1\frac{1}{7} \times 14$ $4\frac{1}{2} \times 10$

C. Find these answers as you did in Lesson 26.

8. $\frac{1}{5}$ of 45 $\frac{2}{5}$ of 45 $\frac{1}{7}$ of 35 $\frac{4}{7}$ of 35

9. $\frac{3}{4}$ of 24 $\frac{2}{3}$ of 15 $\frac{4}{5}$ of 25 $\frac{3}{8}$ of 16

10. $\frac{5}{8}$ of 32 $\frac{3}{4}$ of 12 $\frac{8}{9}$ of 54 $\frac{1}{4}$ of 48

D. Do these exercises.

11. Reduce to lowest terms.

   a. $\frac{5}{15}$ b. $\frac{8}{16}$ c. $\frac{9}{24}$ d. $\frac{6}{24}$ e. $\frac{4}{12}$ f. $\frac{10}{12}$

12. Subtract. Reduce answers to lowest terms.

$$\frac{7}{9} - \frac{4}{9} \qquad \frac{3}{4} - \frac{1}{4} \qquad \frac{11}{12} - \frac{3}{12} \qquad 6\frac{7}{8} - 2\frac{1}{8} \qquad 4\frac{13}{16} - 1\frac{3}{16}$$

General Review

E. *Write the answers only.*

13.
9	8	12	11	7	9	12	8	12
× 7	× 9	× 8	× 11	× 8	× 9	× 7	× 8	× 11

14.
8	5	4	9	3	7
7	4	8	9	7	5
3	8	6	5	7	2
5	8	3	7	9	4
+ 5	+ 6	+ 2	+ 4	+ 6	+ 3

F. *Copy and follow the signs.*

15.
6,700	8,000	7,437	5,103	6,580
− 4,659	− 3,726	− 5,467	− 4,658	− 1,747

16.
573	679	380	428	586
× 27	× 45	× 83	× 67	× 43

17. 6)4,738   5)8,635   4)7,548   7)3,056   3)5,610

G. *Do these exercises.*

18. Write with Roman numerals.

   a. 327   b. 680   c. 943   d. 1,534   e. 1,058

19. Write numerals for these number words.

   a. eleven billion, three hundred million, fifty thousand

   b. 890 billion, 72 million, 276 thousand, 19

   c. six billion, two hundred seventy-four thousand

20. Father and Mother are thankful for the privilege of having a Christian school. They drive 15 miles each day to take their children to and from school. How many miles do Mother and Father drive to and from school in one school week? (Think: How many days are in a school week?)

28. Dividing a Small Number by a Larger One

You know that to find a fourth of a number, you divide the number by 4. One fourth of 16 is 4; one fourth of 28 is 7. But how can you find one fourth of 3?

$\frac{1}{4}$ of 16 = 4

$\frac{1}{4}$ of 28 = 7

$\frac{1}{4}$ of 3 = ?

Dividing a small number, like 3, by a larger number, like 4, results in a fraction. The number being divided (the dividend) becomes the numerator of the fraction, and the number it is divided by (the divisor) becomes the denominator.

One fourth of 3 = 3 ÷ 4 = $\frac{3}{4}$ 1 divided by 5 = $\frac{1}{5}$

One third of 2 = 2 ÷ 3 = $\frac{2}{3}$ 3 divided by 10 = $\frac{3}{10}$

4 is what part of 5?   4 ÷ 5 = $\frac{4}{5}$

Fractions should be reduced to lowest terms.

Example: What is $\frac{1}{8}$ of 2? $\frac{1}{8}$ of 2 = 2 ÷ 8 = $\frac{2}{8}$ = $\frac{1}{4}$

A. *Write the answers as fractions in lowest terms.*

1. 2 ÷ 5   1 ÷ 8   3 ÷ 7   5 ÷ 6   4 ÷ 9

2. 4 ÷ 6   3 ÷ 9   6 ÷ 12   4 ÷ 10   5 ÷ 16

3. $\frac{1}{3}$ of 1 $\frac{1}{5}$ of 3 $\frac{1}{8}$ of 7 $\frac{1}{4}$ of 2

4. $\frac{1}{7}$ of 4 $\frac{1}{8}$ of 4 $\frac{1}{6}$ of 2 $\frac{1}{12}$ of 9

5. 2 is what part of 3?   4 is what part of 12?

6. 6 is what part of 10?   5 is what part of 8?

Ordinary division problems often have remainders. The remainder can be expressed as a fraction by dividing the remainder by the divisor. The remainder becomes the numerator of the fraction, and the divisor becomes the denominator. Then the fraction should be reduced.

$$\begin{array}{r} 45 \text{ R } 6 \\ 8{\overline{)366}} \\ 32 \\ \hline 46 \\ 40 \\ \hline 6 \end{array}$$

$$\begin{array}{r} 45\frac{3}{4} \\ 8{\overline{)366}} \\ 32 \\ \hline 46 \\ 40 \\ \hline 6 \end{array}$$

B. *Copy and divide. Express remainders as fractions in lowest terms.*

7. $3{\overline{)761}}$ $6{\overline{)500}}$ $4{\overline{)563}}$ $8{\overline{)444}}$

8. $5{\overline{)372}}$ $7{\overline{)640}}$ $9{\overline{)375}}$ $4{\overline{)622}}$

C. *Follow the signs and work carefully. Reduce all fractions in your answers to lowest terms.*

9.

$$\frac{7}{11} \atop + \frac{3}{11}$$
$\qquad$
$$\frac{4}{9} \atop + \frac{2}{9}$$
$\qquad$
$$\frac{8}{12} \atop + \frac{1}{12}$$
$\qquad$
$$3\frac{1}{4} \atop + 2\frac{1}{4}$$
$\qquad$
$$5\frac{3}{8} \atop + 4\frac{3}{8}$$

10.

$$\frac{7}{8} \atop - \frac{3}{8}$$
$\qquad$
$$\frac{15}{16} \atop - \frac{3}{16}$$
$\qquad$
$$\frac{9}{10} \atop - \frac{3}{10}$$
$\qquad$
$$5\frac{3}{8} \atop - 4\frac{1}{8}$$
$\qquad$
$$6\frac{5}{7} \atop - 3\frac{2}{7}$$

D. *Write the answers only.*

11. $\frac{1}{5}$ of 40 $\qquad$ $\frac{3}{5}$ of 40 $\qquad$ $\frac{1}{8}$ of 48 $\qquad$ $\frac{5}{8}$ of 48

12. $\frac{3}{7}$ of 28 $\qquad$ $\frac{5}{6}$ of 36 $\qquad$ $\frac{2}{3}$ of 27 $\qquad$ $\frac{3}{4}$ of 16

13. $\frac{2}{5}$ of 20 $\qquad$ $\frac{1}{2}$ of 22 $\qquad$ $\frac{5}{9}$ of 45 $\qquad$ $\frac{3}{8}$ of 24

14. $1\frac{1}{2} \times 20$ $\qquad$ $2\frac{1}{5} \times 10$ $\qquad$ $4\frac{1}{4} \times 4$ $\qquad$ $3\frac{1}{3} \times 9$

15. $2\frac{1}{4} \times 8$ $\qquad$ $1\frac{1}{8} \times 24$ $\qquad$ $3\frac{1}{2} \times 6$ $\qquad$ $1\frac{1}{9} \times 36$

General Review

E. *Do these exercises.*

16. Change these Roman numerals to Arabic numerals.

a. CLXXIV   b. DCCLIX   c. CMXVII   d. MCCCXXVI   e. MLXIII

17. Write the value of the 3 in each number.

a. 890,345,710   b. 13,908,724,561   c. 5,936,170,842

18. What number is 50,000 + 4,000 + 300 + 90 + 6?

19. Write 349,251 in expanded form.

20. Copy each number, and write the next three numbers that come after it. Think: Add 1 each time.

a. 2,097 $\qquad\qquad$ c. 35,089

b. 12,000 $\qquad\qquad$ d. 47,998

29. Changing Improper Fractions to Mixed Numbers

In an improper fraction, the numerator is equal to or larger than the denominator. That means an improper fraction is equal to one whole thing or more. To change an improper fraction to a whole number or mixed number, divide the numerator by the denominator. Express any remainder as a fraction in lowest terms.

> Examples: Change $\frac{6}{2}$ to a whole number. $6 \div 2 = 3$ $\frac{6}{2} = 3$
>
> Change $\frac{10}{4}$ to a mixed number. $4\overline{)10}$ $\;2\frac{1}{2}$ $\frac{10}{4} = 2\frac{1}{2}$

A. *Change these improper fractions to whole or mixed numbers. Reduce all fractions in your answers to lowest terms.*

1. a. $\frac{5}{3}$ b. $\frac{7}{4}$ c. $\frac{10}{5}$ d. $\frac{8}{6}$ e. $\frac{6}{4}$ f. $\frac{9}{3}$ g. $\frac{4}{4}$

2. a. $\frac{8}{2}$ b. $\frac{12}{5}$ c. $\frac{9}{6}$ d. $\frac{16}{7}$ e. $\frac{7}{3}$ f. $\frac{11}{4}$ g. $\frac{14}{4}$

> When fractions are added, the answer may be an improper fraction. Then the answer must be changed to a whole number or a mixed number with the fraction part reduced to lowest terms. Such an answer is in **simplest form**.
>
> $\frac{3}{8}$
> $+ \frac{7}{8}$
> $\frac{10}{8} = 1\frac{2}{8} = 1\frac{1}{4}$

B. *Add these fractions. If the answer is an improper fraction, change it to a whole number or mixed number in simplest form.*

3.
$\frac{5}{8}$ $\quad$ $\frac{3}{4}$ $\quad$ $\frac{7}{9}$ $\quad$ $\frac{2}{3}$ $\quad$ $\frac{7}{12}$
$+\frac{3}{8}$ $\quad$ $+\frac{3}{4}$ $\quad$ $+\frac{4}{9}$ $\quad$ $+\frac{2}{3}$ $\quad$ $+\frac{11}{12}$

C. *Do these exercises.*

4. Subtract these fractions. Reduce answers to lowest terms.

$\frac{7}{9}$ $\qquad$ $\frac{11}{16}$ $\qquad$ $\frac{7}{8}$ $\qquad$ $5\frac{2}{3}$ $\qquad$ $4\frac{5}{6}$
$-\frac{1}{9}$ $\qquad$ $-\frac{3}{16}$ $\qquad$ $-\frac{5}{8}$ $\qquad$ $-1\frac{1}{3}$ $\qquad$ $-3\frac{1}{6}$

5. Find the missing numbers to make equivalent fractions.

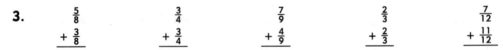

a. $\frac{1}{4} = \frac{4}{?}$ b. $\frac{1}{3} = \frac{?}{6}$ c. $\frac{2}{3} = \frac{?}{15}$ d. $\frac{3}{4} = \frac{9}{?}$ e. $\frac{1}{8} = \frac{?}{16}$

6. Copy and divide. Express remainders as fractions.

$$5\overline{)398} \qquad 4\overline{)6,741} \qquad 6\overline{)7,154} \qquad 8\overline{)4,324}$$

7. Answer **yes** or **no**.

　a. Are $\frac{3}{8}$ and $\frac{5}{8}$ like fractions?

　b. Are $\frac{3}{8}$ and $\frac{5}{8}$ equivalent fractions?

　c. Is 12 the product of 3 and 4?

　d. Is 7 the difference between 3 and 4?

　e. Is the answer to a division problem called the difference?

　f. Are the numerator and denominator the terms of the fraction?

　g. Is the fraction $\frac{5}{5}$ equal to one whole?

Reading Problems

In reading problems solved by division, you must decide whether to change the remainder to a fraction. Think which makes sense. Is it sensible to think of a part?

Example:	Douglas and Aaron found a quarter along the road. Their father told them to share the money. How many cents will each boy have?
	$25 \div 2 = 12$ R1. The boys could not divide the leftover cent. The remainder must be left as R1. Each boy can have 12¢, and 1¢ is left over.
Example:	Three girls are sharing 8 sheets of yellow constuction paper. How many sheets of paper will each of them have?
	$8 \div 3 = 2$ R2. The girls can cut the leftover sheets into pieces. Change the remainder to $\frac{2}{3}$. Each girl can have $2\frac{2}{3}$ sheets of paper.

D. *Solve these reading problems. Divide the remainder to make a fraction* if it is sensible to do so.

8. Father drove 198 miles in 4 hours. At that rate, how far did he drive in one hour?

9. Patricia, Kathleen, and Wendy collected 79 leaves. If they share them, how many leaves will each girl have?

10. Melvin and Jeffrey are marking lines for a game. The playground area is 85 feet long. They want to mark a center line to divide the length of the playground area in half. The center line should be _____ feet from each end.

30. Chapter 3 Review

A. *Do these exercises.*

1. Write these fractions.

    a. numerator—4; denominator—9   e. 3 divided by 7

    b. seven-eighths   f. $1 \div 8$

    c. 2 parts out of 3   g. $\frac{1}{9}$ of 5

    d. 3 is what part of 5?

2. Reduce to lowest terms.

    a. $\frac{3}{9}$ b. $\frac{4}{6}$ c. $\frac{6}{12}$ d. $\frac{10}{16}$ e. $\frac{12}{18}$ f. $\frac{9}{24}$ g. $\frac{16}{20}$

3. Write the missing terms to make equivalent fractions.

    a. $\frac{1}{6} = \frac{?}{12}$ b. $\frac{2}{5} = \frac{4}{?}$ c. $\frac{1}{3} = \frac{*5}{?}$ d. $\frac{3}{4} = \frac{?}{16}$ e. $\frac{1}{8} = \frac{?}{24}$

4. Count by thirds to 4. Begin: $\frac{1}{3}$, $\frac{2}{3}$,   1, $1\frac{1}{3}$ . . .

5. Count by fourths to 3. Reduce all fractions to lowest terms.

6. Write **P** for proper fraction, **I** for improper fraction, and **M** for mixed number.

    a. $\frac{5}{3}$ b. $\frac{3}{5}$ c. $3\frac{1}{5}$ d. $\frac{6}{6}$ e. $4\frac{7}{8}$ f. $\frac{4}{11}$ g. $\frac{15}{16}$

7. Change these improper fractions to whole or mixed numbers in simplest form.

    a. $\frac{12}{5}$ b. $\frac{6}{3}$ c. $\frac{9}{4}$ d. $\frac{4}{4}$ e. $\frac{10}{6}$ f. $\frac{7}{3}$ g. $\frac{8}{7}$

8. Write the letter of each pair of like fractions.

    a. $\frac{3}{8}$ $\frac{5}{8}$ b. $\frac{1}{3}$ $\frac{1}{13}$ c. $\frac{2}{3}$ $\frac{3}{4}$ d. $\frac{2}{5}$ $\frac{4}{5}$ e. $\frac{1}{7}$ $\frac{6}{7}$

B. *Write the answers only.*

9. $\frac{1}{5}$ of 35	$\frac{1}{8}$ of 64	$\frac{1}{4}$ of 24	$\frac{1}{3}$ of 30
10. $\frac{2}{5}$ of 35	$\frac{3}{8}$ of 64	$\frac{3}{4}$ of 24	$\frac{2}{3}$ of 30
11. $\frac{4}{7}$ of 42	$\frac{2}{9}$ of 18	$\frac{5}{8}$ of 32	$\frac{5}{6}$ of 36
12. $1\frac{1}{2} \times 14$	$1\frac{1}{4} \times 16$	$2\frac{1}{3} \times 12$	$1\frac{1}{8} \times 40$
13. $3\frac{1}{4} \times 4$	$2\frac{1}{3} \times 6$	$4\frac{1}{2} \times 8$	$2\frac{1}{5} \times 10$

C. Follow the signs. Write all answers in simplest form.

14. $\frac{3}{8}$ $\frac{2}{9}$ $\frac{3}{16}$ $\frac{7}{12}$ $\frac{5}{8}$
    $+\frac{1}{8}$ $+\frac{5}{9}$ $+\frac{11}{16}$ $+\frac{5}{12}$ $+\frac{7}{8}$

15. $2\frac{1}{4}$ $1\frac{5}{8}$ $3\frac{5}{12}$ $4\frac{1}{6}$ $1\frac{1}{9}$
    $+3\frac{1}{4}$ $+5\frac{1}{8}$ $+6\frac{1}{12}$ $+3\frac{1}{6}$ $+2\frac{5}{9}$

16. $\frac{11}{12}$ $\frac{13}{16}$ $\frac{9}{10}$ $4\frac{7}{8}$ $6\frac{7}{9}$
    $-\frac{7}{12}$ $-\frac{5}{16}$ $-\frac{3}{10}$ $-1\frac{5}{8}$ $-2\frac{4}{9}$

D. Express remainders as fractions in lowest terms.

17. $4\overline{)654}$ $3\overline{)875}$ $6\overline{)378}$ $8\overline{)740}$

18. $5\overline{)3,840}$ $2\overline{)7,543}$ $7\overline{)8,734}$ $6\overline{)5,832}$

E. Copy and multiply.

19.   795   478   937   518   840
     × 46   × 13   × 38   × 98   × 62

Reading Problem Review

F. Write add, subtract, multiply, or divide.

20. To find the difference between numbers, you _____.

21. To find the total of two or more different numbers, you _____.

22. To find the cost of several articles each marked the same price, you _____.

23. You know how much a Bible costs and how much money you have. To find how much more money you need to buy the Bible, you _____.

24. You know the total cost and how many people are sharing the cost. To find each one's share, you _____.

25. You know how much one hymnbook costs. To find the cost of hymnbooks for everyone in your class, you _____.

(continued on next page)

26. You know how many eggs you had and how many you used in baking. To find how many eggs are left, you _____.

27. You know how much money you have. To find how many 5¢ erasers you can buy, you _____.

G. *Solve these problems.*

28. Roy has three mother ducks and one drake. Each of the mother ducks hatched a nest of 17 ducklings. How many ducklings were hatched?

29. Some of the ducklings died before they were grown. Of the ducks Roy raised, he gave 8 to the Hollow Tree Rest Home. He has 38 left. How many ducks did he raise?

30. If 5 doughnuts are shared equally by 3 boys, how many doughnuts will each boy get?

31. Mother spent $23.57 at the grocery store and $9.39 at the dry goods store. If she had $40.00 when she started shopping, how much money does she have left?

32. Construction of the White House, where the President lives, was begun in 1792. Years later, in 1948, a complete rebuilding of the White House was begun. How long was it from the first building of the White House until the rebuilding?

33. How many 8¢ pencils can you buy for 50¢?

- -

31. Chapter 3 Test

Chapter 4

Measures

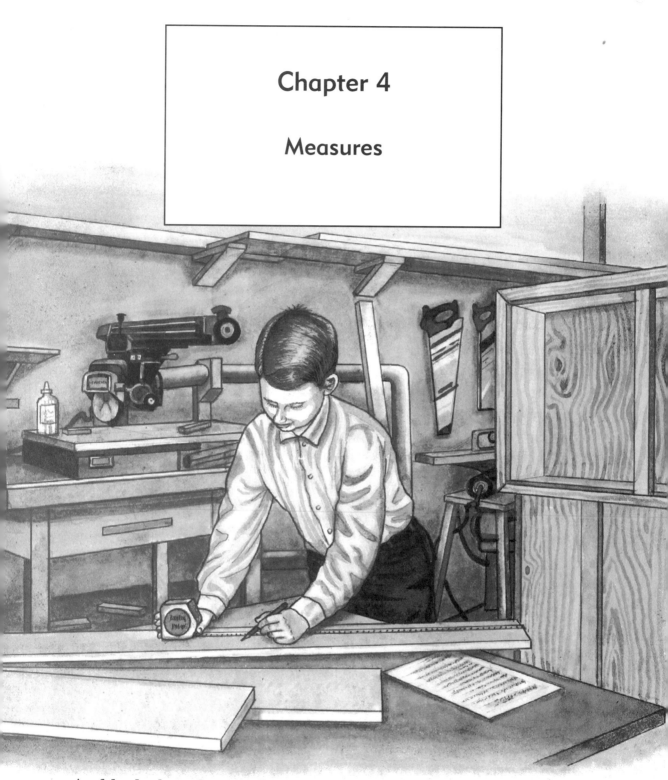

And look that thou make them after their pattern, which was
shewed thee in the mount.
(Exodus 25:40)

32. English Units of Linear Measure

Units of linear measure are used to measure length. Study the table below. Only the last equivalent should be new for you.

> 1 foot (ft. or ') = 12 inches (in. or ")
>
> 1 yard (yd.) = 3 feet = 36 inches
>
> 1 mile (mi.) = 5,280 feet = **1,760 yards**

You should also remember the two rules used to change from one unit of measure to another. In each case the **key number** is the number of the smaller unit in the larger unit. The key number when working with feet and yards is 3. The key number for inches and yards is 36.

> Rule 1:   To change from a larger unit of measure to a smaller unit, **multiply** by the key number.   Example: 4 feet = _____ inches
>
> Multiply by 12 to change feet to inches.   4 × 12 = 48, so 4 ft. = 48 in.
>
> Rule 2:   To change from a smaller unit of measure to a larger unit, **divide** by the key number.   Example: 9 feet = _____ yards
>
> Divide by 3 to change feet to yards.   9 ÷ 3 = 3, so 9 ft. = 3 yd.

A. *Write the larger unit in each pair.*

1. a. foot, inch   **b.** foot, yard   **c.** mile, yard

B. *Write the missing numbers. You will be changing from a larger unit of measure to a smaller one.*

2. 1 yard = _____ ft.   1 mile = _____ ft.   1 mile = _____ yd.

3. 1 yard = _____ in.   1 foot = _____ in.   8 yards = _____ ft.

4. 5 feet = _____ in.   4 yards = _____ in.   2 miles = _____ ft.

5. 3 feet = _____ in.   3 miles = _____ yd.   12 feet = _____ in.

6. 10 yards = _____ in.   12 yards = _____ ft.   4 miles = _____ ft.

C. *Write the answers.*

7. There are 12 inches in a foot, so how many inches are in
a. $\frac{1}{2}$ foot?   **b.** $\frac{1}{3}$ foot?   **c.** $\frac{2}{3}$ foot?   **d.** $\frac{1}{4}$ foot?   **e.** $\frac{3}{4}$ foot?   **f.** $\frac{1}{6}$ foot?

8. There are 36 inches in a yard, so how many inches are in
a. $\frac{1}{2}$ yard?   **b.** $\frac{1}{6}$ yard?   **c.** $\frac{1}{3}$ yard?   **d.** $\frac{2}{3}$ yard?   **e.** $\frac{1}{4}$ yard?   **f.** $\frac{3}{4}$ yard?

9. How many feet are in?   **a.** $\frac{1}{2}$ mile?   **b.** $\frac{1}{4}$ mile?   **c.** $\frac{1}{8}$ mile?
(Show your work.)

General Review

D. *Write the answers in as few words as possible.*

10. What is the answer to an addition problem called?
11. What is the answer to a subtraction problem?
12. What is the answer to a multiplication problem?
13. Another name for multiplier or multiplicand is _____.
14. What is the answer to a division problem?
15. What process is the opposite of subtraction?
16. Like fractions have the same _____.
17. Is 7:00 P.M. in the morning or in the evening?
18. How many thousands are in a million?
19. In a fraction, the _____ tells how many parts are in a whole thing.

E. *Follow the directions.*

20. Add or subtract, as the signs indicate.

$$
\begin{array}{r} 49{,}387 \\ 65{,}892 \\ +\ 36{,}163 \\ \hline \end{array}
\qquad
\begin{array}{r} 92{,}635 \\ 16{,}549 \\ +\ 23{,}894 \\ \hline \end{array}
\qquad
\begin{array}{r} 9{,}012 \\ 8{,}753 \\ 3{,}679 \\ +\ 4{,}564 \\ \hline \end{array}
\qquad
\begin{array}{r} 8{,}300 \\ -\ 2{,}785 \\ \hline \end{array}
\qquad
\begin{array}{r} 7{,}481 \\ -\ 3{,}649 \\ \hline \end{array}
$$

21. Multiply, and check by exchanging the factors.

$$
\text{a.} \quad \begin{array}{r} 68 \\ \times\ 35 \\ \hline \end{array}
\qquad
\text{b.} \quad \begin{array}{r} 43 \\ \times\ 98 \\ \hline \end{array}
\qquad
\text{c.} \quad \begin{array}{r} 27 \\ \times\ 76 \\ \hline \end{array}
\qquad
\text{d.} \quad \begin{array}{r} 19 \\ \times\ 87 \\ \hline \end{array}
$$

22. Divide, and check by multiplying.

$$
5\overline{)6{,}900} \qquad 7\overline{)4{,}664} \qquad 9\overline{)3{,}840} \qquad 4\overline{)9{,}623}
$$

F. *Solve these reading problems.*

so am I

23. The fifth grade class at Bradford Christian School is studying insects in science. Sister Lora told the fifth graders to bring insects for a collection. If each of the 18 pupils brings 15 insects, how many insects will they have in their collection?

24. Among the insects the fifth graders brought were 57 butterflies, 32 moths, 18 crickets, and 149 beetles. How many insects was that altogether?

25. In one week the fifth graders collected 210 small creatures, including 14 spiders. Sister Lora said spiders are not insects. How many of the small creatures were insects?

33. Measuring to the Nearest Eighth Inch

Below is a ruler divided into eighth inches. Hold your own ruler below it, and find the marked points on your ruler.

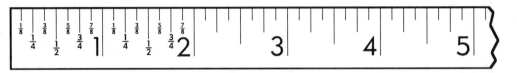

The ruler below is divided into sixteenth inches like your own ruler. Notice that a tiny sixteenth-inch mark is between every two eighth-inch marks. The magnified portion has the same markings labeled as the ruler above.

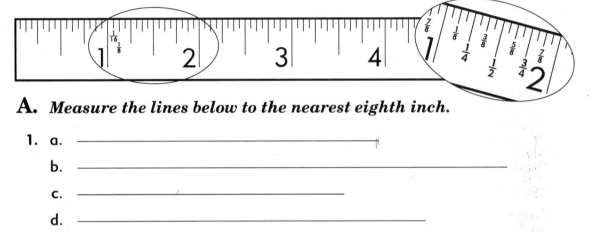

A. *Measure the lines below to the nearest eighth inch.*

1. a. _____

    b. _____

    c. _____

    d. _____

B. *Write the lengths to which the arrows point on the rulers below. Notice that the last ruler does not begin with 1 inch.*

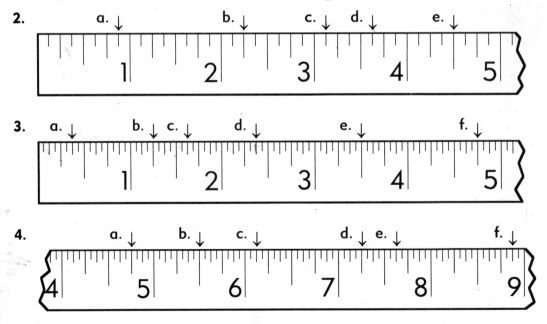

Scale Drawings

Study the scale drawing below. The **scale** on this drawing is "1 inch = 1 mile." That means every inch on the drawing stands for a mile in actual distance.

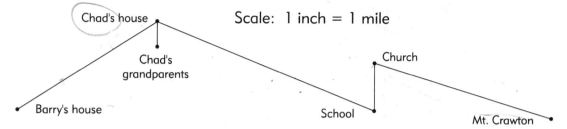

C. *Answer the questions below by measuring the lines on the scale drawing to the nearest $\frac{1}{4}$ inch.*

5. How far does Chad have to school?

6. How far does Barry have to school?

7. What is the distance between the school and the church?

8. How far does Chad live from his grandparents?

9. What is the distance from Chad's house to Mt. Crawton?

General Review

D. *Find and write the missing numbers.*

10. 1 yd. = _____ in.   1 mi. = _____ ft.   1 mi. = _____ yd.

11. 6 ft. = _____ in.   8 yd. = _____ ft.   3 mi. = _____ ft.

12. 3 yd. = _____ in.   4 ft. = _____ in.   2 mi. = _____ yd.

E. *Do these exercises.*

13. Change these improper fractions to whole or mixed numbers.
a. $\frac{5}{5}$ b. $\frac{3}{2}$ c. $\frac{9}{6}$ d. $\frac{13}{4}$ e. $\frac{11}{3}$ f. $\frac{14}{8}$

14. Reduce these fractions to lowest terms.
a. $\frac{6}{8}$ b. $\frac{10}{16}$ c. $\frac{12}{16}$ d. $\frac{14}{16}$ e. $\frac{6}{16}$ f. $\frac{8}{16}$

15. Add or subtract. Write all answers in simplest form.

$3\frac{3}{8} + 3\frac{1}{8}$ $2\frac{5}{16} + 1\frac{9}{16}$ $5\frac{7}{12} + 6\frac{1}{12}$ $8\frac{7}{9} - 2\frac{4}{9}$ $5\frac{11}{16} - 1\frac{3}{16}$

16. Divide, and check by multiplying.

$7\overline{)3{,}784}$ $5\overline{)8{,}620}$ $8\overline{)9{,}854}$ $4\overline{)6{,}314}$ $6\overline{)4{,}600}$

34. Sixteenth Inches on a Ruler

You already know that the smallest lines on your ruler measure sixteenth inches. Study the ruler below and the enlarged section that shows the names of the points on the ruler. With your teacher's help, find those points on your own ruler.

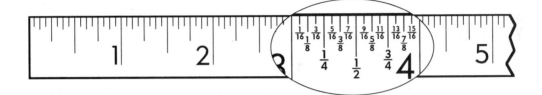

A. *Do these exercises.*

1. Write by sixteenths to 2. Begin: $\frac{1}{16}$, $\frac{2}{16}$, $\frac{3}{16}$ . . .

2. Write by sixteenths to 2 again. This time reduce any of the fractions that you can. Begin: $\frac{1}{16}$, $\frac{1}{8}$, $\frac{3}{16}$, $\frac{1}{4}$ . . .

3. Measure these lines to the nearest sixteenth inch.

   a. _____

   b. _____

   c. _____

   d. _____

   e. _____

   f. _____

B. *Write the lengths to which the arrows point on the rulers below.*

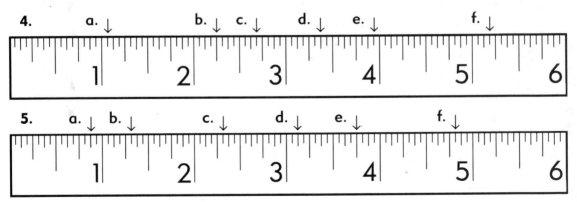

Scale Drawings

The scale on the drawing below is "1 inch = 2 miles." Every inch on the drawing represents 2 miles in actual distance. To change inches to miles, you must think, "Two times as many miles as inches."

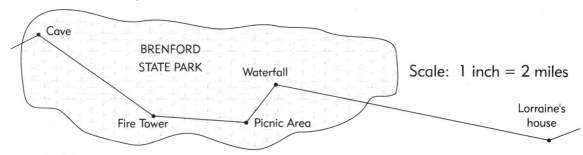

C. *Do these exercises.*

6. Change these measurements to miles. Remember to think, "Two times as many miles as inches."

    a. 3 in.   **b.** 2 in.   **c.** 4 in.   **d.** $\frac{1}{2}$ in.   **e.** $1\frac{1}{2}$ in.

7. Use the scale drawing to find answers for these exercises.

    a. How far does Lorraine live from the edge of the state park?

    b. How far does Lorraine's family need to drive to reach the picnic tables in the park?

    c. One day Lorraine's family hiked from the picnic area to the fire tower. How far did they walk?

    d. What is the distance between the waterfall and the cave by the road?

    e. According to the scale drawing, Brenford State Park is _____ miles across. (Measure from side to side at the widest part.)

General Review

D. *Write the numbers that fit in the blanks.*

8. 1 mi. = _____ yd.   1 yd. = _____ in.   12 ft. = _____ in.

9. 2 mi. = _____ ft.   9 yd. = _____ ft.   4 yd. = _____ in.

E. *Follow the directions.*

10. Copy and multiply. Check by exchanging the factors.

    a.   97   **b.**   50   **c.**   84   **d.**   37   **e.**   26
        × 48   × 87   × 86   × 67   × 19

11. Copy and subtract. Check by addition.

      5,043   9,261   8,304   6,793   7,001
    − 2,879   − 4,536   − 6,258   − 3,697   − 6,824

35. English Units of Capacity

| Pint | Quart | Peck | Bushel |

The amount a container can hold is called its **capacity.** The units of capacity listed in the box indicate some containers and how much they hold. **Liquid measure** is used for things like water, juice, and gasoline. **Dry measure** is used for things like beans, apples, peaches, and strawberries.

Liquid Measure	Dry Measure
1 pint (pt.) = 2 cups	1 quart = 2 pints
1 quart (qt.) = 4 cups	1 peck (pk.) = 8 quarts
1 quart = 2 pints	1 bushel (bu.) = 4 pecks
1 gallon (gal.) = 4 quarts	

A. *Choose the best word to complete each sentence.*

1. If your mother cans applesauce, she will probably buy apples by the (pint, quart, bushel).

2. Strawberries and raspberries are usually sold by the (quart, gallon, bushel).

3. Most milk is sold by the (cup, pint, gallon).

4. A produce farmer may sell potatoes by the (quart, peck, gallon).

B. *Write the larger unit in each pair.*

5. a. quarts, pints   b. quarts, gallons   c. quarts, cups

6. a. pecks, bushels   b. pecks, quarts   c. pints, cups

7. a. yards, feet   b. feet, inches   c. yards, miles

C. *Write the key numbers for these units of measure.*

8. 1 gal. = _____ qt.   1 qt. = _____ pt.   1 qt. = _____ cups

9. 1 pk. = _____ qt.   1 bu. = _____ pk.   1 pt. = _____ cups

10. 1 mi. = _____ ft.   1 mi. = _____ yd.   1 yd. = _____ in.

11. 1 yd. = _____ ft.   1 ft. = _____ in.   1 yr. = _____ wk.

12. 1 min. = _____ sec.   1 day = _____ hr.   1 hr. = _____ min.

D. *Find the missing numbers for the blanks below. You must* divide *because you are changing from smaller units to larger ones. (See Rule 2 in Lesson 32.)*

13. 24 pk. = _____ bu.   16 qt. = _____ pk.   16 qt. = _____ gal.

14. 8 cups = _____ qt.   8 cups = _____ pt.   8 pt. = _____ qt.

15. 8 pk. = _____ bu.   20 pk. = _____ bu.   32 qt. = _____ gal.

16. 32 qt. = _____ pk.   16 cups = _____ qt.   20 cups = _____ pt.

17. 18 ft. = _____ yd.   36 in. = _____ ft.   28 days = _____ wk.

E. *Write the answers only.*

18. $\frac{2}{3}$ of 9 $\frac{1}{6}$ of 24 $\frac{1}{2}$ of 8 $\frac{3}{4}$ of 16

19. $2\frac{2}{3} \times 9$ $1\frac{1}{6} \times 24$ $3\frac{1}{2} \times 8$ $1\frac{3}{4} \times 16$

20. $1\frac{2}{3} \times 6$ $4\frac{1}{2} \times 10$ $2\frac{1}{7} \times 7$ $1\frac{1}{9} \times 18$

21. $3 \div 5$ $4 \div 7$ $\frac{1}{3}$ of 2 $\frac{1}{6}$ of 5

F. *Solve these reading problems.*

22. If you have a whole cake and eat $\frac{5}{8}$ of it, how many eighths will be left?

23. How many nickels can you get for 70 pennies?

24. If 5 sandwiches are shared by 3 boys, how many sandwiches will each boy get?

25. Jim has 3 oranges to divide among 4 boys. Will each boy get a whole orange? What part of an orange will each boy get?

26. The Book of Lamentations has five chapters. One chapter has 66 verses, and the other four have 22 verses each. How many verses are in the entire Book of Lamentations?

27. A jet flew east at a height of 31,880 feet. On its return trip west, it flew at a height of 33,000 feet. How much higher did the jet fly on its trip west?

28. If the jet flew at a speed of 665 miles per hour, how far did it travel in four hours?

29. Mother bought cheese for $4.75, meat for $12.39, dish soap for $1.45, and milk for $2.20. What was her bill?

30. A set of four Ping-Pong paddles costs $13.88. What is the price for one Ping-Pong paddle?

36. English Units of Weight

The three most common units of weight in the English system are the ounce, the pound, and the ton. An ounce is a very small unit, about the same weight as nine pennies. A pound is about the weight of 2 cups of water. A ton is a very large unit. A large workhorse might weigh a ton.

1 pound (lb.) = 16 ounces (oz.)	1 ton = 2,000 pounds (lb.)

Counting	1 dozen (doz.) = 12 items

A. *Write the key numbers that fit in the blanks.*

1. 1 ton = ___ lb.   1 mi. = ___ ft.   1 mi. = ___ yd.   1 lb. = ___ oz.

2. 1 gal. = ___ qt.   1 bu. = ___ pk.   1 qt. = ___ pt.   1 pk. = ___ qt.

3. 1 qt. = ___ cups   1 pt. = ___ cups   1 yd. = ___ in.   1 ft. = ___ in.

B. *Multiply or divide to find the numbers that fit in the blanks.*
Remember: Multiply to change from a larger unit to a smaller one.
Divide to change from a smaller unit to a larger one.

4. 3 yd. = ___ ft.   12 qt. = ___ gal.   12 gal. = ___ qt.   12 ft. = ___ yd.

5. 60 in. = ___ ft.   5 yd. = ___ in.   3 lb. = ___ oz.   3 tons = ___ lb.

6. 3 doz. = ___ items 16 pk. = ___ bu.   16 qt. = ___ pk.   16 qt. = ___ pt.

Finding a Part of a Measure

Example A: How many quarts are in $\frac{1}{2}$ peck?

Think: 1. What is the key number? (8 quarts are in a peck.)

2. What is $\frac{1}{2}$ of 8 quarts?

Answer: $\frac{1}{2}$ of 8 is 4, so 4 quarts are in $\frac{1}{2}$ peck.

Example B: How many ounces are in $\frac{3}{4}$ pound?

Think: 1. What is the key number? (16 ounces are in a pound.)

2. What is $\frac{3}{4}$ of 16 ounces?

Answer: $\frac{3}{4}$ of 16 is 12, so 12 ounces are in $\frac{3}{4}$ pound.

C. *Write the answers.*

7. How many ounces are in   **a.** $\frac{1}{2}$ lb.?   **b.** $\frac{1}{4}$ lb.?   **c.** $\frac{1}{8}$ lb.?   **d.** $\frac{5}{8}$ lb.?

8. How many items are in   **a.** $\frac{1}{2}$ doz.?   **b.** $\frac{1}{3}$ doz.?   **c.** $\frac{2}{3}$ doz.?   **d.** $\frac{1}{4}$ doz.?

9. How many inches are in   **a.** $\frac{1}{6}$ yd.?   **b.** $\frac{1}{4}$ yd.?   **c.** $\frac{3}{4}$ yd.?   **d.** $\frac{1}{2}$ yd.?

Finding What Part One Measure Is of Another

Sometimes when smaller units are changed to larger units, the answers are fractions. If the number in the problem is smaller than the key number, write the two numbers as a fraction. (The key number is always the denominator.) Reduce the fraction to lowest terms.

Examples: 2 cups = _____ qt. (2 ÷ 4)   4 ounces = _____ lb. (4 ÷ 16)

2 cups = $\frac{2}{4}$ = $\frac{1}{2}$ qt.   4 oz. = $\frac{4}{16}$ = $\frac{1}{4}$ lb.

These examples could also be stated as follows:

2 cups is what part of a quart?   4 ounces is what part of a pound?

D. *Write the fractions that fit in the blanks.*

10. 2 ft. = _____ yd.   8 oz. = _____ lb.   2 qt. = _____ gal.

11. 1 cup = _____ pt.   3 qt. = _____ pk.   8 in. = _____ ft.

12. 9 in. = _____ yd.   10 oz. = _____ lb.   3 pk. = _____ bu.

13. 1,000 pounds is what part of a ton?

14. 9 oranges is what part of a dozen?

15. 6 ounces is what part of a pound?

General Review

E. *Do these exercises.*

16. Change these improper fractions to whole or mixed numbers in simplest form.

a. $\frac{13}{8}$ b. $\frac{11}{4}$ c. $\frac{10}{6}$ d. $\frac{8}{4}$ e. $\frac{16}{5}$ f. $\frac{14}{4}$ g. $\frac{9}{2}$

17. Write the lengths to which the arrows point.

a. ↓   b. ↓   c. ↓   d. ↓   e. ↓   f. ↓

```
|1      |2      |3      |4      |5      |6
```

18. Measure these lines to the nearest sixteenth inch.

a. ———————————————————————

b. ———————————————————————————

c. ————————————————————

19. Divide. Express remainders as fractions in lowest terms.

5)4,762   4)9,530   6)946   9)1,191   7)8,229

20. Four boys shared two sandwiches. Did each boy have 2 sandwiches, $1\frac{1}{2}$ sandwiches, $\frac{3}{4}$ sandwich, or $\frac{1}{2}$ sandwich?

37. Units of Time

Study and learn the units in the box. Only the ones marked with a star should be new for you.

1 minute (min.) = 60 seconds (sec.)	1 day = 24 hours
1 hour (hr.) = 60 minutes	1 week (wk.) = 7 days
1 year (yr.) = 365 days	1 year = 52 weeks
*1 leap year = 366 days	1 year = 12 months (mo.)
*1 decade = 10 years	*1 century = 100 years

A. Write the key numbers that fit in the blanks.

1. 1 yr. = _____ days   1 yr. = _____ mo.   1 yr. = _____ weeks
2. 1 hr. = _____ min.   1 day = _____ hr.   1 leap year = _____ days
3. 1 min. = _____ sec.   1 pk. = _____ qt.   1 decade = _____ yr.
4. 1 mi. = _____ yd.   1 lb. = _____ oz.   1 ton = _____ lb.
5. 1 bu. = _____ pk.   1 mi. = _____ ft.   1 century = _____ yr.

You already know that you divide to change from a smaller unit of measure to a larger one. If the answer does not come out even when you divide, change the remainder to a fraction.

Example: 9 pecks = _____ bushels
Answer: $9 \div 4 = 2$ R1, or $2\frac{1}{4}$ 9 pecks = $2\frac{1}{4}$ bushels

B. Divide to find the missing numbers. Some of the answers will be whole numbers, some will be proper fractions as in Lesson 36, and some will be mixed numbers as in the example above.

6. 8 mo. = _____ yr.   10 pk. = _____ bu.   8 qt. = _____ gal
7. 12 pt. = _____ qt.   12 cups = _____ qt.   11 cups = _____ pt.
8. 15 sec. = _____ min.   6 qt. = _____ pk.   8 oz. = _____ lb.
9. 16 in. = _____ ft.   12 days = _____ wk.   48 mo. = _____ yr.

C. Find the parts of these measures.

10. How many minutes are in   a. $\frac{1}{2}$ hour?   b. $\frac{1}{4}$ hour?   c. $\frac{3}{4}$ hour?
11. How many hours are in   a. $\frac{1}{2}$ day?   b. $\frac{1}{4}$ day?   c. $\frac{1}{8}$ day?
12. How many months are in   a. $\frac{1}{2}$ year?   b. $\frac{1}{4}$ year?   c. $\frac{1}{3}$ year?
13. How many years are in   a. $\frac{1}{2}$ century?   b. $\frac{1}{2}$ decade?

Adding and Subtracting Measures

Only like units of measure can be added or subtracted. Minutes can be added to minutes, hours to hours, years to years, and so on.

To add:	4 hours	15 minutes	First add the minutes.
+	5 hours	25 minutes	Then add the hours.
	9 hours	40 minutes	

D. *Add or subtract as indicated.*

14. 28 minutes 35 seconds
    + 15 minutes 15 seconds

                6 days 16 hours
           + 11 days   5 hours

15.   1 peck   4 quarts
    + 2 pecks 2 quarts
     3   6

    8 weeks 2 days
  + 4 weeks 3 days
    12   5

    3 years 6 months
  + 7 years 4 months
    10   10

16. 8 bushels 3 pecks
  − 5 bushels 1 peck
    3   2

  5 yards 20 inches
− 2 yards 12 inches
   3   8

    4 quarts 3 cups
  − 2 quarts 3 cups
    2   0

17. 51 minutes 40 seconds
  − 27 minutes 35 seconds

        18 years 320 days
      − 9 years 165 days

General Review

E. *Do these exercises.*

18. Write the lengths to which the arrows point.

19. Add. Write all answers in simplest form.

$\frac{9}{16}$
$+ \frac{11}{16}$

$\frac{7}{9}$
$+ \frac{4}{9}$

$\frac{7}{12}$
$+ \frac{5}{12}$

$2\frac{3}{8}$
$+ 3\frac{3}{8}$

$1\frac{7}{15}$
$+ 6\frac{2}{15}$

20. Multiply. Check by exchanging the factors.

  78
× 37

  56
× 76

  90
× 98

  75
× 94

  89
× 63

21. Write 780,426 in expanded form.

38.   Regrouping Units in Addition

Sometimes when we add measures, we need to regroup the answer or change it to another form. Study the examples in the box. In the first example, 12 of the 14 months are changed to a year. In the second example, 5,280 of the 6,345 feet are changed to a mile.

6 years 8 months	3 miles 2,890 feet
+ 4 years 6 months	+ 2 miles 3,455 feet
10 years 14 months	5 miles 6,345 feet
= 11 years 2 months	= 6 miles 1,065 feet

If the number of smaller units equals one or more of the larger unit, regroup so that the answer is in simplest form.

A.   *Add these measures. Regroup the answer if necessary.*

1.   3 years 260 days   5 gallons 2 quarts   1 peck 5 quarts
    + 4 years 180 days   + 4 gallons 3 quarts   + 1 peck 3 quarts

2.   2 days 16 hours   5 hours 45 minutes   4 yards 2 feet
    + 3 days 10 hours   + 10 hours 25 minutes   + 2 yards 2 feet

3.   3 feet   8 inches   4 bushels 2 pecks   6 weeks 4 days
    + 1 foot 10 inches   + 4 bushels 2 pecks   + 3 weeks 6 days

4.   4 dozen 6 cookies   8 minutes 35 seconds   3 pounds 12 ounces
    + 3 dozen 8 cookies   + 34 minutes 17 seconds   + 8 pounds   8 ounces

B.   *Solve these reading problems.*

5. God gave Teresa twin baby brothers. Nevin weighed 5 pounds 8 ounces and Nathan weighed 6 pounds 10 ounces. How much did both babies weigh together?

6. One day the Everett family picked 4 bushels and 2 pecks of lima beans. The next time they picked the limas, they got 5 bushels and 3 pecks. How many lima beans did they pick both times?

7. It took the Everetts 1 hour and 45 minutes to pick the limas the first time. The next time it took them 2 hours and 20 minutes. How much time did they spend picking lima beans?

General Review

C. *Write the key number for these measures.*

8. 1 mi. = _____ ft.   1 mi. = _____ yd.   1 decade = _____ yr.

9. 1 bu. = _____ pk.   1 pk. = _____ qt.   1 lb. = _____ oz.

10. 1 ton = _____ lb.   1 yr. = _____ days   1 century = _____ yr.

11. 1 yd. = _____ in.   1 pt. = _____ cups   1 leap year = _____ days

12. 1 qt. = _____ pt.   1 yr. = _____ wk.   1 minute = _____ sec.

D. *Find the missing numbers. Use either measure rule. Some answers will be fractions.*

13. 4 qt. = _____ cups   16 ft. = _____ yd.   3 pk. = _____ bu.

14. 8 oz. = _____ lb.   2 tons = _____ lb.   3 yr. = _____ mo.

15. 72 in. = _____ ft.   10 qt. = _____ gal.   20 days = _____ wk.

16. 5 pt. = _____ cups   5 pt. = _____ qt.   8 in. = _____ ft.

E. *Write the answers only.*

17. $1\frac{1}{8} \times 16$ $1\frac{2}{3} \times 9$ $2\frac{1}{2} \times 4$ $3\frac{1}{6} \times 6$

18. $2\frac{1}{4} \times 8$ $1\frac{1}{5} \times 20$ $2\frac{1}{3} \times 6$ $1\frac{1}{3} \times 24$

19. $\frac{2}{3}$ of 15 $\frac{4}{7}$ of 49 $\frac{3}{4}$ of 48 $\frac{7}{8}$ of 16

20. $\frac{3}{5}$ of 20 $\frac{5}{9}$ of 81 $\frac{1}{2}$ of 40 $\frac{5}{8}$ of 40

21. $3 \div 9$ $4 \div 9$ $\frac{1}{4}$ of 3 $\frac{1}{8}$ of 5

F. *Do these exercises.*

22. Add 6 to each number.

  a. 16   **b.** 29   **c.** 23   **d.** 11   **e.** 14   **f.** 27   **g.** 18

23. Write numerals for these number words.

  a. 250 billion, 384 thousand

  b. 14 billion, 765 million, 3 thousand, 492

  c. 861 billion

  d. six billion, sixty million, six hundred

24. Write Roman numerals for these Arabic numerals.

  a. 389   **b.** 755   **c.** 914   **d.** 1,026   **e.** 2,600   **f.** 847

39. Regrouping Units in Subtraction

Study the problems in the box.

$\begin{array}{r} 6 \\ 7\!\!\!/^{1}0 \\ -\ 35 \\ \hline 35 \end{array}$	$\begin{array}{r} 6 \quad\ \ 12 \\ 7 \text{ years}\ \ 0 \text{ months} \\ -\ 3 \text{ years}\ \ 5 \text{ months} \\ \hline 3 \text{ years}\ \ 7 \text{ months} \end{array}$	$\begin{array}{r} 6 \quad\ \ 7 \\ 7 \text{ weeks}\ \ 0 \text{ days} \\ -\ 3 \text{ weeks}\ \ 5 \text{ days} \\ \hline 3 \text{ weeks}\ \ 2 \text{ days} \end{array}$

These problems show a kind of borrowing, or regrouping. In each problem, one of the larger units is changed to smaller units in order to subtract.

A. *Subtract these units of measure. Regroup as shown in the box.*

1.

6 bushels 1 peck	15 hours 10 minutes	3 pecks 2 quarts
− 3 bushels 3 pecks	− 8 hours 45 minutes	− 1 peck 5 quarts

2.

12 years 150 days	8 days 6 hours	5 quarts 0 pints
− 6 years 287 days	− 2 days 14 hours	− 3 quarts 1 pint

3.

18 pounds 12 ounces	10 weeks 4 days	11 gallons 2 quarts
− 11 pounds 15 ounces	− 4 weeks 5 days	− 5 gallons 3 quarts

4.

4 tons 500 pounds	4 yards 1 foot	6 yards 12 inches
− 2 tons 1,000 pounds	− 1 yard 2 feet	− 5 yards 24 inches

B. *Do these exercises.*

5. Add these measures. Regroup as in Lesson 38.

6 years 8 months	5 pounds 11 ounces	20 hours 55 minutes
+ 4 years 9 months	+ 3 pounds 15 ounces	+ 2 hours 25 minutes

6. Find the missing numbers.

a. 8 min. = _____ sec.   12 qt. = _____ gal.   10 pk. = _____ bu.

b. 9 in. = _____ ft.   9 cups = _____ pt.   4 doz. = _____ items

7. Write the lengths to which the arrows point.

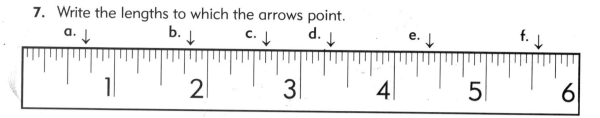

Reading Problems

C. *Write* add, subtract, multiply, or divide. *How would you find . . .*

8. the difference between two numbers?

9. the total cost of 6 bars of soap priced equally?

10. the total cost of 6 items priced differently?

11. how much money you have left after spending $12.79?

12. how much more money you need to buy a book for $7.75

13. how many 6's are in 24?

14. the total of 8, 3, and 24?

15. how many groups of 3 are in a number?

D. *Solve these problems.*

16. Mr. Baker harvested 27 acres of his corn. He got 124 bushels of corn from each acre. How many bushels of corn did he get from the 27 acres?

17. In one field Mr. Baker had trouble with cutworms. He got only 420 bushels of corn from 5 acres. At that rate, how many bushels did he get from one acre?

18. Compare your answer for number 17 with the number of bushels per acre in number 16. Then choose the correct answer: The cutworms caused the loss of (20, 30, 40, 50) bushels of corn per acre.

19. Mr. Baker harvested 2,195 bushels of corn on Monday and 1,980 bushels on Tuesday. Prayer meeting was on Wednesday evening, so Mr. Baker did not work as long in the fields. That day he harvested only 1,560 bushels. How many bushels of corn did Mr. Baker harvest in the three days together?

20. When Mr. Baker is harvesting his corn, he drives 3 miles per hour. One day he harvested corn for six hours. How many miles did he drive during that time?

40. First Quarter Review

A. *Write the answers only.*

1.
$$\begin{array}{c}9\\ \times\,8\end{array}\quad \begin{array}{c}8\\ +\,7\end{array}\quad \begin{array}{c}7\\ \times\,9\end{array}\quad \begin{array}{c}11\\ -\,8\end{array}\quad \begin{array}{c}10\\ -\,6\end{array}\quad \begin{array}{c}12\\ \times\,11\end{array}\quad \begin{array}{c}8\\ +\,6\end{array}\quad \begin{array}{c}5\\ +\,7\end{array}\quad \begin{array}{c}6\\ \times\,8\end{array}$$

2.
$$\begin{array}{c}12\\ \times\,12\end{array}\quad \begin{array}{c}11\\ \times\,10\end{array}\quad \begin{array}{c}8\\ +\,9\end{array}\quad \begin{array}{c}4\\ \times\,7\end{array}\quad \begin{array}{c}12\\ -\,9\end{array}\quad \begin{array}{c}10\\ \times\,10\end{array}\quad \begin{array}{c}7\\ +\,9\end{array}\quad \begin{array}{c}9\\ \times\,6\end{array}\quad \begin{array}{c}12\\ \times\,7\end{array}$$

3.
$$\begin{array}{c}6\\ \times\,7\end{array}\quad \begin{array}{c}12\\ \times\,6\end{array}\quad \begin{array}{c}12\\ \times\,9\end{array}\quad \begin{array}{c}13\\ -\,5\end{array}\quad \begin{array}{c}7\\ \times\,7\end{array}\quad \begin{array}{c}14\\ -\,9\end{array}\quad \begin{array}{c}8\\ \times\,8\end{array}\quad \begin{array}{c}12\\ \times\,8\end{array}\quad \begin{array}{c}18\\ -\,9\end{array}$$

4. $72 \div 8$ $56 \div 7$ $42 \div 6$ $110 \div 10$

5. $120 \div 12$ $99 \div 9$ $121 \div 11$ $60 \div 5$

6. $\frac{1}{2}$ of 24 $\frac{1}{5}$ of 45 $\frac{1}{8}$ of 64 $\frac{1}{7}$ of 21

7. $\frac{3}{4}$ of 20 $\frac{2}{5}$ of 35 $\frac{7}{8}$ of 16 $\frac{4}{9}$ of 54

8. $1\frac{1}{2} \times 20$ $1\frac{1}{8} \times 32$ $2\frac{1}{3} \times 12$ $3\frac{1}{4} \times 4$

9. $3 \div 5$ $1 \div 7$ $\frac{1}{6}$ of 5 $\frac{1}{8}$ of 6

B. *Do these exercises.*

10.   Reduce these fractions to lowest terms.

     a. $\frac{10}{12}$ b. $\frac{8}{20}$ c. $\frac{12}{16}$ d. $\frac{6}{15}$ e. $\frac{4}{12}$ f. $\frac{9}{24}$

11.   Find the missing numbers to make equivalent fractions.

     a. $\frac{1}{2} = \frac{4}{?}$ b. $\frac{3}{4} = \frac{?}{12}$ c. $\frac{2}{3} = \frac{6}{?}$ d. $\frac{1}{8} = \frac{?}{16}$

12.   Tell what time these clocks show.

     a.   b.   c.   d.

13. Write Roman numerals for these Arabic numerals.

    a. 780   b. 346   c. 1,258   d. 864   e. 2,520

14. Write Arabic numerals for these Roman numerals.

    a. MCDLXII   b. MLXXII   c. DXCVII   d. CDXIV   e. DCCCXXXIX

15. Write this number, placing commas correctly: 88888888888
    Circle the 8 in the ten millions' place.

16. Write numerals for these number words.

    a. three hundred eighty-four billion

    b. twenty-seven billion, one hundred million

    c. five billion, sixty-five million, nine hundred three thousand

    d. 17 billion, 255 thousand

    e. 870 billion, 5 million, 60

17. Round to the nearest thousand.

    a. 495,328   b. 73,540   c. 126,499

18. Round to the nearest hundred thousand.

    a. 943,890   b. 1,783,926   c. 173,279

19. Write the lengths to which the arrows point.

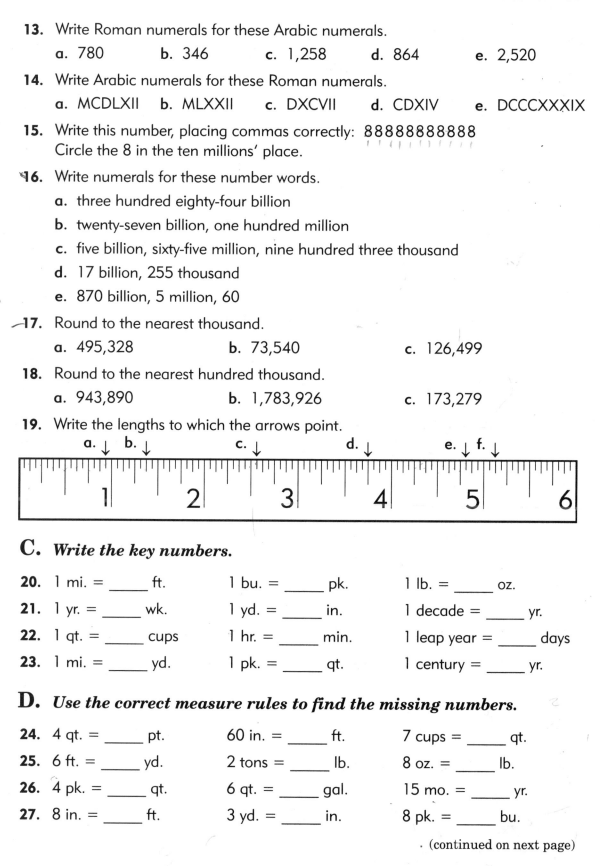

C. Write the key numbers.

20. 1 mi. = _____ ft.   1 bu. = _____ pk.   1 lb. = _____ oz.

21. 1 yr. = _____ wk.   1 yd. = _____ in.   1 decade = _____ yr.

22. 1 qt. = _____ cups   1 hr. = _____ min.   1 leap year = _____ days

23. 1 mi. = _____ yd.   1 pk. = _____ qt.   1 century = _____ yr.

D. Use the correct measure rules to find the missing numbers.

24. 4 qt. = _____ pt.   60 in. = _____ ft.   7 cups = _____ qt.

25. 6 ft. = _____ yd.   2 tons = _____ lb.   8 oz. = _____ lb.

26. 4 pk. = _____ qt.   6 qt. = _____ gal.   15 mo. = _____ yr.

27. 8 in. = _____ ft.   3 yd. = _____ in.   8 pk. = _____ bu.

· (continued on next page)

Computation Practice

E. *Copy and solve these problems.*

28.

8	9	5			
7	3	4	76	486	
2	7	8	93	853	78,372
6	8	9	68	519	65,948
+ 4	+ 5	+ 8	+ 47	+ 244	+ 46,259

29.

7,020	8,326	5,901	$20.00	$45.00
− 4,538	− 2,843	− 3,825	− 17.89	− 36.50

30.

297	8,319	2,476	460	358
× 6	× 4	× 8	× 17	× 83

31.

5 quarts 1 cup	6 years 10 months	3 miles 4,500 feet
+ 3 quarts 3 cups	+ 4 years 6 months	+ 2 miles 3,625 feet

32.

7 bushels 1 peck	4 days 12 hours	18 hours 25 minutes
− 2 bushels 2 pecks	− 1 day 18 hours	− 5 hours 40 minutes

F. *Follow the directions.*

33. Multiply. Check by exchanging factors.

a.   74   b.   93   c.   28   d.   45
    × 15   × 87   × 63   × 77

34. Divide. Check by multiplication.

$6\overline{)947}$ $3\overline{)5,718}$ $5\overline{)1,864}$ $8\overline{)9,184}$

35. Change these improper fractions to whole or mixed numbers.

a. $\frac{9}{2}$ b. $\frac{10}{4}$ c. $\frac{7}{3}$ d. $\frac{18}{6}$ e. $\frac{13}{4}$ f. $\frac{22}{8}$

36. Add or subtract. Write all answers in simplest form.

$\frac{3}{8}$	$\frac{9}{16}$	$3\frac{4}{9}$	$\frac{11}{12}$	$7\frac{13}{16}$
$+ \frac{7}{8}$	$+ \frac{7}{16}$	$+ 2\frac{2}{9}$	$- \frac{5}{12}$	$- 4\frac{9}{16}$

37. Count the money.

38. Tell what pieces of money should be given as change.

a. Total purchase—$2.37; amount given—$5.00

b. Total purchase—$13.69; amount given—$20.00

Reading Problems

G. *Solve these problems.*

39. There are 16 pupils in Doe Run Christian School. One day $\frac{1}{4}$ of them were absent with chicken pox. How many pupils were at school that day?

40. Within two months, $\frac{7}{8}$ of the pupils at Doe Run School had had chicken pox. How many pupils had chicken pox?

41. World War I ended in 1918. President Woodrow Wilson called World War I "the war to end all wars." However by 1939 World War II had begun. How long was it from the end of World War I until the start of World War II?

42. Marla's chocolate chip cookie recipe calls for $\frac{3}{4}$ cup brown sugar and $\frac{3}{4}$ cup white sugar. Altogether, how much sugar does Marla need for a batch of chocolate chip cookies?

43. When Brother Amos and his wife went to fellowship meetings, they drove 2,600 miles in four days. At that rate, how far did they drive each day?

44. Mother bought two loaves of bread marked "2 for $2.15" and three pounds of margarine at $0.79 a pound. What was her total bill?

45. Aunt Julia bought two pieces of dress material for $6.75 and $5.48. She also bought a spool of thread for $0.99. What was her change from a 20-dollar bill?

46. Cindy and Mary Ann want to share 5 sheets of colored paper. How many sheets of paper should each girl receive?

47. One week Henry learned John 14:1–6. If Henry learns 6 Bible verses every week for a whole year, how many verses will he learn?

- -

41. Chapter 4 Test

Interesting Number Facts

Number Patterns

You have learned that when numbers are added, ones must be added to ones, tens must be added to tens, and so on. Have you ever wondered what would happen if you added ones to tens and tens to hundreds? You will not get the correct sum, but you will discover some interesting things about numbers.

A one-digit number can be obtained if the digits of any larger number are added together. If the first sum has more than one digit, add those digits together also. Study the examples below.

One-digit number for 15: $1 + 5 = $ **6**

One-digit number for 89: $8 + 9 = 17$; $1 + 7 = $ **8**

One-digit number for 347: $3 + 4 + 7 = 14$; $1 + 4 = $ **5**

When this process is used on counting numbers, it reveals some interesting number patterns. The box below shows the number patterns for counting by ones and eights, and by twos and sevens. These are grouped in this way because the patterns in counting by ones and by eights are opposite, and the patterns in counting by twos and by sevens are opposite.

Notice another pattern in counting by twos and sevens. First there is a group of even numbers, then a group of odd numbers, and then even numbers again. In counting by sevens, the order is odd group, even group, odd group.

Counting by Ones											
Numbers: 1	2	3	4	5	6	7	8	9	10	11	12
Pattern: 1	2	3	4	5	6	7	8	9	1	2	3
Counting by Eights											
Numbers: 8	16	24	32	40	48	56	64	72	80	88	96
Pattern: 8	7	6	5	4	3	2	1	9	8	7	6

Counting by Twos											
Numbers: 2	4	6	8	10	12	14	16	18	20	22	24
Pattern: 2	4	6	8	1	3	5	7	9	2	4	6
Counting by Sevens											
Numbers: 7	14	21	28	35	42	49	56	63	70	77	84
Pattern: 7	5	3	1	8	6	4	2	9	7	5	3

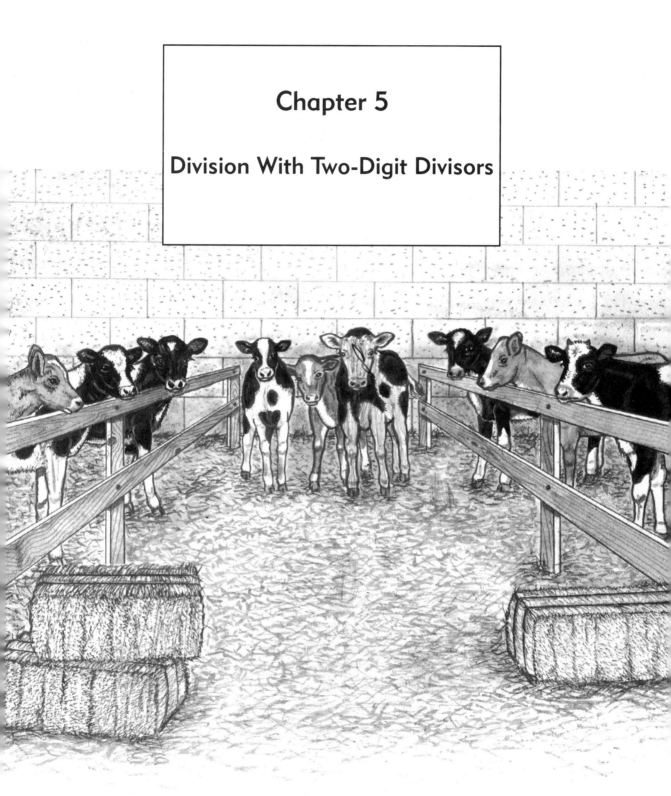

Chapter 5

Division With Two-Digit Divisors

Honour the Lord with thy substance, and with the firstfruits of all
thine increase: so shall thy barns be filled with plenty.
(Proverbs 3:9, 10)

42. Dividing by Multiples of 10

Dividing by multiples of 10 like 20, 30, and 40 is similar to dividing by numbers like 2, 3, and 4. Follow the same steps you use when you divide by one-digit numbers.

```
        3                    7 R 6      To find how many 30's are in 90,
    30)90            20)146             think: How many 3's are in 9?
        90                140
         0                   6          To find how many 20's are in 146,
                                        think: How many 2's are in 14?
                      20
    Check:           × 7
                                        Be very careful to write the quotient
        30           140                figure at the right place.
       × 3           + 6
        90           146                Check by multiplication as usual.
```

A. Copy and divide. Follow the pattern shown above.

1.   40)80   20)60   30)92   20)88   40)47

2.   30)150   20)180   50)200   80)560   40)160

3.   60)184   40)325   70)213   40)284   30)189

4.   50)310   20)91   60)368   90)742   30)244

B. Solve these problems with one-digit divisors.

5.   4)7,541   3)2,682   6)4,638   9)1,239   5)8,340

C. Write the answers only to these division facts.

6.   10)90   12)84   11)66   11)88   12)108   10)100

7.   11)44   10)80   10)30   12)48   11)121   12)144

8.   10)40   12)60   11)77   12)72   12)120   10)110

9.   12)96   10)50   11)22   12)36   11)132   11)110

10. 10)20   11)99   12)24   10)70   10)120   12)132

General Review

D. *Write the missing numbers. Some are key numbers. Use the measure rules to find the others.*

11. 1 yd. = _____ in.   1 mi. = _____ yd.   1 lb. = _____ oz.

12. 1 decade = _____ yr.   1 century = _____ yr.   1 leap year = _____ days

13. 8 bu. = _____ pk.   3 qt. = _____ gal.   3 tons = _____ lb.

14. 24 qt. = _____ pk.   16 mo. = _____ yr.   12 pt. = _____ cups

15. 9 pt. = _____ qt.   15 days = _____ wk.   30 min. = _____ hr.

16. 6 yd. = _____ ft.   72 in. = _____ ft.   20 cups = _____ qt.

E. *Do these exercises.*

17.
```
    8 years  300 days        6 days  12 hours       16 minutes  45 seconds
  + 3 years  180 days      + 8 days  16 hours      + 25 minutes  35 seconds
```

18.
```
   12 pecks  0 quarts       5 tons    200 pounds     10 pounds   6 ounces
  - 5 pecks  2 quarts     - 1 ton  1,000 pounds     - 4 pounds  12 ounces
```

19.
```
     345            829            719            860            937
   × 78           × 36           × 68           × 85           × 19
```

20. Round to the nearest thousand.

a. 5,693   b. 290,345   c. 48,560   d. 394,189

21. Round to the nearest ten thousand.

a. 79,327   b. 290,345   c. 48,560   d. 2,394,189

22. Round to the nearest hundred thousand.

a. 240,345   b. 899,050   c. 3,418,560   d. 2,374,189

23. Write Arabic numerals for these Roman numerals.

a. MDCCCXVI   b. CDLXXXIX   c. DCCXCIII   d. MMDLVII

43. Dividing by Two-Digit Divisors

In Lesson 42 you divided by multiples of 10. Today you will divide by two-digit numbers that are not multiples of 10. Some of the quotients will have only one digit, and some will have two.

A. *Write 1 or 2 to tell how many quotient figures will be in each answer. Do not solve the problems.*

1. a. $14\overline{)638}$ b. $25\overline{)85}$ c. $46\overline{)357}$ d. $18\overline{)150}$ e. $32\overline{)500}$

2. a. $72\overline{)684}$ b. $19\overline{)320}$ c. $51\overline{)473}$ d. $39\overline{)400}$ e. $26\overline{)242}$

B. *Use the 11's and 12's division facts to find the quotient figures. For example, think: How many 12's are in 27?*

3. $12\overline{)276}$ $11\overline{)48}$ $11\overline{)154}$ $12\overline{)79}$ $11\overline{)583}$

4. $12\overline{)648}$ $12\overline{)396}$ $11\overline{)894}$ $12\overline{)984}$ $11\overline{)497}$

The example in the box shows how to divide by a two-digit number that is not a multiple of 10.

$$
\begin{array}{r}
32\,\text{R}\,3 \\
21\overline{)675} \\
63 \\
\hline
45 \\
42 \\
\hline
3
\end{array}
$$

Estimate the first quotient figure by thinking

21 is a little more than 20.

$67 \div 20$ is 3, so $67 \div 21$ is probably 3.

Continue through the other division steps.

C. *Copy and divide. Estimate the quotient figures by rounding the divisor to the nearest ten, as shown in the box.*

5. $22\overline{)90}$ $21\overline{)48}$ $32\overline{)704}$ $21\overline{)888}$ $22\overline{)682}$

6. $20\overline{)480}$ $31\overline{)971}$ $40\overline{)520}$ $30\overline{)570}$ $32\overline{)384}$

General Review

D. *Write the missing numbers.*

7. 1 ton = _____ lb.   1 gal. = _____ qt.   1 min. = _____ sec.

8. 1 mi. = _____ ft.   1 bu. = _____ pk.   1 yr. = _____ wk.

9. 4 ft. = _____ in.   4 ft. = _____ yd.   4 pt. = _____ qt.

10. 9 mo. = _____ yr.   16 qt. = _____ pk.   12 hr. = _____ day

11. 6 cups = _____ pt.   6 cups = _____ qt.   4 decades = _____ yr.

12. 2 mi. = _____ yd.   4 oz. = _____ lb.   25 yr. = _____ century

13. a. $\frac{1}{6} = \frac{4}{?}$ b. $\frac{2}{3} = \frac{?}{15}$ c. $\frac{1}{4} = \frac{?}{16}$ d. $\frac{3}{4} = \frac{9}{?}$ e. $\frac{4}{5} = \frac{?}{20}$

E. *Do these exercises.*

14. Round these numbers to the nearest ten.

   a. 56   b. 89   c. 123   d. 74   e. 235   f. 891

15. Round to the nearest hundred.

   a. 123   b. 235   c. 891   d. 825   e. 5,316   f. 3,460

16. Write the lengths to which the arrows point. Label your answers!

F. *Solve these reading problems.*

17. If a car can go 24 miles on a gallon of gasoline, how far can it go on 12 gallons of gasoline?

18. If a car runs 24 miles on a gallon of gasoline, how many gallons will it take to make a 480-mile trip?

19. When the Good family from Missouri visits their grandparents in Ohio, the trip usually takes 15 hours 30 minutes. One time Father and Mother drove to Ohio themselves without stopping very often. They made the trip in 13 hours 45 minutes. How much less time was that than usual?

44. Multiplying Horizontally

When you divide, you also need to multiply and subtract. The multiplication part is not set up as it is when you do a row of multiplication problems on your paper. Knowing how to multiply horizontally (from side to side) will help you do the multiplication part of division problems.

$3 \times 52 = ?$ Multiply the ones first and then the tens. Think: 3×2 is 6. Write 6.

Think: 3×5 is 15. Write 15 to the left of 6. $3 \times 52 = 156$

A. *Write only the answers, following the pattern in the box.*

1. 3×52 4×21 2×83 2×34 5×71

2. 6×81 3×23 4×42 8×30 4×90

3. 3×13 5×31 2×14 6×40 7×61

B. *Write 1 or 2 to tell how many quotient figures will be in these divisions. Do not solve the problems.*

4. a. $37\overline{)684}$ b. $31\overline{)256}$ c. $42\overline{)870}$ d. $23\overline{)100}$ e. $45\overline{)400}$

5. a. $17\overline{)195}$ b. $52\overline{)648}$ c. $34\overline{)320}$ d. $46\overline{)387}$ e. $22\overline{)500}$

C. *Copy and divide. Estimate quotient figures by rounding divisors as you did in Lesson 43. (Rows 6 and 7 do not have remainders.)*

6. $12\overline{)888}$ $11\overline{)385}$ $60\overline{)960}$ $20\overline{)480}$ $31\overline{)651}$

7. $22\overline{)528}$ $13\overline{)299}$ $21\overline{)714}$ $40\overline{)840}$ $11\overline{)594}$

8. $23\overline{)489}$ $12\overline{)318}$ $50\overline{)625}$ $34\overline{)750}$ $41\overline{)883}$

General Review

D. *Do these exercises.*

9. Write these Arabic numerals as Roman numerals.

   a. 517   b. 849   c. 452   d. 1,900   e. 666   f. 395

10. Write numerals for these number words.

   a. forty-five billion, two hundred fifty thousand
   b. eight hundred ninety-seven million
   c. 12 billion, 619 million, 6 thousand, 75
   d. 8 billion, 50 million, 980

E. *Write the answers only.*

11. $\frac{1}{2}$ of 24 | $\frac{2}{3}$ of 24 | $\frac{7}{8}$ of 24 | $\frac{3}{4}$ of 24

12. $\frac{5}{12}$ of 36 | $\frac{4}{5}$ of 20 | $\frac{3}{7}$ of 42 | $\frac{5}{9}$ of 63

13. $2\frac{1}{2} \times 6$ | $1\frac{1}{3} \times 21$ | $1\frac{1}{7} \times 28$ | $3\frac{1}{4} \times 8$

14. $5 \div 6$ | $1 \div 9$ | $\frac{1}{5}$ of 3 | $\frac{1}{7}$ of 4

Estimating in Reading Problems

Sometimes instead of finding an exact answer to a problem, we round the numbers in the problem and **estimate** the answer. Round numbers are easy to work with, and the estimate helps to show whether the exact answer is sensible.

Example:	Mother has $20.00. Does she have enough to pay for items marked $4.17, $8.95, and $7.60?
	Round the prices to $4.00, $9.00, and $8.00. Think: $4 + $9 + $8 is $21
	Mother will not have enough money.

F. *Choose the most sensible estimate of the three answers. Then find the exact answer.*

15. One bushel of apples makes about 21 quarts of applesauce. How many quart jars will you need if you plan to make applesauce from 7 bushels of apples?
    30   90   140

16. The Brooks family is driving 2,436 miles to visit a mission in Mexico. They have already traveled 1,760 miles. How many more miles do they have to travel?
    600   1,000   4,200

17. What is the total cost of items marked $3.45, $5.76, and $2.82?
    $9.00 $10.00 $12.00

18. Aunt Sarah bought 5 pounds of cheese for $1.95 a pound. What did she pay for the cheese? $3.00 $5.00 $10.00

19. A dozen doughnuts are marked $1.92. What is the price of one doughnut?
    $0.15 $0.50 $13.00

45. More Horizontal Multiplication

The numbers you multiplied horizontally in Lesson 44 did not require carrying. In this lesson you will need to carry. Study the example in the box.

$4 \times 46 = ?$ Multiply the ones first and then the tens.

Think: 4×6 is 24. Write 4; carry 2 in your mind.

Think: 4×4 is 16. Add the carried 2.

Write 18 to the left of 4.

$4 \times 46 = 184$

A. Write the answers, following the pattern in the box.

1. 4×53 5×34 2×85 3×17 4×26

2. 5×25 7×32 8×13 4×43 6×53

3. 3×54 8×61 4×27 2×36 5×92

B. Write 1 or 2 to tell how many quotient figures will be in these divisions. Do not solve the problems.

4.   a. $45\overline{)390}$ b. $13\overline{)511}$ c. $38\overline{)420}$ d. $28\overline{)254}$ e. $17\overline{)156}$

5.   a. $23\overline{)308}$ b. $12\overline{)135}$ c. $35\overline{)170}$ d. $48\overline{)350}$ e. $27\overline{)249}$

C. Copy and divide. Estimate to find the quotient figures. These answers have no remainders.

6. $21\overline{)168}$ $34\overline{)714}$ $23\overline{)736}$ $12\overline{)504}$ $30\overline{)240}$

7. $51\overline{)408}$ $22\overline{)484}$ $14\overline{)294}$ $33\overline{)198}$ $41\overline{)615}$

D. Copy, divide, and check by multiplication.

8.   a. $60\overline{)435}$ b. $32\overline{)362}$ c. $11\overline{)468}$ d. $21\overline{)435}$ e. $31\overline{)160}$

General Review

E. *Write the missing numbers. Be careful! Some answers are fractions.*

9. 1 mi. = _____ yd.   1 yr. = _____ days   1 century = _____ yr.

10. 1 yr. = _____ wk.   1 qt. = _____ cups   1 lb. = _____ oz.

11. 1 pt. = _____ cups   1 pk. = _____ qt.   1 leap year = _____ days

12. 12 pk. = _____ bu.   12 hr. = _____ day   12 days = _____ wk.

13. 3 min. = _____ sec.   24 ft. = _____ yd.   3 in. = _____ ft.

14. 7 cups = _____ pt.   2 qt. = _____ gal.   4 doz. = _____ items

F. *Do these exercises.*

15. Write the lengths to which the arrows point.

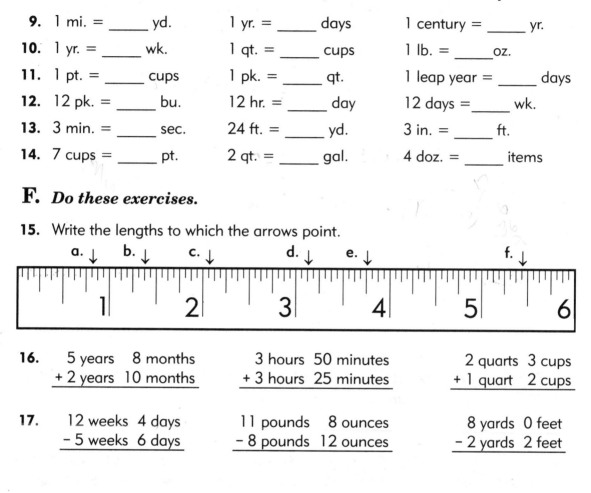

16.
```
   5 years   8 months          3 hours  50 minutes          2 quarts  3 cups
+ 2 years  10 months        + 3 hours  25 minutes        + 1 quart   2 cups
```

17.
```
  12 weeks  4 days           11 pounds    8 ounces          8 yards  0 feet
-  5 weeks  6 days          -  8 pounds  12 ounces        - 2 yards  2 feet
```

18. Add or subtract. Write all answers in simplest form.

a. $\dfrac{7}{8}$ b. $\dfrac{13}{16}$ c. $3\dfrac{2}{9}$ d. $\dfrac{11}{12}$ e. $8\dfrac{9}{10}$

   $+\dfrac{1}{8}$ $+\dfrac{5}{16}$ $+1\dfrac{4}{9}$ $-\dfrac{1}{12}$ $-4\dfrac{3}{10}$

19. What is the value of all the money pictured below?

46. More About Estimating Quotient Figures

In the last several lessons you estimated quotient figures by rounding the divisor down to the nearest ten. In those lessons the first digit you found was the correct one, but in many division problems that is not the case. Instead, when you multiply, you discover that your first estimate is too large or too small. Then you must try another quotient figure. The example in the box is a problem like this.

$$
\begin{array}{r}
6 \\
34\overline{)194} \\
204
\end{array}
$$

Round 194 ÷ 34 to 190 ÷ 30.

Think: 190 ÷ 30 (19 ÷ 3) is about 6.

Multiply: 6 × 34 = 204. 6 is too large.

$$
\begin{array}{r}
5\,\text{R}\,24 \\
34\overline{)194} \\
170 \\
\hline
24
\end{array}
$$

Try 5. Multiply: 5 × 34 = 170.

Subtract: 194 − 170 = 24.

The correct answer is 5 R 24.

Sometimes you may need to try three or four times before you find the right quotient figure. However, you will usually be able to get the correct digit the first or second time.

A. *Copy and divide. If the first quotient figure does not work, try again until you get the right one. These rows have no remainders.*

1. 13)546   14)126   32)480   52)260   14)322

2. 34)918   24)144   13)845   51)255   22)198

3. 31)589   13)312   33)924   23)161   64)448

B. *Write the answers only.*

4. 4 × 58   3 × 39   6 × 16   2 × 89   3 × 75

5. 7 × 54   4 × 69   5 × 58   8 × 90   6 × 37

Computation Review

C. *Use folded paper for rows 6–10.*

6.

6	8	9	4	3	7	4
5	3	6	7	3	9	6
4	9	4	6	7	8	2
8	5	7	6	9	5	8
+ 4	+ 6	+ 2	+ 7	+ 8	+ 4	+ 7

7.

89	47	943	842	4,985	
71	68	39	674	3,453	32,870
35	35	781	2,539	7,357	71,689
+ 64	+ 27	+ 375	+ 4,158	+ 624	+ 68,795

8.

9,000	7,420	5,912	8,030	6,428
− 5,621	− 568	− 4,536	− 4,957	− 5,895

9.

$5.00	$6.17	$20.25	$43.00	$35.95
− 2.97	− 4.96	− 17.58	− 37.50	− 29.75

10.

862	478	3,850	8,375	7,598
× 9	× 6	× 8	× 7	× 4

11.

93	17	84	520	638
× 24	× 79	× 48	× 97	× 36

12. 5)685   3)2,517   6)8,144   9)2,317

13. 4)$2.64   7)$8.19   5)$4.20   8)$8.32

47. Working With Money

On this page are illustrations of the fronts and backs of United States coins, shown almost actual size. The half dollar coin is not used very much, and the dollar coin is almost never used. Perhaps you have never seen a real one.

The men pictured on the coins are famous in United States history. Their names are given below the coins. You may already have heard of some of them.

Be sure you are familiar with these coins.

penny

Abraham Lincoln

quarter

George Washington

nickel

Thomas Jefferson

half dollar

John F. Kennedy

dime

Franklin D. Roosevelt

dollar

Dwight D. Eisenhower

Below are illustrations of the fronts and backs of the most common United States bills. These are much smaller than actual size. United States also has a two-dollar bill, but it is rarely used.

The names of the men pictured on the fronts of the bills are given for your interest. Notice that some of the men pictured on the bills are also pictured on a coin. (Thomas Jefferson is pictured on the two-dollar bill.)

one-dollar bill
George Washington

five-dollar bill
Abraham Lincoln

ten-dollar bill
Alexander Hamilton

twenty-dollar bill
Andrew Jackson

fifty-dollar bill
Ulysses Grant

one-hundred-dollar bill
Benjamin Franklin

A. *Follow the directions.*

1. Write the value of each bill, using the pictures for help.

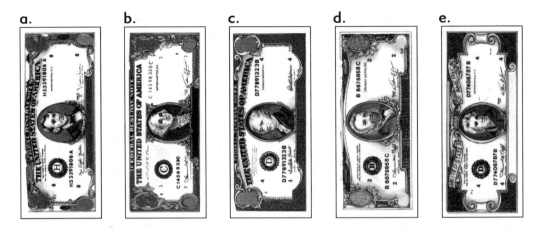

a.   b.   c.   d.   e.

2. Write the value for each combination of coins.

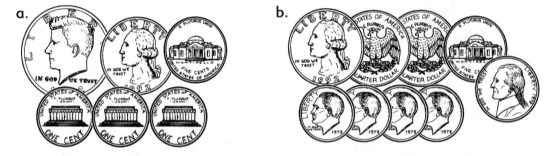

a.   b.

3. Write what bills and coins should be given as change. Use as few pieces as possible.

   a. Amount of purchase—$2.65; amount given to clerk—$5.00
   b. Amount of purchase—$3.17; amount given to clerk—$20.00
   c. Amount of purchase—$26.71; amount given to clerk—$50.00

4. Write each price in two ways.

   a. seventeen cents
   b. eleven dollars
   c. six dollars
   d. fifty-nine cents

5. Write the value of each combination of bills.

   a. three 20-dollar bills, one 10-dollar bill, four 1-dollar bills
   b. four 5-dollar bills, three 10-dollar bills
   c. eight 10-dollar bills, three 5-dollar bills, five 1-dollar bills
   d. two 50-dollar bills, one 20-dollar bill
   e. one 100-dollar bill, two 20-dollar bills, three 5-dollar bills

B. *Copy the problems, and follow the signs. Be sure the decimal points are in straight columns. Remember that when you add or subtract, you must write $7.00 for a dollar amount like $7.*

6. $65.38 + $19 + $3.84 $4 + $55 + $7.99 $0.87 + $36.47 + $9
7. $3.60 + $46.81 + $0.56 $12.98 + $89.02 $13 + $0.64 + $8.75
8. $28 + $0.78 + $34.90 $6.53 + $10 + $4 $389.50 + $578.97

9. $75 − $49.35 $8 − $2.76 $56.80 − $28
10. $21.25 − $18.98 $8.39 − $2.65 $50 − $49.78
11. $20.50 − $4.75 $68.95 − $59 $87.40 − $64.69

General Review

C. *Do these exercises.*

12. 14)210   34)918   22)924   13)338   43)387

13. Round to the nearest hundred: a. 598   b. 4,836   c. 17,452

14. Round to the nearest ten thousand: a. 945,362   b. 1,489,200

15. Round to the nearest hundred thousand: a. 945,362   b. 1,489,200

16. Write the number that is 1,000 more than 56,783,921.

17. Write 45,708 in expanded form.

18. My great-grandfather was born in the year MDCCCLXIX. In what year was he born?

19. 1 mi. = _____ yd.   1 pk. = _____ qt.   1 lb. = _____ oz.
20. 3 pt. = _____ qt.   3 qt. = _____ cups   3 in. = _____ ft.
21. 9 yd. = _____ ft.   9 ft. = _____ yd.   9 cups = _____ pt.

22.   16 yr. 8 mo.   9 days   4 hr.   25 min. 15 sec.
      + 7 yr. 5 mo.   − 6 days 12 hr.   − 18 min. 50 sec.

48. Dividing Money by Two-Digit Divisors

The examples in the box below show how to divide money. Dividing amounts of money is the same as dividing other numbers except for the following things.

1. A dollar sign and a decimal point are placed in the quotient directly above the dollar sign and the decimal point in the dividend.

2. There must be **two** digits to the right of the decimal point. If the quotient has only one digit, a zero must be placed between the decimal point and the one digit. A zero is also placed between the dollar sign and the decimal point to indicate "no dollars." Study the examples in the box.

```
      $0.03          $0.47          $1.45          $0.24          $0.07
  4)$0.12        8)$3.76        5)$7.25       12)$2.88       34)$2.38
      12             32             5              24             2 38
       0             56             22             48              0
                     56             20             48
                      0             25              0
                                    25
                                     0
```

A. *Copy and divide, following the pattern in the box.*

1.   5)$1.25   4)$6.00   8)$0.64   3)$7.17   7)$0.28

2. 11)$3.85   23)$1.38   12)$1.56   41)$7.79   33)$2.31

3. 14)$0.98   43)$2.15   32)$8.64   24)$3.84   13)$1.82

B. *Multiply carefully. Remember to put dollar signs and decimal points in the answers.*

4. $5.16 $1.87 $92.36 $24.50 $31.28
    x   7   x   4   x   3   x   6   x   9

5. $0.97 $0.85 $4.18 $8.29 $6.70
    x 43   x 35   x 28   x 67   x 17

C. *Write the answers only.*

6. 6 × 24   9 × 13   4 × 73   3 × 87   5 × 48

7. $\frac{2}{3}$ of 18 $\frac{4}{5}$ of 20 $\frac{3}{7}$ of 21 $\frac{5}{8}$ of 32 $\frac{3}{4}$ of 12

8. $1\frac{1}{6}$ × 12 $1\frac{1}{3}$ × 24 $2\frac{1}{2}$ × 8 $2\frac{1}{4}$ × 12 $3\frac{1}{9}$ × 9

D. *Change to Roman numerals.*

9. a. 417   b. 790   c. 1,358   d. 524   e. 2,075

E. *Solve these reading problems.*

10. Mother bought 5 pounds of tomatoes for 79¢ a pound, a pound of cheese for $2.39, and a loaf of bread for $1.15. What was her total bill?

11. Kevin saw a new bicycle advertised for $89.95. Instead of a new one, Father bought Kevin a good used bicycle for $25.00. How much money was saved by buying the used bicycle?

12. Mr. Harris has an apple orchard. One day he sold all the half pecks of Golden Delicious apples that he had prepared. He took a bushel of apples and used that to fill some more half pecks. How many half-peck measures could he fill from the bushel? (First think: How many whole pecks can Mr. Harris fill from a bushel?)

13. Mr. Harris sells Golden Delicious apples for $5.50 a half bushel and McIntosh apples for $4.95 a half bushel. How much does he charge for two half bushels of Golden Delicious apples and a half bushel of McIntosh?

14. A half bushel of Golden Delicious apples costs _____ more than a half bushel of McIntosh apples. (See number 13.)

15. Mr. Harris sells apples to stores at a wholesale price of $7.50 a bushel. What is the wholesale price of a half bushel?

16. One week Mr. Harris sold 21 bushels of Macoun apples, 18 bushels of McIntosh, 25 bushels of Golden Delicious, 32 bushels of Red Delicious, and 23 bushels of Grimes Golden. How many bushels of apples did Mr. Harris sell that week?

49. Chapter 5 Review

A. *Write the answers only.*

1.
10	11	12	10	12	11	11	12	10
× 8	× 11	× 10	× 7	× 6	× 12	× 3	× 5	× 10

2.
12	10	12	11	12	10	11	12	10
× 4	× 2	× 3	× 10	× 12	× 6	× 5	× 8	× 4

3.
10	11	12	12	10	11	12	12	10
× 11	× 9	× 2	× 9	× 5	× 2	× 7	× 11	× 12

4. $10\overline{)90}$ $12\overline{)48}$ $11\overline{)44}$ $12\overline{)84}$ $10\overline{)100}$ $12\overline{)120}$

5. $11\overline{)77}$ $10\overline{)60}$ $12\overline{)96}$ $12\overline{)12}$ $11\overline{)132}$ $12\overline{)108}$

6. $12\overline{)60}$ $11\overline{)22}$ $12\overline{)72}$ $10\overline{)30}$ $12\overline{)144}$ $10\overline{)120}$

7. $11\overline{)55}$ $10\overline{)80}$ $12\overline{)24}$ $12\overline{)36}$ $11\overline{)110}$ $11\overline{)121}$

8. $10\overline{)50}$ $11\overline{)88}$ $10\overline{)20}$ $11\overline{)66}$ $10\overline{)110}$ $12\overline{)132}$

9. 4 × 67   8 × 23   9 × 16   5 × 35   6 × 53
10. 2 × 79   4 × 39   8 × 44   7 × 90   3 × 98
11. 6 × 30   7 × 14   5 × 28   8 × 40   2 × 46

B. *Do these exercises.*

12. Round these numbers to the nearest ten.
    a. 56   b. 23   c. 74   d. 129   e. 362   f. 4,591

13. Round to the nearest thousand: a. 4,591 b. 9,389 c. 12,750 d. 345,827

14. Write the value of each bill pictured here. Look in Lesson 47 if you need help.

    a.   b.   c.

15. What is the value of each set of money?

    a. 3 quarters, 2 dimes, 3 nickels

    b. two 20-dollar bills, three 10-dollar bills, one 5-dollar bill

    c. 1 half dollar, 3 quarters, 7 pennies

    d. 6 dimes, 5 nickels, 9 pennies

    e. two 5-dollar bills, 3 dollar bills, 7 nickels

16. Write each price in two ways: **a.** thirty-five cents   **b.** eight dollars

C. *Copy in straight columns. Follow the signs.*

17. $4.56 + $9 + $12.98 $18.95 + $3.65 + $0.19

18. $7.18 + $74.92 + $329.25 $47 + $0.06 + $8.59

19. $52.45 - $43 $75 - $38.27 $21.05 - $16.85

20. $7 - $0.07 $34.12 - $5.68 $8.29 - $0.60

21.
$0.38 × 27 $0.72 × 49 $4.69 × 34 $56.78 × 2 $19.40 × 8

D. *Copy and divide.*

22. 5)$1.40   6)$0.48   8)$9.20   12)$3.84   34)$2.38

23. 30)150   50)700   20)840   60)360   40)925

24. 12)564   11)396   31)713   43)602   14)364

25. 22)95   32)800   11)798   13)598   24)192

Reading Problem Review

E. *How would you find the answers? Write* add, subtract, multiply, *or* divide.

26. a. How many are left?   **b.** Find the product of two numbers.

27. a. How many 5's are in 25?   **b.** How many are five 25's?

28. What is the difference between two numbers?

29. Find the total of several different numbers.

30. What is the price for 8 pounds of bananas if you know the price per pound?

31. How much older am I than my brother?

32. What is the price per pound if you buy a roast for $8.37?

(continued on next page)

F. *Choose the best estimate for each problem.*

33. Columbus discovered America in 1492. The first permanent English settlement in America was founded in 1607, which was _____ years later.

     100   200   300

34. Each of the 28 fifth graders needs 3 sheets of paper for a paper-folding project. How many sheets of paper do the fifth graders need in all?

     25   33   60   90

35. A package of four drinking glasses is priced at $3.95. What is the price of one glass? $16.00 $1.00 $0.50

36. The area of Rhode Island is 1,055 square miles; of Delaware, 1,932 square miles; and of Connecticut, 4,872 square miles. What is the total area of the three states? 6,000 8,000 9,000

G. *Solve these problems.*

37. The price for an 11-ounce box of cereal is $1.98. What is the price per ounce?

38. A 20-ounce box of the same kind of cereal is marked $3.20. What is the price per ounce?

39. Mother saves 2 cents per ounce when she buys a large box. How much does she save on three 20-ounce boxes?

40. What is the price for 25 pounds of flour at $0.18 a pound?

41. What is the cost of 3 bars of soap at $0.89 each and a dish towel for $2.29?

42. Mother had $80.00 when she began shopping. She spent $57.18 at the grocery store, $14.77 at the dry goods store, and $2.90 at the post office. How much money did Mother have left?

50. Chapter 5 Test

Chapter 6

Multiplication by Three-Digit Multipliers

But he that received seed into the good ground is he that heareth
the word, and understandeth it; which also beareth fruit, and
bringeth forth, some an hundredfold, some sixty, some thirty.
(Matthew 13:23)

51. Practice With Larger Numbers

This chart names the longest river on each continent. Use the chart to do the exercises below.

Continent	River	Length in Miles
Africa	Nile River	4,180
South America	Amazon River	3,912
Asia	Yangtze River	3,602
North America	Mississippi River	2,348
Europe	Danube River	1,766
Australia	Darling River	1,702

A. *Write the answers.*

1. Which river is the longest in the world?

2. What is the longest river in North America?

3. How long is the Nile River, to the nearest thousand miles?

4. How long is the Amazon River, rounded to the nearest thousand?

5. The Nile River is _____ longer than the Amazon River. (Use exact numbers.)

6. Round the lengths of the Danube River and the Darling River to the nearest ten miles.

7. Using the rounded numbers, estimate the difference in length between the Danube and the Darling rivers.

8. Find the exact difference in length between the Danube and the Darling rivers.

9. Using numbers rounded to the nearest hundred, estimate how much longer the Yangtze River is than the Mississippi.

10. Now find the exact difference between the Yangtze and the Mississippi.

Study these rules to multiply numbers by 10, 100, or 1,000 easily.

---

1. To multiply a number by 10, place one zero after the number. $10 \times 85 = 850$
2. To multiply a number by 100, place two zeroes after the number. $100 \times 17 = 1,700$
3. To multiply a number by 1,000, place three zeroes after the number.

$1,000 \times 42 = 42,000$

B. *Write the answers only.*

11. 10×18	10×90	10×784	10×810	10×500
12. 100×47	100×50	100×825	$1,000 \times 15$	$1,000 \times 620$
13. 6×17	4×35	7×24	9×13	5×45

C. *Do these exercises.*

14. Write by tens from 1,300 to 1,400. All the numbers end with 0.

15. Which numbers are multiples of 10?   420   605   1,068   3,290

16. Write numerals for these number words.
   a. 114 billion, 350 million
   b. 12 million, 865 thousand, 17
   c. six billion, sixty thousand, six hundred
   d. one hundred billion, one million, eleven thousand, ten

17. Copy each pair of numbers, and put < or > between them.
   a. 14,500,000 _____ 14,509,999   b. 6,740,005 _____ 6,739,889

18. Round to the nearest ten thousand.
   a. 67,304   b. 94,889   c. 123,670   d. 965,371   e. 2,406,385

19. Write the number that is
   a. 10 more than 725,684.   d. 300 more than 725,684.
   b. 100,000 more than 725,684.   e. 40,000 more than 725,684.
   c. 2,000 more than 725,684.   f. 1,000,000 more than 725,684.

20. Copy and subtract. Check by adding.

60,000	18,200	83,004	70,307	96,274
- 35,829	- 9,513	- 54,896	- 9,724	- 45,484

52. Multiplying by Multiples of 10 or 100.

To multiply any number by 10, you place a zero at the end of the number. So any number that ends with 0 is a multiple of 10.

To multiply a number by 100, you place two zeroes at the end of the number. So any number that ends with 00 is a multiple of 100.

Study the information in the box to find a shortcut for multiplying numbers by multiples of 10 or multiples of 100.

When you write a problem like 40 × 68 in column form, write the multiplier with the zero off to the right side.

$$\begin{array}{r} 68 \\ \times\,40 \\ \hline \end{array} \qquad \begin{array}{r} 68 \\ \times\,40 \\ \hline 2{,}720 \end{array}$$

Now multiply. Write 0 first, and then multiply 4 × 68.

Here are several more examples. Can you explain how each is done?

$$\begin{array}{r} 80 \\ \times\,70 \\ \hline 5{,}600 \end{array} \qquad \begin{array}{r} 394 \\ \times\ \ 30 \\ \hline 11{,}820 \end{array} \qquad \begin{array}{r} 72 \\ \times\,600 \\ \hline 43{,}200 \end{array} \qquad \begin{array}{r} 589 \\ \times\ \ 400 \\ \hline 235{,}600 \end{array}$$

A. *Copy and multiply. Follow the pattern in the box for all the problems, including those in row 3.*

1.	70 × 30	43 × 90	715 × 50	849 × 30	280 × 60
2.	80 × 800	16 × 700	360 × 700	724 × 400	698 × 200
3.	25 × 50	86 × 500	419 × 70	370 × 300	396 × 600

B. *Copy and divide.*

4. 60)480   70)840   30)930   50)350   20)520

5. 32)512   13)719   12)388   11)517   24)192

Two-Step Reading Problems

Sometimes a reading problem has a "hidden step" that you must do before you can find the final answer.

> **Example:** Mrs. Weaver bought a 12-pound turkey for $0.79 a pound. What was her change from $10.00?
>
> **First step:**   Cost of turkey = 12 × $0.79 = $9.48
> **Second step:**   Change = $10.00 – $9.48 = $0.52

C. *Two steps are needed to solve these problems. Think and work carefully. Show both steps on your paper.*

6. Mother bought four half-bushel baskets of peaches for $6.25 a basket. She also bought a basket of early apples for $4.75. What was Mother's total bill?

7. Rebecca needs 1 yard of knit material to make pillowcases for her room. She also needs $\frac{1}{2}$ yard of the same material for dresser scarves. If Rebecca buys material for $3.20 a yard, how much will it cost altogether?

8. Brother Elmer goes to a produce auction to buy vegetables to sell at his roadside stand. One week he paid $2.00 apiece for several boxes containing eight heads of cabbage each. He sold the cabbage at his stand for $0.75 a head How much did he gain on one head of cabbage? (The money he made is profit.)

9. One woman who stopped at Brother Elmer's stand bought 3 heads of cabbage at $0.75 each, a quart of turnips for $1.00, and a half peck of apples for $2.50. How much should Brother Elmer charge the woman?

10. Another customer bought a half bushel of broccoli for $4.95 and one head of cabbage for $0.75. The customer paid with a 10-dollar bill. How much change should Brother Elmer give?

11. The Myer family started on a 2,765-mile trip to visit their cousins in British Columbia. The first day they drove 780 miles. The next day they drove 745 miles. How far did they still have to go to reach their cousins' home?

12. The Myers estimated that each day of traveling cost them about $60.00 in gasoline and $25.00 in food. What was their estimated cost for gasoline and food in four days of travel?

53. Practice With Mental Arithmetic

When you solve problems by mental arithmetic, you do all the work "in your head." This page will help to improve your skill in adding and subtracting mentally.

Helps for Mental Addition	
17 + 30 = ?	Think: 10 + 30 = 40; 40 + 7 = 47
13 + 25 = ?	Think: 10 + 20 = 30; 3 + 5 = 8; 30 + 8 = 38
26 + 28 = ?	Think: 20 + 20 = 40; 6 + 8 = 14; 40 + 14 = 54

A. Add mentally, and write the answers only.

1.	12 + 40	13 + 70	40 + 58	50 + 25	36 + 40
2.	14 + 25	13 + 12	38 + 11	63 + 23	34 + 44
3.	19 + 11	16 + 16	18 + 19	36 + 14	27 + 18

Helps for Mental Subtraction	
17 − 2 = ?	Think: 7 − 2 = 5, so 17 − 2 = 15
28 − 7 = ?	Think: 8 − 7 = 1, so 28 − 7 = 21
48 − 17 = ?	Think: 40 − 10 = 30; 8 − 7 = 1; 48 − 17 = 31
28 − 9 = ?	Think: 18 − 9 = 9, so 28 − 9 = 19

B. Subtract mentally, and write the answers only.

4.	29 − 5	18 − 3	48 − 8	57 − 6	36 − 4
5.	58 − 20	77 − 10	35 − 20	69 − 40	43 − 40
6.	35 − 11	46 − 25	27 − 17	66 − 23	79 − 36
7.	16 − 8	26 − 8	36 − 8	56 − 8	86 − 8
8.	24 − 6	30 − 5	40 − 7	32 − 6	55 − 8
9.	43 − 5	22 − 3	31 − 6	41 − 4	37 − 9

C. Write the answers only.

10.	5 × 17	4 × 39	6 × 13	2 × 79	8 × 25
11.	3 × 97	5 × 24	7 × 32	4 × 18	9 × 72

12. $\frac{3}{4}$ of 16 $\frac{2}{3}$ of 15 $\frac{5}{8}$ of 32 $\frac{1}{2}$ of 22 $\frac{4}{5}$ of 30

13. $1\frac{1}{2} \times 14$ $1\frac{1}{8} \times 40$ $2\frac{1}{3} \times 9$ $1\frac{1}{5} \times 30$ $3\frac{1}{6} \times 6$

14. $4 \div 7$ $1 \div 3$ $2 \div 8$ $3 \div 5$ $4 \div 12$

D. *Write these numbers with words. Use hyphens and commas correctly. A sample is done for you.*

S. 267,518   two hundred sixty-seven thousand, five hundred eighteen

15. 13,045,000

16. 86,500,231,006

17. 8,000,320,799

E. *Round first to the nearest thousand and then to the nearest ten thousand.*

18. a. 56,439   b. 134,720   c. 588,588   d. 2,067,482

F. *Estimate answers to these problems by rounding addends to the nearest hundred. Write the estimated answers only.*

19.	540	387	421	308	849
	78	412	906	358	676
	284	985	375	827	438
	+ 394	+ 267	+ 582	+ 31	+ 125

G. *Estimate by rounding to the nearest thousand. Write the estimated answers only.*

20.	5,490	3,947	6,288	45,782	63,392
	4,528	2,377	8,467	28,200	45,428
	+ 8,927	+ 4,185	+ 7,824	+ 17,839	+ 61,565

21.	8,932	5,643	9,351	45,903	21,174
	- 2,358	- 4,725	- 6,899	- 17,261	- 8,798

Your teacher may also want you to find exact answers in rows 19–21.

54. Multiplying by Three-Digit Multipliers

Problems with three-digit multipliers require three separate multiplications. Follow the steps below to multiply 726 by 342.

1. Multiply 2 × 726. Begin the partial product in the ones' place.	726 × 342
2. Multiply 4 × 726. Begin the partial product in the tens' place below the first partial product.	1452 2904
3. Multiply 3 × 726. Begin the partial product in the hundreds' place below the first two partial products.	2178 248,292
4. Add the three partial products.	

A. *Copy and work carefully. Your teacher may have you use graph paper to keep the columns straight.*

1.
783   650   213   967
× 243   × 351   × 786   × 214

2.
582   971   460   835
× 123   × 534   × 675   × 374

3.
4,593   9,750   6,827   1,732
× 45   × 17   × 36   × 49

4.
853   978   480   351
× 700   × 400   × 800   × 600

5. 32)704   11)825   24)192   43)344

6. 5)7,300   6)1,368   3)5,832   8)5,000

General Review
B. *Do these exercises.*

7. Write four number facts with the numbers 8, 4, and 32.

8. Write four number facts with the numbers 7, 9, and 63.

C. Write the missing numbers. Use related facts to help you.

9. ____ × 7 = 35   8 × ____ = 72   9 × ____ = 36   ____ × 2 = 14

10. 9 × 6 = ____   ____ × 7 = 21   4 × ____ = 24   8 × 8 = ____

11. 27 ÷ 3 = ____   42 ÷ ____ = 6   ____ ÷ 8 = 2   ____ ÷ 4 = 5

12. 56 ÷ ____ = 8   ____ ÷ 3 = 8   48 ÷ 6 = ____   32 ÷ ____ = 8

D. Write the answers only.

13. 25 + 15   16 + 13   18 + 14   38 + 13

14. 15 + 30   14 + 15   26 + 10   27 + 17

15. 75 – 30   48 – 14   37 – 25   56 – 6

16. 19 – 7   21 – 6   33 – 4   24 – 8

17. 1 century = ____ yr.   1 leap year = ____ days   1 mo. = ____ days

18. 1 day = ____ hr.   1 mi. = ____ ft.   1 decade = ____ yr.

19. 1 ton = ____ lb.   1 pk. = ____ qt.   1 bu. = ____ pk.

20. 5 wk. = ____ days   9 ft. = ____ yd.   3 cups = ____ pt.

21. 8 qt. = ____ gal.   8 gal. = ____ qt. $\frac{1}{3}$ ft. = ____ in.

E. Follow the directions.

22. Identify these bills. Look in Lesson 47 if you need help.

a.   b.   c.

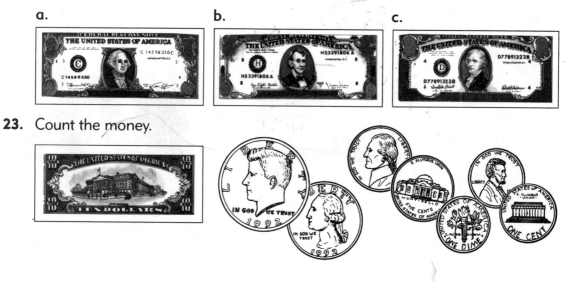

23. Count the money.

55. More Practice With Three-Digit Multipliers

A. *Copy and multiply carefully. Keep the columns straight!*

1.
```
   914          627          890          436
 × 325        × 412        × 324        × 600
```

2.
```
   743          821          765          930
 × 271        × 756        × 300        × 263
```

3.
```
 6,748        3,280        4,109        3,254
 ×   24       ×   43       ×   62       ×   17
```

4.
```
   728          516          162          890
 × 340        × 730        × 650        × 320
```

5. 12)868   33)198   41)861   13)455

6. 8)9,128   2)1,734   9)6,417   6)8,244

B. *Solve these reading problems.*

7. Ernest picked 445 pounds of tomatoes from 5 rows. At that rate, how many pounds of tomatoes did he pick from one row?

8. During a 1-inch rainfall, about 5 pounds of water fall on each square foot of area. How many pounds of water fall on a roof that contains 875 square feet of area?

9. About 113 tons of water fall on each acre of land during a 1-inch rainfall. At that rate, how many tons of water fall on 175 acres during a 1-inch rainfall?

10. A bushel of apples weighs about 50 pounds. How many bushels of apples would be needed to make a ton (2,000 pounds)?

General Review

C. *Do these exercises.*

11. Reduce to lowest terms.

    a. $\frac{6}{16}$ b. $\frac{10}{20}$ c. $\frac{12}{16}$ d. $\frac{9}{15}$ e. $\frac{8}{24}$

12. Change to whole or mixed numbers in simplest form.

    a. $\frac{4}{3}$ b. $\frac{8}{5}$ c. $\frac{10}{4}$ d. $\frac{12}{3}$ e. $\frac{13}{6}$

13. Follow the signs. Write all the answers in simplest form.

$$\frac{3}{8} + \frac{7}{8} \qquad \frac{7}{16} + \frac{9}{16} \qquad 2\frac{1}{5} + 4\frac{3}{5} \qquad 1\frac{5}{12} + 2\frac{1}{12} \qquad 5\frac{7}{9} - 2\frac{1}{9}$$

D. *Write the numbers that fit in the blanks.*

14. $18 \div \underline{\quad} = 3$ $\underline{\quad} \div 4 = 4$ $36 \div 6 = \underline{\quad}$ $\underline{\quad} \div 8 = 5$

15. $\underline{\quad} \div 7 = 7$ $30 \div \underline{\quad} = 5$ $63 \div \underline{\quad} = 9$ $60 \div 10 = \underline{\quad}$

16. $8 \times \underline{\quad} = 48$ $3 \times 8 = \underline{\quad}$ $\underline{\quad} \times 12 = 36$ $\underline{\quad} \times 4 = 8$

17. $6 \times 12 = \underline{\quad}$ $\underline{\quad} \times 4 = 20$ $8 \times \underline{\quad} = 64$ $9 \times \underline{\quad} = 27$

E. *Follow the directions.*

18. Write numerals for these number words.

    a. sixty-five billion

    b. one hundred eighty-two million

    c. 290 billion, 75 million, 376 thousand, 500

    d. 34 billion, 860 million

    e. seventeen million, three hundred fifty-nine

19. Round to the nearest hundred.

    a. 675   b. 342   c. 5,229   d. 36,872

20. Round to the nearest ten thousand.

    a. 56,438   b. 34,198   c. 290,367   d. 728,425

56. Checking Multiplication by Exchanging Factors

The larger the problem, the more careful you must be to make sure you have the right answer. Reversing factors is a good way to check multiplication problems. Study the box.

824	Check: 371
× 371	× 824
824	1484
5768	742
2472	2968
305,704	305,704

A. *Copy, multiply, and check by exchanging the factors.*

1. a. 640   b. 932   c. 517
           × 362   × 147   × 436

2. a. 835   b. 760   c. 219
           × 634   × 265   × 543

3. a. 941   b. 366   c. 487
           × 460   × 824   × 135

4. a. 250   b. 839   c. 624
           × 986   × 451   × 970

B. *Write how many digits are in each quotient. Do not find the answers.*

5. 35)467   14)593   22)178   43)900   32)200

6. 13)156   34)278   51)346   23)894   12)384

C. *Copy and divide carefully.*

7. 11)783   14)854   32)224   21)357   60)720

Mental Arithmetic Practice

D. *Write the answers only. Give fraction answers in simplest form.*

8.

9	12	6	10	12	7	8	12	11
×7	×8	×7	×10	×9	×8	×9	×5	×10

9.

8	12	11	12	10	9	7	6	8
×8	×12	×11	×7	×12	×9	×7	×9	×6

10. ___ × 8 = 32   9 × ___ = 45   7 × ___ = 63   6 × 12 = ___

11. 9 × 4 = ___   ___ × 6 = 36   ___ × 9 = 72   8 × ___ = 56

12. 18 ÷ ___ = 6   27 ÷ ___ = 3   ___ ÷ 4 = 7   ___ ÷ 12 = 4

13. ___ ÷ 2 = 6   48 ÷ 8 = ___   24 ÷ ___ = 8   ___ ÷ 6 = 7

14. 8 × 15   7 × 26   3 × 89   4 × 81   5 × 75

15. 14 + 17   19 + 30   12 + 15   22 + 34   35 + 15

16. 19 − 5   24 − 4   20 − 8   23 − 7   38 − 17

17. $\frac{2}{3}$ of 30 $\frac{1}{2}$ of 16 $\frac{3}{4}$ of 32 $\frac{5}{8}$ of 16 $\frac{2}{5}$ of 25

18. $1\frac{1}{3} × 9$ $1\frac{1}{2} × 12$ $2\frac{1}{4} × 8$ $1\frac{1}{7} × 21$ $3\frac{1}{3} × 6$

19. 3 ÷ 8   2 ÷ 7   1 ÷ 5   4 ÷ 12   8 ÷ 10

20. 1 yr. = ___ days   1 yr. = ___ wk.   1 yr. = ___ mo.

21. 1 bu. = ___ pk.   1 qt. = ___ pt.   1 leap year = ___ days

22. 1 lb. = ___ oz.   1 mi. = ___ yd.   1 ft. = ___ in.

23. 8 cups = ___ qt.   8 cups = ___ pt.   8 pt. = ___ cups

24. 8 qt. = ___ cups   8 qt. = ___ gal.   8 qt. = ___ pk.

25. 3 ft. = ___ yd.   3 ft. = ___ in.   3 yd. = ___ ft.

26. $\frac{1}{2}$ ft. = ___ in. $\frac{1}{4}$ yr. = ___ mo. $\frac{1}{8}$ lb. = ___ oz.

57. Checking Division With Multiplication

Multiply the quotient and the divisor to check division problems. The product should equal the dividend unless there is a remainder. In that case, add on the remainder.

```
        25      Check:    34
  34)850                × 25
     68                  170
    170                   68
    170                  850
      0
```

A. *Copy, divide, and check by multiplying. There are no remainders.*

1. 21)966	40)960	11)528
2. 32)288	14)336	23)161
3. 12)288	30)720	13)598
4. 60)480	42)588	22)176

B. *Copy, multiply, and check by exchanging the factors.*

5. a. 367
      × 350

  b. 590
      × 423

  c. 416
      × 628

6. a. 145
      × 793

  b. 298
      × 312

  c. 732
      × 876

C. *Write the answers only.*

7.
```
  8     6     4     9     3     2     7
  4     2     7     8     6     4     8
  3     5     6     3     7     8     3
  5     4     8     7     2     9     4
+ 6   + 7   + 9   + 5   + 4   + 8   + 2
```

8. 6 × ____ = 42   5 × 9 = ____   ____ × 7 = 63   8 × ____ = 24

9. ____ ÷ 7 = 7   7 ÷ ____ = 7   96 ÷ 8 = ____   ____ ÷ 8 = 6

Practice With Money

D. *Do these exercises.*

10. Write each price in two ways.
   a. forty-nine cents   **b.** eight cents   **c.** eleven dollars

11. Write the missing numbers.
   a. 1 dollar = _____ quarters   **f.** 1 half dollar = _____ nickels
   b. 1 quarter = _____ nickels   **g.** 1 dime = _____ pennies
   c. 1 dollar = _____ nickels   **h.** 2 dollars = _____ quarters
   d. 1 half dollar = _____ dimes   **i.** 2 dollars = _____ half dollars
   e. 1 half dollar = _____ quarters   **j.** 1 dollar = _____ dimes

12. Write these missing numbers, with the labels shown.
   a. 7 nickels = _____ cents   **f.** 7 quarters = $ _____ . _____
   b. 12 nickels = _____ cents   **g.** 2 dimes and 2 nickels = _____ ¢
   c. 8 dimes = _____ cents   **h.** 3 quarters and 1 dime = _____ ¢
   d. 28 pennies = _____ cents   **i.** 5 half dollars = $ _____ . _____
   e. 5 quarters = $ _____ . _____   **j.** 6 dimes and 1 quarter = _____ ¢

13. Write the total value of each set.
   a. four 5-dollar bills   **e.** six 10-dollar bills
   b. three 20-dollar bills   **f.** two 50-dollar bills
   c. two 10-dollar bills, three five-dollar bills
   d. one 20-dollar bill, one 5-dollar bill, four 1-dollar bills

14. Write what pieces of money should be given as change to the following customers. Use the smallest number of pieces possible.

Name of Customer	Amount of Purchase	Amount Given
a. Mrs. Greene	$3.70	$5.00
b. Mrs. Jackson	$1.42	$5.00
c. Mr. Boyd	$4.35	$10.00
d. Miss Martin	$7.64	$20.00

15. Count the money.

58. Two-Digit Divisors and Remainders

You have been dividing by two-digit divisors for several weeks. In this lesson the divisions will have remainders.

Study the box to review how to divide and check problems with remainders.

```
        47 R 7    Check:    13
 13)618                    x 47
     52                      91
     98                      52
     91                     611
      7                    +  7
                           618
```

A. *Copy, divide, and check by multiplication. These problems have remainders.*

1. 20)310   40)335   60)700

2. 11)719   12)800   21)745

3. 13)446   32)520   24)149

4. 23)102   14)343   42)770

B. *Copy, multiply, and check by exchanging the factors.*

5. a.   687   b.   960   c.   412
        x 325   x 786   x 467

C. *Write the answers only.*

6. 10×89 10×450 100×17 100×60 $1,000 \times 35$
7. 4×56 7×82 9×93 5×68 3×78
8. $15 + 23$ $14 + 16$ $28 + 9$ $34 + 30$ $26 + 15$
9. $19 - 5$ $25 - 5$ $25 - 7$ $38 - 11$ $43 - 20$
10. $1\frac{1}{3} \times 9$ $2\frac{1}{2} \times 4$ $\frac{3}{4}$ of 20 $\frac{2}{5}$ of 30 $5 \div 8$

D. *Follow the directions.*

11. Use the numbers 8, 6, and 14 to write four arithmetic facts.

12. Use 7, 6, and 42 to write four arithmetic facts.

Reading Problems

E. ***How do you find the answers? Write*** *add,* *subtract,* *multiply,* **or** *divide.*

13. **a.** How much less?

b. How many 5's are in 15?

c. How much more?

d. How many are left?

e. How many are six 7's?

f. How much change?

g. How many in 7 groups of 4?

h. How much for both?

i. How many in three groups of the same size?

j. How many groups of 4 in a number?

k. How many altogether in three groups of different sizes?

F. ***The reading problems on this page require very simple arithmetic. You can probably solve most of them mentally, but be sure your answers are sensible. Write the answers on your paper.***

14. David became king when he was 30 years old. He was king for 40 years. How old was David then?

15. How much did Mother spend for 3 boxes of Kleenex at $0.80 each?

16. Ten boys and 6 girls are in the fifth grade class at Rafton Christian School. There are _____ fewer girls than boys.

17. The school buys copier paper in large cases with ten packages of paper in each case. If the cost of one package is 3 dollars, what is the cost of a whole case?

18. There are 500 sheets in each package of copier paper. One day Sister Joyce opened a new package and used 50 sheets. How many sheets of paper were left in the package?

19. If Sister Joyce uses 50 sheets of paper each day, in how many days will she use a package of 500 sheets?

20. Brother Wilmer copied a three-page history test for each of his seventh graders. If there are 9 pupils in seventh grade, how many sheets of paper did Brother Wilmer use?

21. One day Brother Wilmer used 40 sheets of paper to copy music tests, 20 sheets for math drills, and 18 sheets for English worksheets. How many sheets of paper did he use altogether?

59. Chapter 6 Review

A. *Write the answers only.*

1.
11	12	8	12	9	11	12	7	12
× 10	× 7	× 9	× 12	× 7	× 12	× 8	× 8	× 9

2. $110 \div 11$ $108 \div 12$ $64 \div 8$ $120 \div 10$

3. $132 \div 12$ $45 \div 5$ $24 \div 3$ $100 \div 10$

4.   ___ × 6 = 48   7 × ___ = 21   ___ × 4 = 8   6 × 9 = ___

5.   12 × ___ = 60   ___ × 4 = 32   ___ × 7 = 56   5 × ___ = 35

6.   72 ÷ ___ = 9   81 ÷ 9 = ___   42 ÷ ___ = 7   ___ ÷ 9 = 4

7.   ___ ÷ 6 = 5   12 ÷ ___ = 4   ___ ÷ 3 = 9   28 ÷ ___ = 7

8. 7×24 8×16 4×15 2×38 6×73

9. 10×32 10×50 100×19 100×48 $1,000 \times 61$

10. $12 + 7$ $23 + 4$ $18 + 8$ $35 + 5$ $27 + 9$

11. $14 + 11$ $23 + 15$ $20 + 14$ $34 + 14$ $18 + 30$

12. $17 - 5$ $25 - 11$ $64 - 10$ $37 - 20$ $48 - 23$

13. $20 - 4$ $30 - 7$ $23 - 6$ $31 - 5$ $45 - 8$

B. *Do these exercises.*

14. Round each number to the nearest ten.
     a. 452   b. 3,675   c. 7,428   d. 14,824

15. Round to the nearest hundred.
     a. 452   b. 3,675   c. 7,428   d. 14,824

16. Round to the nearest thousand.
     a. 3,675   b. 7,428   c. 14,824   d. 275,149

17.

7	4	8	3	7	6
8	6	9	8	5	3
2	8	5	6	4	9
4	2	3	9	3	4
+ 5	+ 7	+ 5	+ 7	+ 8	+ 2

18.

26,300	80,000	50,201	75,391
− 8,506	− 45,329	− 32,974	− 28,467

C. Copy and multiply. Check by going over your work.

19.

548	219	350	178	672
× 400	× 600	× 500	× 300	× 600

D. Copy, multiply, and check by reversing the factors.

20. a. 513 × 428   b. 746 × 327   c. 392 × 145

21. a. 360 × 168   b. 912 × 780   c. 463 × 728

E. Copy, divide, and check by multiplication.

22. 31)465   12)864   23)966

23. 60)960   30)210   80)960

24. 41)328   24)144   32)256

25. 14)490   33)825   22)814

26. 13)172   21)950   34)953

(continued on next page)

Reading Problems

F. *Write whether you would* add, subtract, multiply, *or* divide. ***Then find the answers.***

27. Myra bought a box of greeting cards for $3.85. She paid for it with a 5-dollar bill. What was her change?

28. Brother Gary counts the people in church on Sunday mornings. This Sunday morning he counted 14 in the preschool class, 9 in the primary class, 12 in the junior class, 8 in the intermediate class, 10 in the youth class, and 37 in the adult class. How many people were in the classes altogether?

29. Last Sunday Brother Gary counted 102 people in church. The Sunday before, there were 95 people in church. How many more people were in church last Sunday than the Sunday before?

30. The price of a dozen Gospel tracts is $0.60. At that rate, what is the price of one tract?

31. At the price of $0.60 a dozen, what is the total price for 13 dozen tracts?

32. If 300 tracts are packed in bundles of one dozen each, how many bundles are there?

G. *The following problems require two steps. Solve them carefully on your paper.*

33. At $0.60 a dozen, what is the cost of 300 tracts?

34. One hundred of the same kind of tract costs $1.75. How much money can be saved by buying 600 tracts in bundles of 100 instead of paying $30.00 for them if purchased by the dozen?

35. One hundred 4-page tracts cost $1.75, and one hundred 8-page tracts cost $2.10. How much will Brocker's Mennonite Church pay for 500 4-page tracts and 100 8-page tracts?

36. Some of the brethren from Brocker's Mennonite Church passed out tracts on Saturday afternoon. In one hour they handed out 75 copies of the tract *Be Ready*, 123 copies of *Meet My Friend*, and 97 copies of *The Perfect Gift*. How many tracts did the brethren hand out in 3 hours?

37. On another Saturday, 6 brethren passed out 936 tracts in 3 hours. At that rate, how many tracts did each brother hand out in one hour?

- -

60. Chapter 6 Test

Chapter 7

Factors, Multiples, and Prime Numbers

Then said Boaz unto Ruth, . . .
Go not to glean in another field,
neither go from hence,
but abide here fast by my maidens.
(Ruth 2:8)

61. Multiples

---

1. A **multiple** of a number is a product of that number.

  $2 \times 4 = 8$ $5 \times 4 = 20$ $8 \times 4 = 32$

  Some multiples of 4 are 8, 20, and 32.

  The multiples of 4 are 4, 8, 12, 16 . . .
  The multiples of 9 are 9, 18, 27, 36 . . .
      (The dots mean "continuing in the same way.")

2. Some multiples are easy to recognize.
  Multiples of 10 end with 0. Multiples of 100 end with 00.
  Multiples of 5 end with 0 or 5.
  Multiples of 2 end with 0, 2, 4, 6, or 8.

3. Multiples of 2 are called **even numbers.** Numbers that are not
  multiples of 2 are called **odd numbers.**

A. *Do these exercises.*

1. Write six multiples of each number below.

  a. 6   b. 10   c. 2   d. 12   e. 5   f. 8

2. Which of the following numbers are multiples of 3?

  24   20   15   30   14   27   3   13   9   25

3. Which are multiples of 7?

  24   70   14   30   42   45   27   28   35   3

4. Which are multiples of 11?

  33   88   100   121   35   77   11   81   99

5. Write all the even numbers between 11 and 29.

6. Write all the odd numbers between 40 and 60.

B. *Answer each question with yes or no.*

7. Is 24 a multiple

  a. of 6?   b. of 7?   c. of 4?   d. of 3?   e. of 8?   f. of 9?

8. Is 40 a multiple

  a. of 8?   b. of 6?   c. of 4?   d. of 5?   e. of 3?   f. of 10?

General Review

C. *Do these exercises.*

9. Write the lengths to which the arrows point.

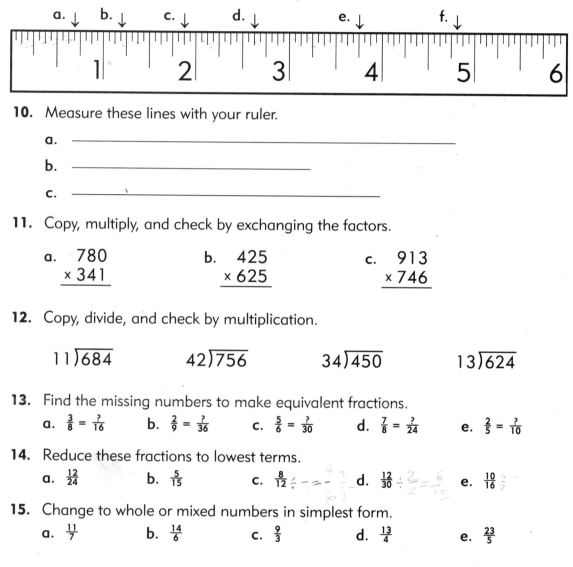

10. Measure these lines with your ruler.

    a. _____

    b. _____

    c. _____

11. Copy, multiply, and check by exchanging the factors.

    a.   780   b.   425   c.   913
        × 341   × 625   × 746

12. Copy, divide, and check by multiplication.

    11)684   42)756   34)450   13)624

13. Find the missing numbers to make equivalent fractions.

    a. $\frac{3}{8} = \frac{?}{16}$ b. $\frac{2}{9} = \frac{?}{36}$ c. $\frac{5}{6} = \frac{?}{30}$ d. $\frac{7}{8} = \frac{?}{24}$ e. $\frac{2}{5} = \frac{?}{10}$

14. Reduce these fractions to lowest terms.

    a. $\frac{12}{24}$ b. $\frac{5}{15}$ c. $\frac{8}{12}$ d. $\frac{12}{30}$ e. $\frac{10}{16}$

15. Change to whole or mixed numbers in simplest form.

    a. $\frac{11}{7}$ b. $\frac{14}{6}$ c. $\frac{9}{3}$ d. $\frac{13}{4}$ e. $\frac{23}{5}$

D. *Solve these reading problems.*

16. Each day Clarence feeds the chickens and gathers the eggs. In five days he gathered the following numbers of eggs: 41, 38, 42, 39, and 44. How many eggs did he gather altogether?

17. How many dozen eggs did Clarence gather in the five days? Choose the correct answer: (15 doz., 16 doz., 17 doz., 18 doz.).

62. Common Multiples

---

1. A **common multiple** is a multiple of more than one smaller number.
   A common multiple of 4 and 9 is 36.
   A common multiple of 2, 3, 4, and 6 is 12.

2. The **lowest common multiple** of two numbers is the smallest number that is a multiple of both.

   Example: Find the lowest common multiple of 4 and 6.
   Multiples of 4: 4, 8, (12) 16, 20, (24) . . .
   Multiples of 6: 6, (12) 18, (24) 30 . . .
   Common multiples of 4 and 6: 12, 24
   Lowest common multiple: 12

A. *Write the answers.*

1. Write all the multiples of 3 from 1 to 40.

2. Write all the multiples of 4 from 1 to 40.

3. Write all the multiples of 8 from 1 to 100.

4. List all the common multiples of 3 and 4 that you have in your lists (numbers 1 and 2).

5. What is the lowest common multiple of 3 and 4?

6. What is the lowest common multiple of 4 and 8? of 3 and 8?

7. Which are multiples of 12?   24   30   48   56   72   81   84

8. Which are multiples of 5?   36   40   55   86   158   420   375

9. Write O for odd numbers and E for even numbers.
   a. 32   b. 85   c. 70   d. 127   e. 489   f. 764

B. *Do these exercises.*

10.
287	574		8,936		
415	387	7,432	7,664	29,564	32,917
368	126	9,564	1,375	31,427	75,419
+ 526	+ 483	+ 5,943	+ 3,452	+ 26,463	+ 48,365

11. Write numerals for these number words.

    a. seventy-two billion, four hundred thirty-five million

    b. 689 billion, 42 thousand, 711

C. *Solve these reading problems on your paper. Some of them require two steps. Always think: Is my answer sensible?*

12. One spring Benjamin was allowed to pick strawberries for a neighbor, Mr. Stevens. Benjamin earned 25¢ for each quart of berries he picked. How much did he earn for picking 45 quarts of berries?

13. Mr. Stevens sold the berries for $1.50 a quart. How much money did he get from the sale of 45 quarts of strawberries?

14. After Mr. Stevens paid Benjamin for picking the berries, how much money did he have left? Choose the correct answer: ($46.25, $49.75, $56.25, $58.75).

15. When Benjamin worked diligently, he could pick 12 quarts of strawberries in 1 hour. At that rate, how many berries could he pick in 4 hours?

16. If people picked their own strawberries, they paid Mr. Stevens $0.80 a quart for them. One family picked 20 quarts of berries for themselves. How much did they save over the ready-picked price of $1.50 a quart?

17. Benjamin's mother wants to make strawberry jam. The recipe calls for 2 quarts of berries to make one batch of jam. How many berries will Benjamin's mother need for 4 batches of jam?

18. It takes 7 cups of sugar to make a batch of strawberry jam. Mother knows that a 5-pound bag of sugar contains 11 cups. How many 5-pound bags of sugar should Mother buy to have enough sugar for 4 batches of jam? (Give the answer as a whole number. Mother cannot buy part of a bag.)

19. Mother made 18 jars of jam at one time and 17 jars of jam at another time. How many more jars will Mother need to fill if she wants to have 50 jars of jam in all?

20. Mother and the girls picked 50 quarts of strawberries one day. They gave 5 quarts to a widowed neighbor. What part of the berries did they give away? (Your answer should be a fraction reduced to lowest terms.)

63. Factors and Prime Numbers

1. **Pairs of factors** are multiplied to form a product. One factor is the multiplier and the other is the multiplicand.

   Pairs of factors for 20 are 1×20, 2×10, and 4×5.

2. The factors of a number are all the different numbers by which the number can be divided evenly.

3. The factors of a number are usually listed in numerical order.

   Factors of 20: 1, 2, 4, 5, 10, 20

4. A number is a **multiple** of each of its **factors.** Factors and multiples are opposites.

5. A number that has no factors except itself and 1 is a **prime number.**

   One prime number is 7; it cannot be divided evenly by any number except 7 and 1. The number 4 is not a prime number; it can be divided by 2.

A. *Do these exercises.*

1. Copy and complete the pairs of factors that form these products.

a. 6	b. 15	c. 18	d. 7	e. 9	f. 12
$1 \times$ ____	$1 \times$ ____	$1 \times$ ____	$1 \times$ ____	$1 \times$ ____	$1 \times$ ____
$2 \times$ ____	$3 \times$ ____	$2 \times$ ____		$3 \times$ ____	$2 \times$ ____
		$3 \times$ ____			$3 \times$ ____

2. Now list the factors in numerical order (order of size). The first one is done for you.

   a. 6 _1_ _2_ _3_ _6_   b. 15   c. 18   d. 7   e. 9   f. 12

3. List all the factors for these numbers. The numbers in ( ) tell how many factors you should have.

   a. 14 (4)   b. 22 (4)   c. 11 (2)   d. 25 (3)   e. 24 (8)   f. 16 (5)

4. Write the products for which these are pairs of factors.

a.	b.	c.	d.	e.
1×8	1×5	1×35	1×30	1×28
2×4		5×7	2×15	2×14
			3×10	4×7
			5×6	

5. Copy the prime numbers.

2   5   8   9   13   16   19   21   25   27   29

6. Which numbers are multiples of 4?   14   16   24   32   44   54

7. Write all the multiples of 7 between 20 and 50.

8. Write all the odd numbers between 40 and 50.

9. Write the lowest common multiple for each number pair.

a. 4 and 5   b. 3 and 9   c. 4 and 12   d. 6 and 8

General Review

B. *Follow the directions.*

10. Find the missing numbers to make equivalent fractions.

a. $\frac{7}{12} = \frac{?}{24}$ b. $\frac{3}{5} = \frac{?}{25}$ c. $\frac{2}{7} = \frac{?}{28}$ d. $\frac{5}{9} = \frac{?}{36}$ e. $\frac{7}{8} = \frac{?}{40}$

11. Write the lengths to which the arrows point.

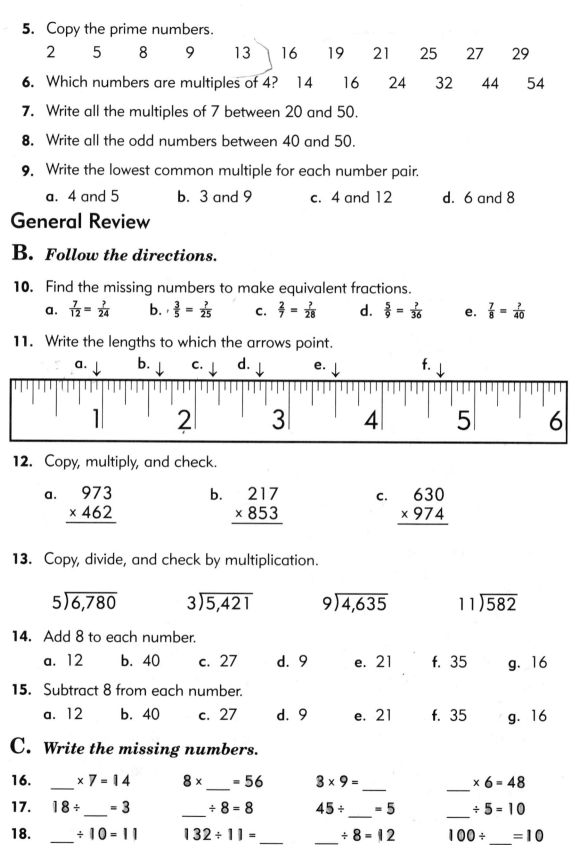

12. Copy, multiply, and check.

a.   973
    × 462

b.   217
    × 853

c.   630
    × 974

13. Copy, divide, and check by multiplication.

5)6,780   3)5,421   9)4,635   11)582

14. Add 8 to each number.

a. 12   b. 40   c. 27   d. 9   e. 21   f. 35   g. 16

15. Subtract 8 from each number.

a. 12   b. 40   c. 27   d. 9   e. 21   f. 35   g. 16

C. *Write the missing numbers.*

16.   ___ × 7 = 14   8 × ___ = 56   3 × 9 = ___   ___ × 6 = 48

17.   18 ÷ ___ = 3   ___ ÷ 8 = 8   45 ÷ ___ = 5   ___ ÷ 5 = 10

18.   ___ ÷ 10 = 11   132 ÷ 11 = ___   ___ ÷ 8 = 12   100 ÷ ___ = 10

64. Common Factors and Factor Trees

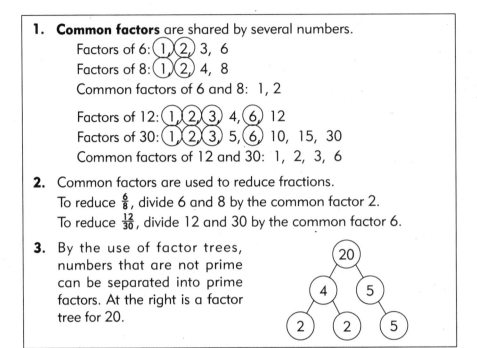

1. **Common factors** are shared by several numbers.
    Factors of 6: (1) (2) 3, 6
    Factors of 8: (1) (2) 4, 8
    Common factors of 6 and 8: 1, 2

    Factors of 12: (1) (2) (3) 4, (6) 12
    Factors of 30: (1) (2) (3) 5, (6) 10, 15, 30
    Common factors of 12 and 30: 1, 2, 3, 6

2. Common factors are used to reduce fractions.
    To reduce $\frac{6}{8}$, divide 6 and 8 by the common factor 2.
    To reduce $\frac{12}{30}$, divide 12 and 30 by the common factor 6.

3. By the use of factor trees, numbers that are not prime can be separated into prime factors. At the right is a factor tree for 20.

A. *Do these exercises.*

1. List all the factor pairs for these numbers. The numbers in ( ) tell how many pairs of factors you should have.

    a. 8 (2)   **b.** 17 (1)   **c.** 14 (2)   **d.** 27 (2)   **e.** 30 (4)   **f.** 36 (5)

2. Now list in order all the factors for these numbers. If you have trouble, look at the factor pairs you wrote for number 1.

    a. 8 ___ ___ ___ ___   **d.** 27 ___ ___ ___ ___
    b. 17 ___ ___   **e.** 30 ___ ___ ___ ___ ___ ___ ___ ___
    c. 14 ___ ___ ___ ___   **f.** 36 ___ ___ ___ ___ ___ ___ ___ ___ ___

3. Using the lists of numbers above, find common factors for each of these pairs.
    a. 8 and 14   **b.** 27 and 30   **c.** 30 and 36   **d.** 8 and 36

4. What is the **greatest common factor** for each of these pairs?
    a. 30 and 36   **b.** 8 and 36   **c.** 6 and 30   **d.** 18 and 27

5. Reduce these fractions to lowest terms. To make reducing easier, divide both terms by the greatest common factor.

    a. $\frac{8}{14}$ **b.** $\frac{27}{30}$ **c.** $\frac{30}{36}$ **d.** $\frac{8}{36}$ **e.** $\frac{6}{30}$ **f.** $\frac{18}{27}$

6. Copy and complete these factor trees. Do not use 1 as a factor.

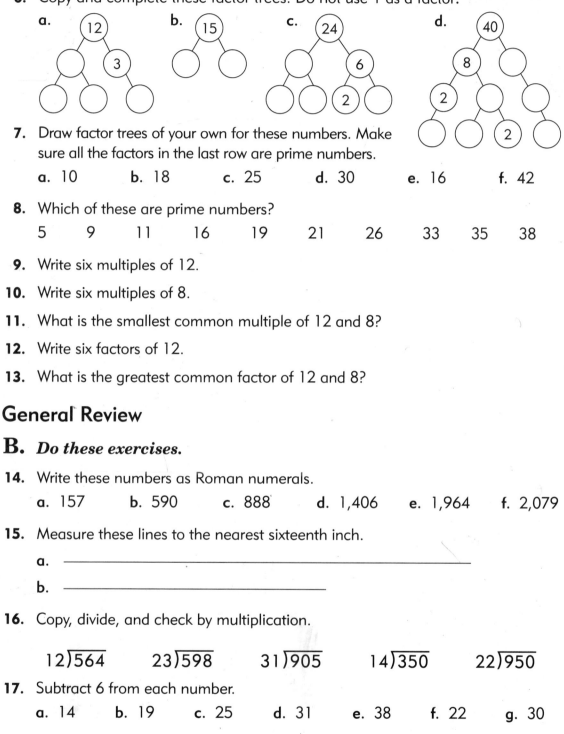

a. 12, 3

b. 15

c. 24, 6, 2

d. 40, 8, 2, 2

7. Draw factor trees of your own for these numbers. Make sure all the factors in the last row are prime numbers.

    a. 10   **b.** 18   **c.** 25   **d.** 30   **e.** 16   **f.** 42

8. Which of these are prime numbers?

    5   9   11   16   19   21   26   33   35   38

9. Write six multiples of 12.

10. Write six multiples of 8.

11. What is the smallest common multiple of 12 and 8?

12. Write six factors of 12.

13. What is the greatest common factor of 12 and 8?

General Review

B. *Do these exercises.*

14. Write these numbers as Roman numerals.

    a. 157   **b.** 590   **c.** 888   **d.** 1,406   **e.** 1,964   **f.** 2,079

15. Measure these lines to the nearest sixteenth inch.

    a. _____

    b. _____

16. Copy, divide, and check by multiplication.

    12)564   23)598   31)905   14)350   22)950

17. Subtract 6 from each number.

    a. 14   **b.** 19   **c.** 25   **d.** 31   **e.** 38   **f.** 22   **g.** 30

18. The longest book in the New Testament is Luke, which has 1,151 verses. The shortest book in the New Testament is 2 John, which has only 13 verses. How many more verses are in Luke than in 2 John?

65. More Practice With Factors and Multiples

A. *Copy the two charts below, and fill in the blanks. The first one on each chart is done for you. Reread the boxes in Lessons 61–64 if you need help.*

Multiple Chart

	List 10 Multiples	List Common Multiples	Lowest Common Multiple
1.	4 — 4, 8, 12, 16, 20, 24, 28, 32, 36, 40 8 — 8, 16, 24, 32, 40, 48, 56, 64, 72, 80	8, 16, 24, 32, 40	8
2.	4 — 6 —		
3.	3 — 5 —		
4.	8 — 12 —		

Factor Chart

	List All Factors	List Common Factors	Greatest Common Factor
5.	8 — 1, 2, 4, 8 12 — 1, 2, 3, 4, 6, 12	1, 2, 4	4
6.	4 — 16 —		
7.	12 — 30 —		
8.	15 — 20 —		

B. *Do these exercises.*

9. Reduce these fractions to lowest terms. Use greatest common factors.

    a. $\frac{12}{20}$ b. $\frac{11}{33}$ c. $\frac{15}{30}$ d. $\frac{8}{24}$ e. $\frac{9}{12}$ f. $\frac{14}{35}$

10. Are these prime numbers? Write **yes** or **no**.

    a. 14   b. 17   c. 5   d. 26   e. 33   f. 13

11. Draw factor trees for these numbers. The first one is done for you.

    a. 56   b. 21   c. 32   d. 45   e. 18

General Review

C. *Copy and work carefully.*

12.
```
  12,000          27,403          75,010          59,046
 - 3,479        - 24,750        - 36,842        - 27,955
```

13.
```
    913             376             380             425
  x  78           x 234           x 500           x 768
```

14. $31\overline{)775}$ $14\overline{)476}$ $11\overline{)759}$ $23\overline{)360}$

D. *Write the answers only.*

15.   34 + 15   13 + 17   12 + 40   28 + 14
16.   22 – 5   25 – 10   34 – 8   46 – 13
17.   10 × 54   10 × 90   100 × 62   1,000 × 78

E. *Solve these reading problems.*

18. God made some kinds of whales grow to be 80 feet long. How much longer is an 80-foot whale than the height of a 4-foot boy?

19. An 80-foot whale is _____ times as long as a 4-foot boy is tall.

66. Expressing Fractions With Common Denominators

You should remember that **like fractions** are fractions with the same denominators. Fractions can be added only if they are like fractions. This lesson will help you to change **unlike fractions** to fractions with **common denominators** (same denominators).

Common denominators are the same as common multiples. To find the **lowest common denominator** for two fractions, use the **lowest common multiple** of those denominators. Study the examples in the box.

Example A: Change $\frac{1}{2}$ and $\frac{1}{3}$ to like fractions.
    Think: The lowest common multiple of 2 and 3 is 6.
    Use 6 as the new denominator. $\frac{1}{2}=\frac{3}{6}$ $\frac{1}{3}=\frac{2}{6}$

Example B: Change $\frac{3}{4}$ and $\frac{5}{8}$ to like fractions.
    Think: The lowest common multiple of 4 and 8 is 8.
    Use 8 as the new denominator.
    Notice that $\frac{5}{8}$ is not changed at all. $\frac{3}{4}=\frac{6}{8}$, $\frac{5}{8}=\frac{5}{8}$

A. Follow the directions.

1. Copy the pairs of **unlike fractions**.
   a. $\frac{3}{4}$ $\frac{1}{4}$ b. $\frac{5}{12}$ $\frac{12}{24}$ c. $\frac{5}{8}$, $\frac{7}{8}$ d. $\frac{2}{3}$ $\frac{3}{4}$ e. $\frac{1}{2}$ $\frac{2}{3}$

2. Write the lowest common denominator for each pair of fractions. Think: What is the smallest number which both denominators can divide evenly?
   a. $\frac{3}{8}$ $\frac{3}{4}$ b. $\frac{7}{12}$ $\frac{2}{3}$ c. $\frac{1}{3}$ $\frac{3}{4}$ d. $\frac{7}{9}$ $\frac{1}{3}$ e. $\frac{1}{2}$ $\frac{2}{3}$

B. Express both fractions in each pair with the denominator in ( ). Then circle the larger fraction. The first one is done for you.

3. a. $\frac{1}{2}$ $\frac{3}{4}$ (4) $\frac{2}{4}$ $\frac{3}{4}$ b. $\frac{5}{6}$ $\frac{1}{3}$ (6)   c. $\frac{7}{12}$ $\frac{1}{4}$ (12)   d. $\frac{2}{3}$ $\frac{3}{4}$ (12)
4. a. $\frac{2}{3}$ $\frac{5}{9}$ (9)   b. $\frac{1}{2}$ $\frac{2}{5}$ (10)   c. $\frac{5}{6}$ $\frac{1}{4}$ (12)   d. $\frac{5}{16}$ $\frac{3}{8}$ (16)

C. Find the lowest common denominator for each fraction pair, and express the fractions with common denominators.

5. a. $\frac{1}{2}$ $\frac{3}{8}$ b. $\frac{5}{16}$ $\frac{1}{4}$ c. $\frac{2}{3}$ $\frac{1}{2}$ d. $\frac{1}{4}$ $\frac{3}{5}$ e. $\frac{2}{3}$ $\frac{1}{8}$

D. *Do these exercises.*

6. a. Write the multiples of 3 from 3 to 30.
b. Write the multiples of 5 from 5 to 50.

7. Copy the two common multiples of 3 and 5 that you see in your lists for number 6.

8. What is the lowest common multiple of 3 and 5?

9. Change $\frac{1}{3}$ and $\frac{3}{5}$ to like fractions, using the lowest common denominator.

10. Write the factors: **a.** of 8.   **b.** of 12.

11. What common factors do 8 and 12 have?

12. What is the greatest common factor of 8 and 12?

13. Reduce $\frac{8}{12}$ to lowest terms. Divide by the greatest common factor.

14. Change $\frac{12}{8}$ to a mixed number in simplest form.

E. *Solve these problems. In row 20, be sure to write all answers in simplest form.*

15. After dinner, $\frac{2}{3}$ of a pumpkin pie and $\frac{3}{4}$ of a cherry pie were left over. Was more pumpkin pie left over or more cherry pie? (Change the two fractions to like fractions to find the answer.)

16. When Israel was traveling to Canaan, God told Moses to count all the men 20 years old and older. Here are the numbers of men in four tribes: Simeon—59,300; Judah—74,600; Reuben—46,500; and Dan—62,700. How many men were counted in these four tribes?

17. Round your answer for number 16 to the nearest hundred thousand.

18.

67	395	4,972	836	915
× 84	× 27	× 63	× 800	× 436

19.

900	3,700	8,020	24,000	83,516
− 458	− 3,649	− 2,385	− 17,437	− 28,492

20.

$\frac{3}{8}$	$\frac{5}{9}$	$3\frac{5}{16}$	$\frac{11}{12}$	$4\frac{3}{4}$
$+\frac{7}{8}$	$+\frac{7}{9}$	$+2\frac{3}{16}$	$-\frac{1}{12}$	$-3\frac{1}{4}$

67. Finding Averages

Finding an **average** is the process of dividing several unequal amounts into equal groups. For example, if your family uses 3 dozen eggs one week, 4 dozen eggs another week, and 2 dozen eggs the third week, your family uses an average of 3 dozen eggs per week.

To average 3 dozen, 4 dozen, and 2 dozen eggs, we could move 1 dozen eggs from the group of 4 dozen to the group of 2 dozen. Then each group would have 3 dozen eggs.

Instead of actually moving items from one group to another, we normally use a two-step process to find an average. First we **add** the numbers, and then we **divide** by the number of addends.

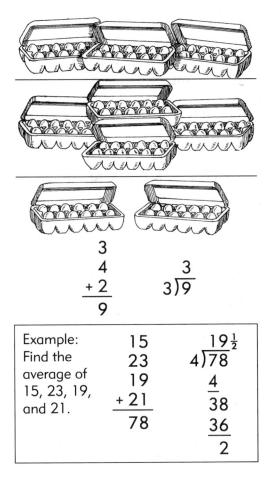

$$\begin{array}{r} 3 \\ 4 \\ +\,2 \\ \hline 9 \end{array} \qquad 3\overline{)9}\;\;^{3}$$

Example:
Find the average of 15, 23, 19, and 21.

$$\begin{array}{r} 15 \\ 23 \\ 19 \\ +\,21 \\ \hline 78 \end{array} \qquad \begin{array}{r} 19\frac{1}{2} \\ 4\overline{)78} \\ 4 \\ \hline 38 \\ 36 \\ \hline 2 \end{array}$$

A. *Use the two steps to find the averages for these sets of numbers. Express any remainders as fractions.*

1. a. 9, 6, 5, 4   **b.** 16, 9, 7, 12   **c.** 75, 59, 82

2. a. 15, 27, 33   **b.** 37, 41, 35, 44, 48   **c.** 14, 13, 9, 12

3. a. 79, 95, 89   **b.** 76, 82, 88, 84, 79, 83   **c.** 2, 8, 6, 4, 7, 9

4. a. 27, 34, 26, 31   **b.** 924; 1,016; 1,036; 1,022; 592

B. *Solve these reading problems involving averages.*

5. On his way to a ministers' meeting, Brother Leon drove 50 miles the first hour, 38 miles the second hour, and 53 miles the third hour. What was his average speed in miles per hour?

6. Sally read 54 Bible verses in 3 days. What was the average number of verses she read each day? (This time the **total** is given. You need to do only the second step.)

7. Bethany had the following grades on six spelling tests: 70%, 64%, 68%, 72%, 56%, and 78%. What was her average score?

8. The next six weeks Bethany studied her spelling words more diligently. Her grades on the next six tests were 78%, 84%, 82%, 80% 88%, and 92%. What was her average score?

General Review

C. *Do these exercises.*

9. List all the factors of each number: a. 10   b. 16

10. What is the greatest common factor of 10 and 16?

11. Draw factor trees for each number: a. 27   b. 14   c. 30

12. Name six multiples of each number: a. 8   b. 12

13. What is the smallest common multiple of 8 and 12?

14. Write the lowest common denominator for each pair of fractions.
   a. $\frac{2}{3}$ $\frac{4}{9}$ b. $\frac{1}{12}$ $\frac{1}{2}$ c. $\frac{2}{3}$ $\frac{1}{4}$ d. $\frac{1}{2}$ $\frac{2}{3}$ e. $\frac{5}{6}$ $\frac{1}{4}$

15. Change each pair of fractions to like fractions.
   a. $\frac{1}{3}$ $\frac{3}{5}$ b. $\frac{3}{4}$ $\frac{7}{16}$ c. $\frac{5}{8}$ $\frac{1}{2}$ d. $\frac{1}{2}$ $\frac{4}{5}$ e. $\frac{3}{8}$ $\frac{1}{12}$

16. Copy each pair of fractions, and write < or > between them. Change the fractions in a pair to like fractions if you are not sure which one is larger.
   a. $\frac{1}{2}$ $\frac{1}{3}$ b. $\frac{3}{8}$ $\frac{5}{16}$ c. $\frac{5}{6}$ $\frac{2}{3}$ d. $\frac{1}{2}$ $\frac{5}{8}$ e. $\frac{3}{4}$ $\frac{2}{3}$

17. Reduce these fractions to lowest terms.
   a. $\frac{12}{32}$ b. $\frac{16}{40}$ c. $\frac{16}{28}$ d. $\frac{18}{24}$ e. $\frac{10}{15}$ f. $\frac{18}{36}$

D. *Write the numbers that fit in the blanks.*

18. 1 yr. = _____ mo.   1 day = _____ hr.   1 min. = _____ sec.

19. 1 yd. = _____ in.   1 lb. = _____ oz.   1 century = _____ yr.

20. 1 pt. = _____ cups   1 mi. = _____ ft.   1 leap year = _____ days

21. 3 gal. = _____ qt.   3 qt. = _____ pt.   3 pt. = _____ qt.

22. 4 bu. = _____ pk.   16 qt. = _____ pk.   28 days = _____ wk.

23. 6 cups = _____ qt.   9 yd. = _____ ft.   9 ft. = _____ yd.

24. 4 ft. = _____ in.   2 hr. = _____ min. $\frac{1}{2}$ lb. = _____ oz.

68. Rules of Divisibility

If a number is **divisible** by 3, it can be divided evenly by 3. The **rules of divisibility** will help you to tell whether one number is divisible by another number. Study the rules in the box.

Rules of Divisibility

Rule for 2: A number is divisible by 2 if it ends with an even digit (0, 2, 4, 6, 8).
>   The number 3,564 ends with 4. It is divisible by 2.
>   The number 6,187 ends with 7. It is not divisible by 2.

Rule for 3: A number is divisible by 3 if the sum of its digits is divisible by 3.
>   For the number 713, the sum of the digits is 11 (7 + 1 + 3).
>>   Since 11 is not divisible by 3, 713 is not divisible by 3.
>   For 2,571, the sum of the digits is 15 (2 + 5 + 7 + 1).
>>   Since 15 is divisible by 3, 2,571 is divisible by 3.

Rule for 4: A number is divisible by 4 if the last two digits are zeroes or if they are divisible by 4.
>   The number 3,000 ends with two zeroes. It is divisible by 4.
>   The number 5,628 ends with 28, which is divisible by 4.
>>   So, 5,628 is divisible by 4.

Rule for 5: A number is divisible by 5 if it ends with 5 or 0.
>   The numbers 540 and 3,785 are both divisible by 5.

Rule for 6: A number is divisible by 6 if it is an even number and the sum of its digits is divisible by 3.
>   The number 816 is even, and the sum of its digits (15) is divisible by 3.
>>   So 816 is divisible by 6.
>   The number 681 is not even. It is not divisible by 6.
>   The number 4,352 is even, but the sum of its digits (14) is not divisible by 3.
>>   So 4,352 is not divisible by 6.

Rule for 9: A number is divisible by 9 if the sum of its digits is divisible by 9.
>   For 612, the sum of the digits (9) is divisible by 9.
>>   So 612 is divisible by 9.
>   For 483, the sum of the digits (15) is not divisible by 9.
>>   So 483 is not divisible by 9.

Rule for 10: A number is divisible by 10 if it ends with 0.
>   The numbers 50, 890, and 47,190 are all divisible by 10.

A. *Write* yes *or* no.

1. Are these numbers divisible by 2?
   a. 58   b. 386   c. 450   d. 2,791   e. 5,963   f. 1,076

2. Are these numbers divisible by 3?
   a. 58   b. 84   c. 450   d. 378   e. 1,265   f. 3,561

3. Are these numbers divisible by 4?
   a. 300   b. 748   c. 136   d. 514   e. 7,912   f. 4,430

4. Are these numbers divisible by 5?
   a. 58   b. 300   c. 485   d. 553   e. 7,915   f. 4,430

5. Are these numbers divisible by 6?
   a. 96   b. 84   c. 261   d. 972   e. 417   f. 714

6. Are these numbers divisible by 9?
   a. 127   b. 840   c. 666   d. 423   e. 1,521   f. 6,786

7. Are these numbers divisible by 10?
   a. 800   b. 705   c. 750   d. 318   e. 4,000   f. 675,840

General Review

B. *Do these exercises.*

8. Are these prime numbers? Write **yes** or **no**.
   a. 17   b. 26   c. 48   d. 31   e. 39   f. 19

9. Draw factor trees for these numbers.
   a. 21   b. 22   c. 24   d. 25   e. 27   f. 30

10. Change each pair of fractions to like fractions.
    a. $\frac{3}{4}$ $\frac{7}{12}$ b. $\frac{1}{2}$ $\frac{7}{9}$ c. $\frac{7}{10}$ $\frac{1}{3}$ d. $\frac{2}{7}$ $\frac{3}{14}$ e. $\frac{5}{8}$ $\frac{2}{3}$

11. Change these fractions pairs to like fractions. Then write $<$ or $>$ between each pair.
    a. $\frac{3}{10}$ $\frac{2}{5}$ b. $\frac{1}{2}$ $\frac{5}{8}$ c. $\frac{4}{9}$ $\frac{2}{3}$ d. $\frac{7}{8}$ $\frac{2}{3}$ e. $\frac{5}{6}$ $\frac{3}{4}$

12. Find the average of each set of numbers.
    a. 8, 7, 8, 5   b. 99, 85, 42, 68, 81   c. $4.35, $6.88, $9.26

13. Copy and multiply.

456	2,839	9,130	784	462
× 64	× 7	× 59	× 325	× 718

14. Write the answers only.
    a. 100×467 b. $1,000 \times 12$ c. 70×9 d. 9×14 e. 7×25

69. Chapter 7 Review

A. *Do these exercises.*

1. Write twelve multiples of 4.

2. Write twelve multiples of 7.

3. Write twelve multiples of 9.

4. Write twelve multiples of 12.

5. Write twelve multiples of 8.

6. What common multiples of 4 and 12 do you have in your lists?

7. Is 36 a common multiple of 8 and 12?

8. What is the lowest common multiple of each pair?

   a. 4, 12   b. 4, 8   c. 8, 12   d. 4, 9   e. 9, 12

9. Write factor pairs for these numbers. The number in ( ) tells how many pairs you should have.

   a. 14 (2)   b. 16 (3)   c. 18 (3)   d. 19 (1)   e. 28 (3)

10. List in order the factors of these numbers.

    a. 14   b. 16   c. 18   d. 19   e. 28

11. Make factor trees for these numbers.

    a. 6   b. 16   c. 18   d. 28   e. 36

12. Write the greatest common factor of each pair.

    a. 6 and 16   b. 6 and 18   c. 16 and 28   d. 12 and 36

13. Are these prime numbers? Write **yes** or **no**.

    a. 7   b. 9   c. 11   d. 18   e. 21   f. 23

14. Use greatest common factors to reduce these fractions to lowest terms.

    a. $\frac{14}{21}$ b. $\frac{6}{16}$ c. $\frac{16}{28}$ d. $\frac{12}{36}$ e. $\frac{10}{25}$ f. $\frac{18}{20}$

15. Write the lowest common denominators.

   a. $\frac{1}{2}$ $\frac{1}{3}$ b. $\frac{1}{4}$ $\frac{1}{3}$ c. $\frac{1}{6}$ $\frac{1}{2}$ d. $\frac{1}{5}$ $\frac{1}{10}$ e. $\frac{1}{9}$ $\frac{1}{6}$

16. Change to fractions with common denominators.

   a. $\frac{1}{2}$ $\frac{1}{8}$ b. $\frac{1}{3}$ $\frac{1}{2}$ c. $\frac{2}{3}$ $\frac{1}{4}$ d. $\frac{5}{12}$ $\frac{1}{3}$ e. $\frac{4}{5}$ $\frac{1}{2}$

17. Also write these pairs with common denominators.

   a. $\frac{3}{4}$ $\frac{7}{12}$ b. $\frac{3}{5}$ $\frac{3}{10}$ c. $\frac{1}{3}$ $\frac{5}{9}$ d. $\frac{11}{16}$ $\frac{3}{4}$ e. $\frac{5}{6}$ $\frac{1}{4}$

18. Copy the fraction pairs, and write < or > between them.

   a. $\frac{1}{2}$ $\frac{5}{12}$ b. $\frac{2}{3}$ $\frac{4}{9}$ c. $\frac{2}{3}$ $\frac{1}{2}$ d. $\frac{1}{4}$ $\frac{7}{12}$ e. $\frac{3}{8}$ $\frac{1}{3}$

B. *Answer* yes *or* no.

19. Are these numbers divisible by 2?
   a. 81   b. 465   c. 800   d. 1,386   e. 7,524

20. Are these numbers divisible by 5?
   a. 81   b. 465   c. 800   d. 1,386   e. 7,524

21. Are these numbers divisible by 3?
   a. 81   b. 465   c. 800   d. 1,386   e. 7,524

22. Are these numbers divisible by 6?
   a. 81   b. 465   c. 800   d. 1,386   e. 7,524

23. Are these numbers divisible by 9?
   a. 81   b. 465   c. 800   d. 1,386   e. 7,524

24. Are these numbers divisible by 10?
   a. 90   b. 465   c. 800   d. 1,386   e. 8,432,160

25. Are these numbers divisible by 4?
   a. 932   b. 465   c. 800   d. 1,346   e. 7,524

C. *Find the average of each set of numbers.*

26. a. 4, 5, 5, 7, 9, 6   b. 16, 12, 20, 24, 18   c. 65, 50, 64, 53

27. a. 26¢, 22¢, 28¢, 24¢, 25¢   b. $5.83, $4.95, $5.25, $5.53

(continued on next page)

D. *Solve these reading problems.*

28. The highest temperature on record in the United States is 134°, recorded in Death Valley, California. The highest temperature on record in Canada is 113°, recorded in Saskatchewan. What is the difference between the two temperatures?

29. Matthew wrote down the temperature each afternoon when he got home from school. In one week he recorded the following temperatures: 52°, 49°, 51°, 57°, and 61°. What was the average afternoon temperature for the week?

30. Mt. Waialeale, Hawaii, receives an average of 460 inches of rain per year. If the same amount of rain falls each month, how much rain falls there during one month?

31. Most parts of Pennsylvania receive about 40 inches of rain per year. About how many years would it take for Pennsylvania to receive as much rain as Mt. Waialeale receives in one year? Choose the best estimate.

      12 yr.   20 yr.   50 yr.   400 yr.   500 yr.

32. At Mt. Waialeale it rains almost every day of the year. During a year when Mt. Waialeale has 347 days with rain, only _____ days of the year have no rain.

33. For three years in a row, numerous tornadoes struck the United States on November 15 and 16. There were 49 tornadoes on those dates in 1987, 44 tornadoes in 1988, and 39 tornadoes in 1989. What was the average number of tornadoes that struck each year on November 15 and 16?

34. When Hurricane Hugo hit South Carolina, it caused billions of dollars of damage. Six congregations each sent a van load of 12 workers to help clean up after the storm. Altogether, how many workers from those six churches went to help?

70. Chapter 7 Test

Chapter 8

Adding and Subtracting Unlike Fractions

But thou shalt have a perfect and just weight, a perfect and just measure shalt thou have: that thy days may be lengthened in the land which the Lord thy God giveth thee.
(Deuteronomy 25:15)

71. Changing Whole Numbers and Mixed Numbers to Improper Fractions

To change a whole number to an improper fraction, multiply the number by the denominator of the fraction.

$2 = \frac{?}{3}$ $(3 \times 2 = 6)$ $2 = \frac{6}{3}$

The example in the box shows how to change a mixed number to an improper fraction.

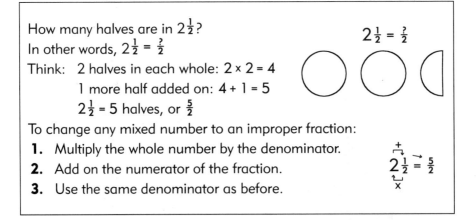

How many halves are in $2\frac{1}{2}$?
In other words, $2\frac{1}{2} = \frac{?}{2}$

Think: 2 halves in each whole: $2 \times 2 = 4$
       1 more half added on: $4 + 1 = 5$
     $2\frac{1}{2} = 5$ halves, or $\frac{5}{2}$

To change any mixed number to an improper fraction:
1. Multiply the whole number by the denominator.
2. Add on the numerator of the fraction.
3. Use the same denominator as before.

$2\frac{1}{2} = \frac{?}{2}$ $2\frac{1}{2} = \frac{5}{2}$

A. Change these whole numbers and mixed numbers to improper fractions as shown above.

1. a. $1 = \frac{?}{2}$ b. $1 = \frac{?}{5}$ c. $1 = \frac{?}{4}$ d. $2 = \frac{?}{2}$ e. $4 = \frac{?}{3}$ f. $3 = \frac{?}{5}$

2. a. $1\frac{1}{2}$ b. $2\frac{1}{4}$ c. $1\frac{2}{3}$ d. $3\frac{1}{2}$ e. $2\frac{1}{6}$ f. $3\frac{2}{5}$

3. a. $4\frac{1}{3}$ b. $6\frac{1}{8}$ c. $5\frac{1}{2}$ d. $1\frac{3}{10}$ e. $2\frac{4}{5}$ f. $1\frac{7}{8}$

B. Do these exercises.

4. Write a pair of like fractions.

5. Change these improper fractions to whole or mixed numbers.
   a. $\frac{10}{2}$ b. $\frac{11}{3}$ c. $\frac{6}{4}$ d. $\frac{10}{6}$ e. $\frac{15}{4}$ f. $\frac{12}{5}$

6. Write the lowest common denominator for each pair of fractions.
   a. $\frac{1}{2}$ $\frac{2}{3}$ b. $\frac{5}{12}$ $\frac{3}{4}$ c. $\frac{7}{16}$ $\frac{1}{2}$ d. $\frac{3}{5}$ $\frac{1}{2}$ e. $\frac{5}{6}$ $\frac{3}{4}$

L G

7. Express these fraction pairs as like fractions. Write < or > between each pair.

a. $\frac{1}{3}$ $\frac{3}{4}$ b. $\frac{7}{8}$ $\frac{1}{2}$ c. $\frac{5}{16}$ $\frac{1}{4}$ d. $\frac{7}{9}$ $\frac{2}{3}$ e. $\frac{3}{4}$ $\frac{2}{5}$

8. Copy the larger one in each pair.

a. 2 $\frac{3}{2}$ b. $1\frac{3}{4}$ $\frac{9}{4}$ c. $\frac{8}{3}$ 3 d. $\frac{12}{5}$ $2\frac{1}{5}$ e. $1\frac{2}{3}$ $\frac{6}{3}$

9. Reduce these fractions to lowest terms.

a. $\frac{12}{24}$ b. $\frac{16}{24}$ c. $\frac{10}{16}$ d. $\frac{18}{30}$ e. $\frac{15}{20}$ f. $\frac{12}{15}$

C. *Follow the signs. Write answers in simplest form.*

10. $\frac{2}{3} + \frac{1}{3}$ $\frac{3}{8} + \frac{7}{8}$ $\frac{5}{12} + \frac{1}{12}$ $2\frac{1}{4} + 1\frac{1}{4}$ $3\frac{5}{16} + 3\frac{7}{16}$

11. $\frac{7}{9} - \frac{1}{9}$ $\frac{11}{16} - \frac{3}{16}$ $\frac{7}{8} - \frac{1}{8}$ $4\frac{2}{3} - 3\frac{1}{3}$ $3\frac{7}{10} - 1\frac{3}{10}$

D. *Use the rules of divisibility to answer numbers 12–18. Write yes or no. Each exercise should have four answers.*

a. 1,544   b. 3,720   c. 7,281   d. 1,215

12. Can the numbers above by divided by 2?

13. Can these numbers be divided by 5?

14. Can the numbers be divided by 10?

15. Can they be divided by 3?

16. Can they be divided by 6?

17. Can they be divided by 9?

18. Can they be divided by 4?

E. *Do these exercises.*

19. Draw a factor tree for each number: a. 24   b. 16   c. 27

20. What is the greatest common factor of each pair?   a. 24 and 16   b. 24 and 27

72. Adding More Difficult Like Fractions

A. *Do these exercises.*

1. Change these mixed numbers to improper fractions as you did in Lesson 71.

   a. $2\frac{1}{2}$ b. $1\frac{7}{16}$ c. $1\frac{3}{5}$ d. $3\frac{1}{8}$ e. $2\frac{3}{4}$ f. $1\frac{2}{3}$

2. Change these improper fractions to whole or mixed numbers.

   a. $\frac{11}{4}$ b. $\frac{7}{2}$ c. $\frac{8}{4}$ d. $\frac{13}{5}$ e. $\frac{5}{3}$ f. $\frac{12}{8}$

If the sum of two or more mixed numbers includes an improper fraction, the answer should be changed to the simplest form. The improper fraction part is changed to a whole number and added to the first part of the answer.

Study the examples at the right.

$$\begin{array}{r} 1\frac{3}{4} \\ + 1\frac{1}{4} \\ \hline 2\frac{4}{4} = 2 + 1 = 3 \end{array} \qquad \begin{array}{r} 3\frac{5}{12} \\ + 1\frac{11}{12} \\ \hline 4\frac{16}{12} = 4 + 1\frac{1}{3} = 5\frac{1}{3} \end{array}$$

B. *Change these mixed numbers to the simplest form.*

3. a. $3\frac{2}{2}$ b. $1\frac{3}{3}$ c. $2\frac{5}{4}$ d. $1\frac{7}{5}$ e. $2\frac{6}{6}$ f. $3\frac{6}{4}$

4. a. $1\frac{4}{3}$ b. $2\frac{5}{5}$ c. $4\frac{3}{2}$ d. $3\frac{5}{3}$ e. $1\frac{7}{4}$ f. $4\frac{4}{4}$

C. *Follow the directions.*

5. Add these mixed numbers. Write the answers in simplest form.

$$\begin{array}{r} 2\frac{1}{2} \\ + 1\frac{1}{2} \\ \hline \end{array} \qquad \begin{array}{r} 3\frac{5}{8} \\ + 2\frac{3}{8} \\ \hline \end{array} \qquad \begin{array}{r} 1\frac{2}{3} \\ + 3\frac{2}{3} \\ \hline \end{array} \qquad \begin{array}{r} 2\frac{7}{8} \\ + \frac{5}{8} \\ \hline \end{array} \qquad \begin{array}{r} 5\frac{7}{9} \\ + 2\frac{4}{9} \\ \hline \end{array}$$

6. Express these fractions with common denominators.

   a. $\frac{1}{2}$ $\frac{1}{8}$ b. $\frac{1}{2}$ $\frac{3}{5}$ c. $\frac{3}{4}$ $\frac{5}{16}$ d. $\frac{3}{8}$ $\frac{5}{6}$ e. $\frac{3}{10}$ $\frac{1}{2}$

D. *Solve these reading problems.*

7. The Statue of Liberty, located at New York City, was made in France and given to the United States in 1884. How many years ago was that?

8. The statue stands 151 feet high from the feet to the torch. How high is that in yards?

9. The Statue of Liberty stands on a base, or pedestal, that is 154 feet high. What is the combined height of the pedestal and the statue?

10. The width of the statue's mouth is 3 feet, which is _____ yard or _____ inches.

11. The statue's longest finger is 8 feet long, or _____ yards.

12. The statue weighs 225 tons. What is that weight in pounds?

13. The pupils from Sunlight Christian Day School visited the Statue of Liberty on their school trip. In the group were 38 pupils, three teachers, and six parents. How many people were in the group altogether?

14. The Statue of Liberty is located on Liberty Island, which can be reached only by a ferry boat. The cost for the ferry ride was $3.00 for each student and $6.00 for each adult. How much was the cost for the whole school group (38 pupils and 9 adults)?

15. The school group arrived at the statue at 12:15, but they had to wait in line for 2 hours and 15 minutes before their turn came to climb the statue. What time was it then?

16. At the statue an elevator took the group from the ground to the top of the pedestal. From there they climbed 171 steps to the crown on the statue's head. Esther said, "At home we have only 14 steps in our stairway." Esther had climbed how many times as many steps as were at home? (Drop the remainder in your answer.)

17. The guide at the statue allowed only 30 people to stand on the statue's crown at one time. How many in the school group had to wait to get on the crown until some of the group left?

18. The teachers bought two post cards for each of the 38 pupils. The cards cost $0.25 each. How much did the teachers spend for the post cards?

73. Adding and Subtracting Unlike Fractions

To add or subtract unlike fractions, find the lowest common denominator and express the fractions as like fractions. Study the examples in the box.

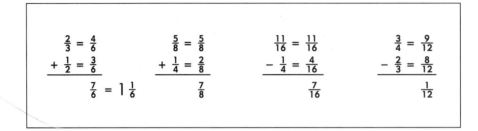

$$\frac{2}{3} = \frac{4}{6}$$
$$+ \frac{1}{2} = \frac{3}{6}$$
$$\overline{\frac{7}{6} = 1\frac{1}{6}}$$

$$\frac{5}{8} = \frac{5}{8}$$
$$+ \frac{1}{4} = \frac{2}{8}$$
$$\overline{\frac{7}{8}}$$

$$\frac{11}{16} = \frac{11}{16}$$
$$- \frac{1}{4} = \frac{4}{16}$$
$$\overline{\frac{7}{16}}$$

$$\frac{3}{4} = \frac{9}{12}$$
$$- \frac{2}{3} = \frac{8}{12}$$
$$\overline{\frac{1}{12}}$$

A. *Change these mixed numbers to simplest form.*

1. a. $3\frac{2}{2}$ b. $1\frac{5}{5}$ c. $2\frac{12}{9}$ d. $1\frac{7}{4}$ e. $4\frac{5}{3}$ f. $3\frac{15}{12}$

B. *Copy, change to like denominators, and add or subtract. Be sure to write the answers in simplest form.*

2.
$$\frac{3}{8}$$
$$+ \frac{1}{2}$$

$$\frac{1}{5}$$
$$+ \frac{2}{3}$$

$$\frac{3}{4}$$
$$+ \frac{1}{3}$$

$$\frac{7}{12}$$
$$+ \frac{2}{3}$$

3.
$$\frac{9}{16}$$
$$+ \frac{1}{4}$$

$$\frac{3}{4}$$
$$+ \frac{5}{12}$$

$$\frac{7}{10}$$
$$+ \frac{1}{2}$$

$$\frac{1}{2}$$
$$+ \frac{1}{3}$$

4.
$$\frac{8}{9}$$
$$- \frac{2}{3}$$

$$\frac{5}{6}$$
$$- \frac{1}{3}$$

$$\frac{5}{8}$$
$$- \frac{3}{16}$$

$$\frac{3}{4}$$
$$- \frac{1}{6}$$

C. *Add these mixed numbers as you did in Lesson 72.*

5.
$$3\frac{3}{4}$$
$$+ 1\frac{3}{4}$$

$$2\frac{7}{8}$$
$$+ 4\frac{5}{8}$$

$$4\frac{1}{12}$$
$$+ 3\frac{11}{12}$$

$$1\frac{2}{3}$$
$$+ 5\frac{2}{3}$$

6. Change these improper fractions to whole or mixed numbers in simplest form.

   a. $\frac{11}{2}$ b. $\frac{9}{5}$ c. $\frac{12}{4}$ d. $\frac{7}{3}$ e. $\frac{14}{8}$ f. $\frac{5}{2}$

7. Change these mixed numbers to improper fractions.

   a. $4\frac{1}{2}$ b. $3\frac{2}{3}$ c. $1\frac{5}{8}$ d. $1\frac{9}{16}$ e. $2\frac{3}{5}$ f. $3\frac{1}{4}$

General Review

D. *Do these exercises.*

8. Change these Roman numerals to Arabic numerals.

   a. CDLVIII   b. MCLXXV   c. CCXLIX   d. MDXXXII   e. DCLXIV

9. Copy the numbers that are multiples of 6.

   2   3   6   10   12   21   24   30

10. Copy the numbers that are factors of 6.

    2   3   6   10   12   21   24

11. Is 3,420 divisible by these numbers? Write **yes** or **no** for each.

    a. by 3   b. by 9   c. by 5   d. by 4   e. by 2   f. by 6

12. Find the average of 17, 25, 46, 32, and 35.

13. a. Copy the following number, and place commas correctly: 43921756

    b. What is the value of the 2 in the number you wrote?

14. Copy and divide.

$$32\overline{)256} \qquad 13\overline{)195} \qquad 24\overline{)600} \qquad 40\overline{)960} \qquad 21\overline{)975}$$

E. *Write the answers only.*

15. 13 + 15   16 + 9   25 + 7   34 + 6   15 + 17
16. 35 + 20   27 + 12   18 + 12   26 + 16   18 + 29
17. 17 − 6   22 − 8   30 − 4   25 − 7   34 − 9
18. 10 × 854   30 × 9   7 × 80   100 × 57   1,000 × 60
19. 4 × 18   7 × 23   8 × 13   3 × 29   6 × 65
20. $\frac{1}{2}$ of 14 $\frac{1}{3}$ of 18 $\frac{1}{7}$ of 56 $\frac{1}{9}$ of 81 $\frac{1}{5}$ of 40

74. Adding and Subtracting Mixed Numbers With Unlike Fractions

The examples in the box show how to add or subtract mixed numbers with unlike fractions.

---

1. Change the fractions to like fractions.

2. Add or subtract the fractions.

3. Add or subtract the whole numbers.

4. Write the answer in simplest form.

$$3\tfrac{5}{8} = 3\tfrac{5}{8}$$
$$+ 1\tfrac{1}{4} = 1\tfrac{2}{8}$$
$$\overline{\qquad 4\tfrac{7}{8}}$$

$$5\tfrac{7}{10} = 5\tfrac{7}{10}$$
$$- 2\tfrac{1}{2} = 2\tfrac{5}{10}$$
$$\overline{\qquad 3\tfrac{2}{10} = 3\tfrac{1}{5}}$$

A. Work carefully. Follow the examples in the box.

1.

$4\tfrac{1}{2}$ 　　 $3\tfrac{2}{5}$ 　　 $1\tfrac{1}{9}$ 　　 $2\tfrac{1}{2}$ 　　 $2\tfrac{7}{16}$

$+ 1\tfrac{1}{4}$ 　 $+ \tfrac{1}{2}$ 　 $+ 1\tfrac{2}{3}$ 　 $+ 1\tfrac{1}{3}$ 　 $+ 3\tfrac{1}{4}$

2.

$3\tfrac{5}{8}$ 　　 $5\tfrac{11}{16}$ 　　 $2\tfrac{11}{12}$ 　　 $6\tfrac{4}{5}$ 　　 $4\tfrac{3}{4}$

$- 1\tfrac{1}{2}$ 　 $- 4\tfrac{1}{2}$ 　 $- 1\tfrac{3}{4}$ 　 $- 2\tfrac{2}{3}$ 　 $- 2\tfrac{1}{3}$

B. Do the following exercises.

3.

$\tfrac{9}{10}$ 　　 $\tfrac{4}{5}$ 　　 $\tfrac{3}{4}$ 　　 $\tfrac{7}{8}$ 　　 $\tfrac{1}{4}$

$+ \tfrac{1}{2}$ 　 $+ \tfrac{1}{4}$ 　 $+ \tfrac{3}{4}$ 　 $+ \tfrac{3}{16}$ 　 $+ \tfrac{5}{6}$

4.

$3\tfrac{1}{2}$ 　　 $1\tfrac{5}{8}$ 　　 $2\tfrac{5}{9}$ 　　 $4\tfrac{7}{16}$ 　　 $3\tfrac{7}{10}$

$+ \tfrac{1}{2}$ 　 $+ 2\tfrac{5}{8}$ 　 $+ 5\tfrac{7}{9}$ 　 $+ \tfrac{9}{16}$ 　 $+ 1\tfrac{1}{10}$

5. Change to improper fractions.

a. $3\tfrac{1}{2}$ 　　 b. $1\tfrac{3}{10}$ 　　 c. $4 = \tfrac{?}{2}$ 　　 d. $2\tfrac{4}{5}$ 　　 e. $3 = \tfrac{?}{3}$ 　　 f. $1\tfrac{5}{6}$

6. Change to whole or mixed numbers.

a. $\tfrac{12}{7}$ 　　 b. $\tfrac{20}{8}$ 　　 c. $\tfrac{8}{3}$ 　　 d. $\tfrac{16}{4}$ 　　 e. $\tfrac{15}{6}$ 　　 f. $\tfrac{18}{16}$

7. Write in simplest form.

a. $1\tfrac{5}{5}$ 　　 b. $2\tfrac{3}{2}$ 　　 c. $1\tfrac{8}{6}$ 　　 d. $3\tfrac{5}{4}$ 　　 e. $4\tfrac{4}{4}$ 　　 f. $2\tfrac{12}{8}$

8. Write what time each clock shows.

a.   b.   c.   d.

9. Copy and multiply.

358	147	3,960	845	269
× 47	× 96	× 36	× 800	× 415

10. Copy and subtract.

7,030	5,621	8,409	40,000	75,100
− 3,428	− 4,916	− 2,427	− 17,184	− 8,650

11. Write the lengths to which the arrows point.

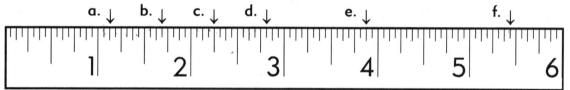

a. ↓   b. ↓   c. ↓   d. ↓   e. ↓   f. ↓

1   2   3   4   5   6

C. *Use these numbers for the following exercises. You should have three yes or no answers for each one.*

a. 5,140   b. 2,742   c. 3,285

12. Can the numbers be divided by 2?

13. Can the numbers be divided by 10?

14. Are the numbers divisible by 5?

15. Are they divisible by 3?

16. Are they divisible by 6?

17. Are they divisible by 9?

18. Are they divisible by 4?

D. *Solve these reading problems.*

19. Some clouds are 6 miles high. How many yards is that? (Remember that 1 mile = 1,760 yards.)

20. Moses spent $\frac{1}{3}$ of his life in Egypt. If he lived to be 120 years old, how many years did he live in Egypt?

75. Adding Harder Mixed Numbers

Sometimes mixed numbers have unlike denominators, and they also have answers that need to be regrouped. The example in the box shows how to solve such problems.

---

1. Change the fractions to like fractions.

2. Add the fractions.

3. Add the whole numbers.

4. Regroup the improper fraction part.

5. Add the regrouped part to the whole number.

$$2\frac{7}{8} = 2\frac{14}{16}$$
$$+\ 3\frac{5}{16} = 3\frac{5}{16}$$
$$5\frac{19}{16} = 5 + 1\frac{3}{16} = 6\frac{3}{16}$$

A. Write in simplest form.

1. a. $3\frac{2}{2}$ b. $1\frac{10}{8}$ c. $2\frac{6}{6}$ d. $1\frac{18}{16}$ e. $4\frac{3}{2}$ f. $2\frac{15}{12}$

B. Copy and add as shown in the box.

2. $\quad 2\frac{3}{4}$ $3\frac{5}{8}$ $1\frac{3}{4}$ $2\frac{3}{5}$
    $+\ 1\frac{1}{2}$ $+\ 3\frac{7}{16}$ $+\ 4\frac{2}{3}$ $+\ 3\frac{1}{2}$

3. $\quad 5\frac{1}{2}$ $1\frac{7}{12}$ $2\frac{4}{5}$ $4\frac{2}{3}$
    $+\ 2\frac{7}{8}$ $+\ 1\frac{1}{2}$ $+\ 2\frac{1}{4}$ $+\ 2\frac{1}{2}$

4. $\quad 3\frac{3}{4}$ $4\frac{2}{3}$ $3\frac{1}{2}$ $2\frac{11}{12}$
    $+\ \ \frac{7}{16}$ $+\ 5\frac{5}{9}$ $+\ 4\frac{9}{10}$ $+\ \ \frac{2}{3}$

C. Do these exercises.

5. Reduce to lowest terms.

   a. $\frac{12}{48}$ b. $\frac{15}{30}$ c. $\frac{20}{24}$ d. $\frac{30}{40}$ e. $\frac{16}{36}$ f. $\frac{28}{42}$

6. Copy and subtract.

   $\quad \frac{15}{16}$ $\frac{4}{5}$ $4\frac{1}{2}$ $5\frac{5}{6}$
   $-\ \frac{7}{16}$ $-\ \frac{1}{2}$ $-\ 3\frac{1}{8}$ $-\ 2\frac{1}{4}$

7. Copy and add. Check by going over your work.

65					
73	490	857	4,592	3,718	75,356
26	289	167	3,780	6,364	67,924
45	382	456	6,978	7,452	13,453
+ 38	+ 527	+ 344	+ 5,143	+ 2,067	+ 50,648

D. *Write the answers only.*

8. $8 + 4 + 5 + 3 + 9$ $\qquad\qquad$ $4 + 6 + 8 + 6 + 7$

9. $42 - 5 - 4 - 10 - 3$ $\qquad\qquad$ $35 - 5 - 6 - 8 - 7$

10. $7 \times 9 + 8$ $\qquad$ $8 \times 6 + 7$ $\qquad$ $4 \times 9 + 6$ $\qquad$ $8 \times 8 + 5$

11. $1\frac{1}{4} \times 12$ $\qquad$ $1\frac{1}{8} \times 24$ $\qquad$ $2\frac{1}{2} \times 4$ $\qquad$ $3\frac{1}{3} \times 9$

12. 100×56 $\qquad$ 10×497 $\qquad$ $1,000 \times 35$ $\qquad$ 8×37

13. $\frac{2}{3}$ of 15 $\qquad$ $\frac{3}{7}$ of 28 $\qquad$ $\frac{5}{8}$ of 64 $\qquad$ $\frac{3}{4}$ of 32

14. $16 + 17$ $\qquad$ $18 + 12$ $\qquad$ $25 + 19$ $\qquad$ $42 + 25$

15. $35 - 20$ $\qquad$ $28 - 11$ $\qquad$ $30 - 7$ $\qquad$ $24 - 8$

16. 1 mi. = _____ ft. $\qquad$ 1 yr. = _____ days $\qquad$ 1 century = _____ yr.

17. 2 bu. = _____ pk. $\qquad$ 5 qt. = _____ pt. $\qquad$ 6 yd. = _____ ft.

18. 5 cups = _____ qt. $\qquad$ $\frac{1}{4}$ lb. = _____ oz. $\qquad$ $\frac{1}{2}$ ton. = _____ lb.

E. *Find the answers.*

19. Find the average of 99, 85, 42, 68, and 81.

20. Eight packs of snack crackers cost $2.16. What is the cost of one pack?

21. Joab counted one million, one hundred thousand men of Israel and four hundred seventy thousand men of Judah. How many men did Joab count altogether? (Write the numbers as numerals first.)

76. Subtracting Fractions From Whole Numbers

How much pie is left from 2 pies after $\frac{3}{4}$ pie is eaten? Cut one pie into fourths to take away $\frac{3}{4}$. You can see from the pictures that $1\frac{1}{4}$ pies are left.

To find the answer without cutting pies, borrow 1 from 2 as shown in the first problem in the box. Then change the borrowed 1 to 4 fourths and subtract.

How many bananas are left from 4 bananas if $2\frac{1}{2}$ bananas are eaten? Change 4 to $3\frac{2}{2}$ and subtract.

$$
\begin{array}{rcl}
2 &=& 1\frac{4}{4} \\
-\frac{3}{4} &=& \frac{3}{4} \\
\hline
&& 1\frac{1}{4}
\end{array}
\qquad
\begin{array}{rcl}
4 &=& 3\frac{2}{2} \\
-2\frac{1}{2} &=& 2\frac{1}{2} \\
\hline
&& 1\frac{1}{2}
\end{array}
$$

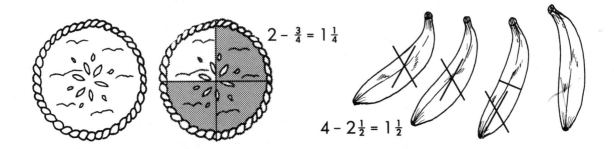

$$2 - \tfrac{3}{4} = 1\tfrac{1}{4}$$

$$4 - 2\tfrac{1}{2} = 1\tfrac{1}{2}$$

A. Copy and subtract as shown in the box.

1.

$$
\begin{array}{r} 6 \\ -\frac{2}{3} \\ \hline \end{array}
\qquad
\begin{array}{r} 3 \\ -\frac{1}{4} \\ \hline \end{array}
\qquad
\begin{array}{r} 2 \\ -\frac{3}{5} \\ \hline \end{array}
\qquad
\begin{array}{r} 4 \\ -\frac{5}{8} \\ \hline \end{array}
\qquad
\begin{array}{r} 5 \\ -\frac{7}{10} \\ \hline \end{array}
$$

2.

$$
\begin{array}{r} 4 \\ -1\frac{3}{4} \\ \hline \end{array}
\qquad
\begin{array}{r} 2 \\ -1\frac{1}{2} \\ \hline \end{array}
\qquad
\begin{array}{r} 7 \\ -3\frac{7}{8} \\ \hline \end{array}
\qquad
\begin{array}{r} 5 \\ -2\frac{1}{3} \\ \hline \end{array}
\qquad
\begin{array}{r} 6 \\ -3\frac{5}{12} \\ \hline \end{array}
$$

B. Do these exercises.

3. Change to improper fractions.

     a. $3\frac{1}{4}$ b. $1\frac{7}{8}$ c. $2\frac{5}{12}$ d. $1\frac{11}{16}$ e. $3 = \frac{?}{4}$ f. $2 = \frac{?}{3}$

4. Write in simplest form.

     a. $1\frac{4}{4}$ b. $2\frac{3}{2}$ c. $4\frac{16}{12}$ d. $3\frac{6}{5}$ e. $1\frac{11}{8}$ f. $2\frac{10}{10}$

5. $3\frac{1}{2}$ $2\frac{7}{16}$ $5\frac{2}{3}$ $1\frac{7}{10}$ $2\frac{3}{5}$
     $+\,4\frac{5}{8}$ $+\,1\frac{9}{16}$ $+\,3\frac{1}{2}$ $+\,4\frac{1}{2}$ $+\,2\frac{2}{3}$

6. $6\frac{7}{12}$ $4\frac{3}{4}$ $5\frac{7}{8}$ $8\frac{11}{12}$ $7\frac{2}{3}$
     $-\,2\frac{1}{2}$ $-\,1\frac{7}{16}$ $-\,3\frac{1}{4}$ $-\,\frac{1}{3}$ $-\,4\frac{1}{4}$

C. *These reading problems contain fractions. Solve them carefully.*

7. Mother had a 5-pound bag of brown sugar. She used $1\frac{1}{2}$ pounds to make cookies. How many pounds are left in the bag?

8. Nancy used $\frac{2}{3}$ cup of margarine in a cake and $1\frac{1}{4}$ cup in cookies. How much margarine did she use?

9. Kenneth lives $3\frac{1}{2}$ miles from school. Jay lives $2\frac{7}{10}$ miles farther from the school than Kenneth does. How far does Jay live from school?

10. When Joseph was ruler in Egypt, he gathered grain to be used when the seven-year famine came. He collected $\frac{1}{5}$ of the grain that the people raised. If an Egyptian of that time raised 340 bushels of grain, how much did he give to Joseph?

11. Mother needs $2\frac{1}{2}$ yards of cloth to make a dress for Amy and $\frac{3}{4}$ yard to make a dress for baby Judith. How many yards does she need for the two dresses?

12. Mother bought a 6-yard piece of cloth. After she makes herself a dress with $4\frac{1}{4}$ yards, how much of the cloth will be left?

13. A rope that is $2\frac{1}{4}$ yards long is how many inches long?

14. Warren has $\frac{2}{3}$ can of white paint. If he uses $\frac{1}{2}$ can to paint a shelf, how much paint will he have left?

15. How many pounds are in $\frac{3}{4}$ ton?

16. Aunt Grace had a rooster that weighed $8\frac{3}{4}$ pounds. After it was dressed to eat, it weighed $6\frac{1}{8}$ pounds. How much weight was lost?

77. Borrowing to Subtract From Mixed Numbers

Aunt Ruth had $2\frac{1}{4}$ pounds of butter. She used $\frac{3}{4}$ pound to make cookies. How much was left?

As you can see in the picture below, Aunt Ruth had to open one of the full boxes of butter in order to have enough for the cookies. The picture shows that $1\frac{2}{4}$, or $1\frac{1}{2}$, pounds of butter were left.

Study the first problem in the box to learn how to solve the problem without pictures. Borrow 1 from the 2 and change the 1 to $\frac{4}{4}$. Add $\frac{4}{4}$ to the $\frac{1}{4}$ already in the minuend. Now take $\frac{3}{4}$ away from $1\frac{5}{4}$. Reduce the fraction.

$$\begin{array}{r} 2\frac{1}{4} = 1\frac{5}{4} \\ -\ \frac{3}{4} = \ \frac{3}{4} \\ \hline 1\frac{2}{4} = 1\frac{1}{2} \end{array}$$

$$\begin{array}{r} 4\frac{3}{16} = 3\frac{19}{16} \\ -\ 2\frac{9}{16} = 2\frac{9}{16} \\ \hline 1\frac{10}{16} = 1\frac{5}{8} \end{array}$$

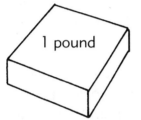
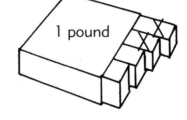
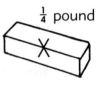

A. Copy and subtract as shown in the box.

1.
$$5\frac{3}{8} \qquad 4\frac{3}{16} \qquad 3\frac{1}{3} \qquad 6\frac{5}{12} \qquad 5\frac{1}{6}$$
$$-\ \frac{5}{8} \qquad -\ \frac{7}{16} \qquad -\ \frac{2}{3} \qquad -\ \frac{11}{12} \qquad -\ \frac{5}{6}$$

2.
$$4\frac{1}{8} \qquad 7\frac{2}{9} \qquad 6\frac{3}{5} \qquad 8\frac{5}{16} \qquad 3\frac{3}{10}$$
$$-\ 2\frac{5}{8} \qquad -\ 3\frac{5}{9} \qquad -\ 2\frac{4}{5} \qquad -\ 4\frac{13}{16} \qquad -\ 1\frac{7}{10}$$

B. Do these exercises.

3. Subtract as you did in Lesson 76.
$$6 \qquad 4 \qquad 5 \qquad 3 \qquad 9$$
$$-\ \frac{7}{16} \qquad -\ \frac{3}{8} \qquad -\ 2\frac{1}{4} \qquad -\ 2\frac{7}{12} \qquad -\ 4\frac{2}{3}$$

4. Copy and add.
$$3\frac{1}{2} \qquad 6\frac{3}{4} \qquad 4\frac{5}{16} \qquad 2\frac{7}{9} \qquad 5\frac{5}{6}$$
$$+\ 2\frac{7}{8} \qquad +\ \frac{1}{3} \qquad +\ 3\frac{5}{8} \qquad +\ 2\frac{2}{3} \qquad +\ \frac{7}{12}$$

5. Find the average of 367, 482, 354, and 429.

C. *Use these numbers for the following exercises. You should have two* yes *or* no *answers for each one.*

        a. 5,940   **b.** 2,145

6. Are the numbers above divisible by 2?

7. Are the numbers above divisible by 5?

8. Are the numbers divisible by 4?

9. Are the numbers divisible by 3?

10. Are they divisible by 6?

11. Are they divisible by 9?

12. Are they divisible by 10?

D. *Write the answers only.*

13. 1 year = _____ days   1 pint = _____ cups   1 decade = _____ years

14. 1 mile = _____ yards   1 yard = _____ inches   1 ton = _____ pounds

15. 1 year = _____ weeks   1 quart = _____ pints   1 bushel = _____ pecks

16. 1 peck = _____ quarts   1 pound = _____ ounces   1 hour = _____ minutes

17. 6 yd. = _____ ft.   6 ft. = _____ yd.   6 ft. = _____ in.

18. $\frac{1}{3}$ ft. = _____ in. $\frac{1}{2}$ lb. = _____ oz. $\frac{1}{4}$ hr. = _____ min.

19. 8 qt. = _____ gal.   12 days = _____ wk.   9 mo. = _____ yr.

E. *Follow the directions.*

20. Write numerals for these number words.
    a. two hundred thirteen billion, eighty-five million
    b. sixteen billion, four hundred twenty million, ten
    c. one billion, eleven million, ten thousand, one hundred

21. Write these with Roman numerals.
    a. 780   **b.** 459   **c.** 2,342   **d.** 1,615   **e.** 1,936

22. Copy and divide.

    12)564   70)910   24)168   33)870   41)779

78. Borrowing With Unlike Fractions

Titus lives $7\frac{3}{10}$ miles from church. William lives $5\frac{1}{2}$ miles from church. How much closer does William live to church than Titus does?

To subtract $5\frac{1}{2}$ from $7\frac{3}{10}$, first change $\frac{1}{2}$ and $\frac{3}{10}$ to like fractions. Then you can easily see that the larger fraction is the subtrahend. That means you must borrow.

$$7\frac{3}{10} = 7\frac{3}{10} = 6\frac{13}{10}$$
$$-5\frac{1}{2} = 5\frac{5}{10} = 5\frac{5}{10}$$
$$1\frac{8}{10} = 1\frac{4}{5}$$

Borrow 1 from the 7, and change the 7 to 6. Change the borrowed 1 to $\frac{10}{10}$ and add it to the $\frac{3}{10}$ in the minuend. Now subtract.

After you subtract and simplify the answer, you find that William lives $1\frac{4}{5}$ miles closer to church than Titus does.

A. *Copy and subtract as shown in the box.*

1.
$$2\frac{1}{2} \qquad 4\frac{5}{16} \qquad 1\frac{1}{5} \qquad 5\frac{1}{4}$$
$$-\frac{7}{8} \qquad -\frac{3}{4} \qquad -\frac{1}{2} \qquad -\frac{2}{3}$$

2.
$$3\frac{1}{10} \qquad 6\frac{1}{2} \qquad 4\frac{3}{8} \qquad 7\frac{5}{12}$$
$$-1\frac{3}{5} \qquad -3\frac{11}{16} \qquad -3\frac{3}{4} \qquad -2\frac{3}{4}$$

B. *Copy and subtract. You will not need to borrow or change to like fractions in all the problems.*

3.
$$5\frac{1}{3} \qquad 8\frac{3}{4} \qquad 3\frac{5}{6} \qquad 4\frac{1}{9}$$
$$-\frac{7}{12} \qquad -\frac{9}{16} \qquad -\frac{1}{3} \qquad -\frac{5}{9}$$

4.
$$2\frac{7}{8} \qquad 6\frac{1}{6} \qquad 7\frac{1}{12} \qquad 5\frac{1}{3}$$
$$-1\frac{1}{3} \qquad -4\frac{5}{6} \qquad -3\frac{1}{2} \qquad -2\frac{3}{5}$$

General Review

C. *Do these exercises.*

5. Change to whole numbers or mixed numbers in simplest form.

a. $3\frac{5}{5}$ b. $2\frac{9}{8}$ c. $5\frac{6}{4}$ d. $1\frac{16}{16}$ e. $4\frac{14}{12}$ f. $2\frac{12}{9}$

6. Copy and add.

$$5\tfrac{1}{2}\qquad 4\tfrac{7}{8}\qquad 1\tfrac{7}{16}\qquad 3\tfrac{4}{5}\qquad 4\tfrac{7}{12}$$
$$+\ \tfrac{3}{4}\qquad +3\tfrac{1}{8}\qquad +2\tfrac{3}{8}\qquad +2\tfrac{3}{10}\qquad +1\tfrac{11}{12}$$

7. List all the factors of each number: a. 18   b. 27

8. What is the greatest common factor of 18 and 27?

9. Reduce $\tfrac{18}{27}$ to lowest terms.

10. Draw a factor tree for each number: a. 18   b. 42

11. List 10 multiples for each number: a. 4   b. 6

12. What is the smallest common multiple of 4 and 6?

13. What is the lowest common denominator that you can use to add $\tfrac{3}{4}$ and $\tfrac{5}{6}$?

14. Change these Roman numerals to Arabic numerals.

  a. XCVII   b. DCCCLIII   c. MMLXXIV   d. CMXVI   e. MCDXXIX

D. *Write the answers only.*

15. 15 + 16   21 + 17   32 + 9   18 + 9   14 + 26

16. 19 – 5   21 – 4   30 – 8   24 – 6   32 – 9

17. 40 × 9   6 × 70   100 × 27   3 × 28   5 × 47

18. $\tfrac{2}{3}$ of 15 $\tfrac{3}{8}$ of 24 $\tfrac{4}{5}$ of 20 $1\tfrac{1}{2} \times 16$ $2\tfrac{1}{3} \times 6$

E. *Solve these reading problems.*

19. One Saturday morning Faye spent $1\tfrac{1}{2}$ hours hoeing corn in the garden. Then she helped Mother in the kitchen for $2\tfrac{3}{4}$ hours. How much time did Faye spend in the garden and in the kitchen?

20. How much more time did Faye spend in the kitchen than in the garden?

21. Mother had a 10-pound bag of flour. She used $6\tfrac{1}{4}$ pounds to make bread and $1\tfrac{1}{2}$ pounds to make pies. How much flour was left in the bag?

79. Review of Fractions

A. *Do the following exercises.*

1. Reduce to lowest terms.

   a. $\frac{12}{36}$ b. $\frac{20}{24}$ c. $\frac{15}{25}$ d. $\frac{16}{24}$ e. $\frac{18}{42}$ f. $\frac{12}{16}$

2. Change to whole or mixed numbers in simplest form.

   a. $\frac{13}{6}$ b. $\frac{9}{3}$ c. $\frac{18}{4}$ d. $\frac{10}{8}$ e. $\frac{7}{2}$ f. $\frac{21}{16}$

3. Change to improper fractions.

   a. $3 = \frac{?}{4}$ b. $2 = \frac{?}{10}$ c. $4\frac{1}{2}$ d. $5\frac{2}{3}$ e. $3\frac{3}{4}$ f. $1\frac{7}{16}$

4. Write in simplest form.

   a. $4\frac{3}{3}$ b. $1\frac{11}{8}$ c. $2\frac{18}{16}$ d. $3\frac{12}{12}$ e. $1\frac{10}{6}$ f. $5\frac{23}{20}$

5. Write the lowest common denominator for each pair.

   a. $\frac{2}{3}$ $\frac{4}{9}$ b. $\frac{1}{2}$ $\frac{5}{12}$ c. $\frac{5}{8}$ $\frac{1}{3}$ d. $\frac{11}{16}$ $\frac{3}{4}$ e. $\frac{3}{5}$ $\frac{2}{3}$

B. *Subtract. Write all answers in simplest form.*

6. 6 5 3 5 4
   $-\frac{5}{8}$ $-2\frac{1}{4}$ $-1\frac{3}{10}$ $-4\frac{7}{16}$ $-2\frac{5}{12}$

7. $2\frac{1}{8}$ $4\frac{1}{3}$ $6\frac{1}{9}$ $3\frac{5}{16}$ $5\frac{2}{5}$
   $-\frac{5}{8}$ $-1\frac{2}{3}$ $-2\frac{7}{9}$ $-\frac{7}{16}$ $-3\frac{4}{5}$

8. $7\frac{1}{4}$ $3\frac{1}{2}$ $5\frac{1}{10}$ $4\frac{1}{4}$ $2\frac{1}{4}$
   $-2\frac{2}{3}$ $-1\frac{5}{6}$ $-\frac{1}{2}$ $-3\frac{1}{6}$ $-\frac{9}{16}$

C. *Add. Write all answers in simplest form.*

9. $3\frac{7}{8}$ $2\frac{1}{2}$ $4\frac{11}{16}$ $1\frac{3}{4}$ $5\frac{7}{10}$
   $+\frac{3}{8}$ $+4\frac{1}{2}$ $+1\frac{7}{16}$ $+3\frac{3}{4}$ $+2\frac{1}{10}$

10. $2\frac{7}{8}$ $5\frac{1}{2}$ $1\frac{5}{9}$ $4\frac{13}{16}$ $3\frac{3}{4}$
   $+2\frac{1}{4}$ $+3\frac{2}{3}$ $+2\frac{1}{3}$ $+\frac{1}{4}$ $+1\frac{2}{3}$

General Review

D. *Follow the directions.*

11. Copy and multiply.

459	3,926	7,140	836	572
× 25	× 71	× 78	× 600	× 346

12. Write the lengths to which the arrows point.

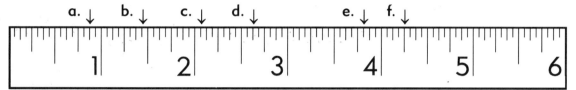

E. *Answer yes or no.*

13. Is 4,316 divisible by:
a. 2? b. 3? c. 4? d. 5? e. 9?

14. Are $\frac{3}{4}$ and $\frac{12}{16}$ equivalent fractions?

15. Does 1 mile equal 1,760 feet?

16. Are there four quarts in a cup?

17. Are there four pecks in a bushel?

18. Are there 366 days in a leap year?

19. Does April have 31 days?

20. Is 6:00 A.M. in the morning?

21. Are two dimes and six nickels equal to a half dollar?

22. Does the 3 in 56,730,942,815 mean 30 billion?

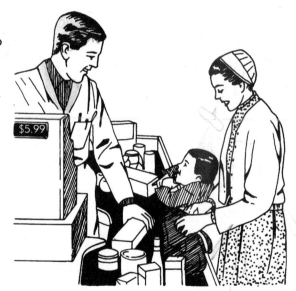

80. Midyear Review

A. *Write the answers only.*

1.
$$
\begin{array}{ccccccccc}
8 & 10 & 12 & 9 & 7 & 6 & 12 & 14 & 3 \\
\times 7 & \times 10 & -7 & +5 & \times 6 & +8 & \times 5 & -5 & +8
\end{array}
$$

2.
$$
\begin{array}{ccccccccc}
9 & 12 & 11 & 16 & 4 & 8 & 7 & 11 & 10 \\
+8 & \times 12 & -9 & -7 & \times 8 & +7 & \times 9 & \times 11 & -6
\end{array}
$$

3.
$$
\begin{array}{ccccccccc}
6 & 10 & 7 & 6 & 9 & 12 & 12 & 15 & 3 \\
\times 9 & \times 11 & +6 & \times 5 & \times 9 & \times 8 & -4 & -6 & \times 9
\end{array}
$$

4. $56 \div 7$ $84 \div 12$ $100 \div 10$ $42 \div 6$

5. $18 \div 3$ $28 \div 7$ $35 \div 5$ $132 \div 11$

6. $15 + 14$ $16 + 30$ $21 + 9$ $18 + 12$ $25 + 16$

7. $18 - 5$ $23 - 10$ $27 - 12$ $25 - 7$ $32 - 6$

8. 10×48 100×30 $1{,}000 \times 12$ 40×7 9×80

9. $\frac{1}{3}$ of 36 $\frac{2}{5}$ of 20 $\frac{3}{8}$ of 64 $1\frac{1}{2} \times 14$ $2\frac{1}{3} \times 6$

10. $1 \div 6$ $3 \div 7$ $2 \div 8$ 4 is what part of 12?

11. 1 yr. = _____ days   1 yr. = _____ wk.   1 century = _____ yr.

12. 1 mi. = _____ ft.   1 bu. = _____ pk.   1 ton = _____ lb.

13. 1 lb. = _____ oz.   1 qt. = _____ cups   1 gal. = _____ qt.

14. 1 yd. = _____ in.   1 doz. = _____ items   1 qt. = _____ pt.

15. 1 pk. = _____ qt.   1 hr. = _____ min.   1 day = _____ hr.

16. 6 ft. = _____ in.   6 ft. = _____ yd.   3 wk. = _____ days

17. 8 cups = _____ pt.   5 pt. = _____ qt.   6 mo. = _____ yr.

18. What is the lowest common denominatior for each fraction pair?
    a. $\frac{1}{2}$ $\frac{2}{3}$ b. $\frac{3}{4}$ $\frac{7}{16}$ c. $\frac{11}{12}$ $\frac{1}{2}$ d. $\frac{3}{5}$ $\frac{1}{3}$ e. $\frac{5}{6}$ $\frac{7}{8}$

B. *Do these exercises.*

19. Copy each pair of fractions, and write < or > between them. Change them to like fractions if you are not sure.

    a. $\frac{3}{4}$ $\frac{1}{2}$ b. $\frac{3}{4}$ $\frac{7}{12}$ c. $\frac{2}{3}$ $\frac{5}{6}$ d. $\frac{1}{2}$ $\frac{3}{5}$ e. $\frac{2}{3}$ $\frac{5}{8}$

20. Reduce to lowest terms: a. $\frac{5}{20}$ b. $\frac{12}{36}$ c. $\frac{18}{24}$ d. $\frac{16}{40}$

21. Change to whole or mixed numbers in simplest form: a. $\frac{12}{3}$ b. $\frac{14}{5}$ c. $\frac{12}{8}$

22. Change to improper fractions: a. $4 = \frac{?}{2}$ b. $1\frac{1}{2}$ c. $2\frac{3}{8}$ d. $3\frac{2}{3}$

23. Change to simplest form: a. $3\frac{4}{4}$ b. $1\frac{10}{8}$ c. $2\frac{19}{16}$ d. $5\frac{9}{5}$

24. Write all the factors of each number: a. 15   b. 24

25. Draw a factor tree for 24.

26. Write six multiples of each number: a. 7   b. 8

27. What is the lowest common multiple of 7 and 8?

28. Is 3,915 divisible by these numbers? Write **yes** or **no** for each.

    a. 2   b. 3   c. 4   d. 5   e. 6   f. 9   g. 10

29. What time is shown on the clocks?   a.   b.

30. Measure this line.

    _____

31. What measurement is $\frac{1}{16}$ inch after $\frac{1}{4}$ inch?

32. What is $\frac{1}{16}$" after $\frac{7}{16}$"?

33. Write numerals for these number words and Roman numerals.

    a. two million, seventy-nine thousand
    b. thirteen billion, six hundred million, eighteen thousand, two
    c. 470 billion, 3 million, 295 thousand, twenty-six
    d. MMMCLV
    e. MCMXCIV

34. What is the value of the 9 in this number?   328,904,217,685

35. Count the money.

(continued on next page)

Computation Practice

C. *Follow the signs. Your teacher may let you use folded paper for some of the exercises.*

36.

5	8	4	9	5	3	6
6	3	9	6	5	9	2
4	9	4	5	7	8	7
8	4	6	8	9	2	3
+ 3	+ 9	+ 6	+ 4	+ 8	+ 4	+ 7

37.

$\frac{9}{16}$	$3\frac{3}{4}$	$2\frac{7}{8}$	$4\frac{2}{5}$	$1\frac{5}{9}$
$+ \frac{3}{4}$	$+ 1\frac{3}{4}$	$+ \frac{5}{16}$	$+ 2\frac{1}{2}$	$+ 2\frac{2}{3}$

38.

$\frac{11}{12}$	2	$4\frac{1}{4}$	$5\frac{7}{10}$	$3\frac{1}{2}$
$- \frac{2}{3}$	$- \frac{5}{8}$	$- 1\frac{7}{12}$	$- 3\frac{9}{10}$	$- \frac{5}{6}$

39.

	569		4,327	62,871
493	876	9,903	4,634	18,378
945	137	8,519	5,147	32,464
+ 528	+ 627	+ 5,672	+ 6,917	+ 56,035

40.

5,048	8,612	90,000	27,003	56,020
- 3,665	- 5,384	- 29,850	- 18,627	- 36,431

41.

6,748	593	2,960	875	364
× 8	× 47	× 36	× 500	× 429

42.   6)4,596   4)5,930   50)900   23)184   14)378

43.

12 minutes 18 seconds		7 feet 8 inches
- 5 minutes 45 seconds		+ 8 feet 9 inches

Reading Problems

D. *Find the answers.*

44. What is the average of each set of numbers?
   a. 17, 25, 43, 36, 29
   b. 458, 367, 424, 383

45. Mrs. Jones spent $23.63 at the book store and gave the clerk $30.00. How much change did she receive?

46. What coins and bills would Mrs. Jones receive if she gave the clerk $20.00 for a bill of $7.46 and the clerk gave her as few pieces as possible?

47. God gave Martha twin sisters. Melanie weighed 5 pounds 12 ounces, and Marlene weighed 7 pounds 6 ounces. How much did the twins weigh together?

48. How much more did Marlene weigh than Melanie?

49. Warren read 45 pages in *Home Fires* one Sunday. On Monday he read only 17 pages, on Tuesday 38 pages, and on Wednesday none at all (0 pages). On Thursday he read 35 pages. What was the average number of pages he read per day?

50. To make one batch of sugar cookies, Norma uses 4 cups of flour. How much flour does Norma use for $2\frac{1}{2}$ batches of sugar cookies?

51. Norma used 8 cups of flour for sugar cookies, $4\frac{1}{2}$ cups of flour for chocolate chip cookies, and $3\frac{3}{4}$ cups of flour for peanut butter cookies. How much flour did Norma use altogether?

52. Norma gave some of the cookies to widows in the community. She put $1\frac{1}{2}$ dozen cookies on each plate. How many cookies were on a plate?

53. How many cookies were needed to fill 6 plates as described in number 52?

54. At the bookstore Mother bought 5 New Testaments at $3.95 each to give to the neighbor children. She also bought a new Bible for Father for $35.65. What was her total bill?

55. The family bought a 48-pound case of oranges. Ernest put oranges in bags for needy families. If he had 80 oranges and put 8 oranges in each bag, how many bags could he fill?

---

81. Chapter 8 Test

Interesting Number Facts

A Printing Press Number

The number 12,345,679 works like a printing press. If it is multiplied by certain numbers, it will produce many copies of the same digit. Look at these problems.

12,345,679	12,345,679	12,345,679
x 18	x 45	x 72
98 765 432	61 728 395	24 691 358
123 456 79	493 827 16	864 197 53
222,222,222	555,555,555	888,888,888

Notice that the multiplier in each problem is a multiple of 9. The first problem repeats 2 in the answer. The multiplier is 18, or 2 × 9. The second problem repeats 5 in the answer. The multiplier is 45, or 5 × 9. Do you see the pattern?

Ask one of your friends to choose a digit from 1 to 9. Mentally multiply the number he gives you by 9. Then have him multiply 12,345,679 by the number you got. If your friend multiplies correctly, his answer will be a whole line of the digit he chose.

The reason for this interesting result is the order that God has placed in numbers. Our number system is based on 10; therefore, special things happen with the number 9, one less than 10. If 12,345,679 is multiplied by 9, the product is 111,111,111. Then of course, if it is multiplied by 2 × 9 (18), the result is 222,222,222. If is is multiplied by 3 × 9 (27), the answer is 333,333,333—and so on. Multiplying the printing press number by 9 and its multiples is just another way of multiplying 111,111,111 by a digit from 1 to 9.

Do you remember how to tell if a number divides evenly by 9? the sum of its digits is always a multiple of 9. Add the digits in 111,111,111. The sum is 9, so 111,111,111 is divisible by 9. The sums of the digits in 222,222,222 or 555,555,555 or 777,777,777 are also divisible by 9. Isn't 9 an interesting number?

Chapter 9

More Division
by Two-Digit Divisors

He looked up to heaven, and blessed, and brake the loaves, . . .
and the two fishes divided he among them all.
(Mark 6:41)

82. Two-Digit Divisors Ending With 7, 8, or 9

You have been dividing by two-digit numbers for some time. So far all the divisors have ended with 0, 1, 2, 3, or 4. To estimate the quotient figure, you rounded the divisor **down** to the nearest ten.

In this lesson some divisors end with 7, 8, or 9. To estimate quotient figures, you will round **up** to the nearest ten. As you learned earlier, your first estimate may not be right and you will need to try another number. Remember that the remainder must never be as large as the divisor. Study the problem in the box.

```
Think: 28 rounds up to 30           24 (Wrong)          25 (Right)
Divide: 70 ÷ 30 = 2           28)700              28)700
Multiply: 2 × 28 = 56              56                  56
Subtract: 70 – 56 = 14           140                 140
Bring down the 0.                 112                 140
Think: 140 ÷ 30 = 4               28                    0
Multiply: 4 × 28 = 112
Subtract: 140 – 112 = 28; remainder is too large.
Think: 5 × 28 = 140; correct answer is 25.
```

A. *Solve these problems.*

1. Write 1, 2, or 3 to tell the number of quotient figures. Do not solve the problems.

$$17\overline{)190} \qquad 39\overline{)286} \qquad 48\overline{)440} \qquad 27\overline{)578} \qquad 37\overline{)2,459} \qquad 28\overline{)2,912}$$

2. Copy and work carefully. These answers have no remainders.

$$18\overline{)810} \qquad 49\overline{)637} \qquad 38\overline{)190} \qquad 27\overline{)729} \qquad 47\overline{)141}$$

3. Divide. These answers have remainders.

$$29\overline{)220} \qquad 17\overline{)215} \qquad 28\overline{)660} \qquad 47\overline{)453} \qquad 39\overline{)160}$$

4. Divide. Some answers have remainders and some do not.

$$19\overline{)722} \qquad 39\overline{)930} \qquad 48\overline{)1,728} \qquad 27\overline{)130} \qquad 18\overline{)2,330}$$

General Review

B. *Write the answers only.*

5. 15 – 8	34 – 7	42 – 9	21 – 6	43 – 5
6. 30 – 7	41 – 8	25 – 7	46 – 9	37 – 8
7. 22 – 4	36 – 5	51 – 7	40 – 6	26 – 7
8. 5 × 38	6 × 19	4 × 27	7 × 17	3 × 39
9. 7 × 28	4 × 49	3 × 18	6 × 36	5 × 29
10. 3 × 47	5 × 17	6 × 47	8 × 28	4 × 38

11. 8 × 7 + 5   9 × 6 + 4   3 × 9 + 6   7 × 9 + 3

12. 4 × 7 + 5   8 × 4 + 6   6 × 8 + 5   3 × 7 + 4

13. Round to the nearest ten: 78   365   8,294   94,728

14. Round to the nearest hundred: 365   8,294   94,728

15. Round to the nearest thousand: 8,294   94,728   136,195

16. Round to the nearest ten thousand: 94,728   136,195   208,352

C. *Find the answers.*

17.

358	4,913	7,328	450	682
× 64	× 8	× 53	× 179	× 700

18.

3 feet 8 inches	6 gallons 2 quarts	9 weeks 5 days
+ 4 feet 10 inches	+ 3 gallons 3 quarts	+ 5 weeks 4 days

D. *Solve these reading problems.*

19. The town of Hershey had 11,860 people living in it in 1980. By 1990 the population was 13,250. How many more people lived in Hershey in 1990 than in 1980?

20. If the population of Hershey grows by 1,530 people in the next ten years, the growth will be at an average rate of _____ persons per year.

83. More Practice With Two-Digit Divisors

The hardest divisors to estimate are those ending with 4, 5, or 6. If you round downward, your estimated quotient figure is often too large. If you round upward, your estimated figure is often too small.

As you gain practice with divisions like this, you will learn to subtract 1 from your estimate if you rounded down the divisor. If you rounded up, you will learn to add 1 to your estimate. Study the problem in the box to see how this works.

```
      1 ? R ?    Think: 50 ÷ 35 = 1
  35)500
      35         Subtract: 50 - 35 = 15; bring down the 0.
     ───
     150         Think: Round 35 to 30. 150 ÷ 30 = 5, so use 4.
     ? ? ?           Or: Round 35 to 40. 150 ÷ 40 = 3, so use 4.
     ───
      ??         (You should be able to finish the problem.)
```

A. *The problems in row 1 have been done, but each of them has a mistake. Copy and solve the problems correctly.*

```
1.          4 R 36          19 R 7            21            93 R 5              66 R 6
       36)180          47)800          34)728     15)1,300          26)1,612
          144             47              68            135              146
          ───             ───             ──            ───              ───
           36            430              48             50              152
                         423              34             45              146
                         ───              ──             ──              ───
                           7              14              5                6
```

B. *Copy, work carefully, and check by multiplication.*

2.   14)39   25)950   46)322   37)695

3.   35)560   16)848   27)172   34)986

4.   17)1,100   26)1,612   45)5,535   24)7,616

General Review

C. *Write the answers only.*

5. $54-6$ $23-7$ $30-8$ $42-5$ $21-8$
6. $37-9$ $25-5$ $41-7$ $50-4$ $43-20$
7. 6×85 3×19 7×48 8×29 4×86
8. 4×93 5×28 2×27 6×15 9×45

9. $1\frac{1}{4}\times16$ $2\frac{1}{2}\times10$ $1\frac{1}{6}\times24$ $3\frac{1}{3}\times6$
10. $\frac{3}{5}$ of 35 $\frac{4}{7}$ of 56 $\frac{2}{3}$ of 36 $\frac{5}{8}$ of 32

11. Round to the nearest hundred: 785 6,349 57,452
12. Round to the nearest thousand: 6,349 57,452 128,701
13. Round to the nearest hundred thousand: 128,701 3,561,980

D. *Copy and solve.*

14.
    12 years 6 months
   + 9 years 8 months

    5 pecks 5 quarts
   + 1 peck   3 quarts

    15 hours 45 minutes
   + 6 hours 25 minutes

E. *Do these three things with each problem below. The first one is started for you.*

(1) Round the numbers in the problem.

(2) Use the rounded numbers to find an estimated answer.

(3) Find the exact answer.

15. a.
```
  5,793      6,000
  6,845      7,000
  3,275      3,000
+ 4,926    + 5,000
           21,000
```
b.
```
  2,398
  8,467
  6,873
+ 8,729
```
c.
```
 35,609
 23,487
 41,764
+19,361
```
d.
```
 64,827
 28,561
  7,293
+33,426
```

16. a.
```
  9,302
- 6,896
```
b.
```
 72,510
-17,365
```
c.
```
 6,349
×   87
```
d.
```
   527
× 473
```

84. Multipliers Ending With Zero

Some fifth graders
find 690 × 375 this way:

Here is a shorter way of finding 690 × 375. The
second partial product begins in the hundreds'
column.

First Way:
$$\begin{array}{r} 375 \\ \times\,690 \\ \hline 000 \\ 3375 \\ 225000 \\ \hline 258{,}750 \end{array}$$

Second Way:
$$\begin{array}{r} 375 \\ \times\,690 \\ \hline 33750 \\ 2250 \\ \hline 258{,}750 \end{array}$$

A. *Copy and multiply in the second way shown above.*

1.	964 × 370	387 × 230	641 × 760	953 × 420	780 × 840
2.	857 × 520	419 × 980	390 × 560	526 × 640	166 × 810

B. *To solve these problems, first write 00 and then multiply by the
hundreds' digit. You may offset the multiplier if you wish.*

3.	947 × 400	590 × 600	713 × 800	628 × 300	340 × 700

C. *Copy, divide, and check by multiplication.*

4.   16)384   25)950   38)228   19)1,235   47)1,576

D. *Write the numbers that fit in the blanks.*

5. 1 yard = _____ inches   1 peck = _____ quarts   1 quart = _____ pints

6. 1 decade = _____ years   1 year = _____ days   1 pound = _____ ounces

7. 5 yards = _____ feet   5 feet = _____ yards   6 cups = _____ pints

8. 4 dozen = _____ items   2 tons = _____ pounds   6 pecks = _____ bushels

Remainders in Reading Problems

1. In some reading problems solved by division, the remainder is changed to a fraction.

    Problem A: Mother had a 3-yard piece of cloth. She used $\frac{1}{2}$ of the piece to make a dress for the Anderson's little girl. How much cloth did Mother use for the dress?

    $$\begin{array}{r} 1 \\ 2\overline{)3} \\ 2 \\ \hline 1 \end{array}$$

    Think: The 1 leftover yard can be divided. Mother used **$1\frac{1}{2}$ yards** of cloth for the dress.

    Note: **When a remainder is a unit of measure, it is almost always changed to a fraction.**

2. In some reading problems solved by division, the remainder is stated as R or is even dropped completely.

    Problem B: Sister Joan has a box of 500 craft sticks. She is planning an art project that takes 48 sticks per project. How many such projects can be made with the sticks in Sister Joan's box?

    $$\begin{array}{r} 10 \\ 48\overline{)500} \\ 48 \\ \hline 20 \end{array}$$

    Think: The 20 left over sticks cannot be used. There are enough for **10 projects.**

3. In some problems the remainder is changed to one and added to the quotient.

    Problem C: Harrington Christian School has 168 pupils. They are using buses to go on their school trip. If each bus holds 44 pupils, how many buses are needed for all the pupils?

    $$\begin{array}{r} 3 \\ 44\overline{)168} \\ 132 \\ \hline 36 \end{array}$$

    Think: The 36 extra pupils need a bus too. It takes **4 buses** for the trip.

E. *Solve these reading problems. Make sure your answers are sensible.*

9. Kevin sawed a 10-foot board into 4 equal pieces. How long was each piece?

10. On Sunday afternoon 21 members met at church to pass out the *Star of Hope* in Trenton. If 6 people can ride in a car, how many cars were needed to carry the people to Trenton?

11. The group at church had 1,000 copies of the *Star of Hope*. The papers were counted into packets with 80 in each packet, and the leftover ones were put on the table at church. How many packets were made, and how many copies were put on the table?

12. If the 21 members passed out 960 copies of the *Star of Hope*, what was the average number that each person distributed? (The answer is an average, so the remainder should be changed to a fraction.)

STAR OF HOPE

85. Multiplying With Zero in the Tens' Place

Study the examples in the box below.

Multiplicand With Zero in Tens' Place		Multiplier With Zero in Tens' Place	
806	309	527	480
× 386	× 457	× 706	× 907
4 836	2 163	3 162	3 360
64 48	15 45	3689	4320
241 8	123 6	372,062	435,360
311,116	141,213		

A. *Write the answers only.*

1.
$$
\begin{array}{cccccccc}
0 & 5 & 4 & 8 & 0 & 5 & 0 & 3 & 1 \\
\times 7 & \times 0 & + 0 & \times 0 & + 6 & + 0 & \times 0 & \times 0 & + 0
\end{array}
$$

2. $4 \times 9 + 6$ $8 \times 8 + 5$ $3 \times 6 + 7$ $8 \times 0 + 6$

3. $5 \times 7 + 4$ $9 \times 1 + 4$ $4 \times 0 + 5$ $7 \times 7 + 7$

4. $8 \times 9 + 0$ $3 \times 9 + 6$ $9 \times 9 + 3$ $8 \times 7 + 4$

B. *Copy and solve the problems.*

5.
$$
\begin{array}{cccc}
703 & 208 & 406 & 809 \\
\times 942 & \times 674 & \times 271 & \times 593
\end{array}
$$

6.
$$
\begin{array}{cccc}
145 & 763 & 849 & 650 \\
\times 709 & \times 306 & \times 403 & \times 904
\end{array}
$$

C. *Multiply. Check by exchanging the factors.*

7. a. $\begin{array}{r} 678 \\ \times 305 \end{array}$ b. $\begin{array}{r} 420 \\ \times 800 \end{array}$ c. $\begin{array}{r} 907 \\ \times 260 \end{array}$ d. $\begin{array}{r} 702 \\ \times 754 \end{array}$

General Review

D. *Copy and solve.*

8. $16\overline{)720}$ $37\overline{)841}$ $48\overline{)816}$ $19\overline{)900}$

9. $53\overline{)3,286}$ $24\overline{)1,390}$ $60\overline{)5,640}$ $32\overline{)4,576}$

10.
```
   20 days  10 hours          14 yards  0 feet          6 feet    7 inches
 - 14 days  16 hours        -  5 yards  2 feet        - 3 feet  10 inches
```

11.
```
   4 gallons  1 quart         16 years  13 weeks         6 pecks  4 quarts
 - 3 gallons  3 quarts      - 12 years  30 weeks       - 2 pecks  6 quarts
```

E. *Answer with one of the underlined words or numbers.*

12. Is 12 a <u>factor</u> or a <u>multiple</u> of 4?

13. Is $\frac{4}{5}$ a <u>proper</u> or an <u>improper</u> fraction?

14. Is 9:00 A.M. in the <u>morning</u> or the <u>evening</u>?

15. Does the Roman numeral DC mean <u>400</u> or <u>600</u>?

16. Does the 4 in 17,054,923,896 mean <u>4 billion</u> or <u>4 million</u>?

17. Does one quart contain <u>2 cups</u> or <u>4 cups</u>?

18. Do most years have <u>365 days</u> or <u>366 days</u>?

19. Does April have <u>30</u> or <u>31</u> days?

20. Is <u>7,143</u> or <u>3,810</u> divisible by 6?

F. *Solve these reading problems.*

21. Psalm 90:10 says that a man usually lives about 70 years. The first men on the earth lived much longer than that. For example, Adam's great-grandson Cainan lived 910 years. Cainan lived _____ times as long as man's usual 70 years.

22. Adam, the first man, lived 930 years after the Creation. Noah was born 126 years after Adam died, and he was 600 years old when the Flood came. According to these figures, how many years were between the Creation and the Flood?

23. Enoch was 65 years old when his son Methuselah was born, and he lived on earth for 300 years afterward. Methuselah lived 969 years. How much longer did Methuselah live on earth than his father Enoch?

86. Multiplying Units of Measure

The examples in the box show how to multiply measures.

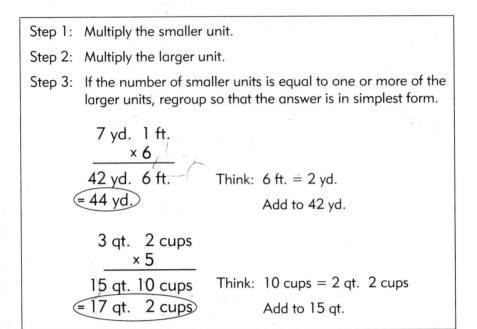

Step 1: Multiply the smaller unit.

Step 2: Multiply the larger unit.

Step 3: If the number of smaller units is equal to one or more of the larger units, regroup so that the answer is in simplest form.

$$\begin{array}{r} 7 \text{ yd. } 1 \text{ ft.} \\ \times 6 \\ \hline 42 \text{ yd. } 6 \text{ ft.} \\ = 44 \text{ yd.} \end{array}$$ Think: 6 ft. = 2 yd.

Add to 42 yd.

$$\begin{array}{r} 3 \text{ qt. } 2 \text{ cups} \\ \times 5 \\ \hline 15 \text{ qt. } 10 \text{ cups} \\ = 17 \text{ qt. } 2 \text{ cups} \end{array}$$ Think: 10 cups = 2 qt. 2 cups

Add to 15 qt.

A. *Write the numbers that fit in the blanks. Do the work in your head.*

1. a. 10 cups = _____ qt. _____ cups   b. 10 pt. = _____ qt. _____ pt.

2. a. 16 days = _____ wk. _____ days   b. 16 ft. = _____ yd. _____ ft.

3. a. 8 qt. = _____ gal. _____ qt.   b. 18 mo. = _____ yr. _____ mo.

B. *Copy and multiply.*

4.
$$\begin{array}{r} 3 \text{ gal. } 1 \text{ qt.} \\ \times 4 \\ \hline \end{array}$$
$$\begin{array}{r} 2 \text{ ft. } 3 \text{ in.} \\ \times 5 \\ \hline \end{array}$$
$$\begin{array}{r} 1 \text{ pt. } 1 \text{ cup} \\ \times 3 \\ \hline \end{array}$$

5.
$$\begin{array}{r} 5 \text{ bu. } 2 \text{ pk.} \\ \times 3 \\ \hline \end{array}$$
$$\begin{array}{r} 4 \text{ wk. } 3 \text{ days} \\ \times 4 \\ \hline \end{array}$$
$$\begin{array}{r} 1 \text{ pk. } 4 \text{ qt.} \\ \times 6 \\ \hline \end{array}$$

6.
$$\begin{array}{r} 2 \text{ yr. } 6 \text{ mo.} \\ \times 5 \\ \hline \end{array}$$
$$\begin{array}{r} 3 \text{ qt. } 1 \text{ pt.} \\ \times 4 \\ \hline \end{array}$$
$$\begin{array}{r} 4 \text{ yd. } 2 \text{ ft.} \\ \times 5 \\ \hline \end{array}$$

Review of Multiplication and Division

C. *Copy and multiply. Be careful with zeroes!*

7.
704	687	850	400	602
× 563	× 307	× 340	× 784	× 860

8.
395	176	800	903	980
× 504	× 700	× 804	× 295	× 603

D. *Write 1, 2, or 3 to tell how many digits will be in each quotient. Do not find the answers.*

9. 72)148   43)932   15)746   38)304   69)548

10. 47)392   56)708   24)5,840   17)1,377   33)4,200

E. *Copy and solve the problems.*

11. 12)916   35)875   48)288   6)806

12. 19)766   8)6,744   53)5,989   24)1,992

Review of Large Numbers

F. *Write numerals for these number words.*

13. two billion, eight hundred million, twenty-five thousand

14. 45 billion, 250 million, 8 thousand, 17

15. eleven billion, one million, ten thousand, one hundred

16. nine hundred sixty-seven billion, fifty-two

G. *Read this number to yourself: 251,043,602. Then answer the following questions about it.*

17. What number is 1,000 more than this number?

18. What number is 200 less than this number?

19. What number is 3,000,000 more than this number?

20. What number is 100,000 more than this number?

87. Zeroes in the Quotient

Study the steps used to solve the problem in the box.

```
      ???   Do before anything else: Notice that there will be 3 digits
  17)3,519  in the quotient.
```

Step 1

```
        2
  17)3,519
     34
```

Step 2

```
       20
  17)3,519
     34
     11
```

Step 3

```
      207
  17)3,519
     34
     119
     119
```

Divide to find the digit in the hundreds' place. Write 2.

Subtract; bring down the 1. Think: There are no 17's in 11. Write 0 in the tens' place.

Bring down the 9; write it beside 11. Divide to find the digit in the ones' place. Write 7.

Notice that you do not need to multiply and subtract if the quotient figure is 0. Just bring down the next digit from the dividend.

Here are some more problems and their solutions for you to study.

```
      406 R 30
  51)20,736
     20 4
       336
       306
        30
```

```
      2,006
  36)72,216
     72
        216
        216
```

A. Copy and solve as shown in the box. Check by multiplication.

1. 32)9,856   25)5,075   56)8,978   44)9,056

2. 19)5,776   46)9,558   27)4,865   36)7,344

3. 43)8,619   15)9,045   22)6,613   39)4,212

4. 62)21,121   35)45,710   17)68,102   28)11,216

General Review

B. *Copy and work carefully.*

5.
$$549 \times 603 \qquad 708 \times 136 \qquad 807 \times 507 \qquad 564 \times 109 \qquad 208 \times 950$$

6.
```
   7 bushels  2 pecks          13 hours  40 minutes
 + 8 bushels  3 pecks        + 5 hours  36 minutes
```

7.
```
  18 years  3 months           6 yards  12 inches
- 12 years  9 months         - 2 yards  24 inches
```

8.
```
4 quarts  1 pint       3 yards  2 feet       5 gallons  3 quarts
         x 4                    x 4                     x 2
```

9.
$$2\tfrac{1}{2} + 3\tfrac{9}{16} \qquad 4\tfrac{3}{4} + 6\tfrac{7}{12} \qquad 6 - 2\tfrac{5}{8} \qquad 5\tfrac{5}{9} - 1\tfrac{8}{9} \qquad 8\tfrac{1}{3} - 3\tfrac{3}{4}$$

C. *Reduce to lowest terms.*

10. a. $\frac{15}{21}$ b. $\frac{18}{30}$ c. $\frac{24}{36}$ d. $\frac{10}{40}$ e. $\frac{16}{36}$ f. $\frac{12}{22}$

D. *Solve these reading problems.*

11. After Zacchaeus met Jesus, he promised to give half of his goods to the poor. If Zacchaeus had $75,000 in the value of our money today, how much did he give to the poor?

12. Zacchaeus also promised to give back four times as much as he had taken. If Zacchaeus had taken $489 from someone, how much did he promise to give back?

13. Mother bought a flat of 24 small tomato plants for $6.00. How much did she pay per plant?

14. Nine of the tomato plants died before they produced any tomatoes. Since the plants that died were not worth anything, what was Mother's cost for each living plant?

88. Practice With Zeroes in the Quotient

A. *For rows 1 and 2, write the number of quotient figures that will be in each answer. Do not solve the problems.*

1. $8\overline{)950}$ $7\overline{)489}$ $9\overline{)6,521}$ $23\overline{)950}$ $65\overline{)379}$

2. $17\overline{)6,940}$ $39\overline{)3,740}$ $78\overline{)79,123}$ $46\overline{)32,096}$ $54\overline{)63,100}$

B. *Copy, divide, and check as in Lesson 87. Be careful with zeroes!*

3. $7\overline{)843}$ $9\overline{)9,261}$ $6\overline{)2,418}$ $4\overline{)8,032}$

4. $12\overline{)3,708}$ $28\overline{)3,928}$ $35\overline{)7,280}$ $49\overline{)3,457}$

5. $24\overline{)72,048}$ $17\overline{)51,765}$ $62\overline{)24,986}$ $58\overline{)75,412}$

C. *Copy and multiply.*

6. $\begin{array}{r} 284 \\ \times\,104 \\ \hline \end{array}$ $\begin{array}{r} 806 \\ \times\,300 \\ \hline \end{array}$ $\begin{array}{r} 367 \\ \times\,630 \\ \hline \end{array}$ $\begin{array}{r} 190 \\ \times\,875 \\ \hline \end{array}$ $\begin{array}{r} 408 \\ \times\,607 \\ \hline \end{array}$

General Review

D. *Answer yes or no.*

7. Is 7,810 divisible by 4?

8. Is 4,185 divisible by 3?

9. Is 149 + 327 equal to 327 + 149?

10. Is 840 – 235 equal to 235 – 840?

11. Does $\frac{3}{4}$ mean the whole was divided into 3 parts?

12. Is $\frac{3}{8}$ a proper fraction?

13. Are $\frac{3}{8}$ and $\frac{3}{4}$ like fractions?

14. Is CM equal to 1,000?

15. Are 12 quarters equal to 3 dollars?

16. To write a number that is 10,000 more than 37,824,015, would you write 37,834,015?

Three-Step Reading Problems

Some reading problems have several hidden steps. For any reading problem, always ask the following questions.

What do I need to find out?

What must I do first before I can find it out?

Sample Problem: Mother bought a sweater for $12.95 and two cards of buttons at $0.65 each. How much change did she receive if she gave the clerk a 20-dollar bill?

Think: **1.** I need to find how much change. To do that, I must first know how much Mother spent. She spent $12.95 plus $0.65 each for two cards of buttons. How much did the buttons cost?

2. How much did Mother spend in all?

3. What was Mother's change?

$$\begin{array}{r} \$0.65 \\ \times\quad 2 \\ \hline \$1.30 \end{array} \qquad \begin{array}{r} \$12.95 \\ +\quad 1.30 \\ \hline \$14.25 \end{array} \qquad \begin{array}{r} \$20.00 \\ -\ 14.25 \\ \hline \$5.75 \end{array}$$

E. *Solve the problems below. Show all the number steps on your paper.*

17. In Mr. Lind's orchard are 18 rows of peach trees with 25 trees in a row. There are also 14 rows of apple trees with 25 trees in a row. Altogether, how many peach trees and apple trees are in Mr. Lind's orchard?

18. Mr. Lind sells peaches for $6.95 a half bushel and apples for $4.75 a half bushel. How much does Mr. Lind receive for 62 half bushels of peaches and 48 half bushels of apples?

19. When Mr. Lind sells peaches for $6.95 a basket, that is not all profit. He pays his hired men $1.35 a basket for picking peaches. He also has other expenses amounting to $3.00 per basket of peaches sold. How much does Mr. Lind have left from 62 baskets after the expenses are paid? (Hint: Figure the expenses for one basket first.)

20. One week Mr. Lind and his men picked an average of 36 bushels of peaches per day. The next week they picked the following amounts: Monday—65 bushels, Tuesday—48 bushels, Wednesday—51 bushels, Thursday—46 bushels, Friday—55 bushels, and Saturday—59 bushels. How much higher was the average amount picked each day the second week than the week before?

89. Chapter 9 Review

A. *Write the answers only.*

1. 5 × 9 + 4	3 × 8 + 6	7 × 7 + 5	8 × 9 + 4
2. 4 × 0 + 7	1 × 8 + 3	6 × 9 + 6	3 × 9 + 5
3. 6 × 6 + 4	0 × 7 + 5	5 × 7 + 5	4 × 1 + 7
4. 4 × 56	6 × 17	5 × 26	4 × 83
5. 8 × 14	3 × 39	9 × 46	7 × 35
6. 5 × 40	6 × 28	8 × 38	2 × 87

7. Round to the nearest ten.

   a. 48   b. 24   c. 37   d. 721   e. 3,906   f. 45,423

8. Round to the nearest hundred.

   a. 721   b. 3,906   c. 45,423   d. 63,760   e. 148,353

B. *Write the numbers that fit in the blanks.*

9. a. 20 days = _____ wk. _____ days   b. 16 ft. = _____ yd. _____ ft.

10. a. 7 cups = _____ pt. _____ cup   b. 12 qt. = _____ gal. _____ qt.

11. a. 16 mo. = _____ yr. _____ mo.   b. 10 pk. = _____ bu. _____ pk.

12. a. 26 hr. = _____ day _____ hr.   b. 28 in. = _____ ft. _____ in.

13. a. 6 pt. = _____ qt. _____ pt.   b. 12 qt. = _____ pk. _____ qt.

Review of Computation

C. *Copy and work carefully.*

14.
```
   13 hours  45 minutes          15 years   6 months
 +  6 hours  23 minutes        −  8 years  10 months
 _____            _____
```

15.
```
   5 yards  2 feet          3 pecks 2 quarts          4 quarts  1 cup
         × 4                        × 6                        × 4
 _____          _____          _____
```

16. 705   496   200   702   870
    x 619   x 406   x 809   x 390   x 480

17. 346   816   409   280   903
    x 800   x 704   x 507   x 495   x 609

D. Write the number of digits in each quotient. Do not solve the problems.

18. 3)786   8)456   8)4,926   9)9,140   7)41,382

19. 14)632   43)259   52)4,027   38)4,168   27)22,690

E. Solve these problems.

20. 28)168   36)756   13)845   45)645

21. 17)7,259   64)3,840   38)7,752   26)9,112

22. 32)6,528   18)9,013   29)59,305   51)16,575

Review of Reading Problems

F. You will need to divide to solve these problems. Change remainders to fractions for some of the answers. Express some answers as whole numbers. Think: What is sensible?

23. Sister Anna needs 26 cups of tomato juice to make soup for the students at Bible school. How many quart jars of tomato juice will she need to open?

24. Sister Anna uses 10 quarts of water to cook noodles for the soup. How many gallons of water is that?

25. Sister Lucy, another cook at Bible school, is putting cookies on plates for lunch. If she puts 12 cookies on each plate, how many full plates can she make with 200 cookies?

(continued on next page)

26. In the dining room at the Bible school, 8 people can sit at each table. How many tables are needed to seat 126 students and teachers?

27. Two boys at one table decided to share the last 5 cookies on the plate. How many cookies will each boy have if they share the cookies equally?

G. *Solve these problems. You will need to do more than one step.*

28. A watering tank holds 90 gallons of water. Two hoses carry water to the tank. One hose can carry 5 gallons of water a minute, and the second hose can carry 4 gallons of water per minute. How long will it take for the two hoses to fill the tank?

29. Mr. Maxwell bought 175 feet of pine lumber at $1.10 a foot and 360 feet of cedar lumber at $0.95 a foot. What was his total bill?

30. Brother James ordered the following books by mail: *Strong's Concordance*—$19.75, *Vine's Expository Dictionary*—$20.45, and *Manners and Customs of Bible Lands*—$12.60. The book company charges postage equal to $\frac{1}{10}$ of the price of the books ordered. What was Brother James's total bill for the books and postage?

31. Apples weigh about 45 pounds a bushel. Ryan picked six bushels of apples and weighed each bushel separately. The weights he recorded were 46 pounds, 48 pounds, 44 pounds, 47 pounds, 45 pounds, and 49 pounds. Did Ryan's apples average more or less than 45 pounds per bushel? How much more or less?

90. Chapter 9 Test

Chapter 10

Decimals

The Lord shall preserve thy going out and thy coming in.
(Psalm 121:8)

91. Adding Three Fractions

When three fractions are added, they must all be expressed with the same denominator. Use the lowest common multiple of all three.

Study the problems in the box.

$$\frac{3}{4} = \frac{9}{12}$$
$$\frac{2}{3} = \frac{8}{12}$$
$$+\frac{1}{2} = \frac{6}{12}$$
$$\overline{\quad\frac{23}{12} = 1\frac{11}{12}}$$

$$\frac{9}{10} = \frac{27}{30}$$
$$\frac{3}{5} = \frac{18}{30}$$
$$+\frac{2}{3} = \frac{20}{30}$$
$$\overline{\quad\frac{65}{30} = 2\frac{5}{30} = 2\frac{1}{6}}$$

A. *Find lowest common denominators and add carefully. Write all answers in the simplest form.*

1.

$\frac{1}{2}$	$\frac{2}{5}$	$\frac{5}{8}$	$\frac{2}{3}$	$\frac{1}{2}$
$\frac{2}{3}$	$\frac{7}{10}$	$\frac{3}{4}$	$\frac{11}{12}$	$\frac{5}{16}$
$+\frac{1}{4}$	$+\frac{1}{2}$	$+\frac{7}{16}$	$+\frac{1}{2}$	$+\frac{7}{8}$

2.

$\frac{3}{8}$	$\frac{1}{2}$	$\frac{1}{4}$	$\frac{5}{9}$	$\frac{5}{8}$
$\frac{1}{2}$	$\frac{5}{6}$	$\frac{2}{5}$	$\frac{1}{3}$	$\frac{3}{4}$
$+\frac{3}{4}$	$+\frac{2}{3}$	$+\frac{7}{10}$	$+\frac{1}{2}$	$+\frac{1}{3}$

3.

$3\frac{1}{2}$	$2\frac{2}{3}$	$4\frac{7}{8}$	$1\frac{5}{6}$	$6\frac{1}{2}$
$+4\frac{11}{12}$	$+1\frac{5}{9}$	$+2\frac{3}{16}$	$+3\frac{2}{3}$	$+2\frac{4}{5}$

B. *Write the lowest common denominator for each set of fractions.*

4. a. $\frac{1}{2}$ $\frac{2}{3}$ $\frac{3}{8}$ b. $\frac{3}{4}$ $\frac{1}{2}$ $\frac{7}{12}$ c. $\frac{1}{3}$ $\frac{1}{4}$ $\frac{1}{2}$ d. $\frac{4}{5}$ $\frac{1}{2}$ $\frac{2}{3}$

C. *Find the missing numerators.*

5. a. $\frac{2}{3} = \frac{?}{30}$ b. $\frac{1}{2} = \frac{?}{24}$ c. $\frac{2}{3} = \frac{?}{15}$ d. $\frac{3}{4} = \frac{?}{24}$ e. $\frac{5}{6} = \frac{?}{18}$

6. a. $\frac{1}{2} = \frac{?}{30}$ b. $\frac{3}{5} = \frac{?}{20}$ c. $\frac{1}{3} = \frac{?}{24}$ d. $\frac{7}{9} = \frac{?}{18}$ e. $\frac{3}{4} = \frac{?}{20}$

Adding and Multiplying Money

Remember the following points when solving problems about money.

1. Keep the decimal points in a straight column for addition or subtraction.	$ 6.48 $4.85
2. Add, subtract, or multiply as you do with other numbers.	0.15 × 1.67
3. Place a dollar sign and decimal point in the answer. Always have two digits to the right of the decimal point.	+ 29.35 33 95
	$35.98 291 0
4. Remember that only the multiplicand in a multiplication problem has a dollar sign and decimal point, never both factors.	485
	$809.95

D. *Copy in straight columns and add.*

7. $5.80 + $0.17 + $24.79 + $356 $93.64 + $65 + $725.19

8. $78.39 + $3.75 + $246.05 + $4.58 $18 + $4.95 + $0.53 + $29.45

9. $236.24 + $6.70 + $450 + $15.99 $75.35 + $8 + $116.08 + $0.57

10.
```
$  56.78    $903.51    $  5.97    $  63.80
  375.29       6.95      80.00      485.67
   10.52      59.00     348.25        6.29
    3.84     375.50      72.64      590.35
+ 452.00   +  22.48    +    .39   +    3.45
```

E. *Copy and multiply.*

11.
```
$0.95      $0.38      $7.46      $8.00
×  35      ×  74      ×  47      ×  36
```

12.
```
$6.19      $3.98      $6.09      $4.82
× 900      × 417      × 380      × 802
```

F. *Solve this reading problem.*

13. Elvin and Joseph picked strawberries for 3 hours 50 minutes in the forenoon and 2 hours 15 minutes in the afternoon. How much time did the boys spend picking strawberries?

92. Practice With Adding and Subtracting Fractions

A. *Write the lowest common denominator for each set of fractions.*

1. a. $\frac{3}{4}$ $\frac{1}{3}$ $\frac{5}{6}$ b. $\frac{7}{8}$ $\frac{2}{3}$ $\frac{1}{4}$ c. $\frac{9}{16}$ $\frac{1}{2}$ $\frac{5}{8}$ d. $\frac{7}{9}$ $\frac{1}{3}$ $\frac{1}{2}$

B. *Write the missing numerators.*

2. a. $\frac{3}{4} = \frac{?}{16}$ b. $\frac{1}{2} = \frac{?}{20}$ c. $\frac{3}{5} = \frac{?}{30}$ d. $\frac{2}{3} = \frac{?}{24}$ e. $\frac{1}{3} = \frac{?}{18}$

3. a. $\frac{1}{2} = \frac{?}{18}$ b. $\frac{3}{4} = \frac{?}{36}$ c. $\frac{2}{3} = \frac{?}{18}$ d. $\frac{1}{6} = \frac{?}{30}$ e. $\frac{3}{10} = \frac{?}{30}$

C. *Copy and solve carefully.*

4.
$$\begin{array}{r} \frac{2}{3} \\ \frac{1}{2} \\ +\ \frac{3}{4} \\ \hline \end{array} \qquad \begin{array}{r} \frac{3}{5} \\ \frac{1}{2} \\ +\ \frac{9}{10} \\ \hline \end{array} \qquad \begin{array}{r} \frac{3}{4} \\ \frac{7}{8} \\ +\ \frac{1}{2} \\ \hline \end{array} \qquad \begin{array}{r} \frac{2}{3} \\ \frac{1}{4} \\ +\ \frac{5}{6} \\ \hline \end{array}$$

5.
$$\begin{array}{r} \frac{3}{8} \\ \frac{2}{3} \\ +\ \frac{1}{4} \\ \hline \end{array} \qquad \begin{array}{r} \frac{1}{2} \\ \frac{1}{6} \\ +\ \frac{1}{3} \\ \hline \end{array} \qquad \begin{array}{r} \frac{1}{3} \\ \frac{4}{5} \\ +\ \frac{1}{6} \\ \hline \end{array} \qquad \begin{array}{r} \frac{9}{16} \\ \frac{3}{4} \\ +\ \frac{7}{8} \\ \hline \end{array}$$

6. $6\frac{1}{8} + 5\frac{11}{16}$ $3\frac{7}{9} + 4\frac{1}{2}$ $1\frac{7}{12} + 3\frac{3}{4}$

7.
$$\begin{array}{r} 7 \\ -\ 5\frac{3}{16} \\ \hline \end{array} \qquad \begin{array}{r} 4\frac{7}{10} \\ -\ 2\frac{9}{10} \\ \hline \end{array} \qquad \begin{array}{r} 4\frac{1}{2} \\ -\ 3\frac{11}{16} \\ \hline \end{array} \qquad \begin{array}{r} 6\frac{1}{5} \\ -\ 1\frac{2}{3} \\ \hline \end{array}$$

8. $8\frac{2}{3} - 5$ $7\frac{1}{6} - 3\frac{7}{12}$ $7\frac{1}{2} - 2\frac{4}{5}$

9. $3\frac{5}{16} - 1\frac{3}{4}$ $3 - 2\frac{11}{12}$ $6\frac{1}{3} - 1\frac{3}{4}$

Subtracting and Dividing Money

D. *Copy in straight columns and subtract.*

10. $100 – $54.97 $428.10 – $327.75 $920.67 – $13

11. $89.32 – $15.49 $520 – $327.50 $703.25 – $69.30

12.
$90.30	$70.00	$365.00	$829.05	$670.89
– 37.87	– 19.40	– 48.15	– 375.95	– 88.00

E. *Copy and divide. Place the decimal point in the quotient directly above the decimal point in the dividend.*

13.   15)$93.00   42)$14.70   51)$83.64   28)$85.68

14.   39)$122.46   26)$130.52   18)$378.90   45)$461.25

F. *Answer yes or no.*

15. Is 5,416 divisible by 6?

16. Is 4 a multiple of 20?

17. Is $\frac{6}{5}$ an improper fraction?

18. Does $\frac{5}{8}$ plus $\frac{1}{16}$ equal $\frac{11}{16}$?

19. Are there 100 years in a decade?

20. Does 40 × 8 equal 8 × 40?

21. Does the 6 in 14,632,905,870 mean 60 million?

22. If 100,000 is taken from 32,560,974, is the answer 32,460,974?

G. *Solve these reading problems.*

23. The Mennonite Church operated a mission in the area around Madhya Pradesh, India, for 53 years. How many weeks is that?

24. A case of 24 cans of crushed pineapple sells for $12.00. What was the price per can?

25. At the flour mill Mother bought 100 pounds of bread flour for $0.19 a pound and 25 pounds of whole wheat flour for $0.27 a pound. How much change did Mother receive from $30.00?

93. Reading Problems With Distance, Rate, and Time

The word **per** is often used to express rate. **Cost per pound** means the cost for 1 pound. To find the cost per pound, divide the total cost by the number of pounds.

3 pounds for $1.65
 cost ÷ pounds
 = cost per pound

Rates are used in travel. The **rate of travel** is also called the **speed**. Speed is often expressed in **miles per hour** (m.p.h.), but it can also be expressed as miles per day, feet per hour, or feet per minute.

miles ÷ hours
 = miles per hour

Distance, rate, and time are used together to solve many reading problems. Learn the information in the box.

To find the **distance** traveled, **multiply** the time by the rate. **distance = rate × time**	**Example A** Rate = 55 m.p.h. Time = 3 hours Distance = 55 × 3 = 165 miles
To find **rate** of travel, **divide** the distance by the time. **rate = distance ÷ time**	**Example B** Distance = 200 miles Time = 4 hours Rate = 200 ÷ 4 = 50 m.p.h.
To find **time** of travel, **divide** the distance by the rate. **time = distance ÷ rate**	**Example C** Distance = 200 miles Rate = 40 m.p.h. Time = 200 ÷ 40 = 5 hours

A. *Solve these reading problems about distance, rate, and time. Be sure to label your answers properly.*

1. In the Old Testament the expression "from Dan even to Beersheba" meant the entire length of the land of Israel, a distance of about 140 miles. If a horse could travel directly from Dan to Beersheba at a rate of 35 miles per day, how long would it take to make the journey?

2. If a group of foot soldiers traveled the 140 miles from Dan to Beersheba in 7 days, what was their rate of travel in miles per day?

3. Suppose a car travels at a speed of 50 miles per hour for 3 hours. How much farther would it travel than the distance from Dan to Beersheba?

B. *Also solve these problems about distance, rate, and time.*

4. In 1492, Columbus sailed across the Atlantic Ocean from Spain to the West Indies in 70 days. This is a distance of about 5,110 miles. How many miles per day did Columbus and his men travel?

5. Some passenger trains today travel about 70 miles per hour. How far could such a train go in one 24-hour day?

6. In the 1800s, a stagecoach could travel from New York to a point in Indiana, a distance of 714 miles, in two weeks (14 days). How many miles per day did the stagecoach travel?

7. In the 1800s, mail was carried by pony express along a 1,710-mile route from St. Joseph, Missouri, to Sacramento, California. If it took the ponies 9 days to make the trip, what was the ponies' average rate in miles per day?

8. If a mail truck today travels 1,710 miles at an average speed of 45 miles per hour, how many hours would be required to make the trip?

9. In the early 1900s, an automobile could travel from New York City to San Francisco, a distance of 2,944 miles, in 64 days. How many miles per day did it travel?

10. Today we drive automobiles at speeds of 55 miles or more each hour. At 55 miles per hour, how long does it take to travel 2,944 miles? (Express the remainder as a fraction.)

11. At 55 miles per hour, how far can an automobile travel in 14 hours?

12. In the early days of the automobile, a person could travel faster by train. Then the 2,944 miles from New York City to San Francisco could be covered in 96 hours (4 days). In that case, what was the train's average speed in miles per hour? (Express the remainder as a fraction.)

13. Now jets can travel at speeds of hundreds of miles per hour. Suppose a jet begins flying the 2,944 miles from New York City to San Francisco at 660 miles per hour. After it flies 4 hours, how much farther does the jet need to travel?

14. The earth is about 25,000 miles around at the equator. If there could be an "equator highway" where cars could drive 65 miles per hour around the earth, how many hours would it take to make the trip, if they drove day and night without stopping? Drop the remainder this time.

94. Decimal Places to Thousandths

Our number system is based on tens. Each place has a value 10 times the value of the place to its right. Our tens system is also called a **decimal system.**

You have learned the names of 12 places, starting with the ones' place and going to the **left.** A decimal point can be written after the ones' place, and then new places can be added to the **right.** These new places are called **decimal places.**

The box below gives more information about decimal places.

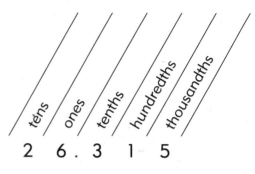

2 6 . 3 1 5

---

1. The first place to the right of the decimal point is **tenths.** The second place is **hundredths,** and the third place is **thousandths.** The decimal point is read "and."

   1.5 is read "one and five tenths"

   3.06 is read "three and six hundredths"

   14.022 is read "fourteen and twenty-two thousandths"

2. **Decimal fractions** are less than one whole. A zero is usually written in the ones' place. A decimal fraction means the same as a common fraction.

   $0.5 = \frac{5}{10}$

   $0.128 = \frac{128}{1,000}$

3. **Decimals** are any numbers that contain decimal fractions. Their value may be more or less than 1. Mixed numbers with common fractions can be written as decimals.

   $13.25 = 13\frac{25}{100}$

   $7.009 = 7\frac{9}{1,000}$

A. Read these decimals when your teacher tells you to.

1.   0.5   0.05   0.005   5.15   15.500   50.055

2.   82.14   0.068   194.3   60.06   4.129   37.8

B. Do these exercises.

3. Write these fractions and mixed numbers as decimals.

   a. $\frac{6}{10}$ b. $\frac{89}{100}$ c. $4\frac{250}{1,000}$ d. $16\frac{3}{100}$ e. $9\frac{2}{10}$ f. $2\frac{29}{1,000}$

4. Write each of these in two ways: first with a common fraction, and then as a decimal.

   a. thirteen hundredths   e. eleven and six hundredths
   b. eight tenths   f. twenty-four thousandths
   c. seven thousandths   g. ninety-nine and four tenths
   d. nine and three hundred fifteen thousandths

5. Write these decimals as common fractions or mixed numbers.

    a. 15.07   b. 4.091   c. 350.3   d. 0.225   e. 6.39   f. 21.005

General Review

C. *Solve these problems about distance, rate, and time.*

6. The Mastons are planning to drive to a mission in Guatemala. They are hoping to drive 750 miles per day. How far will they travel in 4 days at that rate?

7. The distance to Guatemala is about 3,100 miles. How far will the Mastons still have to travel after they have driven 750 miles per day for 4 days?

8. Suppose the Mastons could drive the whole 3,100 miles at an average speed of 50 miles per hour. How many hours of travel time would it take to reach Guatemala?

9. When Brother Titus flew to Guatemala, the plane traveled on a direct route of 2,100 miles. The trip by air took 4 hours. What was the speed of the plane in miles per hour?

D. *Copy and solve these problems.*

10. $62\overline{)\$93.00}$ $17\overline{)\$52.19}$ $35\overline{)\$721.70}$ $29\overline{)\$423.40}$

11.

$5.06	$1.47	$4.09	$3.57
× 482	× 780	× 609	× 305

12.

$ 47.80	$738.05		
288.49	6.75		
17.65	84.37		
3.25	461.20	$510.00	$364.50
+ 354.13	+ 0.69	− 246.70	− 38.95

13.

$\frac{1}{3}$	$\frac{5}{8}$	$\frac{9}{10}$	$\frac{5}{6}$
$\frac{1}{4}$	$\frac{1}{2}$	$\frac{4}{5}$	$\frac{3}{4}$
$+\frac{3}{8}$	$+\frac{3}{4}$	$+\frac{1}{2}$	$+\frac{2}{3}$

E. *Write all these fractions in simplest form.*

14. a. $\frac{25}{4}$ b. $\frac{34}{10}$ c. $\frac{16}{24}$ d. $\frac{24}{16}$ e. $\frac{30}{15}$ f. $\frac{15}{30}$ g. $\frac{15}{24}$

95. Working With Decimals

Counting by tenths, hundredths, or thousandths is much like counting by ones. Whenever a place is "full" with a 9, carry one to the place to the left. Study the numbers below.

Counting by tenths:

  0.1, 0.2, 0.3, 0.4, 0.5, 0.6, 0.7, 0.8, 0.9, 1.0, 1.1

Counting by hundredths:

  4.05, 4.06, 4.07, 4.08, 4.09, 4.10, 4.11, 4.12, 4.13, 4.14

Counting by thousandths:

  2.009, 2.010, 2.011, 2.012, 2.013, 2.014, 2.015, 2.016, 2.017

A. Copy these lists, filling in the missing numbers.

1. 5.6, 5.7, _____, _____, _____, 6.1, 6.2, _____, _____, _____

2. 0.08, 0.09, _____, _____, 0.12, 0.13, _____, _____, _____, 0.17

3. 3.005, _____, 3.007, 3.008, _____, _____, 3.011, _____, _____

4. 8.83, 8.84, _____, _____, _____, 8.88, _____, _____, _____, 8.92

5. 4.095, 4.096, _____, _____, _____, 4.100, _____, _____, 4.103

6. 12.6, 12.7, _____, 12.9, _____, _____, _____, 13.3, _____

B. Read these numbers, or write them with words when your teacher tells you to.

7. 3.01   4.175   92.6   108.011   7.2

8. 850.9   48.12   27.003   6.09   92.065

C. Write each of these in two ways: first as a decimal, and then with a common fraction.

9. a. twelve and thirty-five thousandths   b. sixteen hundredths

10. a. three and eight tenths   b. four and two hundredths

11. a. seven and ninety-eight hundredths   b. thirteen thousandths

12. a. nine hundred five thousandths   b. one and four thousandths

13. forty-one and six hundred eighteen thousandths

Study the examples below to see how decimals can be changed to common fractions or mixed numbers in simplest form.

$$0.6 = \frac{6}{10} = \frac{3}{5}$$
$$0.25 = \frac{25}{100} = \frac{1}{4}$$

$$3.5 = 3\frac{5}{10} = 3\frac{1}{2}$$
$$0.750 = \frac{750}{1,000} = \frac{3}{4}$$

D. Reduce to lowest terms.

14. a. $\frac{50}{100}$ b. $\frac{5}{100}$ c. $\frac{80}{100}$ d. $\frac{75}{100}$ e. $\frac{40}{1,000}$ f. $\frac{250}{1,000}$

E. Change these decimals to common fractions or mixed numbers in simplest form. Follow the pattern shown in the box.

15. 0.5   0.8   7.10   0.50   4.75

16. 0.025   0.300   0.250   0.400   0.070

17. 0.4   8.60   0.08   0.500   0.200

General Review

F. Copy and work carefully.

18. $5,000 – $459.35 $672.05 – $345.25 $920 – $39.75

19. $328.94 + $5.60 + $14.27 + $6 $56.78 + $832 + $175.99

20.
$14.27
×   45

$53.90
×   63

$7.09
× 268

$3.98
× 406

21.

$\frac{3}{8}$
$\frac{1}{4}$
$+ \frac{9}{16}$

$\frac{2}{3}$
$\frac{1}{2}$
$+ \frac{11}{12}$

$3\frac{7}{8}$
$+ 1\frac{1}{3}$

$2\frac{5}{6}$
$+ 4\frac{1}{4}$

$1\frac{5}{16}$
$+ 5\frac{5}{8}$

G. Solve these reading problems.

22. Father bought a dozen spark plugs for $21.00. What was the cost of one spark plug?

23. What is the average speed of a car that travels 290 miles in 5 hours?

96. Adding and Subtracting Decimals

Adding and subtracting decimals is much like adding and subtracting money. Keep the decimal points in straight columns. Add or subtract as with ordinary numbers, but **do not forget to place a decimal point in the answer.**

```
   6.015        13.7
  18.678       - 5.8
   0.462         7.9
+ 35.946
  _____
  61.101
```

A. *Copy and follow the signs.*

1.	0.8	3.51	12.8	0.265	5.33
	4.5	0.72	35.4	7.004	2.75
	2.6	4.10	5.7	4.125	3.06
	+ 3.5	+ 0.49	+ 22.3	+ 3.465	+ 0.94

2.	5.67	2.087	4.3	26.43	67.1
	23.04	0.261	3.8	5.29	6.8
	37.41	6.370	12.6	30.53	7.7
	+ 4.86	+ 3.625	+ 5.0	+ 47.20	+ 13.9

3.	820.45	367.1	90.5	3.460	50.017
	- 216.80	- 18.3	- 75.4	- 0.629	- 29.287

4.	35.00	21.015	730.2	903.10	84.116
	- 19.45	- 7.990	- 264.5	- 371.86	- 47.065

B. *Copy and fill in the missing numbers.*

5. 2.4, 2.5, 2.6, _____, _____, _____, _____, 3.1, _____

6. 6.08, 6.09, _____, _____, _____, 6.13, 6.14, _____, _____

7. 3.995, 3.996, _____, _____, 3.999, _____, _____, 4.002, _____

C. *Do these exercises.*

8. Write these as common fractions or mixed numbers in simplest form.

  a. 0.05   b. 0.125   c. 0.75   d. 3.4   e. 5.500   f. 8.20

9. Write each of these in two ways: first as a decimal, and then with a common fraction.

a. sixteen hundredths

b. sixteen thousandths

c. four and five tenths

d. one and twelve hundredths

e. seventeen and four thousandths

f. five and thirty-nine hundredths

g. fifty-five and six tenths

h. two hundred twenty thousandths

General Review

D. *Write the lengths to which the arrows point.*

10.
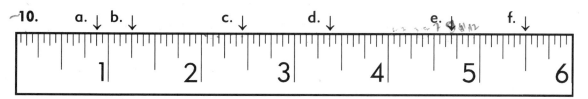

E. *Copy and follow the signs.*

11.

$$3\tfrac{7}{8} \\ +\,2\tfrac{3}{4}$$ $$7\tfrac{2}{3} \\ +\,4\tfrac{11}{12}$$ $$1\tfrac{3}{5} \\ +\,5\tfrac{1}{2}$$ $$8\tfrac{1}{10} \\ -\,2\tfrac{4}{5}$$ $$6 \\ -\,4\tfrac{13}{16}$$

12.

3 bushels 1 peck
            × 5

5 feet 7 inches
        × 4

13. 16)$40.00   24)$41.52   39)$118.56   60)$142.20

F. *Answer* yes *or* no.

14. Is 4,620 divisible by 6?

15. Is 4,620 divisible by 4?

16. Are there 4 cups in a pint?

17. Is 6 a multiple of 24?

18. Is $\tfrac{3}{5}$ a proper fraction?

97. Comparing Decimals

To compare the values of decimals, remember the following facts.

> **1.** Any decimal place has a greater value than the place to its right.
>
> 0.6 > 0.06 because 6 **tenths** is more than 6 **hundredths.**
> 3.06 > 3.006 because 6 **hundredths** is more than 6 **thousandths.**
> 4.17 < 4.71 because **17** hundredths is less than **71** hundredths.
>
> **2.** Zeroes placed at the right of a decimal (**annexed** to the decimal) do not change the value of the decimal.
>
> 6 = 6.0   7.5 = 7.50 = 7.500   0.190 = 0.19
>
> **3.** Zeroes can be dropped or annexed at the right to help compare decimals.
>
> Example: Which is larger—0.4 or 0.37? Change 0.4 to 0.40.
>
> 0.40 > 0.37, so 0.4 > 0.37

A. Copy each pair of decimals, and write >, <, or = between them.

1. 2 _____ 2.0   0.06 _____ 0.60   2.01 _____ 2.001
2. 5.4 _____ 5.04   7.80 _____ 7.8   15.58 _____ 15.60
3. 0.45 _____ 0.54   1.6 _____ 1.55   4.5 _____ 4.399

B. Write each set in order from smallest to largest.

4. 0.09   0.009   0.9   1.11   1.10   1.01
5. 4.4   4.45   4.50   3.7   3.07   3.77
6. 2.09   2.08   2.10   6.01   6.007   6.009

C. Copy and follow the signs.

7.

4.07	23.9	53.105	36.45	8.006
0.95	5.8	27.475	7.27	0.875
18.56	6.4	81.782	10.56	7.238
+ 5.32	+ 64.1	+ 5.035	+ 6.90	+ 1.643

8.

7.050	9.64	628.05	732.0	42.103
- 0.694	- 3.57	- 27.75	- 482.8	- 17.375

General Review

D. *Copy and fill in the missing numbers.*

9. 3.6, 3.7, 3.8, _____, _____, _____, 4.2, 4.3, _____

10. 5.08, 5.09, _____, _____, 5.12, _____, _____, 5.15, _____

11. 6.005, 6.006, _____, _____, 6.009, _____, _____, _____

12. 1.77, 1.78, _____, _____, 1.81, 1.82, _____, _____, 1.85

E. *Do these exercises.*

13. Write these decimals as common fractions or mixed numbers in simplest form.

a. 0.25   b. 4.500   c. 17.8   d. 1.05   e. 0.375   f. 3.40

14. Copy, multiply, and check by exchanging the factors.

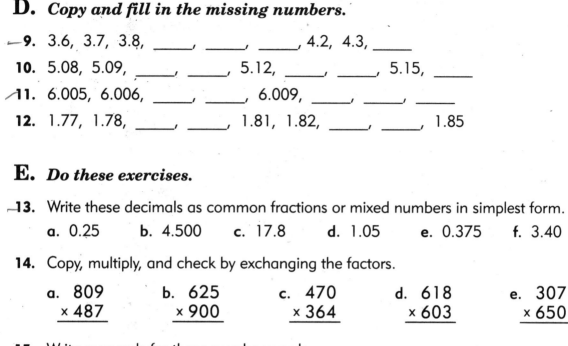

a. 809
  × 487

b. 625
  × 900

c. 470
  × 364

d. 618
  × 603

e. 307
  × 650

15. Write numerals for these number words.

a. thirty-one million, two hundred thousand, four
b. five hundred seventy-three billion
c. one billion, one hundred million, ten thousand, eleven

16. Write the time that is 10 minutes later than that shown on each clock.

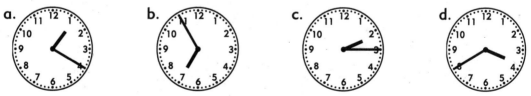

a.   b.   c.   d.

F. *Solve these reading problems.*

17. Cheetahs can run as fast as 70 miles per hour in short bursts. If a cheetah could maintain that speed, how far could it run in 3 hours?

18. The air distance from New York to London is 3,470 miles. If a jet flies the distance in 5 hours, how fast is the jet flying?

19. How long would it take an automobile traveling 55 miles per hour to travel 660 miles?

98. More Practice With Decimals

The example in the box shows how to add a list of decimals.

1. Write the decimals in a column, with the decimal points one below another.	
2. Annex zeroes to fill any gaps at the right of the decimals.	
3. Add as usual. The answer is 333.218.	

$$\begin{array}{r} 54.16 \\ 6.7 \\ 13.058 \\ + \ 259.3 \\ \hline \end{array} \qquad \begin{array}{r} 54.160 \\ 6.700 \\ 13.058 \\ + \ 259.300 \\ \hline 333.218 \end{array}$$

Sometimes whole numbers are included in addition or subtraction problems with decimals. Place a decimal point and zeroes after the whole number, and add or subtract as usual.

Examples: $45 - 28.16 = ?$

$$\text{Write:} \quad \begin{array}{r} 45.00 \\ - \ 28.16 \\ \hline 16.84 \end{array}$$

$5.65 + 72.8 + 35 = ?$

$$\text{Write:} \quad \begin{array}{r} 5.65 \\ 72.80 \\ + \ 35.00 \\ \hline 113.45 \end{array}$$

A. *Copy and solve, annexing zeroes as needed to fill empty places.*

1. $564.35 + 412.607 + 85.9$ $\qquad$ $7.31 + 845.2 + 16.998$

2. $6142.5 + 73.68 + 14.842$ $\qquad$ $8 + 6.5 + 14.927 + 4.28$

3. $4 + 36.7 + 193.459 + 27.18$ $\qquad$ $526.7 + 42.675 + 3.06 + 0.854$

4. $3.075 + 85.6 + 125.16 + 47$ $\qquad$ $63.79 + 4.614 + 5.9 + 75.061$

5. $75.9 + 16 + 4.932 + 0.715$ $\qquad$ $213.78 + 4.5 + 72 + 3.361$

6. $47.6 - 25.72$ $\qquad$ $320 - 80.5$ $\qquad$ $706.254 - 536.79$

7. $86 - 42.479$ $\qquad$ $53.2 - 45.168$ $\qquad$ $285.16 - 78$

8. $17.259 - 5.67$ $\qquad$ $450 - 259.62$ $\qquad$ $60.02 - 19.455$

B. *Copy these decimals, and write <, >, or = between them.*

9. 1.6 ____ 1.60 $\qquad$ 2.05 ____ 2.005 $\qquad$ 4.09 ____ 4.90

10. 17.06 ____ 17.6 $\qquad$ 45.8 ____ 45.85 $\qquad$ 10.50 ____ 10.500

11. 3.7 ____ 3.75 $\qquad$ 6.009 ____ 6.09 $\qquad$ 94.998 ____ 94.89

C. *Solve these reading problems.*

12. Brother Miller, the deacon at Faith Valley Church, counts the offerings given by the congregation each Sunday. One month the offerings amounted to $875.25, $923.48, $843.72, and $1,129.35. What was the total amount given in the offerings that month?

13. What was the average amount given each Sunday? Choose the correct answer: ($932.95, $942.95, $952.95, $962.95)

14. One month Brother Miller paid $1,782.45 for school expenses, $256.84 for electricity and heating, $150 for gifts to Sunday evening speakers, $125.30 for tracts, and $985 toward the Naumans' hospital bill. How much money did Brother Miller have left after expenses were paid if that month's offerings totaled $3,934.95?

15. In Old Testament times, God's people were required to give one-tenth of their earnings to the Lord. Today many Christians also give to the Lord at least a tenth of the money they earn. If a member in Brother Miller's church earned $370.00 in a week and gave a tenth in the offering, how much did he give?

16. If a member who earned $370.00 a week gave one-eighth of his earnings, how much would he give?

17. If the average weekly offering at Faith Valley congregation had been $957.85, how much money would be given in offerings in one year (52 weeks)?

18. Newtown, Connecticut, received the following amounts of rainfall from May through September: May, 7.8 inches; June, 6.2 inches; July, 3 inches; August, 4.1 inches; and September, 5.4 inches. What was the average amount of rainfall per month?

19. A jet and a train traveled the same route. The jet flew at a speed of 645 miles per hour, and the train traveled at 75 miles per hour. It took the jet 3 hours to cover the distance. How far did the jet travel?

20. The train covered the same distance as the jet (number 19). At 75 miles per hour, how long did it take the train to travel the distance? Choose the correct answer: ($25\frac{2}{3}$ hr., $25\frac{4}{5}$ hr., $26\frac{2}{5}$ hr., $26\frac{1}{3}$ hr.)

99. Chapter 10 Review

A. *Read these decimals when your teacher tells you to.*

1.   6.03   17.4   0.18   35.99   22.9
2.   1.003   3.013   4.500   0.017   5.145

B. *Do these exercises.*

3. Reduce these fractions.

   a. $\frac{75}{100}$ b. $\frac{125}{1,000}$ c. $\frac{55}{100}$ d. $\frac{12}{100}$ e. $\frac{6}{10}$ f. $\frac{250}{1,000}$

4. Write in two ways: as decimals and as common fractions or mixed numbers.

   a. sixteen thousandths
   b. four and seven tenths
   c. three and four hundredths
   d. one and forty-six hundredths
   e. seventy-nine and three hundred twenty-five thousandths
   f. three tenths
   g. two and three thousandths
   h. ten and twelve hundredths
   i. eighty-seven thousandths

5. Change these decimals to common fractions. Then reduce the fractions to lowest terms.

   a. 0.25   b. 0.025   c. 0.50   d. 0.4   e. 0.32   f. 0.65

C. *Copy each pair, and write <, >, or = between them.*

6.   0.08 _____ 0.8   5.7 _____ 5.700   6.45 _____ 6.4
7.   25.11 _____ 25.011   0.72 _____ 0.8   3.006 _____ 3.6
8.   14 _____ 14.0   8.210 _____ 8.21   9.3 _____ 9.35

D. *Write each set in order from smallest to largest.*

9. 0.8 0.7 0.9   1.7 1.71 1.72   0.125 0.12 0.025
10. 3.99 4 3.0   4.05 4.5 4.15   2.009 2.090 2.099
11. 7.6 7.18 7.8   8.5 8.4 8.45   3.6 3.06 3.006

Computation Review

E. *Solve these problems.*

12.
$4.29	$75.86	$237.05	$412.64
3.76	8.45	672.94	98.95
0.50	18.35	18.52	336.14
+ 6.37	+ 20.74	+ 164.32	+ 629.47

13.
$40.00	$74.03	$580.00	$926.30
- 37.89	- 19.54	- 265.35	- 75.99

14.
$5.39	$16.75	$8.07	$4.80
× 47	× 56	× 248	× 639

15. $40\overline{)\$26.00}$ $25\overline{)\$87.00}$ $37\overline{)\$39.59}$ $14\overline{)\$50.40}$

16.
$\frac{1}{3}$	$\frac{3}{8}$	$\frac{7}{10}$	$\frac{1}{8}$
$\frac{1}{2}$	$\frac{1}{4}$	$\frac{1}{2}$	$\frac{2}{3}$
$+ \frac{3}{4}$	$+ \frac{7}{16}$	$+ \frac{4}{5}$	$+ \frac{5}{12}$

17.
$3\frac{4}{5}$	8	$4\frac{2}{9}$	$7\frac{1}{2}$
$- 2\frac{2}{3}$	$- 5\frac{11}{16}$	$- 1\frac{5}{9}$	$- 3\frac{5}{6}$

F. *Copy in straight columns to add or subtract. Annex zeroes as needed to fill empty places.*

18.   67.3 + 4.56 + 19.036 + 3.6   5.709 + 15 + 3.52 + 12.8

19.   4.025 + 7.4 + 35.621 + 57   367.4 + 38.009 + 245.85

20.   6 + 42.75 + 3.215 + 495   63.17 + 2.634 + 12 + 0.06

21.   72.08 - 27.007   85 - 34.62   420.087 - 359.2

22.   385.35 - 87.129   6.1 - 4.395   710 - 287.4

(continued on next page)

Reading Problems

G. *Find the answers.*

23. Weekend meetings were planned at the Monroe Church. There were 9 benches on each side of the auditorium. Each bench could seat 7 people. How many people could be seated on all the benches?

24. Marlin and Jacob helped their fathers set up extra chairs. They put a chair at each end of every one of the 18 benches. At the back of the auditorium the boys also set up 8 rows of chairs with 6 chairs in each row. How many chairs did they set up?

25. For the Sunday morning service, 90 chairs were used in the auditorium and 35 chairs in the Sunday school rooms. The Monroe Church owned only 75 folding chairs. How many chairs had to be borrowed from another congregation?

26. Brother Titus drove 318 miles to preach at the meetings. It took him 6 hours to make the trip. What was his average speed?

27. Brother Ivan drove 110 miles to the meetings. Since he did not drive on any four-lane highways, his average speed was only 44 miles per hour. How long did it take Brother Ivan to drive the distance? (Express the remainder as a fraction.)

28. On Sunday morning there were 26 pupils in the preschool Sunday school class, 23 in the primary class, 18 in the junior class, 22 in the intermediate class, 16 in the youth class, and 81 in the adult class. How many people were at church altogether?

29. What was the average number of people in each of the six classes?

30. What was the average number in each of the five children's classes?

100. Chapter 10 Test

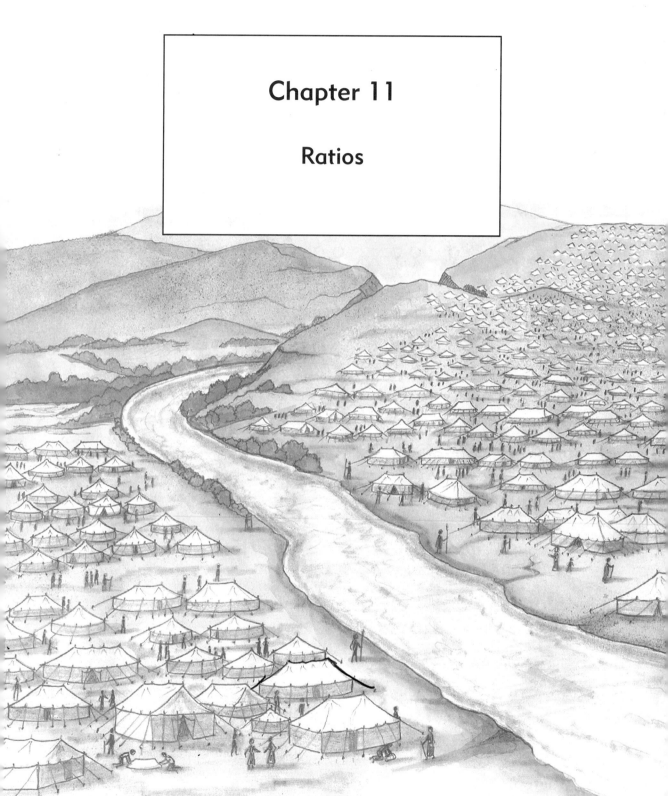

Chapter 11

Ratios

The children of Israel pitched before them like two little flocks of kids; but the Syrians filled the country.
(1 Kings 20:27)

101. Picture Graphs

Graphs are used to compare numbers. A **picture graph** is a simple graph that uses pictures to represent the objects being compared.

The picture graph below shows how many children were present in one Sunday school on five different Sundays. Notice that each small picture is a symbol that stands for **two** children.

Attendance at Sunday School in January

Each symbol represents 2 children present.

A. *Answer the questions by studying the picture graph. (Count by 2's to find the number of pupils present.)*

1. Five symbols on the graph stand for _____ children present at Sunday school.

2. How many children were present at Sunday school on January 9?

3. How many children were present on January 16?

4. On which date was Sunday school attendance the highest?

5. What was the lowest attendance at Sunday school in January?

6. How many more children were present on January 23 than on January 16?

7. What was the difference between the attendance on January 2 and on January 30?

8. What was the average attendance each Sunday?

General Review

B. *Write* add, subtract, multiply, *or* divide. ***Then find the answers.***

9. How many more than 18 is 72?

10. 72 is how many times as much as 18?

11. What is the total of 18 and 72?

12. What is the product of 18 and 72?

13. How many groups of 18 fit in 72?

14. How many fewer is 18 than 72?

15. What is the average of 18 and 72?

16. How many are in 18 groups with 72 in each group?

C. *Do these exercises.*

17. Write **P** for proper fraction, **I** for improper fraction or **M** for mixed number.

   a. $\frac{11}{5}$ b. $\frac{5}{11}$ c. $3\frac{4}{7}$ d. $\frac{8}{8}$ e. $\frac{4}{8}$ f. $\frac{8}{4}$ g. $4\frac{1}{8}$

18. Reduce these fractions to lowest terms.

   a. $\frac{35}{100}$ b. $\frac{24}{30}$ c. $\frac{800}{1,000}$ d. $\frac{4}{50}$ e. $\frac{16}{36}$ f. $\frac{20}{100}$ g. $\frac{250}{1,000}$

19. Change these improper fractions to whole or mixed numbers.

   a. $\frac{28}{12}$ b. $\frac{14}{3}$ c. $\frac{43}{20}$ d. $\frac{60}{30}$ e. $\frac{24}{16}$ f. $\frac{19}{15}$ g. $\frac{26}{10}$

D. *Copy each pair of decimals, and write* <, >, *or* = *between them.*

20. 6.0 ____ 6   5.001 ____ 5.01   0.09 ____ 0.2   1.3 ____ 1.300

21. 4.54 ____ 4.5   9.005 ____ 9.03   8.12 ____ 8.012   3.61 ____ 3.6

E. *Copy in straight columns. Follow the signs.*

22. 6.8 + 13.75 + 2.605 + 47   345.19 + 5.927 + 2.6 + 0.35

23. 720 – 39.47   65.2 – 26.54   93.015 – 8.39

F. *Copy and solve.*

24. 25)$\overline{\$60.00}$ 70)$\overline{\$239.40}$ 18)$\overline{\$265.68}$ 43)$\overline{\$216.72}$

25.

$$\begin{array}{c} \frac{2}{3} \\ \frac{1}{4} \\ +\frac{1}{2} \\ \hline \end{array} \qquad \begin{array}{c} \frac{5}{9} \\ \frac{2}{3} \\ +\frac{1}{2} \\ \hline \end{array} \qquad \begin{array}{c} 3\frac{7}{8} \\ +4\frac{1}{3} \\ \hline \end{array} \qquad \begin{array}{c} 6\frac{13}{16} \\ -1\frac{3}{4} \\ \hline \end{array} \qquad \begin{array}{c} 5\frac{1}{2} \\ -2\frac{9}{10} \\ \hline \end{array}$$

102. Bar Graphs

The picture graph below compares the number of cars in several countries for every thousand people living in the country. Notice that each small car stands for 100 cars. The number of cars has been rounded to the nearest hundred to make the graph.

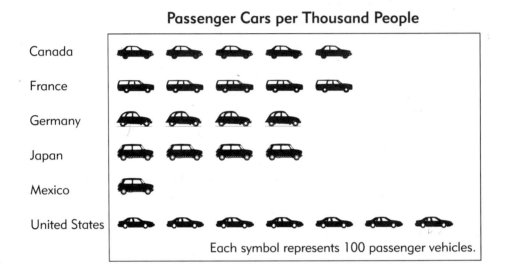

The bar graph below shows the same information as the picture graph, but it uses **bars** to show the different numbers of cars. It is more accurate than the picture graph because it can show numbers between exact hundreds. The numbers on this graph are rounded to the nearest 25.

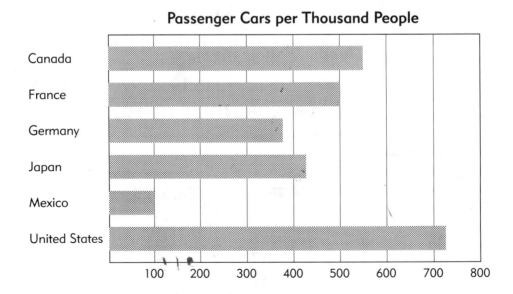

A. *Use the graphs on the first page to answer the questions below.*

1. Each little car on the picture graph stands for _____ cars.

2. Which country has the most vehicles per thousand people?

3. Which country has the fewest passenger vehicles?

4. According to the picture graph, how many cars per thousand people are in each of these countries?
   a. Canada   b. Japan   c. Mexico   d. United States

5. According to the bar graph, how many cars does Canada have per thousand people? Notice that the bar is halfway between 500 and 600.

6. On the picture graph it looks as if Japan and Germany have the same number of cars. According to the bar graph, does Japan or Germany have more cars?

7. Which countries show the same number of cars on both graphs?

8. Count by 25's from 300 to 500.

9. Since you know that the numbers on the bar graph are rounded to the nearest 25, how many cars are shown for Germany?

10. How many cars are shown on the bar graph for Japan?

11. France has _____ fewer cars per thousand people than Canada has.

12. How many cars are shown for the United States on the bar graph?

13. How many more cars per thousand people does the United States have than Canada, according to the bar graph?

14. Which country has closest to half as many cars as people? (Use the bar graph for this one.)

15. How many cars altogether are represented on the picture graph?

16. What is the average number of cars per thousand people for the six countries shown on the picture graph? (Change the remainder to a fraction.)

(continued on next page)

Review of Arithmetic Facts

B. *Write the answers quickly. Use folded paper for rows 17–27.*

17.
$$\begin{array}{cccccccc} 6 & 8 & 12 & 9 & 3 & 10 & 7 & 4 & 0 \\ \times 7 & +5 & -9 & \times 5 & \times 8 & -4 & -7 & \times 9 & +5 \end{array}$$

18.
$$\begin{array}{cccccccc} 4 & 11 & 10 & 8 & 3 & 1 & 8 & 9 & 12 \\ +7 & \times 11 & \times 10 & \times 9 & +7 & +8 & -6 & \times 7 & -5 \end{array}$$

19.
$$\begin{array}{cccccccc} 6 & 3 & 7 & 10 & 12 & 4 & 2 & 12 & 11 \\ \times 6 & \times 5 & +9 & -7 & \times 6 & +9 & \times 8 & \times 4 & -6 \end{array}$$

20.
$$\begin{array}{cccccccc} 5 & 7 & 12 & 11 & 9 & 3 & 10 & 12 & 14 \\ \times 7 & +6 & -8 & \times 10 & \times 9 & +8 & -6 & \times 9 & -9 \end{array}$$

21.
$$\begin{array}{cccccccc} 9 & 16 & 11 & 9 & 4 & 7 & 6 & 13 & 5 \\ \times 6 & -8 & \times 12 & -8 & +5 & +8 & \times 7 & -9 & -0 \end{array}$$

22.
$$\begin{array}{cccccccc} 8 & 12 & 10 & 7 & 3 & 2 & 12 & 15 & 11 \\ -7 & \times 12 & \times 7 & \times 7 & \times 6 & +9 & -3 & -9 & \times 5 \end{array}$$

23.
$$\begin{array}{cccccccc} 4 & 10 & 12 & 9 & 8 & 5 & 11 & 18 & 9 \\ \times 7 & -5 & \times 10 & \times 4 & +8 & \times 5 & -9 & -9 & +6 \end{array}$$

24.
$$\begin{array}{cccccccc} 3 & 15 & 17 & 7 & 5 & 8 & 10 & 9 & 14 \\ \times 4 & -7 & -8 & \times 8 & \times 6 & \times 6 & \times 11 & +4 & -8 \end{array}$$

25. $8\overline{)48}$ $7\overline{)84}$ $6\overline{)24}$ $11\overline{)110}$ $12\overline{)72}$ $10\overline{)120}$

26. $7\overline{)56}$ $4\overline{)20}$ $3\overline{)9}$ $10\overline{)100}$ $11\overline{)121}$ $12\overline{)96}$

27. $9\overline{)36}$ $6\overline{)18}$ $5\overline{)40}$ $12\overline{)132}$ $10\overline{)110}$ $12\overline{)108}$

28. $7 \times \underline{\quad} = 35$ $\underline{\quad} \times 4 = 8$ $\underline{\quad} \times 5 = 60$ $9 \times \underline{\quad} = 27$

29. $8 \div \underline{\quad} = 2$ $72 \div \underline{\quad} = 9$ $\underline{\quad} \div 6 = 9$ $\underline{\quad} \div 3 = 6$

General Review

C. *Do these exercises.*

30. Write as decimals and as common fractions or mixed numbers.
  a. fifty-six and seventy-nine thousandths
  b. two hundred eighty and four hundredths
  c. twelve and three hundred forty-five thousandths
  d. ninety-one and seven tenths
  e. eleven thousand, two hundred eighteen and four hundredths

31. Write these fractions in simplest form.
  a. $\frac{12}{3}$ **b.** $\frac{3}{12}$ **c.** $\frac{250}{1,000}$ **d.** $\frac{30}{16}$ **e.** $\frac{42}{20}$ **f.** $\frac{20}{30}$ **g.** $\frac{24}{100}$

32. $8\overline{)1,724}$ $4\overline{)7,100}$ $7\overline{)8,531}$ $9\overline{)38,406}$ $6\overline{)42,031}$

33. $\begin{array}{r} \$15.67 \\ \times\ \ \ 25 \\ \hline \end{array}$ $\begin{array}{r} \$34.80 \\ \times\ \ \ 64 \\ \hline \end{array}$ $\begin{array}{r} \$8.03 \\ \times 569 \\ \hline \end{array}$ $\begin{array}{r} \$6.25 \\ \times 760 \\ \hline \end{array}$ $\begin{array}{r} \$7.39 \\ \times 407 \\ \hline \end{array}$

34. Write these numbers as Roman numerals.
  a. 127   **b.** 439   **c.** 665   **d.** 914   **e.** 1,506   **f.** 2,058

D. *Solve these reading problems.*

35. Eugene laid 714 blocks in 17 hours. At that rate, how many blocks did he lay in one hour?

36. Mr. Jackson sold a hog for $112.00 at a livestock sale. The cost of raising the hog was $27.00 less than the price he received at the sale. What was the cost of raising the hog?

37. The Miller family is traveling to a fellowship meeting in Ontario, a trip of 1,250 miles. On the first day they drove 586 miles, and by 4:30 on the second day they had driven 527 miles. How many miles did they have left to travel?

38. Honey weighs 12 pounds per gallon. Water weighs 8.3 pounds per gallon. How much heavier is a gallon of honey than a gallon of water?

103. Comparing Numbers by Division

Six boys and four girls are in the fifth grade class at the Bethany Christian School. How many more boys than girls are in the class?

To find "how many more" or "how many less," you **subtract**. There are two more boys than girls in fifth grade. Subtraction is one way of comparing two numbers. Subtraction shows the **difference** between two numbers.

Numbers can also be compared by division. To find "how many times as large" or "what part of," you **divide** one number by the other. The answer will usually be a fraction or mixed number, which should be changed to simplest form. Another name for "comparison by division" is **ratio** (rā' shō).

Compare the number of fifth-grade boys at
        Bethany School with the number of girls.
  Think: $6 \div 4 = 1\frac{2}{4}$, or $1\frac{1}{2}$
  There are $1\frac{1}{2}$ times as many boys as girls.
Compare the number of girls with the number of boys.
  Think: $4 \div 6 = \frac{4}{6}$, or $\frac{2}{3}$
  There are $\frac{2}{3}$ as many girls as boys.
What part of the class is boys? What part is girls?
  Think: 10 people in the whole class
        6 out of 10 are boys $\frac{6}{10}$, or $\frac{3}{5}$, of the class is boys
        4 out of 10 are girls $\frac{4}{10}$, or $\frac{2}{5}$, is girls

A. *Use the chart below to do numbers 1–6. Each one has five answers.*

	Family	Boys	Girls
a.	Marcia's family	2	4
b.	Brent's family	4	3
c.	Arnold's family	2	1
d.	Phoebe's family	1	3
e.	Rebecca's family	3	2

1. How many children altogether are in each family listed above?

    a. Marcia's   **b.** Brent's   **c.** Arnold's   **d.** Phoebe's   **e.** Rebecca's

2. Use subtraction to find how many more boys or girls are in each family. For example, Marcia's family has **2 more girls**.

3. Use division to compare the number of boys with the number of girls in each family. You are finding the ratio of boys to girls in each family.

4. Now use division to compare the number of girls in each family with the number of boys.

5. What part of the children in each family are boys?

6. What part of the children are girls?

B. *Do these exercises.*

7. Write the ratio of the first number to the second as a fraction in lowest terms.

    a. 5 is what part of 40?   **d.** 10 is what part of 16?

    b. 500 is what part of 1,000?   **e.** 8 is what part of 24?

    c. 16 is what part of 20?   **f.** 25 is what part of 100?

8. Find the ratio of the first number to the second. Write the answers as whole or mixed numbers.

    a. 6 is _____ times as many as 3.   **d.** 12 is _____ times as many as 8.

    b. 9 is _____ times as many as 4.   **e.** 20 is _____ times as many as 12.

    c. 50 is _____ times as many as 20.   **f.** 30 is _____ times as many as 9.

9. Find the missing numbers to make equivalent fractions. They could be called "equivalent ratios."

    a. $\frac{4}{5} = \frac{?}{20}$ **b.** $\frac{1}{3} = \frac{10}{?}$ **c.** $\frac{75}{100} = \frac{3}{?}$ **d.** $\frac{16}{32} = \frac{?}{8}$ **e.** $\frac{7}{8} = \frac{?}{24}$ **f.** $\frac{24}{36} = \frac{?}{9}$

10. Are these ratios equivalent? Write **yes** or **no**.

    a. $\frac{1}{2}$ $\frac{15}{30}$ **b.** $\frac{3}{4}$ $\frac{7}{8}$ **c.** $\frac{9}{10}$ $\frac{3}{4}$ **d.** $\frac{16}{36}$ $\frac{4}{9}$ **e.** $\frac{7}{12}$ $\frac{16}{24}$ **f.** $\frac{18}{30}$ $\frac{3}{5}$

General Review

C. *Do these problems.*

11.

$129.45	$ 62.09			
47.39	364.53			
630.74	7.83	$573.01	$27.10	$7.48
+ 219.51	75.28	− 263.95	× 67	× 384
	+ 413.70			

12. 9)$11.34   28)$85.40   45)$541.80   33)$271.92

13.

$3\frac{1}{2}$ $8\frac{1}{2}$ $\frac{2}{3}$ $\frac{1}{2}$ $6\frac{2}{3}$ $5\frac{1}{4}$

$+ 5\frac{13}{16}$ $+ 9\frac{4}{5}$ $\frac{5}{6}$ $\frac{4}{9}$ $- 3\frac{5}{12}$ $- 1\frac{11}{16}$

                                        $+ \frac{3}{4}$ $+ \frac{1}{3}$

104. Measures and Ratios

Can you answer the following question?
    What part of a pound is 6 ounces?

The question could also be stated like this:
    What is the ratio of 6 ounces to one pound?

Think: **1.** One pound is 16 ounces.

2. Compare 6 and 16 by division to form a fraction.
6 is the numerator, and 16 is the denominator.

3. Reduce $\frac{6}{16}$ to $\frac{3}{8}$.
Answer: 6 ounces = $\frac{3}{8}$ pound

A. *Compare by division to find the parts of these measures. Write your answers as fractions in lowest terms.*

1. What part of a foot is
   a. 1 inch? **b.** 6 inches? **c.** 8 inches? **d.** 2 inches? **e.** 10 inches? **f.** 3 inches?

2. What part of a quart is: **a.** 1 cup?   **b.** 2 cups?   **c.** 3 cups?

3. What part of a pound is
   a. 1 ounce?   **b.** 4 oz.?   **c.** 8 oz.?   **d.** 10 oz.?   **e.** 7 oz.?   **f.** 12 oz.?

4. What part of a peck is
   a. 1 quart?   **b.** 5 quarts?   **c.** 4 quarts?   **d.** 6 quarts?   **e.** 3 quarts?

5. What part of a yard is
   a. 4 inches?   **c.** 6 inches?   **e.** 16 inches?   **g.** 27 inches?
   b. 9 inches?   **d.** 12 inches?   **f.** 18 inches?

6. What part of a year is
   a. 1 month? **b.** 4 months? **c.** 9 months? **d.** 7 months? **e.** 3 months? **f.** 2 months?

Equivalent fractions are **equivalent ratios.**

A **pair** of equivalent ratios may be called a **proportion.**

Here are some proportions: $\frac{2}{3} = \frac{6}{9}$ $\frac{1}{2} = \frac{15}{30}$ $\frac{1}{8} = \frac{125}{1,000}$

B. *Write the missing numbers to form proportions.*

7.   **a.** $\frac{3}{4} = \frac{?}{40}$ **b.** $\frac{?}{15} = \frac{2}{3}$ **c.** $\frac{1}{?} = \frac{4}{12}$ **d.** $\frac{1}{6} = \frac{5}{?}$ **e.** $\frac{20}{25} = \frac{?}{5}$

Study the bar graph below. Notice that only the tens are marked. Each space from one line to the next represents two verses.

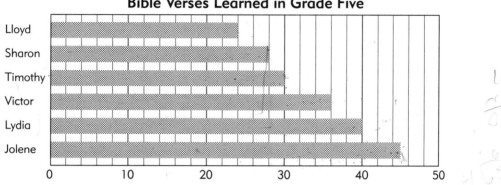

Bible Verses Learned in Grade Five

C. *Use the graph above to do these exercises.*

8. How many verses did Victor learn? How many did Sharon learn?

9. How many verses did Jolene learn? (Be careful! the end of the bar is between two lines.)

10. How many more verses did Timothy learn than Lloyd?

11. How many fewer verses did Sharon learn than Lydia?

12. Write a fraction to compare the number of Sharon's verses with the number of Lydia's.

13. What is the ratio of Timothy's verses to Lydia's?

14. Victor learned how many times the number of verses that Lloyd learned?

15. The number of verses Timothy learned is what part of the number Jolene learned?

16. Did Jolene learn twice as many verses as Lloyd?

General Review

D. *Do these exercises.*

17. Change to Arabic numerals.
    a. XCVIII   b. CCCXLV   c. DCCIX   d. MCLXIV   e. CMXI   f. DXXX

18. Write as decimals and as common fractions or mixed numbers.
    a. sixteen and three hundredths
    b. four and thirty-two thousandths
    c. eight and seven tenths
    d. nine thousandths

19.

$$\frac{5}{6}$$ $\qquad$ $$\frac{7}{12}$$

$$\frac{1}{2}$$ $\qquad$ $$\frac{3}{4}$$ $\qquad$ $11\frac{2}{3}$ $\qquad$ $10\frac{7}{10}$ $\qquad$ 8 $\qquad$ $6\frac{1}{8}$

$$+\frac{2}{3}$$ $\qquad$ $$+\frac{1}{2}$$ $\qquad$ $+12\frac{3}{4}$ $\qquad$ $+6\frac{4}{5}$ $\qquad$ $-4\frac{11}{12}$ $\qquad$ $-2\frac{7}{16}$

105. Rates in Reading Problems

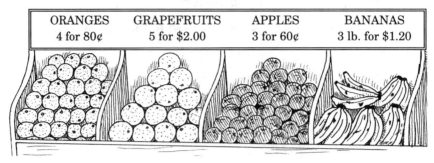

ORANGES	GRAPEFRUITS	APPLES	BANANAS
4 for 80¢	5 for $2.00	3 for 60¢	3 lb. for $1.20

The price of oranges is 4 for 80¢. What is the cost of 10 oranges at that price?

Use two steps to solve problems like the one above. First find the price of one orange. Then find the cost of ten oranges at that price.

4 oranges cost 80¢
1 orange costs 80¢ ÷ 4 or 20¢
10 oranges cost 10 × 20¢ or $2.00

A. *Solve the following problems as shown in the box. Use the information in the picture at the top of the page.*

1. How much would 5 apples cost?
2. Find the price of 7 pounds of bananas.
3. What is the cost of 3 grapefruits?
4. What is the price of $1\frac{1}{2}$ dozen oranges?
5. Find the cost of a dozen grapefruits.

B. *Solve these problems in the same way as for problems 1–5. First find the rate for one, and then find the amount called for in the problem.*

6. If 30 pounds of onions cost $9.00, how much would you pay for 45 pounds of onions?
7. Leslie's car can go 300 miles on 10 gallons of gasoline. How far will it go on 8 gallons of gasoline?
8. Kevin walked 12 miles in 4 hours. At that rate, how many miles could he walk in 7 hours?
9. In 8 days Marcus read 16 chapters in his Bible. At that rate, how many chapters will he read in 3 weeks?
10. Andrew can lay 70 concrete blocks in 2 hours. How many blocks can he lay in 5 hours?

Finding a Part of a Measure

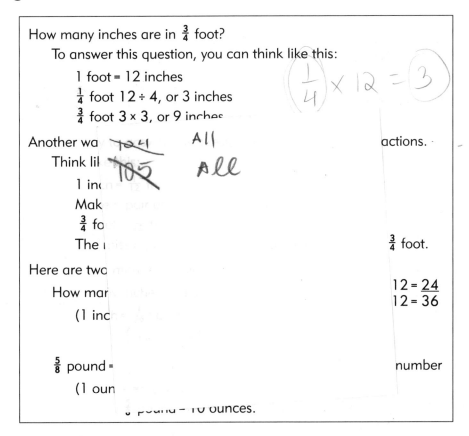

How many inches are in $\frac{3}{4}$ foot?

To answer this question, you can think like this:

1 foot = 12 inches

$\frac{1}{4}$ foot 12 ÷ 4, or 3 inches

$\frac{3}{4}$ foot 3 × 3, or 9 inches

$\left(\frac{1}{4}\right) \times 12 = \boxed{3}$

Another wa ┼д४ᴕ   All ⋯ actions.

Think lil ╲╲╲   All

105

1 inc

Mak

$\frac{3}{4}$ fo

The ⋯ $\frac{3}{4}$ foot.

Here are two

How mar ⋯ 12 = 24

12 = 36

(1 inc

$\frac{5}{8}$ pound = ⋯ number

(1 oun

⋯ pound – 10 ounces.

C. *Use equivalent fractions to find the parts of these measures. Circle your answers. The first one is done for you.*

11. $\frac{5}{6}$ yr. = __10__ mo. $\frac{5}{6} = \frac{10}{12}$ $\frac{1}{3}$ yd. = _____ in. $\frac{3}{4}$ pk. = _____ qt.

12. $\frac{3}{4}$ yd. = _____ in. $\frac{5}{8}$ lb. = _____ oz. $\frac{2}{3}$ hr. = _____ min.

13. $\frac{1}{4}$ century = _____ yr. $\frac{1}{6}$ yd. = _____ in. $\frac{1}{2}$ qt. = _____ cups

14. $\frac{1}{2}$ min. = _____ sec. $\frac{3}{4}$ day. = _____ hr. $\frac{5}{12}$ hr. = _____ min.

15. $\frac{1}{2}$ decade. = _____ yr. $\frac{3}{8}$ lb. = _____ oz. $\frac{1}{4}$ ton = _____ lb.

D. *What part is it? Write the missing fractions (in lowest terms).*

16. 5 oz. = _____ lb.   4 qt. = _____ pk.   8 in. = _____ ft.

17. 20 min. = _____ hr.   3 in. = _____ yd.   12 in. = _____ yd.

18. 2 qt. = _____ gal.   8 hr. = _____ day   4 mo. = _____ yr.

19. 3 days = _____ wk.   50 min. = _____ hr.   12 oz. = _____ lb.

106. Introduction to Percents

Your teacher probably uses percents to grade your lessons. Study the information in the box below to learn about percents.

---

1. The word **percent** means "per hundred." Since **per** means "divided by," percent means "divided by 100" or "out of 100." Percents are ratios based on 100.

> **70 percent** means "70 parts out of 100."

2. The symbol **%** means "percent."

3. 100 percent means 1.00, or one whole.

If you get 100% on an assignment, the whole thing is correct.

If you get a grade of 85%, you have 85 out of 100 correct. The part wrong is 100% − 85%, or 15%.

4. Common fractions or decimals based on 100 can easily be changed to percents. The % sign replaces 2 decimal places.

$$\frac{1}{100} = 0.01 = 1\% \qquad\qquad \frac{75}{100} = 0.75 = 75\%$$

A. *Write the percents that have these meanings.*

1. a. 16 out of 100 parts   d. 89 parts out of 100
    b. seventy parts out of 100   e. thirty-four out of 100
    c. fifty-five divided by 100   f. 97 compared with 100

B. *Change the following fractions to percents.*

2. $\frac{20}{100}$ $\frac{78}{100}$ $\frac{45}{100}$ $\frac{99}{100}$ $\frac{60}{100}$ $\frac{6}{100}$

3. 0.80   0.37   0.59   0.94   0.03   0.15

C. *Do these exercises.*

4. Change these percents to common fractions like those in row 2.
    19%   88%   45%   72%   23%   8%

5. Change these percents to decimals like those in row 3.
    36%   93%   2%   68%   85%   29%

D. *Answer the following questions about percents.*

6. There are 66 books in the Bible. Father and Mother have read 100% of them. How many of the books in the Bible have Father and Mother read?

7. Of all the people in the world, 56% live on the continent of Asia. Write a fraction showing how many parts out of 100 live in Asia.

8. What percent of people in the world live on all the continents other than Asia? (See number 7.)

9. In the United States and Canada, 24% of the people live in rural areas (areas not in towns or cities). What percent of the people do not live in rural areas?

10. On a spelling test of 100 words, Craig had 95 words correct. What percent of the words did Craig have correct?

11. Because of heavy rains and hail, a farmer lost 50% of his wheat crop. That means he lost _____ bushels of wheat out of every 100 bushels that had been in the field.

12. Mr. Young gave $20 out of $100 for mission work. What percent of the money did Mr. Young give?

General Review

E. *Write the fractions that fit in the blanks.*

13. 6 in. = _____ yd.   6 qt. = _____ pk.   6 oz. = _____ lb.

14. 500 lb. = _____ ton   2 cups = _____ qt.   75 yr. = _____ century

15. 27 in. = _____ yd.   16 hr. = _____ day   15 min. = _____ hr.

F. *Find how many are in these parts of measures.*

16. $\frac{5}{8}$ lb. = _____ oz. $\frac{2}{3}$ yr. = _____ mo. $\frac{1}{2}$ hr. = _____ min.

17. $\frac{5}{6}$ yd. = _____ in. $\frac{3}{4}$ bu. = _____ pk. $\frac{1}{8}$ day = _____ hr.

G. *Find the missing numbers in these proportions.*

18. a. $\frac{3}{?} = \frac{18}{24}$ b. $\frac{4}{10} = \frac{?}{5}$ c. $\frac{?}{16} = \frac{4}{8}$ d. $\frac{1}{3} = \frac{10}{?}$ e. $\frac{?}{7} = \frac{8}{28}$

H. *Solve these reading problems.*

19. If Jeffrey can travel 450 miles on 18 dollars' worth of gasoline, how far can he travel on 30 dollars' worth? (Hint: First find how far Jeffrey can travel on 1 dollar's worth of gasoline.)

20. Clyde has 8 boxes of apples. Their total weight is 344 pounds. How many pounds are in 3 boxes of apples if there is an equal weight in each box?

107. Changing Fractions to Percents

In Lesson 106 you changed fractions with denominators of 100 to percents. Since **percent** means "per hundred," the number of hundredths is equal to the percent.

Fractions with denominators other than 100 can be changed to percents if the fraction is first expressed as hundredths. Study the examples in the box.

$$\frac{4}{5} = ?\% \quad \text{Think:} \ \frac{4 \times 20}{5 \times 20} = \frac{80}{100} \qquad \frac{80}{100} = 80\% \qquad \frac{3}{25} = \frac{12}{100} = 12\%$$

A. *Do these exercises.*

1. Finish the factor pairs for 100. You need to know these factors so that you can change fractions to hundredths easily.

$2 \times \underline{50} = 100 \quad 4 \times \underline{25} = 100 \quad 5 \times \underline{20} = 100 \quad 10 \times \underline{10} = 100$

2. Now list these seven factors of 100 in order.

B. *Express these fractions with denominators of 100.*

3. a. $\frac{3}{4} = \frac{?}{100}$ b. $\frac{7}{10} = \frac{?}{100}$ c. $\frac{19}{20} = \frac{?}{100}$ d. $\frac{1}{5} = \frac{?}{100}$ e. $\frac{17}{50} = \frac{?}{100}$

4. a. $\frac{2}{5} = \frac{?}{100}$ b. $\frac{1}{10} = \frac{?}{100}$ c. $\frac{13}{25} = \frac{?}{100}$ d. $\frac{1}{4} = \frac{?}{100}$ e. $\frac{3}{20} = \frac{?}{100}$

C. *Express these fractions as hundredths and then as percents.*

5. a. $\frac{1}{2} = \frac{?}{100} = $ ____% b. $\frac{1}{5} = \frac{?}{100} = $ ____% c. $\frac{7}{20} = \frac{?}{100} = $ ____%

6. a. $\frac{3}{5}$ b. $\frac{9}{10}$ c. $\frac{48}{50}$ d. $\frac{21}{25}$ e. $\frac{3}{4}$ f. $\frac{1}{20}$

7. a. $\frac{1}{10}$ b. $\frac{4}{5}$ c. $\frac{11}{20}$ d. $\frac{3}{10}$ e. $\frac{17}{25}$ f. $\frac{5}{10}$

D. *Write the answers.*

8. Brother Robert gave $\frac{1}{4}$ of his earnings to the church one week. What percent of his earnings did he give to the church?

9. About $\frac{7}{10}$ of the earth's surface is covered with water. What percent is that?

10. The edible parts of the wheat plant consist of about $\frac{3}{25}$ water, $\frac{6}{50}$ protein, $\frac{1}{20}$ fat, $\frac{7}{10}$ carbohydrates, and $\frac{2}{100}$ minerals. Change these fractions to percents, with the correct label for each.

General Review

E. *Follow the directions.*

11. Reduce to lowest terms.

   a. $\frac{20}{100}$ b. $\frac{50}{100}$ c. $\frac{80}{100}$ d. $\frac{75}{100}$ e. $\frac{16}{100}$ f. $\frac{85}{100}$

12. Find the missing numbers in these proportions.

   a. $\frac{1}{6} = \frac{?}{30}$ b. $\frac{?}{5} = \frac{40}{100}$ c. $\frac{21}{24} = \frac{7}{?}$ d. $\frac{27}{?} = \frac{3}{4}$ e. $\frac{?}{16} = \frac{6}{8}$

F. *Find the missing numbers by using equivalent fractions.*

13. $\frac{7}{8}$ lb. = _____ oz. $\frac{1}{2}$ pk. = _____ qt. $\frac{1}{2}$ qt. = _____ cups

14. $\frac{2}{3}$ ft. = _____ in. $\frac{2}{3}$ yd. = _____ in. $\frac{3}{4}$ hr. = _____ min.

15. $\frac{3}{4}$ yr. = _____ mo. $\frac{2}{5}$ min. = _____ sec. $\frac{1}{4}$ day = _____ hr.

G. *Answer with fractions reduced to lowest terms.*

16. 8 oz. = _____ lb.   5 days = _____ wk.   25 yr. = _____ century

17. 16 hr. = _____ day   35 min. = _____ hr.   9 in. = _____ yd.

H. *Solve these problems.*

18. Mr. Williams owns a nursery. He is offering a special this week of 3 trees for $39.00. Mr. Clark wants to buy 7 trees. What is the cost of 7 trees at this rate? (Hint: First find the cost of one tree.)

19.
```
    17.3          670.45          3.749
     4.57          38.6         272.5
   567.8         265.386         67.89          7.028         561
 + 54.275        +  7.82        +14.5         - 3.746       - 48.3
```

20.
```
   $4.09          $7.84          $6.50
   x   86         x  307         x 653        25)$89.25     17)$69.02
```

108. Reading Problem Practice

The problems in Part A include rates like those in Lesson 105. First divide to find the rate for one, and then multiply to find the answer to the problem.

A. *Solve these problems.*

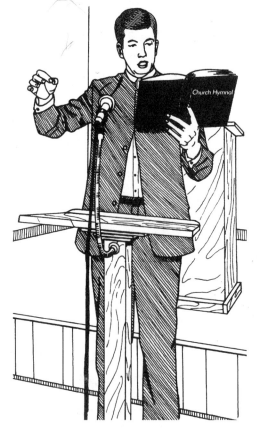

1. Water flows through a pipe into a tank at a rate of 24 gallons in 3 minutes. How many gallons will flow into the tank in 20 minutes?

2. If a car can travel 200 miles on 5 gallons of gasoline, how far can it travel on 14 gallons of gasoline?

3. Raymond sold 6 cords of firewood one week for $210. The next week he sold 11 cords of firewood. How much did he earn the second week?

4. Brother Clifford, the church trustee, noticed that Church Hymnals were on sale at the local bookstore. Knowing that the church needed some new songbooks, he purchased 12 books for a total of $90.00. Later he found that the church could have used 20 books. How much would 20 books have cost at the sale price?

The problems in Part B are distance-rate-time problems like those in Lesson 93.

B. *Solve these problems.*

5. The distance from Mount Carmel to Jezreel is about 20 miles. If Elijah ran that distance in two hours, how fast was he running?

6. A dog team can travel about 25 miles in one day. How many days would it take a dog team to travel the 625 miles from Fairbanks, Alaska, to the Arctic Ocean?

7. How much farther will a jet go in one hour at 625 miles per hour than a car can go in 6 hours at 55 miles per hour? (Be careful! This is a two-step problem.)

8. The distance from Washington, D.C., to Cincinnati, Ohio, is 480 miles. To make the trip in 10 hours, what average speed would you need to travel?

The problems in Part C are solved in a variety of ways. Be sure your answers make sense.

C. *Solve these problems.*

9. The junior Sunday school class at Mt. Joy Church has 15 pupils. Last Sunday 100% of the pupils were present. How many pupils were present?

10. Of all the girls in Sister Sara's classroom, 35% know how to knit. What percent of the girls do **not** know how to knit?

11. Mr. Freeman built the basement walls of his house with concrete blocks that are 8 inches high. If the basement wall is 104 inches high and 8 inches is allowed for mortar between the blocks, how many rows of blocks are there?

12. The rainfall on Sunday was 2.75 inches. On Monday the rainfall was 1.3 inches. What was the rainfall during the two days?

13. If the cost of cutting and wrapping meat is 5¢ a pound, what will be the cost of having a 600-pound beef cut and wrapped?

14. Mr. Ellis sells potatoes for $5.75 a bushel. One day he sold 21 bushels of potatoes, and the next day he sold 18 bushels. In the two days, how much money did he receive for the potatoes?

15. David keeps a record of the eggs he gathers from his father's 25 hens. One week he recorded the following numbers: Sunday—22, Monday—23, Tuesday—21, Wednesday—20, Thursday—21, Friday—24, Saturday—23. What was the average number of eggs he gathered each day?

16. If each of the 25 hens had laid an egg every day, how many eggs would David have gathered in a week?

General Review

D. *Do these exercises.*

17. Change these fractions to percents by first changing them to hundredths.

a. $\frac{4}{25}$ b. $\frac{3}{4}$ c. $\frac{11}{20}$ d. $\frac{8}{10}$ e. $\frac{23}{50}$ f. $\frac{3}{5}$ g. $\frac{24}{25}$

18. Find the missing parts of these proportions.

a. $\frac{4}{5} = \frac{?}{100}$ b. $\frac{?}{10} = \frac{90}{100}$ c. $\frac{13}{20} = \frac{?}{100}$ d. $\frac{16}{?} = \frac{4}{6}$ e. $\frac{5}{6} = \frac{15}{?}$

19.

$$\begin{array}{r} \frac{1}{2} \\ \frac{3}{4} \\ +\ \frac{7}{8} \\ \hline \end{array} \qquad \begin{array}{r} \frac{1}{4} \\ \frac{2}{3} \\ +\ \frac{5}{6} \\ \hline \end{array} \qquad \begin{array}{r} 3\frac{7}{16} \\ +8\frac{3}{4} \\ \hline \end{array} \qquad \begin{array}{r} 7\frac{1}{2} \\ -2\frac{7}{10} \\ \hline \end{array} \qquad \begin{array}{r} 8 \\ -3\frac{11}{16} \\ \hline \end{array}$$

109. Chapter 11 Review

A. *Write the missing numbers in these proportions.*

1. a. $\frac{3}{5} = \frac{?}{10}$ b. $\frac{?}{100} = \frac{19}{20}$ c. $\frac{18}{24} = \frac{3}{?}$ d. $\frac{35}{100} = \frac{?}{20}$ e. $\frac{15}{?} = \frac{3}{8}$

B. *Write a fraction in lowest terms to show the ratio of the first number to the second number.*

2. 6 is what part of 30?   5 is what part of 20?

3. 16 is what part of 40?   8 is what part of 18?

4. 40 is what part of 50?   25 is what part of 100?

C. *Write a fraction in lowest terms to show what part the first measure is of the second one.*

5. 8 oz. = _____ lb.   8 mo. = _____ yr.   8 hr. = _____ day

6. 15 min. = _____ hr.   15 in. = _____ yd.   24 in. = _____ yd.

7. 10 oz. = _____ lb.   18 in. = _____ yd.   25 yr. = _____ century

8. 18 hr. = _____ day   5 in. = _____ ft.   5 yr. = _____ decade

9. 40 min. = _____ hr.   3 qt. = _____ pk.   20 yr. = _____ century

D. *Find the missing numbers by using proportions (equivalent fractions).*

10. $\frac{1}{6}$ yd. = _____ in. $\frac{1}{3}$ hr. = _____ min. $\frac{1}{5}$ century = _____ yr.

11. $\frac{3}{4}$ ft. = _____ in. $\frac{3}{4}$ hr. = _____ min. $\frac{3}{8}$ lb. = _____ oz.

12. $\frac{1}{4}$ ton = _____ lb. $\frac{2}{3}$ day = _____ hr. $\frac{4}{7}$ wk. = _____ days

13. $\frac{4}{9}$ yd. = _____ in. $\frac{3}{4}$ yd. = _____ in. $\frac{2}{3}$ ft. = _____ in.

14. $\frac{5}{6}$ yr. = _____ mo. $\frac{1}{2}$ gal. = _____ qt. $\frac{1}{4}$ doz. = _____ items

E. *Write the whole or mixed numbers to tell the ratio of the first number to the second.*

15. a. 6 is how many times as much as 2?   b. 8 is _____ times 3.

16. a. 11 is how many times as much as 2?   b. 12 is _____ times 2.

17. a. 9 is how many times as much as 4?   b. 7 is _____ times 5.

F. *Do these exercises*

18. Change these percents to decimals.

   a. 81%   b. 90%   c. 45%   d. 3%   e. 72%   f. 29%

19. Change these fractions and decimals to percents.

   a. $\frac{15}{100}$ b. 0.07   c. 0.50   d. $\frac{62}{100}$ e. 0.88

20. Change these fractions to hundredths and then to percents. The first one is done for you.

   a. $\frac{2}{5} = \frac{40}{100} = 40\%$ b. $\frac{1}{2}$ c. $\frac{3}{4}$ d. $\frac{17}{20}$ e. $\frac{37}{50}$ f. $\frac{9}{10}$ g. $\frac{14}{25}$

G. *Study this graph, and answer the questions below it.*

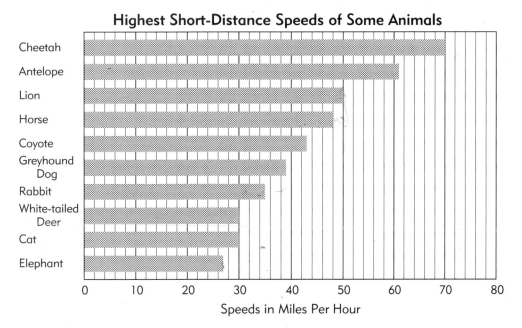

Highest Short-Distance Speeds of Some Animals

Speeds in Miles Per Hour

21. How fast can the fastest animal run?

22. How much faster can a lion run than a rabbit?

23. How much faster can a horse run than a white-tailed deer?

24. Could a lion catch an antelope running at top speed?

25. Could a greyhound dog catch a rabbit running at top speed?

26. How much slower is an elephant's top speed than a cat's?

27. According to the graph, which two animals have the same top speed?

28. The speed limit in Lavelle is 40 miles per hour. Which animals can run faster than this speed limit?

(continued on next page)

H. *Write the answers. For numbers 29–33, write* add, subtract, multiply, *or* divide.

29. To find "how many more," you should _____.

30. To find "what part of," you should _____.

31. To find "how many times as much," you should _____.

32. To find an average, you first _____ and then _____.

33. To find the cost of 8 oranges when 5 oranges cost 75¢, you first _____ to find the cost of one, and then _____ to find the cost of 8.

34. Percent means "per _____."

35. All the parts, or the whole thing, can be expressed as _____ percent.

36. Which is more accurate for comparing large numbers, a bar graph or a picture graph?

I. *Solve these reading problems. For each one ask yourself, Does my answer make sense?*

37. In 1989 the United States produced 41% of the world's total corn crop. What percent of the corn crop was raised in other nations?

38. Fifty out of each hundred acres in the state of Washington are covered by forests. Write the number of forested acres as a percent.

39. Edward spent $\frac{7}{10}$ of his working time one week helping his neighbor build a barn. What percent of his time did Edward spend helping his neighbor that week?

40. Mother bought two yards of material for $5.00. At that price, what would be the cost of five yards of material?

41. On three arithmetic tests Wendell received grades of 79%, 95%, and 84%. What was his average grade on the three tests?

42. Postage for a first-class letter was 29¢. What was the total cost of stamps for 17 letters?

43. If a family spends $474 for food in six weeks, how much is spent for food each week?

44. At $0.60 a dozen, the cost of 18 Gospel tracts is _____.

45. An airplane traveled 2,205 miles in 7 hours of flying time. What was its speed in miles per hour?

----

110. Chapter 11 Test

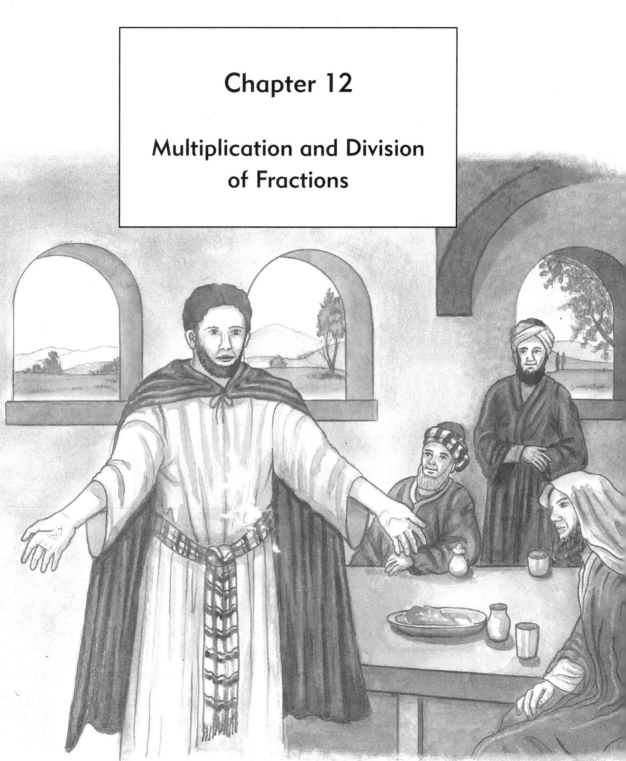

Chapter 12

Multiplication and Division of Fractions

And Zacchaeus stood, and said unto the Lord; Behold, Lord, the
half of my goods I give to the poor; and if I have taken any thing
from any man by false accusation, I restore him fourfold.
(Luke 19:8)

111. Multiplying Whole Numbers by Mixed Numbers

Below are two ways to multiply whole numbers by mixed numbers.

Multiply $2\frac{3}{4} \times 8$.

First way:

$2 \times 8 = 16$

$\frac{3}{4} \times 8 \left(\frac{3}{4} \text{ of } 8\right) = 6$

$2\frac{3}{4} \times 8 = 16 + 6$, or 22

Second way:
$$\begin{array}{r} 8 \\ \times\, 2\frac{3}{4} \end{array}$$

$\frac{24}{4}$ $\frac{3}{4} \times 8 = 6$

$2 \times 8 = \underline{16}$

Add 6 and 16: 22

Use the second way for larger numbers that are hard to multiply in your head. Can you explain the steps in the two problems at the right?

$$\begin{array}{r} 14 \\ \times\, 3\frac{1}{2} \\ \hline 7 \\ 42 \\ \hline 49 \end{array} \qquad \begin{array}{r} 24 \\ \times\, 5\frac{2}{3} \\ \hline 16 \\ 120 \\ \hline 136 \end{array}$$

A. Copy and solve these problems in the second way shown above.

1.
$$\begin{array}{r} 12 \\ \times\, 2\frac{1}{4} \end{array} \qquad \begin{array}{r} 10 \\ \times\, 3\frac{1}{5} \end{array} \qquad \begin{array}{r} 9 \\ \times\, 6\frac{1}{3} \end{array} \qquad \begin{array}{r} 20 \\ \times\, 4\frac{1}{2} \end{array} \qquad \begin{array}{r} 14 \\ \times\, 8\frac{1}{7} \end{array}$$

2.
$$\begin{array}{r} 18 \\ \times\, 3\frac{2}{3} \end{array} \qquad \begin{array}{r} 16 \\ \times\, 4\frac{3}{8} \end{array} \qquad \begin{array}{r} 24 \\ \times\, 2\frac{3}{4} \end{array} \qquad \begin{array}{r} 16 \\ \times\, 7\frac{1}{2} \end{array} \qquad \begin{array}{r} 15 \\ \times\, 5\frac{4}{5} \end{array}$$

B. These problems have small numbers. Find the answers mentally as you did before this lesson.

3. $1\frac{1}{2} \times 6$ $3\frac{1}{4} \times 8$ $2\frac{1}{6} \times 6$ $1\frac{1}{3} \times 15$

4. $2\frac{1}{5} \times 10$ $4\frac{1}{3} \times 6$ $2\frac{1}{3} \times 9$ $2\frac{1}{4} \times 12$

5. $\frac{3}{4}$ of 20 $\frac{2}{3}$ of 24 $\frac{5}{6}$ of 30 $\frac{3}{7}$ of 14

6. $\frac{5}{9}$ of 18 $\frac{7}{8}$ of 24 $\frac{3}{4}$ of 36 $\frac{2}{3}$ of 12

General Review

C. *Do these exercises.*

7. Find the missing numbers in these proportions.

    a. $\frac{3}{8} = \frac{9}{?}$ **b.** $\frac{?}{7} = \frac{16}{28}$ **c.** $\frac{18}{?} = \frac{2}{5}$ **d.** $\frac{15}{18} = \frac{?}{6}$ **e.** $\frac{4}{?} = \frac{20}{25}$

8. Write these ratios as fractions in lowest terms.

    a. 6 compared with 12   **c.** 18 is what part of 30?

    b. 2 is what part of 24?   **d.** 14 out of 21

9. Change these fractions to percents.

    a. $\frac{49}{100}$ **b.** $\frac{1}{4}$ **c.** $\frac{4}{5}$ **d.** $\frac{9}{10}$ **e.** $\frac{7}{20}$ **f.** $\frac{19}{25}$ **g.** $\frac{31}{50}$

D. *Find the answers.*

10. God covered 71% of the earth's surface with water. What percent of the earth's surface is land?

11. Verna studied 30 minutes to prepare for a 10-minute spelling test. At that same rate, how long would Verna need to study for a 40-minute history test?

12. Mother bought $2\frac{1}{2}$ yards of fabric for a tablecloth. At $2.60 a yard, how much did Mother pay for the fabric? (Set up this problem like the ones in rows 1 and 2.)

E. *Copy and work carefully.*

13.
$$\begin{array}{r} 12{,}904 \\ -\ 8{,}247 \\ \hline \end{array} \qquad \begin{array}{r} 70{,}000 \\ -\ 62{,}307 \\ \hline \end{array} \qquad \begin{array}{r} 60{,}502 \\ -\ 43{,}824 \\ \hline \end{array} \qquad \begin{array}{r} 91{,}375 \\ -\ 7{,}936 \\ \hline \end{array}$$

14.
$$\begin{array}{r} \$52.08 \\ \times\ \ \ \ 26 \\ \hline \end{array} \qquad \begin{array}{r} \$83.50 \\ \times\ \ \ \ 38 \\ \hline \end{array} \qquad \begin{array}{r} \$6.39 \\ \times\ 406 \\ \hline \end{array} \qquad \begin{array}{r} \$8.07 \\ \times\ 750 \\ \hline \end{array}$$

15. $8\overline{)\$20.64}$ $6\overline{)\$71.04}$ $23\overline{)\$16.79}$ $45\overline{)\$92.70}$

16.
$$\begin{array}{r} \frac{2}{3} \\ \frac{1}{4} \\ +\ \frac{5}{6} \\ \hline \end{array} \qquad \begin{array}{r} \frac{4}{5} \\ \frac{7}{10} \\ +\ \frac{3}{4} \\ \hline \end{array} \qquad \begin{array}{r} 7\frac{3}{4} \\ +\ 6\frac{1}{6} \\ \hline \end{array} \qquad \begin{array}{r} 11\frac{7}{9} \\ +\ 7\frac{2}{3} \\ \hline \end{array}$$

112. Multiplying Fractions by Whole Numbers

You know that 3×6 equals $6 + 6 + 6$. Both are 18. Multiplication is a quick way of adding the same number over and over.

The same thing is true of fractions. Study the examples below.

$3 \times \frac{2}{5} = ?$ Think: $\frac{2}{5} + \frac{2}{5} + \frac{2}{5} = \frac{6}{5} = 1\frac{1}{5}$ Write: $3 \times \frac{2}{5} = \frac{6}{5} = 1\frac{1}{5}$

$4 \times \frac{3}{4} = ?$ Think: $\frac{3}{4} + \frac{3}{4} + \frac{3}{4} + \frac{3}{4} = \frac{12}{4} = 3$ Write: $4 \times \frac{3}{4} = \frac{12}{4} = 3$

To multiply a fraction by a whole number, multiply the whole number times the numerator of the fraction. Keep the same denominator. Then write the answer in simplest form.

A. *Copy and multiply, following the examples in the box.*

1. $4 \times \frac{2}{3}$ $5 \times \frac{1}{2}$ $2 \times \frac{3}{4}$ $6 \times \frac{2}{3}$

2. $3 \times \frac{5}{16}$ $2 \times \frac{7}{10}$ $5 \times \frac{4}{9}$ $4 \times \frac{3}{16}$

3. $6 \times \frac{1}{2}$ $3 \times \frac{3}{5}$ $2 \times \frac{9}{16}$ $7 \times \frac{3}{10}$

B. *Write these fractions in simplest form.*

4. a. $\frac{12}{8}$ b. $\frac{8}{12}$ c. $\frac{10}{7}$ d. $\frac{4}{24}$ e. $\frac{24}{4}$ f. $\frac{30}{12}$ g. $\frac{12}{30}$

C. *Copy and multiply in row 5. Do the work mentally in rows 6 and 7.*

5.	12	27	28	14	24
	$\times 3\frac{1}{2}$	$\times 2\frac{2}{3}$	$\times 1\frac{3}{4}$	$\times 4\frac{3}{7}$	$\times 3\frac{5}{8}$

6. $\frac{3}{4}$ of 8 $\frac{2}{3}$ of 24 $\frac{4}{5}$ of 15 $\frac{3}{8}$ of 40

7. $1\frac{1}{2} \times 18$ $2\frac{1}{3} \times 9$ $3\frac{1}{2} \times 8$ $1\frac{1}{4} \times 12$

General Review

D. *Do these exercises.*

8. Copy and add.

$$\begin{array}{r} \frac{5}{12} \\ \frac{5}{12} \\ + \frac{5}{12} \end{array} \qquad \begin{array}{r} \frac{5}{12} \\ \frac{1}{4} \\ + \frac{2}{3} \end{array} \qquad \begin{array}{r} \frac{7}{10} \\ \frac{1}{2} \\ + \frac{3}{5} \end{array} \qquad \begin{array}{r} \frac{1}{6} \\ \frac{2}{3} \\ + \frac{1}{2} \end{array} \qquad \begin{array}{r} \frac{3}{5} \\ \frac{1}{4} \\ + \frac{1}{2} \end{array}$$

9. Write the lengths to which the arrows point. Label your answers.

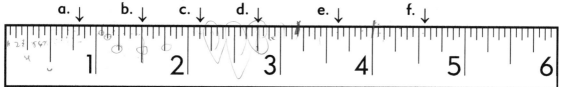

10. Change these fractions to percents.

    a. $\frac{81}{100}$ **b.** $\frac{16}{100}$ **c.** $\frac{47}{50}$ **d.** $\frac{19}{20}$ **e.** $\frac{3}{4}$ **f.** $\frac{1}{5}$ **g.** $\frac{11}{25}$

11. Write in two ways: with decimals and with common fractions or mixed numbers.

    a. three and two tenths   **c.** nine thousandths

    b. five and fourteen thousandths   **d.** forty-eight hundredths

E. *For each purchase below, write (a) how much change should be given and (b) what pieces of money should be given. Be ready to count out the change when your teacher asks you to.*

Sample: Amount of purchase—$4.67; amount given to clerk—$10.00
Change: **a.** $5.33   **b.** 3 pennies, 1 nickel, 1 quarter, 1 five-dollar bill

12. Amount of purchase—$7.58; amount given to clerk—$10.00

13. Amount of purchase—$1.29; amount given to clerk—$5.00

14. Amount of purchase—$12.71; amount given to clerk—$20.00

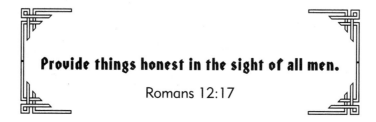

Provide things honest in the sight of all men.

Romans 12:17

113. Multiplying Mixed Numbers by Whole Numbers

The examples in the box show how to multiply mixed numbers by whole numbers. The first step is like the problems you did in Lesson 112.

$12\frac{1}{2}$
$\times 8$
———
4
96
———
100

1. Think: $8 \times \frac{1}{2} = \frac{8}{2}$. $\frac{8}{2} = 4$
2. Think: $8 \times 12 = 96$
3. Add: $4 + 96 = 100$

$13\frac{2}{3}$
$\times 9$
———
6
117
———
123

A. *Multiply as shown by the examples above.*

1. $11\frac{1}{3}$ $9\frac{3}{4}$ $13\frac{7}{8}$ $15\frac{2}{3}$ $23\frac{1}{2}$
    $\times 9$ $\times 8$ $\times 8$ $\times 6$ $\times 4$

2. $12\frac{1}{4}$ $5\frac{2}{3}$ $8\frac{1}{2}$ $17\frac{3}{4}$ $16\frac{4}{5}$
    $\times 8$ $\times 9$ $\times 8$ $\times 4$ $\times 5$

B. *Multiply as in Lesson 111.*

3. 16 32 16 18 12
    $\times 3\frac{7}{8}$ $\times 2\frac{3}{4}$ $\times 4\frac{1}{2}$ $\times 6\frac{2}{3}$ $\times 5\frac{5}{6}$

C. *Multiply as in Lesson 112. Remember to multiply numerators only.*

4. $3 \times \frac{3}{8}$ $4 \times \frac{4}{5}$ $2 \times \frac{7}{16}$ $5 \times \frac{3}{10}$

5. $2 \times \frac{5}{12}$ $5 \times \frac{5}{16}$ $5 \times \frac{3}{4}$ $9 \times \frac{1}{2}$

D. *Add these fractions.*

6. $\frac{3}{4}$ $\frac{3}{10}$ $\frac{7}{8}$
    $\frac{1}{2}$ $\frac{1}{2}$ $\frac{7}{8}$ $12\frac{5}{9}$ $24\frac{7}{12}$
    $+ \frac{7}{8}$ $+ \frac{4}{5}$ $+ \frac{7}{8}$ $+ 15\frac{2}{3}$ $+ 17\frac{1}{4}$

Reading Problems

A number of the reading problems on this page require multiplying a whole number and a mixed number. Study the two examples in the box.

Judith made $6\frac{3}{4}$ dozen chocolate chip cookies. How many cookies did Judith make?

$$
\begin{array}{r}
12 \\
\times 6\frac{3}{4} \\
\hline
9 \\
72 \\
\hline
81
\end{array}
$$

Mother bought $5\frac{1}{2}$ yards of elastic for 28¢ a yard. How much did Mother pay for the elastic?

$$
\begin{array}{r}
\$0.28 \\
\times \quad 5\frac{1}{2} \\
\hline
14 \\
140 \\
\hline
\$1.54
\end{array}
$$

E. *Solve the problems below. Be sure to include dollar signs and decimal points in money answers.*

7. Father said, "I remember when I helped our neighbor bale hay for $0.80 an hour." How much did Father earn when he worked $4\frac{1}{4}$ hours?

8. Grandma said, "When I was 16, I helped a neighbor lady with her housework. She paid me 24¢ an hour." How much did Grandma earn for $6\frac{3}{4}$ hours of work?

9. What is the cost of $3\frac{3}{4}$ yards of bias tape at 28¢ a yard?

10. Glenn is $4\frac{2}{3}$ feet tall. How many inches tall is Glenn?

11. Lavern needs $7\frac{1}{2}$ yards of insulated wire for a science project. How much will the wire cost at $0.24 a yard?

12. How many inches are in $2\frac{1}{4}$ yards?

13. What is the difference between a line $2\frac{1}{4}$ yards long and one that is 80 inches long?

14. How much would you pay for $\frac{3}{4}$ yard of denim at $4.28 a yard? (Hint: First find the cost of $\frac{1}{4}$ yard.)

15. If 6 submarine sandwiches are divided equally among 8 boys, what part of a sandwich will each boy receive? (Think: Will each boy get a whole sandwich?)

16. Father paid $47.88 for 6 rolls of wallpaper. What was the cost per roll?

114. Multiplying Whole Numbers by Fractions

You have already learned how to multiply some whole numbers by fractions. To find $\frac{2}{3}$ of 12, you first divide to find $\frac{1}{3}$ of 12: $12 \div 3 = 4$. Then you multiply to find $\frac{2}{3}$ of 12: $2 \times 4 = 8$.

This method does not work for a problem such as $\frac{3}{4}$ of 5, because you cannot divide 5 evenly by 4. The example below shows how to solve a problem like this. Notice that you first multiply and then divide.

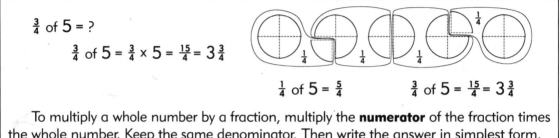

$\frac{3}{4}$ of 5 = ?

$\quad \frac{3}{4}$ of 5 $= \frac{3}{4} \times 5 = \frac{15}{4} = 3\frac{3}{4}$

$\quad\quad\quad\quad \frac{1}{4}$ of 5 $= \frac{5}{4}$ $\quad\quad\quad \frac{3}{4}$ of 5 $= \frac{15}{4} = 3\frac{3}{4}$

To multiply a whole number by a fraction, multiply the **numerator** of the fraction times the whole number. Keep the same denominator. Then write the answer in simplest form.

$$\frac{1}{2} \text{ of } 7 = \frac{7}{2} = 3\frac{1}{2} \quad\quad\quad \frac{3}{8} \text{ of } 2 = \frac{6}{8} = \frac{3}{4}$$

A. *Copy and multiply the numbers below. Write all answers in simplest form.*

1. $\frac{1}{2}$ of 3 $\frac{1}{8}$ of 6 $\frac{1}{4}$ of 7 $\frac{1}{6}$ of 4 $\frac{1}{5}$ of 6

2. $\frac{2}{3}$ of 8 $\frac{5}{8}$ of 12 $\frac{3}{5}$ of 4 $\frac{7}{10}$ of 2 $\frac{1}{2}$ of 11

3. $\frac{3}{4} \times 6$ $\frac{2}{5} \times 10$ $\frac{3}{8} \times 6$ $\frac{4}{7} \times 3$ $\frac{3}{10} \times 9$

B. *Copy and multiply. See Lessons 111 and 113 if you need help.*

4. $\begin{array}{r} 17\frac{3}{4} \\ \times\ 8 \\ \hline \end{array}$ $\begin{array}{r} 7\frac{2}{3} \\ \times\ 6 \\ \hline \end{array}$ $\begin{array}{r} 24\frac{1}{2} \\ \times\ 4 \\ \hline \end{array}$ $\begin{array}{r} 13\frac{3}{4} \\ \times\ 4 \\ \hline \end{array}$ $\begin{array}{r} 16\frac{1}{3} \\ \times\ 6 \\ \hline \end{array}$

5. $\begin{array}{r} 15 \\ \times\ 4\frac{3}{5} \\ \hline \end{array}$ $\begin{array}{r} 36 \\ \times\ 2\frac{5}{6} \\ \hline \end{array}$ $\begin{array}{r} 18 \\ \times\ 5\frac{1}{3} \\ \hline \end{array}$ $\begin{array}{r} 27 \\ \times\ 3\frac{4}{9} \\ \hline \end{array}$ $\begin{array}{r} 21 \\ \times\ 9\frac{3}{7} \\ \hline \end{array}$

Computation Review

C. *Follow the signs. Work carefully.*

6. $\begin{array}{r} 11 \\ -\ 4\frac{5}{8} \\ \hline \end{array}$ $\begin{array}{r} 9\frac{1}{2} \\ -\ 5\frac{7}{16} \\ \hline \end{array}$ $\begin{array}{r} 14 \\ -\ 6\frac{11}{12} \\ \hline \end{array}$ $\begin{array}{r} 12\frac{1}{3} \\ -\ 3\frac{7}{8} \\ \hline \end{array}$

7.
$$\begin{array}{r} 81,000 \\ -16,739 \\ \hline \end{array}\qquad \begin{array}{r} 60,350 \\ -8,945 \\ \hline \end{array}\qquad \begin{array}{r} 37,201 \\ -17,399 \\ \hline \end{array}\qquad \begin{array}{r} 84,093 \\ -32,838 \\ \hline \end{array}$$

8.
$$\begin{array}{r} 6 \\ -3.455 \\ \hline \end{array}\qquad \begin{array}{r} 274.3 \\ -39.59 \\ \hline \end{array}\qquad \begin{array}{r} 80.32 \\ -46.8 \\ \hline \end{array}\qquad \begin{array}{r} 73.7 \\ -6.521 \\ \hline \end{array}$$

9. $7\overline{)4,593}$ $5\overline{)9,260}$ $9\overline{)3,726}$ $6\overline{)34,028}$

10. $18\overline{)3,654}$ $45\overline{)1,845}$ $27\overline{)4,050}$ $32\overline{)33,824}$

11.
$$\begin{array}{r} 4,925 \\ \times\ 7 \\ \hline \end{array}\qquad \begin{array}{r} 6,183 \\ \times\ 8 \\ \hline \end{array}\qquad \begin{array}{r} 9,037 \\ \times\ 6 \\ \hline \end{array}\qquad \begin{array}{r} 8,540 \\ \times\ 9 \\ \hline \end{array}$$

12.
$$\begin{array}{r} 360 \\ \times 635 \\ \hline \end{array}\qquad \begin{array}{r} 709 \\ \times 590 \\ \hline \end{array}\qquad \begin{array}{r} 614 \\ \times 806 \\ \hline \end{array}\qquad \begin{array}{r} 852 \\ \times 700 \\ \hline \end{array}$$

13.
$$\begin{array}{r} 5,509 \\ 17,346 \\ 83,253 \\ +2,840 \\ \hline \end{array}\qquad \begin{array}{r} 39,472 \\ 537 \\ 4,167 \\ +15,335 \\ \hline \end{array}\qquad \begin{array}{r} 78,130 \\ 38,526 \\ 1,243 \\ +19,401 \\ \hline \end{array}\qquad \begin{array}{r} 6,429 \\ 5,444 \\ 51,789 \\ +9,135 \\ \hline \end{array}$$

D. *Solve these problems.*

14. Father cut an 11-foot piece of chain in half to make a swing for the children. How long was each piece of chain? (Use multiplication.)

15. Four children shared the new swing for 30 minutes. If each one had a turn of equal length, how long did each child swing?

115. Multiplying Fractions by Fractions

Sister Mary gave the Beilers an apple pie when Mother was sick. Mother told Janice to cut the pie into fourths and then cut each fourth in half. How big a piece is half of a fourth?

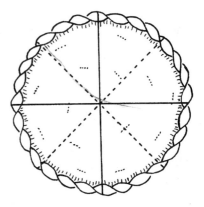

You can see from the picture that if each fourth is cut in half, the pie will be cut into 8 pieces. Each piece is one-eighth of the pie.

Half of a fourth can be written with numbers like this: $\frac{1}{2}$ of $\frac{1}{4}$ or $\frac{1}{2} \times \frac{1}{4}$. The picture shows that $\frac{1}{2} \times \frac{1}{4} = \frac{1}{8}$.

> **To multiply a fraction by a fraction, multiply the numerators and multiply the denominators to make a new fraction. Reduce the fraction to lowest terms.**
>
> Examples: $\frac{1}{3}$ of $\frac{3}{4} = \frac{3}{12} = \frac{1}{4}$ $\frac{3}{8} \times \frac{3}{4} = \frac{9}{32}$ $\frac{5}{8} \times \frac{2}{3} = \frac{10}{24} = \frac{5}{12}$

A. Multiply these fractions as shown in the box. Reduce the answers!

1. $\frac{1}{3}$ of $\frac{2}{3}$ $\frac{1}{2}$ of $\frac{3}{4}$ $\frac{2}{3}$ of $\frac{3}{4}$ $\frac{1}{2}$ of $\frac{7}{8}$ $\frac{3}{4}$ of $\frac{4}{5}$

2. $\frac{2}{3} \times \frac{3}{8}$ $\frac{1}{4} \times \frac{1}{2}$ $\frac{1}{3} \times \frac{1}{3}$ $\frac{4}{5} \times \frac{5}{12}$ $\frac{2}{3} \times \frac{9}{10}$

3. $\frac{1}{6} \times \frac{1}{4}$ $\frac{5}{9} \times \frac{3}{4}$ $\frac{7}{12} \times \frac{3}{5}$ $\frac{2}{3} \times \frac{5}{6}$ $\frac{1}{2} \times \frac{3}{10}$

B. Multiply as in Lessons 111–114.

4. $4 \times \frac{2}{3}$ $3 \times \frac{7}{8}$ $2 \times \frac{9}{16}$ $5 \times \frac{3}{5}$ $4 \times \frac{1}{8}$

5. $\frac{3}{4}$ of 6 $\frac{2}{3}$ of 5 $\frac{7}{8}$ of 4 $\frac{1}{2} \times 7$ $\frac{2}{5} \times 10$

6.
$$15\frac{2}{3} \qquad 21\frac{1}{2} \qquad 7\frac{3}{4} \qquad 25 \qquad 24$$
$$\underline{\times\,6} \qquad \underline{\times\,4} \qquad \underline{\times\,8} \qquad \underline{\times\,5\frac{3}{5}} \qquad \underline{\times\,3\frac{5}{8}}$$

> **As we have therefore opportunity, let us do good unto all men, especially unto them who are of the household of faith.** Galations 6:10

Review of Measures

C. *Write the numbers that belong in the blanks.*

7. 1 pint = _____ cups   1 quart = _____ pints   1 bushel = _____ pecks
8. 1 day = _____ hours   1 peck = _____ quarts   1 hour = _____ minutes
9. 1 quart = _____ cups   1 ton = _____ pounds   1 century = _____ years
10. 1 mile = _____ feet   1 yard = _____ inches   1 gallon = _____ quarts
11. 1 year = _____ days   1 year = _____ months   1 leap year = _____ days
12. 1 mile = _____ yards   1 year = _____ weeks   1 pound = _____ ounces
13. 1 yard = _____ feet   1 foot = _____ inches   1 decade = _____ years
14. 1 week = _____ days   1 dozen = _____ items   1 minute = _____ seconds

D. *Give the answers.*

15. To change 10 feet to inches, do you multiply or divide?
16. To change 10 pints to quarts, do you multiply or divide?
17. To change 10 days to weeks, do you multiply or divide?
18. How many inches are in each measure?
    a. $\frac{2}{3}$ yard   b. $\frac{1}{4}$ yard   c. $\frac{7}{12}$ yard   d. $\frac{1}{6}$ yard
19. How many ounces are in each measure?
    a. $\frac{3}{4}$ pound   b. $\frac{1}{2}$ pound   c. $\frac{7}{8}$ pound   d. $\frac{9}{16}$ pound

E. *Use the correct rule to change each measure. Write any fractions or mixed numbers in simplest form.*

20. 30 in. = _____ ft.   12 gal. = _____ qt.   6 pt. = _____ qt.
21. 4 yr. = _____ mo.   24 days = _____ wk.   8 yd. = _____ in.
22. 8 ft. = _____ yd.   8 in. = _____ ft.   8 in. = _____ yd.
23. 3 pk. = _____ qt.   6 doz. = _____ items   32 oz. = _____ lb.
24. 2 tons = _____ lb.   7 hr. = _____ min.   3 days = _____ hr.
25. 15 min. = _____ hr.   10 cups = _____ qt.   12 ft. = _____ in.

F. *Solve this reading problem.*

26. Dwight needs a board 3 feet 10 inches long to make a shelf for Grandma's flowers. He found a board 6 feet 6 inches long. After he cuts the piece for the shelf, what length of board will be left?

116. Cancellation: A Short Cut for Multiplying Fractions

To simplify multiplication of fractions, we can use a process called **cancellation**. The numerator of one fraction can be canceled by the denominator of another fraction **if they have a common factor**. Study the examples in the box to see how this works.

Canceling once:

$$\frac{\overset{1}{\cancel{2}}}{3} \times \frac{5}{\underset{4}{\cancel{8}}} = \frac{5}{12}$$

1. Divide 2 (a numerator) and 8 (a denominator) by 2. Cross out 2 and 8 and write 1 and 4 instead.

2. Multiply the numerators (1 × 5) and the denominators (3 × 4) for the answer.

Canceling twice:

$$\frac{\overset{1}{\cancel{3}}}{\underset{2}{\cancel{4}}} \times \frac{\overset{1}{\cancel{2}}}{\underset{1}{\cancel{3}}} = \frac{1}{2}$$

Follow the same steps as above, except cancel twice (3 and 3, then 2 and 4.)

Canceling with whole numbers and fractions:

$$\frac{7}{12} \times 2 = \frac{7}{\underset{6}{\cancel{12}}} \times \frac{\overset{1}{\cancel{2}}}{1} = \frac{7}{6} = 1\frac{1}{6}$$

1. Think of the whole number as an improper fraction with a denominator of 1.

$$4 \times \frac{5}{6} = \frac{\overset{2}{\cancel{4}}}{1} \times \frac{5}{\underset{3}{\cancel{6}}} = \frac{10}{3} = 3\frac{1}{3}$$

2. Cancel and multiply as shown above.

A. Copy and multiply. Use cancellation when you can.

1. $\frac{4}{5} \times \frac{5}{7}$ $\frac{1}{6} \times \frac{3}{4}$ $\frac{4}{9} \times \frac{3}{7}$ $\frac{4}{5} \times \frac{5}{16}$ $\frac{1}{4} \times \frac{2}{3}$

2. $\frac{1}{2} \times \frac{1}{3}$ $\frac{1}{12} \times \frac{3}{4}$ $\frac{3}{16} \times \frac{2}{3}$ $\frac{8}{9} \times \frac{9}{16}$ $\frac{7}{10} \times \frac{4}{5}$

3. $\frac{3}{10}$ of 5 $\frac{1}{2}$ of 8 $\frac{3}{4} \times 6$ $\frac{2}{3} \times 12$ $\frac{5}{12} \times 4$

4. $3 \times \frac{2}{3}$ $8 \times \frac{3}{4}$ $2 \times \frac{7}{8}$ $5 \times \frac{9}{10}$ $4 \times \frac{5}{6}$

General Review

B. *Write add, subtract, multiply,* **or** *divide.*

5. To change from a small unit of measure to a large one, you _____.
6. To change from a large unit of measure to a small one, you _____.
7. You _____ to find the amount of change.
8. To find an average, first _____ and then _____.
9. To find the total of a list of numbers, you _____.
10. You _____ to find how many are left.
11. To find the miles per hour when you know the distance and the time, you _____.
12. To find the distance traveled when you know the rate and the time, you _____.
13. To find how many more, you _____.
14. To find $\frac{2}{3}$ of $\frac{3}{4}$, you _____ $\frac{2}{3}$ and $\frac{3}{4}$.
15. To find how many groups of 3 are in 18, you _____.
16. To find how many in three equal groups, you _____.
17. To find the difference between two numbers, you _____.
18. To find what part one number is of another, you _____.
19. To find the cost of 5 pounds of grapes at $0.90 a pound, you _____.
20. To find the price of one pound of apples at 3 pounds for $1.29, you _____.

C. *Write the missing numbers.*

21. 2 yr. = _____ wk.	6 mo. = _____ yr.	3 decades = _____ yr.
22. 1 mi. = _____ ft.	4 min. = _____ sec.	8 ft. = _____ yd.
23. 8 yd. = _____ ft.	8 in. = _____ ft.	3 qt. = _____ pt.
24. 7 cups = _____ qt.	500 lb. = _____ ton	10 oz. = _____ lb.
25. 3 lb. = _____ oz.	2 days = _____ hr.	42 items = _____ doz.
26. 3 cups = _____ qt.	40 min. = _____ hr.	50 yr. = _____ century

D. *Copy and solve.*

27.
```
   10 weeks  4 days        3 tons  1,000 pounds      11 hours  40 minutes
 + 7 weeks  6 days       + 1 ton   1,500 pounds    + 10 hours  35 minutes
```

28.
```
   13 years   3 months      7 yards  12 inches       6 gallons  0 quarts
 - 8 years  10 months     - 2 yards  18 inches     - 4 gallons  2 quarts
```

29.
```
   4 bushels  2 pecks        6 feet  4 inches        2 quarts  3 cups
              x 4                     x 5                      x 3
```

117. Dividing Whole Numbers by Fractions

The Groffs have invited the Hostetters for Sunday dinner. Mother Groff made 4 pumpkin pies. She cut each pie into 6 pieces. How many pieces of pie did Mother have?

You can find how many pieces of pie by looking at the picture. You can also find the number of pieces of pie by thinking, "How many sixths are in 4 wholes?" One pie has 6 sixths, so 4 pies have 24 sixths.

Finding how many sixths are in 4 pies is the same as **dividing** 4 pies by $\frac{1}{6}$. Study the rule below.

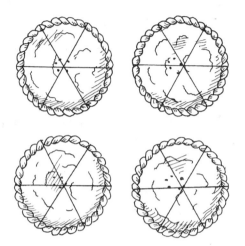

$4 \div \frac{1}{6}$ means "How many sixths are in 4?" $4 \div \frac{1}{6} = 4 \times 6$, or 24

To **divide** a whole number by a fraction with a numerator of **1**, **multiply** the whole number times the denominator of the fraction.

A. *Write the answers to these problems.*

1. $3 \div \frac{1}{3}$	$5 \div \frac{1}{4}$	$6 \div \frac{1}{3}$	$2 \div \frac{1}{8}$	$7 \div \frac{1}{3}$
2. $5 \div \frac{1}{2}$	$8 \div \frac{1}{3}$	$4 \div \frac{1}{4}$	$6 \div \frac{1}{8}$	$3 \div \frac{1}{5}$

Does it seem strange to **multiply** in order to **divide** by a fraction? In Rows 3 and 4 you **divide** in order to **multiply** by a fraction.

3. $\frac{1}{3} \times 9$	$\frac{1}{2} \times 6$	$\frac{1}{4} \times 24$	$\frac{1}{3}$ of 12	$\frac{1}{5}$ of 10
4. $\frac{1}{6} \times 30$	$\frac{1}{2} \times 14$	$\frac{1}{8} \times 32$	$\frac{1}{6}$ of 36	$\frac{1}{10}$ of 40

B. *Write the numbers that belong in the blanks. Be careful!*

5. ____ × 6 = 42	8 × ____ = 16	12 × ____ = 60	____ × 9 = 63
6. 12 ÷ ____ = 4	____ ÷ 7 = 7	____ ÷ 6 = 9	____ ÷ 9 = 3
7. ____ ÷ 5 = 4	____ ÷ 8 = 2	56 ÷ ____ = 8	30 ÷ ____ = 5

General Review

C. *Copy and solve. Use cancellation when you can in rows 8–11.*

8. $\frac{3}{4} \times \frac{7}{9}$ $\frac{1}{3} \times \frac{3}{8}$ $\frac{3}{5} \times \frac{11}{12}$ $\frac{2}{3} \times \frac{3}{4}$ $\frac{13}{16} \times \frac{4}{5}$

9. $\frac{1}{2} \times \frac{2}{3}$ $\frac{7}{12} \times \frac{2}{7}$ $\frac{9}{10} \times \frac{5}{6}$ $\frac{1}{4} \times \frac{1}{8}$ $\frac{1}{6} \times \frac{4}{11}$

10. $3 \times \frac{4}{5}$ $8 \times \frac{1}{6}$ $5 \times \frac{2}{3}$ $4 \times \frac{1}{8}$ $6 \times \frac{2}{3}$

11. $\frac{2}{5} \times 10$ $\frac{4}{7} \times 2$ $\frac{3}{8} \times 2$ $\frac{1}{2} \times 5$ $\frac{3}{4} \times 7$

12.
$\begin{array}{r} 12 \\ \times\,4\frac{2}{3} \\ \hline \end{array}$ $\begin{array}{r} 30 \\ \times\,3\frac{1}{6} \\ \hline \end{array}$ $\begin{array}{r} 28 \\ \times\,2\frac{3}{4} \\ \hline \end{array}$ $\begin{array}{r} 17\frac{1}{3} \\ \times\,9 \\ \hline \end{array}$ $\begin{array}{r} 21\frac{1}{2} \\ \times\,8 \\ \hline \end{array}$

D. *Write the missing numbers.*

13. 3 in. = _____ ft.   15 yd. = _____ ft.   15 sec. = _____ min.

14. 15 qt. = _____ gal.   3 pt. = _____ qt.   2 centuries = _____ yr.

15. 4 lb. = _____ oz.   4 oz. = _____ lb.   90 min. = _____ hr.

E. *Write numerals for these number words.*

16. seventy-five billion, three hundred million

17. eight hundred forty million, seventeen

18. twelve billion, twenty thousand

19. one billion, eleven million, ten thousand, one hundred

20. thirty-six and fifty-nine thousandths

F. *Write as Roman numerals.*

21. a. 47   b. 470   c. 658   d. 914   e. 2,037   f. 1,862

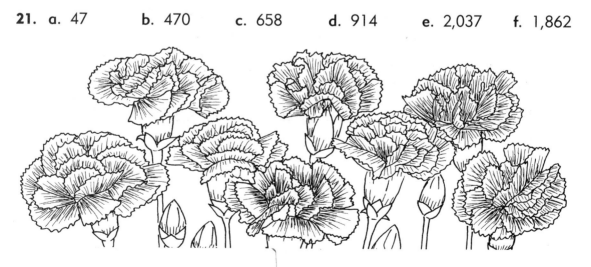

118. Dividing Fractions by Whole Numbers

Four boys shared half of a cherry pie equally. How much of the pie did each boy have?

The picture shows half of the pie divided into 4 equal parts. To solve the problem without a picture, you can think: $\frac{1}{4}$ of $\frac{1}{2} = \frac{1}{4} \times \frac{1}{2} = \frac{1}{8}$.

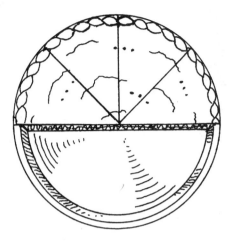

Each boy had $\frac{1}{8}$ of the pie.
The problem can also be stated this way:
$$\frac{1}{2} \div 4 = \frac{1}{8}.$$

The easiest way to divide fractions is to change one number and multiply. In Lesson 117 you multiplied 4×2 in order to divide 4 by $\frac{1}{2}$. You also multiply to divide $\frac{1}{2}$ by 4. You multiply $\frac{1}{2} \times \frac{1}{4}$, because $\frac{1}{2} \div 4$ is the same as $\frac{1}{4}$ of $\frac{1}{2}$.

The box below summarizes how to divide fractions by multiplying.

To divide fractions:

1. Invert the **divisor** in the problem.

    To **invert** means to exchange the numerator and denominator. Thus $\frac{1}{5}$ becomes $\frac{5}{1}$, 4 $(\frac{4}{1})$ becomes $\frac{1}{4}$, and $\frac{2}{3}$ becomes $\frac{3}{2}$.

2. **Multiply** the dividend and the inverted divisor.

    $\frac{1}{5} \div 4 = \frac{1}{5} \div \frac{1}{4}$ Change $\frac{4}{1}$ to $\frac{1}{4}$. Multiply: $\frac{1}{5} \times \frac{1}{4} = \frac{1}{20}$

The same principle was used in Lesson 117. $5 \div \frac{1}{3} = \frac{5}{1} \times \frac{3}{1} = 15$

A. *Divide as shown in the box. Write answers in simplest form.*

1. $\frac{2}{3} \div 5$ $\frac{1}{4} \div 4$ $\frac{3}{5} \div 2$ $\frac{1}{2} \div 8$ $\frac{3}{4} \div 3$

2. $\frac{1}{5} \div 6$ $\frac{1}{4} \div 2$ $\frac{2}{3} \div 4$ $\frac{5}{8} \div 2$ $\frac{6}{7} \div 3$

3. $\frac{5}{9} \div 10$ $\frac{3}{7} \div 12$ $\frac{1}{2} \div 2$ $\frac{5}{6} \div 5$ $\frac{4}{5} \div 2$

4. $7 \div \frac{1}{2}$ $5 \div \frac{1}{3}$ $4 \div \frac{1}{4}$ $2 \div \frac{1}{9}$ $6 \div \frac{1}{5}$

General Review

B. *Copy and solve. Use cancellation when you can in rows 5 and 6.*

5. $6 \times \frac{3}{8}$ $\frac{1}{4} \times \frac{2}{3}$ $\frac{1}{2} \times 7$ $\frac{5}{8} \times \frac{3}{10}$ $4 \times \frac{1}{6}$

6. $\frac{7}{16} \times \frac{4}{5}$ $\frac{1}{3} \times 9$ $\frac{3}{7} \times \frac{1}{2}$ $\frac{7}{8} \times 4$ $6 \times \frac{2}{3}$

7.
$$13\frac{1}{2} \quad\quad 12 \quad\quad 15 \quad\quad 11\frac{1}{3} \quad\quad 14$$
$$\underline{\times 6} \quad\quad \underline{\times 9\frac{3}{4}} \quad\quad \underline{\times 6\frac{1}{3}} \quad\quad \underline{\times 9} \quad\quad \underline{\times 4\frac{3}{7}}$$

8.
$$2{,}309 \quad\quad 4{,}629 \quad\quad 6{,}370 \quad\quad 5{,}829$$
$$\underline{\times \quad 29} \quad\quad \underline{\times \quad 34} \quad\quad \underline{\times \quad 63} \quad\quad \underline{\times \quad 50}$$

9.
$$307 \quad\quad 680 \quad\quad 794 \quad\quad 825$$
$$\underline{\times 250} \quad\quad \underline{\times 637} \quad\quad \underline{\times 307} \quad\quad \underline{\times 416}$$

10. $16\overline{)848}$ $35\overline{)5{,}600}$ $42\overline{)12{,}936}$ $29\overline{)9{,}889}$

Reading Problems

C. *These reading problems contain fractions. Solve them carefully.*

11. Abraham lived $\frac{3}{7}$ of his life before he entered the land of Canaan. Abraham lived to be 175 years old. How old was he when he entered the land of Canaan?

12. An adult should drink about $\frac{1}{2}$ gallon of water a day. How many gallons of water should an adult drink in 30 days?

13. A cookie recipe calls for $\frac{3}{4}$ cup of sugar. Sally is making $\frac{2}{3}$ of a batch of cookies. How much sugar will she need?

14. The recipe calls for 2 cups of flour. How much flour will Sally use for $\frac{2}{3}$ of a batch?

119. Dividing Fractions by Fractions

In Lesson 118 you learned the two-step rule for dividing fractions by whole numbers. The same two steps can be used to divide fractions by fractions. Study the examples in the box.

What is $\frac{1}{2} \div \frac{1}{3}$?   **1.** Invert the divisor; $\frac{1}{3}$ becomes $\frac{3}{1}$.

   2. Multiply. $\frac{1}{2} \times \frac{3}{1} = \frac{3}{2} = 1\frac{1}{2}$

What is $\frac{1}{4} \div \frac{3}{4}$? $\frac{1}{4} \div \frac{3}{4} = \frac{1}{\overset{}{\underset{1}{4}}} \times \frac{\overset{1}{4}}{3} = \frac{1}{3}$

You may be surprised that the quotient in the first division is larger than the dividend and divisor. If the divisor is a fraction smaller than the dividend, the quotient is **always** larger. Think of it this way:

$\frac{1}{2} \div \frac{1}{3}$ means: "How many thirds are in $\frac{1}{2}$?"

There are $1\frac{1}{2}$ thirds in $\frac{1}{2}$.

$\frac{1}{4} \div \frac{3}{4}$ means: "How many $\frac{3}{4}$'s are in $\frac{1}{4}$?"

Only $\frac{1}{3}$ of $\frac{3}{4}$ is in $\frac{1}{4}$.

A. *Copy and divide as shown in the box. Cancel when you can.*

1. $\frac{2}{3} \div \frac{1}{2}$ $\frac{2}{5} \div \frac{2}{3}$ $\frac{3}{4} \div \frac{1}{2}$ $\frac{1}{8} \div \frac{5}{12}$

2. $\frac{4}{5} \div \frac{2}{5}$ $\frac{1}{2} \div \frac{2}{3}$ $\frac{3}{8} \div \frac{3}{8}$ $\frac{3}{7} \div \frac{9}{28}$

3. $\frac{1}{6} \div \frac{1}{2}$ $\frac{7}{15} \div \frac{4}{21}$ $\frac{3}{8} \div \frac{9}{16}$ $\frac{5}{16} \div \frac{1}{4}$

4. $7 \div \frac{1}{4}$ $6 \div \frac{2}{3}$ $3 \div \frac{3}{4}$ $8 \div \frac{6}{7}$

5. $\frac{2}{5} \div 3$ $\frac{3}{4} \div 2$ $\frac{6}{7} \div 4$ $\frac{9}{16} \div 3$

Dividing Fractions in Reading Problems

Before this lesson, whenever you needed to divide in reading problems, you always knew that the larger number was the dividend and the smaller number was the divisor. Now you have learned that small numbers can be divided by larger ones.

When you divide **fractions** to solve reading problems, be very careful to divide the right number in the problem. Think: What is being divided? That number is the **dividend,** which you write first.

Example 1:   Father bought 3 bags of chicken feed. Carmen feeds $\frac{1}{4}$ bag of feed to the chickens each day. How many days will the feed last?

Think: The 3 bags of feed are being divided.

Solution: The feed will last 12 days. $3 \div \frac{1}{4} = \frac{3}{1} \times \frac{4}{1} = \frac{12}{1} = 12$

Example 2:   Three people share $\frac{3}{4}$ apple. What part of the apple will each person have?

Think: The $\frac{3}{4}$ apple is being divided.

Solution: Each person will have $\frac{1}{4}$ apple. $\frac{3}{4} \div \frac{3}{1} = \frac{\cancel{3}^{1}}{4} \times \frac{1}{\cancel{3}_{1}} = \frac{1}{4}$

B. *Solve the following problems.*

6. When Mr. Roberts noticed that his pigs were coughing, he bought $\frac{1}{2}$ pint of antibiotic to mix with the pigs' feed. The directions say that $\frac{1}{10}$ pint of the antibiotic should be used each day. How many days will the $\frac{1}{2}$ pint of antibiotic last?

7. Paula sprinkled $\frac{2}{3}$ cup of sugar on top of 4 small chocolate-applesauce cakes. How much did she sprinkle on each cake?

8. Paula also sprinkled 2 cups of chocolate chips over the 4 cakes. What part of a cup of chocolate chips was on each cake?

9. Mother wants to make cupcakes for everyone at Bible school, but she found that she has only 3 cups of milk. If one batch of cupcakes takes $\frac{3}{4}$ cup of milk, how many batches of cupcakes can Mother make with the milk she has?

10. The cookbook says to allow $\frac{1}{2}$ pound of beef for each person being served. At that rate how many people will a 6-pound roast serve?

120. Reviewing Multiplication and Division of Fractions

A. *Copy and multiply. Use cancellation when you can.*

1. $3 \times \frac{5}{8}$ $\frac{3}{4} \times 4$ $\frac{5}{12} \times \frac{9}{20}$ $\frac{1}{16} \times \frac{2}{3}$

2. $\frac{8}{9} \times \frac{3}{4}$ $\frac{1}{4} \times \frac{1}{3}$ $\frac{11}{16} \times \frac{4}{9}$ $\frac{5}{12} \times 4$

3. $8 \times \frac{1}{3}$ $\frac{3}{10} \times 5$ $\frac{7}{20} \times \frac{5}{7}$ $\frac{2}{3} \times 2$

4. $\frac{3}{4} \times 10$ $\frac{4}{5} \times \frac{5}{7}$ $2 \times \frac{9}{16}$ $\frac{2}{5} \times \frac{5}{12}$

B. *Copy and divide. Remember to invert the divisor and multiply.*

5. $\frac{5}{9} \div 15$ $\frac{3}{4} \div \frac{1}{2}$ $\frac{4}{15} \div \frac{2}{3}$ $8 \div \frac{1}{3}$

6. $\frac{1}{4} \div 8$ $\frac{5}{8} \div 20$ $7 \div \frac{1}{2}$ $\frac{6}{7} \div \frac{3}{14}$

7. $\frac{2}{5} \div \frac{1}{4}$ $\frac{3}{4} \div \frac{3}{8}$ $\frac{7}{16} \div \frac{7}{8}$ $12 \div \frac{3}{4}$

C. *Copy and add. You must first change addends to like fractions.*

8. $7\frac{2}{3}$ $5\frac{7}{8}$ $12\frac{3}{4}$ $10\frac{5}{6}$
   $+6\frac{1}{4}$ $+4\frac{5}{16}$ $+5\frac{3}{5}$ $+13\frac{2}{3}$

9. $\frac{3}{4}$ $\frac{7}{16}$ $\frac{1}{2}$ $\frac{5}{8}$
   $\frac{1}{2}$ $\frac{1}{4}$ $\frac{3}{5}$ $\frac{3}{4}$
   $+\frac{7}{8}$ $+\frac{5}{8}$ $+\frac{7}{10}$ $+\frac{1}{3}$

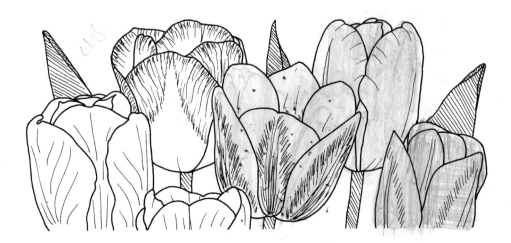

General Review

D. *Do these exercises.*

10. Reduce to lowest terms.

a. $\frac{12}{30}$ b. $\frac{16}{24}$ c. $\frac{15}{45}$ d. $\frac{10}{100}$ e. $\frac{75}{100}$ f. $\frac{32}{40}$

11. Change to percents.

a. $\frac{79}{100}$ b. $\frac{3}{10}$ c. $\frac{1}{4}$ d. $\frac{17}{20}$ e. $\frac{34}{50}$ f. $\frac{21}{25}$

12. Write as Arabic numerals.

a. MLXIX   b. MCMLV   c. DCCCVI   d. MMDXLIII   e. CDLXXXII

13. Round to the nearest hundred: a. 590   b. 4,327   c. 18,654

14. Round to the nearest thousand: a. 8,359   b. 732,814

15. Write as decimals and as common fractions or mixed numbers.

a. sixteen and twenty-five hundredths
b. four hundred twenty and seven thousandths
c. seventy-eight and five tenths
d. nine and three hundredths

E. *Copy each pair of numbers, and write <, >, or = between them.*

16. 3.0 _____ 3   1.7 _____ 1.07   5.3 _____ 5.36

17. 12.4 _____ 12.14   8.7 _____ 7.8   9.2 _____ 9.20

18. 4.16 _____ 4.61   5.5 _____ 5.51   3.008 _____ 3.8

F. *Solve these reading problems.*

19. Charles plowed $\frac{2}{3}$ of a field in the morning. In the afternoon he plowed $\frac{3}{5}$ of the field. Did he plow more of the field in the morning or the afternoon? How much more?

20. A cookie recipe calls for 2 cups of brown sugar. Martha is making $\frac{3}{4}$ batch of cookies. How much brown sugar does she need?

121. Review of Fractions

A. *Copy and multiply. Use cancellation when you can.*

1. $\frac{2}{3} \times \frac{5}{6}$ $11 \times \frac{1}{4}$ $\frac{3}{7} \times 14$ $\frac{4}{5} \times \frac{3}{8}$

2. $10 \times \frac{2}{3}$ $\frac{14}{15} \times \frac{5}{6}$ $\frac{1}{2} \times \frac{7}{12}$ $\frac{5}{6} \times 4$

B. *Copy and divide. Remember to invert the divisor and multiply.*

3. $14 \div \frac{2}{5}$ $\frac{9}{11} \div \frac{3}{5}$ $6 \div \frac{3}{4}$ $\frac{4}{7} \div \frac{2}{3}$

4. $\frac{4}{5} \div \frac{6}{7}$ $\frac{2}{5} \div 10$ $\frac{1}{2} \div \frac{11}{12}$ $9 \div \frac{1}{4}$

C. *Copy and follow the signs.*

5.
$$\frac{1}{2}$$
$$\frac{2}{3}$$
$$+\frac{5}{6}$$

$$\frac{7}{12}$$
$$\frac{1}{4}$$
$$+\frac{1}{2}$$

$$\frac{4}{9}$$
$$\frac{1}{3}$$
$$+\frac{1}{6}$$

$$\frac{3}{10}$$
$$\frac{3}{4}$$
$$+\frac{1}{2}$$

6.
$$3\frac{7}{10}$$
$$+\frac{1}{2}$$

$$7\frac{5}{8}$$
$$+7\frac{9}{16}$$

$$11\frac{3}{5}$$
$$+8\frac{1}{3}$$

$$9\frac{3}{4}$$
$$+6\frac{5}{6}$$

7.
$$10$$
$$-6\frac{5}{8}$$

$$6\frac{3}{4}$$
$$-2\frac{5}{12}$$

$$9\frac{1}{2}$$
$$-\frac{13}{16}$$

$$11$$
$$-4\frac{17}{24}$$

8.
$$12\frac{1}{3}$$
$$-\frac{5}{6}$$

$$14\frac{2}{3}$$
$$-6\frac{11}{12}$$

$$7\frac{8}{9}$$
$$-4\frac{1}{3}$$

$$8\frac{1}{4}$$
$$-3\frac{4}{5}$$

9.
$$18$$
$$\times 4\frac{2}{3}$$

$$15$$
$$\times 6\frac{3}{5}$$

$$21\frac{1}{3}$$
$$\times 9$$

$$8\frac{3}{4}$$
$$\times 8$$

D. *Follow the directions.*

10. Write each fraction in simplest form.

    a. $\frac{17}{3}$ b. $\frac{16}{2}$ c. $\frac{2}{16}$ d. $\frac{35}{40}$ e. $\frac{28}{6}$ f. $\frac{24}{64}$

11. Change these fractions to percents.

    a. $\frac{91}{100}$ b. $\frac{4}{5}$ c. $\frac{1}{2}$ d. $\frac{37}{50}$ e. $\frac{9}{10}$ f. $\frac{11}{20}$

12. Find the missing numbers in these proportions.

    a. $\frac{36}{48} = \frac{?}{8}$ b. $\frac{12}{?} = \frac{3}{9}$ c. $\frac{?}{4} = \frac{8}{16}$ d. $\frac{10}{30} = \frac{2}{?}$ e. $\frac{3}{7} = \frac{?}{56}$

E. *Write the answers only.*

13. $\frac{1}{2}$ of 18 $\frac{1}{3}$ of 33 $\frac{1}{5}$ of 10 $\frac{1}{9}$ of 72

14. $\frac{3}{4}$ of 16 $\frac{2}{3}$ of 30 $\frac{7}{8}$ of 32 $\frac{5}{7}$ of 35

15. $1\frac{1}{2} \times 6$ $2\frac{1}{4} \times 12$ $3\frac{1}{4} \times 8$ $1\frac{1}{7} \times 14$

Reading Problems

Study the problem in the box.

Notebooks are priced at 3 for $1.25. At that rate, what is the price of 6 notebooks?	Think: 6 is twice as much as 3. 6 notebooks will cost twice as much as 3. The cost of 6 notebooks is 2 × $1.25, or $2.50.

F. *Solve these problems like the one in the box.*

16. If grapefruits are priced at 3 for $0.89, what is the price of a dozen grapefruits?

17. Pencils are marked 2 for 25¢. What is the price of 6 pencils?

18. In the *1995 Rod and Staff Catalog*, four "Little Jewel" books cost $7.70. How much would you pay for 8 of the books?

122. Third Quarter Review

A. *Do these exercises.*

1. Write as decimals and as common fractions or mixed numbers.
   a. three and sixty-nine thousandths
   b. fourteen and five tenths
   c. seventy-five and eleven hundredths

2. Change these to decimals.
   a. $13\frac{1}{10}$ b. $6\frac{75}{1,000}$ c. $4\frac{8}{100}$ d. $25\frac{37}{100}$

3. Change these decimals to common fractions or mixed numbers in simplest form.
   a. 3.007   b. 0.25   c. 4.8   d. 9.05   e. 16.500

4. Write the larger number in each pair, or write **same** if the two numbers are equal.
   a. 5.1 5.06   b. 7.3 7.30   c. 6.4 6.45   d. 0.09 0.2

5. Change these percents to fractions.
   a. 77%   b. 50%   c. 25%   d. 80%   e. 6%   f. 48%

6. Change these fractions to percents.
   a. $\frac{17}{20}$ b. $\frac{97}{100}$ c. $\frac{47}{50}$ d. $\frac{3}{10}$ e. $\frac{3}{4}$ f. $\frac{2}{5}$

7. Find the missing numbers in these proportions.
   a. $\frac{17}{20} = \frac{?}{100}$ b. $\frac{?}{5} = \frac{20}{25}$ c. $\frac{16}{?} = \frac{4}{9}$ d. $\frac{6}{8} = \frac{?}{24}$ e. $\frac{18}{48} = \frac{3}{?}$

8. The Harman family has 2 girls and 4 boys. Write fractions in simplest form to show the following ratios.
   a. the girls to the boys
   b. the girls to all the children
   c. the boys to all the children

B. *Write fractions to tell the parts (the ratios) of these measures.*

9. What part of a foot is: a. 6 in.?   b. 9 in.?   c. 4 in.?

10. What part of a pound is: a. 6 oz.?   b. 8 oz.?   c. 10 oz.?

11. What part of a yard is: a. 6 in.?   b. 24.?   c. 9 in.?

C. *Write the missing numbers. Use equivalent fractions to help you.*

12. $\frac{3}{8}$ lb. = _____ oz. $\frac{2}{3}$ doz. = _____ items $\frac{3}{4}$ pk. = _____ qt.

13. $\frac{1}{4}$ ft. = _____ in. $\frac{2}{3}$ day = _____ hr. $\frac{1}{2}$ century = _____ yr.

14. $\frac{1}{2}$ bu. = _____ pk. $\frac{1}{4}$ min. = _____ sec. $\frac{1}{3}$ hr. = _____ min.

D. *Study the bar graph, and do the exercises below it.*

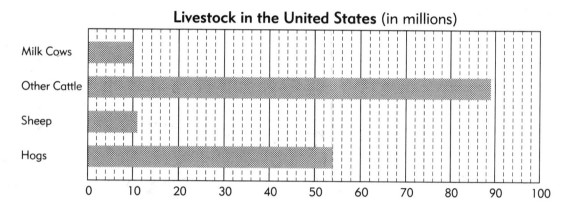

Livestock in the United States (in millions)

15. The distance from one dotted line on the graph to another represents _____ million head of livestock.

16. How many milk cows are in the United States according to the graph?

17. How many sheep are shown on the graph? how many hogs?

18. What is the total of the milk cows and other cattle in the United States?

19. How many more hogs than sheep are shown on the graph?

Computation Practice

E. *Copy and solve.*

20. $3 \times \frac{7}{8}$ $\frac{1}{3} \times 7$ $8 \times \frac{3}{16}$ $\frac{3}{4} \times 6$

21. $\frac{2}{3} \times \frac{7}{8}$ $\frac{5}{12} \times \frac{3}{4}$ $\frac{9}{10} \times \frac{2}{3}$ $\frac{4}{5} \times \frac{5}{16}$

22. $6 \div \frac{1}{2}$ $\frac{3}{4} \div 6$ $8 \div \frac{2}{3}$ $\frac{1}{5} \div 2$

23. $\frac{7}{8} \div \frac{3}{4}$ $\frac{2}{3} \div \frac{3}{7}$ $\frac{9}{16} \div \frac{3}{8}$ $\frac{4}{5} \div \frac{3}{10}$

(continued on next page)

24.

$$12 \times 7\tfrac{3}{4}$$

$$19\tfrac{2}{3} \times 6$$

$$23\tfrac{1}{2} \times 8$$

$$15 \times 7\tfrac{3}{5}$$

25.

$$\tfrac{3}{4} \quad \tfrac{1}{3} \quad +\tfrac{3}{8}$$

$$13\tfrac{1}{4} - 6\tfrac{3}{5}$$

$$9\tfrac{3}{10} - 5\tfrac{1}{2}$$

$$\tfrac{5}{6} \quad \tfrac{1}{2} \quad +\tfrac{3}{4}$$

26. $23 - 17.5$ $6.2 - 0.827$ $231.069 - 39.47$

27. $64.905 + 372.4 + 2.985$ $6.44 + 38.5 + 78.086$

28.

$$\$672.53 - 245.60$$

$$\begin{aligned}\$465.29\\27.64\\328.35\\+173.05\end{aligned}$$

$$\$900.00 - 384.09$$

$$\begin{aligned}\$38.90\\175.00\\4.87\\+522.69\end{aligned}$$

29.

$$806 \times 643$$

$$379 \times 360$$

$$\$3.47 \times 508$$

$$\$4.10 \times 785$$

30. $29\overline{)3{,}886}$ $45\overline{)92{,}745}$ $17\overline{)\$85.51}$ $32\overline{)\$802.24}$

Reading Problem Review

F. *Write* **add,** *subtract,* **multiply,** *or* **divide.**

31. 12 is how many more than 8?

32. How many groups of 6 are in 18?

33. How many are eight 4's?

34. What is one-third of 15?

35. What is the average of 10, 8, and 9?

36. What is the total of 6, 3, 9, and 4?

37. What is the difference between 7 and 9?

38. If you have 17 blocks and lose 5, how many are left?

39. If your bill is $3.50 and you give the clerk $5.00, what is your change?

40. Three pounds of bananas cost $1.20. What is the cost per pound?

41. How far can a train go in 4 hours at 80 miles per hour?

42. What is the cost of 3 bookmarks at 45¢ each?

G. *Solve these reading problems.*

43. Donna's sugar cookie recipe calls for 2 cups of sugar. How much sugar does Donna need to make $\frac{3}{4}$ batch of cookies?

44. From Forest Hill Church to Elm Dale Church is 120 miles. It took Brother Frank 3 hours to travel the distance. What was his speed?

45. If Brother Frank could have averaged 50 miles per hour, how many hours would it have taken him to travel 120 miles?

46. Mother made four quarts of fruit punch for the family's picnic lunch. If each person drinks $\frac{1}{2}$ quart of punch, how many people can be served?

47. Chicken noodle soup is priced at 2 cans for 79¢. What is the price of 4 cans?

48. Mother bought 3 yards of fabric priced at $2.75 a yard, 2 cards of buttons at 69¢ each, and a zipper for $1.20. What was her total bill?

49. In 1920, 27% of the people in America were farmers. What percent of the people were involved in other work?

50. In 1990, only 2% of the people in America were farmers. Write this percent as a fraction.

51. The Upland Christian School has 74 pupils and 4 teachers. They all plan to travel by bus to Washington, D.C., for their school trip. If the buses each hold 44 people, how many buses will be needed?

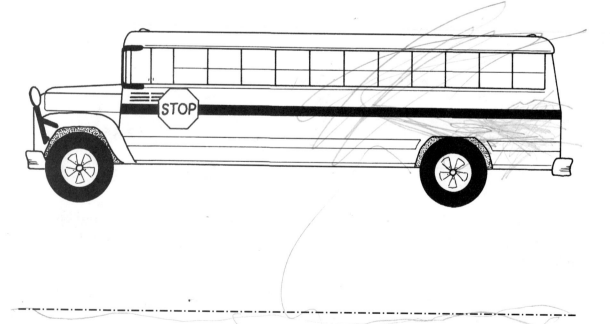

123. Chapter 12 Test

Interesting Number Facts

A Number That Goes in Circles

Multiplying the number 142,857 by 2, 3, 4, 5, or 6 produces some interesting results. The products all contain these digits.

1 - 4 - 2 - 8 - 5 - 7

However, the digits are rearranged so that a different digit is first in each product. It is like going clockwise around this circle, starting with a different digit each time.

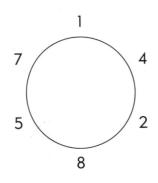

Here are some examples to show what happens.

142,857	142,857	142,857
x 2	x 4	x 5
285,714	571,428	714,285

Like the "printing-press number" (page 178), the "number that goes in circles" is related to the number 9. Multiply 142,857 by 7 to see how this number is related to 9.

Chapter 13

Bible Measure and Metric Measure

[They] sounded, and found it twenty fathoms:
and when they had gone a little further, they sounded again,
and found it fifteen fathoms.
(Acts 27:28)

124. Bible Units of Length

In the United States, English units called inches, feet, yards, and miles are used to measure length. These are **standard units** because men have decided exactly how long each one is. In Bible times, most measuring was done with **indefinite units**, or units that are not exact. Knowing about these units helps us to understand the Bible better.

Some Bible units of length are the **handbreadth**, the **span**, the **cubit**, the **fathom**, and the **furlong**. The span, cubit, and furlong were used to measure distance on land. The fathom was used to measure the depth of water.

Study the pictures to learn how men in Bible times measured a handbreadth, span, cubit, and fathom. Then study the table of equivalent Bible and English units of length.

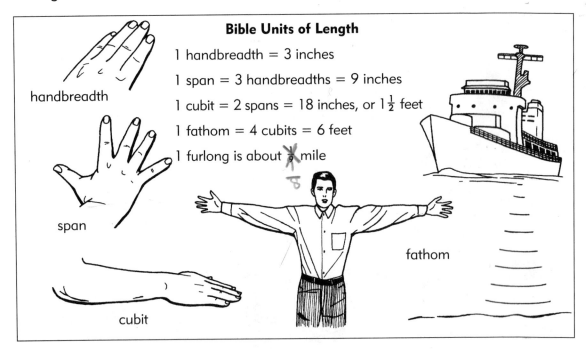

Bible Units of Length

1 handbreadth = 3 inches

1 span = 3 handbreadths = 9 inches

1 cubit = 2 spans = 18 inches, or $1\frac{1}{2}$ feet

1 fathom = 4 cubits = 6 feet

1 furlong is about $\frac{1}{8}$ mile

handbreadth

span

cubit

fathom

A. Write the missing numbers.

1. 1 span = _____ handbreadths

2. 1 furlong = _____ mile

3. 1 handbreadth = _____ inches

4. 1 cubit = _____ spans

5. 1 fathom = _____ feet

1 fathom = _____ cubits

1 cubit = _____ inches

1 cubit = _____ feet

1 span = _____ inches

1 mile = _____ furlongs

B. *Use your Bible and the table of equivalent units to do these exercises.*

6. In Acts 27:28, how many fathoms deep was the water at the first sounding? How many fathoms deep was it at the second sounding?

7. Change the two measures in number 6 to feet.

8. Nebuchadnezzar's golden image in Daniel 3:1 was "threescore cubits" high (60 cubits), and _____ cubits wide. In English units, what was the height and width of the image?

9. Exodus 25:10 gives the dimensions of the ark of the covenant. Write the length and the width (breadth) in inches. (Multiply the number of cubits times 18.)

10. Goliath's height is recorded in 1 Samuel 17:4 as "six cubits and a span." How tall was Goliath in inches?

11. Read John 11:18. About how many miles was the distance from Jerusalem to Bethany? (Think: How many 9's are in 15 furlongs?)

General Review

C. *Find the missing numbers by multiplying or dividing.*

12. 6 min. = _____ sec.   2 mi. = _____ ft.   7 qt. = _____ gal.

13. 4 pt. = _____ qt.   4 qt. = _____ cups   3 yr. = _____ mo.

14. 15 days = _____ wk.   40 min. = _____ hr.   6 bu. = _____ pk.

D. *Follow the signs, and work carefully.*

15.
```
   8 years  250 days          7 days  14 hours         12 yards  20 inches
 + 5 years  300 days        + 9 days  12 hours        + 7 yards  24 inches
```

16.
```
  12 gallons  1 quart          9 weeks  3 days          15 bushels  0 pecks
 - 7 gallons  3 quarts       - 2 weeks  6 days         - 11 bushels  3 pecks
```

17.
```
  6 quarts  2 cups           5 yards  1 foot           3 pounds  6 ounces
            x 3                       x 6                        x 4
```

18. $6 \div \frac{2}{3}$ $\frac{3}{5} \div 3$ $\frac{2}{3} \div \frac{1}{4}$ $\frac{7}{16} \div \frac{7}{8}$

19. $8 \times \frac{2}{7}$ $\frac{3}{4} \times 10$ $\frac{1}{2} \times \frac{6}{7}$ $\frac{5}{12} \times \frac{4}{5}$

125. Metric Units of Length

The metric system has become the main system of measure in all major countries of the world except the United States. Because metric units are based on tens like our decimal number system, it is easier to change from one unit to another than in the English system.

The metric system uses basic units of measure and adds prefixes to them to name larger or smaller units. Today you will be working with the **meter**, which is the basic unit of length. You will also be introduced to six metric prefixes and their meanings.

Study the prefixes and their meanings in the box below. Notice how each prefix combines with the base unit to name another unit. The first three prefixes name units smaller than a meter; the last three name units larger than a meter.

Metric Prefixes	Meaning	Metic Units of Length	
milli-	$\frac{1}{1,000}$, or 0.001	**millimeter (mm)**	0.001 meter
centi-	$\frac{1}{100}$, or 0.01	**centimeter (cm)**	0.01 meter
deci-	$\frac{1}{10}$, or 0.1	decimeter	0.1 meter
—	1	**meter (m)**	Basic Unit
deka-	10	dekameter	10 meters
hecto-	100	hectometer	100 meters
kilo-	1,000	**kilometer (km)**	1,000 meters

The units most commonly used are in boldface, followed by their abbreviations.

Metric–English Equivalents
1 meter is about 39 inches, or about 3 inches more than a yard.
1 centimeter is a little less than $\frac{1}{2}$ inch.
1 millimeter is less than $\frac{1}{16}$ inch.
1 kilometer is about $\frac{5}{8}$ mile (a little over $\frac{1}{2}$ mile).

A. Do these exercises.

1. Write the meaning of each prefix as a whole number or decimal.

   a. hecto-   b. kilo-   c. milli-   d. deci-   e. deka-   f. centi-

2. What is the basic unit of length in the metric system?

3. Is each unit **larger** or **smaller** than a meter?

   a. centimeter   b. kilometer   c. decimeter   d. millimeter

4. Write the unit that means

   a. 1,000 meters   c. $\frac{1}{1,000}$ meter   e. 0.01 meter

   b. 0.1 meter   d. 100 meters   f. 10 meters

B. *Choose the correct words in parentheses.*

5. The distance between my neighbor's house and mine is about one (millimeter, decimeter, hectometer).

6. The width of your finger is about one (millimeter, centimeter, meter).

7. The length of a new pencil might be about two (centimeters, decimeters, kilometers).

8. The height of the classroom door is about two (centimeters, meters, kilometers).

9. A millimeter is (more, less) than a centimeter.

10. A centimeter is (more, less) than a meter.

11. A kilometer is (more, less) than a meter.

12. A kilometer is (more, less) than a mile.

13. A meter is (more, less) than a yard.

14. A centimeter is (more, less) than an inch.

General Review

C. *Do these exercises in your head, and write the answers only.*

15. Multiply each number by 10. (Remember: Annex a zero.)
     a. 67   b. 30   c. 298   d. 400   e. 7,420

16. Multiply each number by 100.
     a. 19   b. 48   c. 70   d. 572   e. 360

17. Multiply each number by 1,000.
     a. 35   b. 80   c. 971   d. 600   e. 214

18. Divide each number by 10.
     a. 130   b. 70   c. 500   d. 470   e. 6,200

19. Add 12 to each number.
     a. 40   b. 37   c. 28   d. 59   e. 16

20. Subtract 8 from each number.
     a. 17   b. 25   c. 40   d. 32   e. 59

D. *Write the numbers that belong in the blanks.*

21. 1 cubit = _____ ft.   1 cubit = _____ in.   1 cubit = _____ spans

22. 1 span = _____ in.   1 fathom = _____ ft.   1 furlong = _____ mi.

23. 1 yard = _____ in.   1 mile = _____ ft.   1 mile = _____ yd.

24. 1 handbreadth = _____ in.   1 span = _____ handbreadths

126. Changing From One Metric Unit
to Another

Because the metric system is based on tens, it is easy to change from one unit in the system to another. For example, 1 centimeter = $\frac{1}{100}$ meter, so 1 meter = 100 centimeters. Study other equivalents in the box.

To change from one unit to another, we use measure rules similar to those used for English units. Let's see how it works.

---

1 meter = 10 decimeters = 100 centimeters = 1,000 millimeters

1 meter = $\frac{1}{10}$ dekameter = $\frac{1}{100}$ hectometer = $\frac{1}{1,000}$ kilometer

---

1. To change meters to a smaller unit, **multiply** times the number of the other unit in 1 meter. (See above.)

   Examples: 3 meters = _____ decimeters   Think: $3 \times 10 = 30$

                 5 meters = _____ centimeters   Think: $5 \times 100 = 500$

                 2 meters = _____ millimeters   Think: $2 \times 1,000 = 2,000$

2. To change meters to a larger unit, **divide** by the number of meters in the larger unit. (See prefixes in Lesson 125.)

   Examples: 6,000 meters = _____ dekameters   Think: $6,000 \div 10 = 600$

                 6,000 meters = _____ hectometers   Think: $6,000 \div 100 = 60$

                 6,000 meters = _____ kilometers   Think: $6,000 \div 1,000 = 6$

3. To change any unit to the next smaller unit, multiply by 10.

   Example: 12 centimeters = 120 millimeters

4. To change any unit to the next larger unit, divide by 10.

   Example: 250 millimeters = 25 centimeters

A. Write the numbers that belong in the blanks.

1. 4 meters = _____ centimeters   17 meters = _____ millimeters

2. 900 meters = _____ hectometers   4,000 meters = _____ kilometers

3. 8 meters = _____ decimeters   120 meters = _____ dekameters

4. 12 meters = _____ millimeters   12 meters = _____ centimeters

5. 20 centimeters = _____ millimeters

6. 6 centimeters = _____ millimeters

7. 20 millimeters = _____ centimeters

8. 300 millimeters = _____ centimeters

9. 10 centimeters = _____ millimeters

10. 10 millimeters = _____ centimeters

B. *Write T for true or F for false.*

11. A meter is less than a yard.

12. The meter is the basic metric unit of length.

13. A kilometer is less than a yard.

14. There are 100 centimeters in a meter.

15. There are 10 millimeters in a centimeter.

16. There are 1,000 kilometers in a meter.

17. A centimeter is less than an inch.

18. A centimeter is less than a millimeter.

General Review

C. *Copy and solve.*

19. $\frac{4}{7} \times \frac{7}{12}$	$4 \times \frac{3}{16}$	$\frac{5}{6} \times 4$	$\frac{1}{4} \times \frac{2}{5}$
20. $\frac{3}{4} \div 6$	$\frac{3}{5} \div \frac{1}{6}$	$4 \div \frac{5}{6}$	$\frac{7}{8} \div \frac{3}{8}$

21. $7\overline{)27,426}$ $4\overline{)61,420}$ $28\overline{)\$60.48}$ $35\overline{)\$358.75}$

22.
$$
\begin{array}{r} 32\frac{3}{4} \\ \times\ 8 \\ \hline \end{array}
\qquad
\begin{array}{r} 14 \\ \times\ 5\frac{2}{7} \\ \hline \end{array}
\qquad
\begin{array}{r} 609 \\ \times\ 274 \\ \hline \end{array}
\qquad
\begin{array}{r} 357 \\ \times\ 270 \\ \hline \end{array}
$$

23.
$$
\begin{array}{r} 74,012 \\ -\ 18,735 \\ \hline \end{array}
\qquad
\begin{array}{r} 90,030 \\ -\ 25,760 \\ \hline \end{array}
\qquad
\begin{array}{r} \$312.50 \\ -\ 64.28 \\ \hline \end{array}
\qquad
\begin{array}{r} \$590.44 \\ -\ 383.54 \\ \hline \end{array}
$$

24.
$$
\begin{array}{r} 792 \\ 154 \\ 358 \\ +\ 472 \\ \hline \end{array}
\qquad
\begin{array}{r} 5,082 \\ 3,941 \\ 2,873 \\ +\ 4,537 \\ \hline \end{array}
\qquad
\begin{array}{r} 57,145 \\ 25,387 \\ +\ 17,840 \\ \hline \end{array}
\qquad
\begin{array}{r} 46,394 \\ 71,056 \\ 37,578 \\ +\ 52,913 \\ \hline \end{array}
$$

127. Working With Metric Units

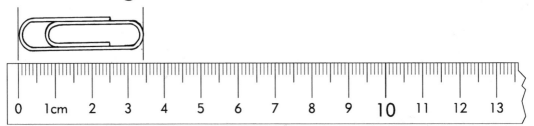

How long is this paper clip in metric units? There are three ways to express its length.
1. In millimeters: 34 mm
2. In centimeters and millimeters: 3 cm 4 mm
3. In centimeters only: 3.4 cm

The three expressions are very similar. That is because a millimeter is **one-tenth** of a centimeter.

A. *Write the missing numbers to make equivalent expressions.*
   Sample: 51 mm = 5 cm 1 mm = 5.1 cm

   1. 75 mm = _____ cm _____ mm = _____ cm

   2. _____ mm = 4 cm 8 mm = _____ cm

   3. 12 mm = _____ cm _____ mm = _____ cm

   4. _____ mm = 3 cm 9 mm = _____ cm

B. *Measure each line with your metric ruler, and write its length to the nearest tenth of a centimeter. Sample answer: 6.4 cm*

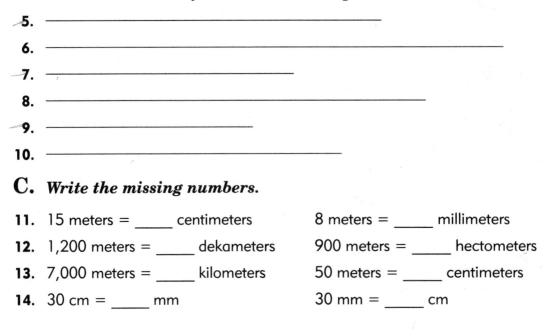

   5. _____

   6. _____

   7. _____

   8. _____

   9. _____

   10. _____

C. *Write the missing numbers.*

   11. 15 meters = _____ centimeters   8 meters = _____ millimeters

   12. 1,200 meters = _____ dekameters   900 meters = _____ hectometers

   13. 7,000 meters = _____ kilometers   50 meters = _____ centimeters

   14. 30 cm = _____ mm   30 mm = _____ cm

D. Write the metric units that have these lengths.

15. a. a little more than a yard   b. about $\frac{5}{8}$ mile
16. a. less than $\frac{1}{16}$ inch   b. about a half inch
17. a. 39 inches   b. 1,000 meters   c. $\frac{1}{1,000}$ meter

E. Write the Bible units nearest to the lengths given.

18. a. 9 inches   b. 6 feet   c. $\frac{1}{9}$ mile
19. a. 18 inches   b. 3 inches   c. $1\frac{1}{2}$ feet
20. a. 2 spans   b. 4 cubits   c. 3 handbreadths

Reading Problems

We use money to buy things we need and to give to others. To earn the money your family needs, your father either works for someone else or has his own business. The money he earns is his **income**.

If a man has his own business, he must pay the business **expenses** out of his income. The money left after expenses are paid is **profit**.

To find the profit, first find the total income and the total expenses. Subtract expenses from income to find profit.

Income − Expenses = Profit

F. Do these reading problems.

21. The Jones family makes baked goods to sell. They sell bread for $1.25 a loaf and pies for $3.75 each. What is their **total income** when they sell 26 loaves of bread and 8 pies?

22. Mother Jones figures that expenses for ingredients are about 48¢ for each loaf of bread and $1.65 for each pie. What are the expenses for ingredients in 26 loaves of bread and 8 pies?

23. Besides the expense of ingredients, the Joneses have other expenses, such as gas for the stove and rent for their market stand. They figure that these expenses are about $9.20 for 40 loaves of bread and 10 pies. What are their **total expenses** for 40 loaves of bread and 10 pies?

24. If the total expenses for 15 loaves of bread and 5 pies is $19.15, what is the **profit**?

128. Metric Units of Weight

The **gram** is the basic unit of weight in the metric system. The six metric prefixes you learned can be combined with *gram* to name other units of weight. Study the information in the box below. The units that are used most are in boldface.

Metric Units of Weight	Meanings
milligram (mg)	0.001 gram
centigram (cg)	0.01 gram
decigram	0.1 gram
gram (g)	Basic Unit
dekagram	10 grams
hectogram	100 grams
kilogram (kg)	1,000 grams

grams

One gram is about 0.035 ounce, or the weight of one regular-sized paper clip. Grams are used to weigh rather small items like cereal and butter.

One kilogram is about 2.2 pounds. Kilograms are used to weigh heavy objects like apples and flour.

The milligram is used to weigh very small amounts, like the ingredients in vitamin pills.

A. Answer with yes or no.

1. Might a person weigh 50 centigrams?
2. Could a person weigh 50 kilograms?
3. Could you carry 2,000 grams?
4. Is a milligram more than a centigram?
5. Is a kilogram the same as a thousand milligrams?
6. Are most men less than 100 centimeters tall?
7. Could a very tall man be 2 meters tall?
8. Are 2 kilometers less than a mile?
9. Is 60 miles per hour faster than 60 kilometers per hour?
10. Is 4 inches more than 4 centimeters?
11. Is a furlong about the same as four cubits?
12. Is a yard about the same as two cubits?
13. Is a fathom used to measure the distance between cities?

kilograms

milligrams

B. Write the prefixes that have these meanings.

14. a. 100   b. $\frac{1}{100}$ c. 10   d. $\frac{1}{10}$ e. 1,000   f. $\frac{1}{1,000}$

C. *Measure to the nearest tenth of a centimeter.*
   Sample answer: 8.2 cm

15. _____

16. _____

17. _____

D. *Write the missing numbers. Refer to Lessons 126–128 for help.*

18. 11 meters = _____ centimeters   24 meters = _____ decimeters

19. 7,000 meters = _____ kilometers   800 meters = _____ dekameters

20. 1,500 meters = _____ hectometers   9 meters = _____ millimeters

21. 3,000 grams = _____ kilograms   5 grams = _____ centigrams

22. 8 grams = _____ milligrams   1 kilogram = _____ grams

23. 16 centimeters = _____ millimeters   40 mm = _____ cm

24. 27 mm = ___ cm ___ mm = ___ cm   84 mm = ___ cm ___ mm = ___ cm

E. *Write as decimals and as common fractions or mixed numbers.*

25. a. thirteen and five thousandths
    b. eighty-five and eleven hundredths
    c. nine and seventy-eight thousandths
    d. fifty and three tenths

F. *Solve these problems.*

26. $894.5 + 3.982 + 74.354$ $60.81 + 563.956 + 4.9$

27. $970.35 - 62.57$ $800 - 254.6$ $45.1 - 26.25$

28. $3 \times \frac{7}{8}$ $\frac{1}{6} \times 3$ $\frac{4}{5} \times \frac{5}{12}$ $\frac{7}{8} \times \frac{2}{3}$

29. $8 \div \frac{2}{3}$ $\frac{3}{4} \div 2$ $\frac{7}{16} \div \frac{1}{4}$ $\frac{3}{8} \div \frac{3}{16}$

30.
$$3\frac{7}{16} \atop + 8\frac{5}{8}$$
$$\frac{3}{4} \atop \frac{5}{6} \atop + \frac{2}{3}$$
$$18\frac{1}{2} \atop - 14\frac{7}{10}$$
$$9\frac{1}{6} \atop - 3\frac{5}{9}$$

31. The Corner Grocery sold $2,473.18 worth of groceries one week. That week their expenses were $1,356.49 for groceries to sell in the store, $146.27 for electricity and telephone, and $572.00 for wages. What was their profit for the week?

129. Measuring Liquids With Metric Units

In the English system, liquids are measured with cups, pints, quarts, and gallons. The **liter** is the basic unit for measuring liquids in the metric system. Study the information in the box to learn more about metric units of liquid measure. The two most common units are in boldface.

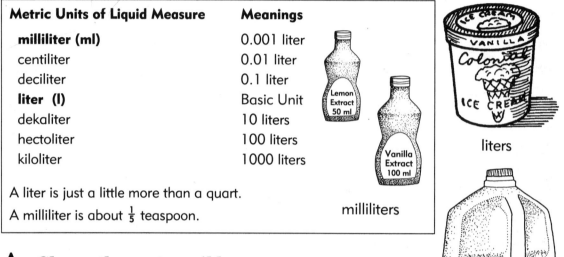

Metric Units of Liquid Measure	Meanings
milliliter (ml)	0.001 liter
centiliter	0.01 liter
deciliter	0.1 liter
liter (l)	Basic Unit
dekaliter	10 liters
hectoliter	100 liters
kiloliter	1000 liters

A liter is just a little more than a quart.

A milliliter is about ⅕ teaspoon.

milliliters

liters

A. *Choose the most sensible answers.*

1. A thirsty cow might drink (20 liters, 20 milliliters) of water.

2. Father put (50 liters, 50 milliliters) of gasoline into the car.

3. You might drink (500 liters, 500 milliliters) if you are thirsty.

4. A baby chick might drink (1 liter, 1 milliliter) when it dips its beak into the water.

5. A large family would probably eat (2 liters, 2 milliliters) of peaches at a meal.

6. A big book weighs about (2 grams, 2 kilograms, 2 centigrams).

7. A package of butter would probably weigh about (500 kilograms, 500 milligrams, 500 grams).

8. A vitamin C tablet would be most likely to contain (100 milligrams, 100 grams, 100 kilograms) of vitamin C.

9. The page of a book might be (15 millimeters, 15 centimeters, 15 meters) across.

10. The coast-to-coast distance across the United States is about 3,000 miles. In metric units the distance is about (4,800 kilometers, 4,800 meters, 4,800 centimeters).

B. *Do these excercises.*

11. Write the measurements to which the arrows point. Sample answer: 4.5 cm

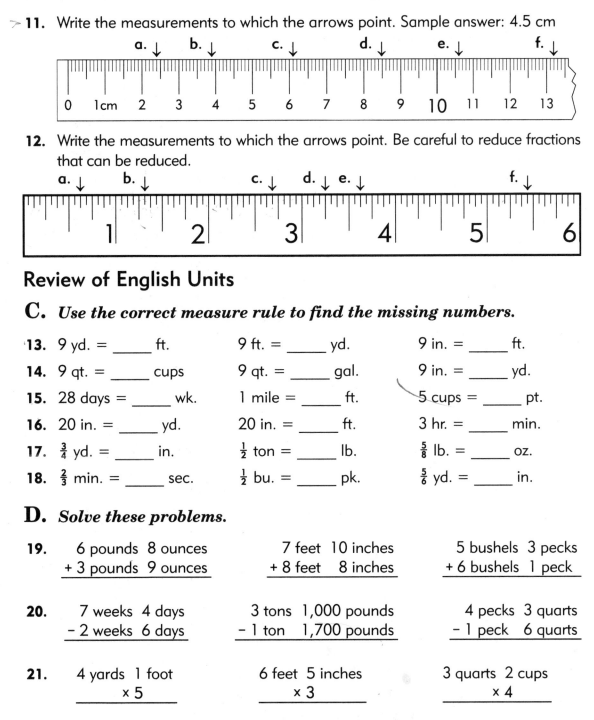

12. Write the measurements to which the arrows point. Be careful to reduce fractions that can be reduced.

Review of English Units

C. *Use the correct measure rule to find the missing numbers.*

13. 9 yd. = _____ ft.   9 ft. = _____ yd.   9 in. = _____ ft.

14. 9 qt. = _____ cups   9 qt. = _____ gal.   9 in. = _____ yd.

15. 28 days = _____ wk.   1 mile = _____ ft.   5 cups = _____ pt.

16. 20 in. = _____ yd.   20 in. = _____ ft.   3 hr. = _____ min.

17. $\frac{3}{4}$ yd. = _____ in. $\frac{1}{2}$ ton = _____ lb. $\frac{5}{8}$ lb. = _____ oz.

18. $\frac{2}{3}$ min. = _____ sec. $\frac{1}{2}$ bu. = _____ pk. $\frac{5}{6}$ yd. = _____ in.

D. *Solve these problems.*

19.   6 pounds 8 ounces   7 feet 10 inches   5 bushels 3 pecks
         + 3 pounds 9 ounces   + 8 feet   8 inches   + 6 bushels 1 peck

20.   7 weeks 4 days   3 tons 1,000 pounds   4 pecks 3 quarts
         − 2 weeks 6 days   − 1 ton   1,700 pounds   − 1 peck   6 quarts

21.   4 yards 1 foot   6 feet 5 inches   3 quarts 2 cups
                    × 5   × 3   × 4

22. Richard lives $6\frac{7}{10}$ miles from church. On Sunday mornings his family takes elderly Mrs. Greene along to church. The trip to church is $3\frac{1}{2}$ miles farther when they pick up Mrs. Greene. How far does Richard's family drive when they go to church on Sunday mornings?

130. Two Kinds of Thermometers

Thermometers are used to measure temperature, which is measured in **degrees** (°).

Two kinds of thermometer scales are in common use. The **Fahrenheit** scale is most common in the United States. The **Celsius** scale is most common in countries that use the metric system.

Learn these important temperatures on the two scales.

	Freezing Point of Water	Boiling Point of Water
Fahrenheit Scale	32°	212°
Celsius Scale	0°	100°

The thermometer pictured above has the Fahrenheit scale marked with **F** and the Celsius scale marked with **C**. Notice that only the tens are labeled on the thermometer. The spaces between the unmarked lines stand for **two** degrees. Thus, 32° F. is only one line above 30° F.

A. *Write the answers.*

1. These thermometers have only one scale, not both. Write the temperature shown by each thermometer.

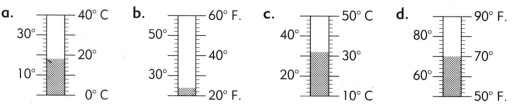

B. *Write the words that belong in the blanks.*

2. The _____ point of water is 32° F.

3. The boiling point on the _____ scale is 100°.

4. The _____ scale is most common in the United States.

5. The _____ scale goes with the metric system of measure.

6. A _____ is the distance from elbow to finger tips.

7. A _____ was used to measure the depth of water in Bible times.

8. The _____ is the basic metric unit of weight.

9. The _____ is the basic metric unit of length.

10. The _____ is the basic metric unit of liquid measure.

C. *Write the meanings of these metric prefixes.*

11. **a.** deka-   **b.** milli-   **c.** kilo-   **d.** hecto-   **e.** deci-   **f.** centi-

D. *Write the missing numbers.*

12. 3 kilometers = _____ meters   8 centimeters = _____ millimeters

13. 4 meters = _____ centimeters   7 meters = _____ millimeters

14. 5,000 grams = _____ kilograms   6 liters = _____ milliliters

15. 1,000 meters = _____ kilometer   5 grams = _____ milligrams

16. 35 mm = ___ cm ___ mm = ___ cm   19 mm = _____ cm

17. 3 ft. = _____ in.   7 weeks = _____ days   4 pt. = _____ qt.

18. 12 bu. = _____ pk.   12 qt. = _____ pk.   9 in. = _____ ft.

19. 20 min. = _____ hr.   5 gal. = _____ qt.   1 decade = _____ years

General Review

E. *Do these exercises.*

20. Copy and multiply.

138	9,264	679	528	906
× 57	× 35	× 400	× 608	× 639

21. Write with Arabic numerals.
  a. CCCXLV   **b.** DCLIX   **c.** MCCVIII   **d.** CMXII   **e.** MCDLXXIV

22. Write numerals for these number words.
  a. one hundred twelve billion, sixty-five million, three
  b. thirty-seven million, eight hundred fifty thousand
  c. forty-one and twenty-six thousandths

23. Reduce to lowest terms.
  a. $\frac{36}{48}$ **b.** $\frac{15}{45}$ **c.** $\frac{12}{32}$ **d.** $\frac{6}{20}$ **e.** $\frac{18}{30}$ **f.** $\frac{56}{72}$

F. *Solve these reading problems.*

24. Brother Harold bought 4 plow shares at $5.95 each. How much did he pay for the plow shares?

25. Brother Harold also bought 12 bolts at $0.29 each and 4 heavier bolts at $0.31 each. How much did he pay for the 16 bolts?

131. Chapter 13 Review

A. *Write the words that fit in the blanks.*

1. The _____ is the basic metric unit of length.

2. The _____ is the basic metric unit of liquid measure.

3. The _____ is the basic metric unit of weight.

4. The _____ is a Bible unit for measuring the depth of water.

5. The _____ is the distance from the elbow to the tip of the finger.

6. The _____ is the distance across the outstretched hand.

7. The _____ is the distance across the closed fingers.

8. The _____ scale for measuring temperature is part of the metric system.

B. *Write the numbers that fit in the blanks. Turn to Lessons 124, 125, 128, and 129 if you need help.*

9. A kilometer is _____ meters.

10. A centimeter is _____ millimeters.

11. A meter is _____ centimeters or _____ millimeters.

12. A kilogram is _____ grams.

13. A kilogram is about _____ pounds.

14. A meter is about _____ inches.

15. A gram is about _____ ounces.

16. A cubit is about _____ inches or _____ feet.

17. A span is about _____ inches.

18. A handbreadth is about _____ inches.

19. A furlong is about _____ mile.

20. A kilometer is about _____ mile.

21. A fathom is about _____ feet.

22. A centimeter is a little less than _____ inch.

23. On the Celsius scale the freezing point is _____° and the boiling point is _____°.

24. On the Fahrenheit scale the freezing point is _____° and the boiling point is _____°.

C. *Give the answers.*

25. Write the meanings of these metric prefixes.

    a. deka-   **b.** hecto-   **c.** centi-   **d.** kilo-   **e.** deci-   **f.** milli-

26. Which is the larger unit in each pair?

    a. kilometer or mile   **e.** meter or yard
    b. centimeter or millimeter   **f.** kilogram or pound
    c. gram or ounce   **g.** gram or kilogram
    d. liter or quart   **h.** decimeter or dekameter

D. *Choose the most sensible answers.*

27. A toothpick is about (5 millimeters, 5 centimeters) long.

28. A baby is about ($\frac{1}{2}$ meter, $\frac{1}{2}$ kilometer) long.

29. It might take you 15 minutes to walk (1 centimeter, 1 meter, 1 kilometer).

30. (Your English book, a weed seed, a paper clip) weighs about a gram.

31. (A large rock, a large book, a pencil) weighs about a kilogram.

32. Father put (500 milliliters, 50 liters, 500 liters) of gasoline into the car.

33. A teaspoon holds about (5 milliliters, 500 milliliters, 5 liters).

E. *Write the numbers that fit in the blanks.*

34. 17 meters = _____ millimeters   25 meters = _____ centimeters

35. 6 kilograms = _____ grams   13 centimeters = _____ millimeters

36. 9 kilometers = _____ meters   7,000 meters = _____ kilometers

37. 29 meters = _____ decimeters   900 meters = _____ dekameters

38. 12 liters = _____ milliliters   43 grams = _____ centigrams

39. 56 mm = ___ cm ___ mm = ___ cm   32 mm = ___ cm ___ mm = ___ cm

40. 8 ft. = _____ yd.   8 yd. = _____ ft.   8 in. = _____ ft.

41. 4 lb. = _____ oz.   4 oz. = _____ lb.   4 qt. = _____ gal.

42. 4 gal. = _____ qt.   4 qt. = _____ pt.   4 pt. = _____ qt.

F. *Do these exercises.*

43.
```
   7 feet  5 inches        8 gallons  1 quart        3 pecks  4 quarts
 + 5 feet  9 inches      - 3 gallons  3 quarts              x 3
```

(continued on next page)

44. Write the temperatures shown on these thermometers.

a. 60° C   b. 40° C   c. 60° C   d. 70° C

G. Solve these reading problems.

45. A thirsty camel can drink 75 liters of water at one time. Rebekah drew water for the ten camels of Abraham's servant. If each camel drank 75 liters of water, how many liters of water did Rebekah draw from the well?

46. Job had 3,000 camels. If each drank 75 liters, how many liters of water could they drink at once?

47. A large bottle of medicine holds 250 milliliters. A small bottle holds 50 milliliters. How many small bottles will it take to fill one large bottle?

48. In John 6, the disciples of Jesus took a ship to go across the Sea of Galilee. After they had rowed about 25 furlongs, Jesus came to them, walking on the water. About how many miles had the disciples rowed before Jesus came to them? (Remember, a furlong equals about $\frac{1}{9}$ mile.)

49. Father and Mother bought 3 rabbits for Kevin and Loren. The boys were allowed to keep any profit they made on their rabbits. Out of the first few litters, Kevin and Loren sold 12 rabbits for $2.35 each. By that time the boys had spent $21.95 for rabbit feed. How much profit did they have?

50. Mr. Benson sells strawberries for $1.75 a quart at his roadside stand. On some days he sells 250 quarts of berries. What is Mr. Benson's income from the strawberries?

51. David thought Mr. Benson would get rich from selling so many strawberries. Father explained that Mr. Benson paid his workers $0.45 a quart for picking the berries. He paid $0.06 for each box that the berries were sold in. He also had other expenses like fertilizer, sprays, and machinery, amounting to about $0.75 per quart of berries sold. If Mr. Benson sold the berries at $1.75 per quart, what was his actual profit on each quart?

132. Chapter 13 Test

Chapter 14

Multiplication and Division of Decimals

The Lord thy God is with thee whithersoever thou goest.
(Joshua 1:9)

133. Review of Multiplying Fractions

A. *Multiply these fractions and whole numbers. Cancel when you can.*

1. $\frac{3}{4} \times \frac{8}{9}$ $\frac{7}{12} \times \frac{4}{5}$ $\frac{2}{3} \times \frac{3}{8}$ $\frac{9}{16} \times \frac{1}{2}$

2. $5 \times \frac{2}{3}$ $8 \times \frac{3}{4}$ $9 \times \frac{5}{12}$ $6 \times \frac{1}{4}$

3. $10 \times \frac{3}{5}$ $4 \times \frac{1}{2}$ $3 \times \frac{1}{6}$ $12 \times \frac{2}{9}$

B. *Do you remember how to multiply whole numbers and mixed numbers? For the first problem below, multiply $8 \times \frac{3}{4}$, then multiply 8×8, and finally add the two products. Follow the same pattern for the other problems.*

4. $8\frac{3}{4}$ $13\frac{1}{3}$ $16\frac{1}{2}$ $24\frac{2}{5}$
     $\times 8$ $\times 9$ $\times 4$ $\times 5$

5. $9\frac{2}{3}$ $11\frac{1}{2}$ $23\frac{2}{3}$ $14\frac{3}{7}$
     $\times 9$ $\times 8$ $\times 6$ $\times 7$

C. *Do these exercises.*

6. Reduce these fractions to lowest terms.

   a. $\frac{21}{28}$ b. $\frac{25}{100}$ c. $\frac{40}{48}$ d. $\frac{28}{36}$ e. $\frac{20}{40}$

7. Change these improper fractions to whole or mixed numbers in simplest form.

   a. $\frac{21}{8}$ b. $\frac{10}{3}$ c. $\frac{80}{20}$ d. $\frac{18}{12}$ e. $\frac{21}{15}$

8. Copy and subtract.

   18 $12\frac{5}{6}$ $9\frac{1}{3}$ $14\frac{1}{2}$
  $-9\frac{7}{16}$ $-6\frac{3}{4}$ $-5\frac{7}{9}$ $-11\frac{4}{5}$

General Review

D. *Follow the directions.*

9. Change these fractions to hundredths and then to percents.

    a. $\frac{1}{2}$ b. $\frac{2}{5}$ c. $\frac{21}{25}$ d. $\frac{3}{4}$ e. $\frac{3}{20}$ f. $\frac{47}{50}$

10. Write all the factors of 18. (See Lesson 63.)

11. Draw factor trees for 18 and 42. (See Lesson 64.)

12. Copy the prime numbers. (A prime number has no factors except itself and 1. See Lesson 63.)

    7   8   9   10   11   12   13   15   17

E. *Write T for true and F for false.*

13. A centimeter equals 10 millimeters.

14. A meter equals 10 centimeters.

15. The prefix **kilo-** means $\frac{1}{1,000}$.

16. The boiling point on the Celsius scale is 100°.

17. The freezing point on the Fahrenheit scale is 32°.

18. The liter is used to measure weight.

19. A meter is a little more than a yard.

20. A cubit is about a foot and a half.

21. There are 1,000 grams in a kilogram.

22. A gram is equal to about a pound.

23. A kilometer is less than a mile.

24. A three-year-old boy may be about one meter tall.

25. A three-year-old boy may weigh about 50 grams.

F. *Solve these reading problems.*

26. Mother bought 12 pounds of bananas at 3 pounds for $1.00. What did Mother pay for the bananas?

27. Mother also bought $3\frac{1}{2}$ pounds of ground beef at $1.38 a pound. What was the cost of the meat?

28. Uncle Ray drove 324 miles on 12 gallons of gasoline. How many miles per gallon did he drive?

134. Working With Money

A. *Do these exercises.*

1. Write each price in two ways.

   a. thirty-five cents   b. sixteen dollars

2. Write these amounts with dollar signs and decimal points.

   a. five hundred ninety-nine dollars and twenty-five cents
   b. three hundred eighteen dollars and seven cents

3. Write the total value of each set.

   a. 3 quarters, 6 dimes
   b. 5 quarters, 4 nickels, 7 pennies
   c. 3 five-dollar bills, 1 half dollar
   d. 2 twenty-dollar bills, 2 five-dollar bills, 6 nickels
   e. 4 one-dollar bills, 4 quarters, 5 dimes, 5 nickels
   f. 1 half dollar, 3 quarters, 2 dimes, 3 nickels

4. List the pieces of money that should be returned as change in each situation. Start with the smallest pieces.

   a. Your purchase—$3.82; amount given—$5.00
   b. Your purchase—$12.44; amount given—$20.00
   c. Your purchase—$23.65; amount given—two 20-dollar bills

B. *Copy in straight columns. Follow the signs.*

5. $5.79 + $17 + $48.32 + $7.25 $659.30 + $35.78 + $863.46
6. $980.36 – $375.98 $741 – $57.28 $53.02 – $47

C. *Copy and multiply carefully. Remember the dollar signs and decimal points in the answers.*

7.
$$\begin{array}{r} \$3.48 \\ \times\ \ \ 8 \\ \hline \end{array} \qquad \begin{array}{r} \$5.67 \\ \times\ \ 25 \\ \hline \end{array} \qquad \begin{array}{r} \$8.09 \\ \times\ \ 18 \\ \hline \end{array} \qquad \begin{array}{r} \$78.50 \\ \times\ \ \ \ 9 \\ \hline \end{array} \qquad \begin{array}{r} \$40.65 \\ \times\ \ \ 64 \\ \hline \end{array}$$

8.
$$\begin{array}{r} \$5.00 \\ \times\ 830 \\ \hline \end{array} \qquad \begin{array}{r} \$7.30 \\ \times\ 269 \\ \hline \end{array} \qquad \begin{array}{r} \$4.08 \\ \times\ 437 \\ \hline \end{array} \qquad \begin{array}{r} \$3.29 \\ \times\ 604 \\ \hline \end{array} \qquad \begin{array}{r} \$7.25 \\ \times\ 735 \\ \hline \end{array}$$

Reading Problems

D. *Solve the reading problems below. Use the chart for numbers 9–15.*

Highest Mountain Peaks on the Seven Continents		
Location	Name of Peak	Height in Feet
Asia (Nepal-Tibet)	Mount Everest	29,028
South America (Argentina)	Mount Aconcagua	22,834
North America (Alaska)	Mount McKinley	20,320
Africa (Tanzania)	Mount Kilimanjaro	19,340
Antarctica	Vinson Massif Peak	16,864
Europe (France)	Mont Blanc	15,771
Australia	Mount Kosciusko	7,310

9. What is the name of the highest mountain peak in North America?

10. Mount Everest is _____ feet higher than the highest peak in North America.

11. The difference in height between Mount Kilimanjaro and Mont Blanc is _____ feet.

12. The highest mountain in Australia is _____ feet lower than the highest peak in Antarctica.

13. About how many miles high is Mount Aconcagua? Choose the most sensible estimate. (2 miles, 4 miles, 5 miles, 7 miles)

14. In 1958 Edmund Hillary and Tenzing Norgay first climbed Mount Everest. How many years ago was that?

15. The deepest point yet discovered in the Pacific Ocean is the Mariana Trench, east of the Philippines. There the ocean is 35,840 feet deep. If the highest mountain could be placed at the bottom of the Mariana Trench, how many feet of water would still be above the mountain?

16. Two pounds of plums are marked $1.59. What is the price of eight pounds?

17. What is the cost of a dozen light bulbs at 4 for $1.89?

18. If a package of 12 pencils costs $1.56, what is the price of 6 pencils?

135. Multiplying Decimals

Sister Helen wants to make a border for her bulletin board. She has strips of blue paper each 30.5 centimeters long. How long a strip can Sister Helen make if she tapes 12 of the strips together?

To find the answer to this question, you need to multiply 12 times 30.5, a decimal.

Decimals are multiplied in the same way as amounts of money. First multiply as if there were no decimal point. After you multiply, place the decimal point in the answer. There are as many decimal places in the answer as in the problem. Study the problems below.

6.8	0.375	64.8	5.29	1.809
× 6	× 4	× 37	× 465	× 28
40.8	1.500	4536	2645	14472
		1944	3174	3618
		2,397.6	2116	50.652
			2,459.85	

A. *Do this exercise.*

1. Find the answer to the problem at the top of the page. (How long a strip of paper will Sister Helen have if she tapes together 12 strips of paper each 30.5 centimeters long?)

B. *Copy and multiply. Remember the decimal points in the answers!*

2.
8.3	4.5	0.67	5.96	9.138
× 7	× 9	× 4	× 6	× 7

3.
0.57	9.3	71.6	0.325	6.490
× 35	× 64	× 70	× 89	× 58

4.
4.23	16.2	8.06	0.915	7.29
× 163	× 850	× 498	× 205	× 349

General Review

C. *Follow the directions.*

5. Write as decimals and as common fractions or mixed numbers.
   a. six and three tenths
   b. ninety-five and seventeen thousandths
   c. forty and fifty-eight hundredths
   d. two hundred thirty-seven thousandths

6. Copy each set of decimals in order of size, beginning with the smallest. (Annex zeroes if you need help.)
   a. 4.7 4.07 4.007
   b. 0.037 0.2 0.03
   c. 5.50 5.9 5.95
   d. 0.67 6.7 0.067
   e. 1.15 1.51 1.151
   f. 0.009 0.01 0.1

7. Copy the following number, and place commas correctly. Circle the digit in hundred millions' place.   80345291760

8. Write the number that means 80,000 + 4,000 + 300 + 50 + 8.

D. Write yes or no.

9. Is 18 a prime number?

10. Are 6 and 4 factors of 12?

11. Is 8 a multiple of 12?

12. Is $\frac{6}{4}$ an improper fraction?

13. Are there 8 halves in 4 wholes?

14. Is a span about 9 inches?

15. Is a centimeter equal to 10 millimeters?

16. Is a kilometer equal to 10 meters?

17. Are there 1,000 millimeters in a meter?

18. Is a kilogram equal to about 2.2 pounds?

19. Could you drink 30 liters of water if you were very thirsty?

20. Was a furlong used to measure long distances on land?

E. Solve these reading problems.

21. King Solomon built the "house of the forest of Lebanon." The house was 100 cubits long, 50 cubits wide, and 30 cubits high. What are these three measurements in feet?

22. What is the cost of $2\frac{1}{2}$ yards of oilcloth at $3.50 per yard?

23. What is the cost of 6 pounds of ripe bananas at 4 pounds for $1.00?

136. Practice With Multiplying Decimals

In Lesson 135 you multiplied decimals by whole numbers. The decimal was the multiplicand in all those problems. But in this lesson, the decimal is sometimes the multiplier. These problems are solved in the same way as the ones in Lesson 135.

Study the two problems in the box. Notice that the factors in the two problems are exchanged. Therefore, both have the same answer, including the placement of the decimal point.

```
      51.8              638
    x 638            x 51.8
     4144             5104
     1554              638
    3108              3190
   33,048.4          33,048.4
```

A. Copy and multiply. Remember the decimal points in the answers!

1.
4.5	0.72	6.8	8.3	0.96
x 78	x 65	x 48	x 79	x 50

2.
3.75	0.208	73.1	40.9	0.438
x 9	x 7	x 569	x 248	x 602

3.
509	725	430	817	626
x 4.6	x 0.57	x 7.8	x 1.26	x 0.643

B. Solve these reading problems.

4. Planing makes the surfaces of lumber smooth. A rough board one inch thick will often be reduced to 0.75 inch thick in the planing process. How high is a stack of twenty planed boards each 0.75 inch thick?

5. A board 12 inches wide is reduced to 11.5 inches when it is planed. What is the total width of twenty 12-inch boards after planing?

6. To repair a broken section of the porch, Father bought 26 planed one-by-fours each 3.5 inches wide. He plans to place the boards side by side on the porch. How wide an area will the boards cover?

General Review

C. *Do these exercises.*

7. 6)51,304   8)16,368   5)73,210   4)27,318

8. 25)6,100   17)8,534   46)57,960   31)63,178

9. Write the meanings of these metric prefixes.
   a. kilo-   **b.** centi-   **c.** hecto-   **d.** deci-   **e.** milli-   **f.** deka-

D. *Write the numbers that belong in the blanks.*

10. 1 kilometer = _____ meters   1 liter = _____ milliliters
11. 1 meter = _____ centimeters   1 centimeter = _____ millimeters
12. 1 gram = _____ milligrams   1 kilogram = _____ grams
13. 1 meter = _____ millimeters   1 gram = _____ centigrams
14. 18 cm = _____ mm   70 mm = _____ cm

15. On the Celsius scale, the freezing point of water is _____° and the boiling point is _____°.

16. On the Fahrenheit scale, the freezing point of water is _____° and the boiling point is _____°.

17. 3 bushels = _____ pk.   3 pecks = _____ qt.   3 quarts = _____ pt.
18. 3 pints = _____ qt.   3 quarts = _____ cups   3 yards = _____ ft.
19. 3 inches = _____ ft.   3 quarts = _____ gal.   3 days = _____ hr.
20. 30 minutes = _____ hr.   30 feet = _____ yd.   30 days = _____ wk.

137. Dividing Money

The Bethel Bible School offers three-week courses for young people to come and study the Bible. Each student pays $95.00 per term to help cover the costs of the Bible school. If the students are at Bible school for 20 days during the three weeks, how much do they pay per day?

To find the answer, divide $95.00 by 20. Notice that the decimal point in the quotient is placed directly above the decimal point in the dividend.

```
       $  4.75
  20)$95.00
      80
      150
      140
       100
       100
```

A. *Copy and divide. Be sure to place dollar signs and decimal points correctly in the quotients.*

1. 9)$14.76   5)$74.00   3)$82.14   8)$90.56

2. 25)$78.50   38)$40.28   53)$24.91   17)$37.23

3. 42)$128.52   12)$189.84   30)$522.00   26)$110.50

B. *Solve these reading problems.*

4. Students who attend Bethel Bible School for only part of a term pay more per day than those who go for the whole term. Trudy attended Bible school for 12 days and paid $75.00. How much did she pay per day?

5. Offerings are given to help support the Bible school. Four offerings amounted to $327.80, $540.75, $483.55, and $395.10. What was the average of the four offerings?

6. The cooks at Bible school served 85 people at one meal. Food for the meal would have cost $109.65 if it had all been purchased. How much would the meal have cost for each person served?

7. Much of the food was given to the Bible school, so the actual cost of the meal for 85 people was only $22.95. What was the cost to the Bible school per person served?

General Review

C. *Do these exercises.*

8.   0.365   617   8.79   40.8   750
    ×   46   × 8.4   × 36   × 489   × 0.178

9. a. $\frac{4}{5} \times 30$ b. $15 \times \frac{3}{4}$ c. $\frac{3}{8} \times \frac{11}{12}$ d. $\frac{4}{7} \times \frac{7}{16}$

10. a. $\frac{3}{4} \div 2$ b. $\frac{7}{12} \div \frac{1}{3}$ c. $6 \div \frac{2}{3}$ d. $\frac{9}{16} \div \frac{3}{8}$

11. List the prime numbers between 20 and 30.

12. List all the factors of 24.

D. *Subtract to find the amount of change.*

13. Your purchase—$4.68;   amount given—$10.00

14. Your purchase—$5.12;   amount given—$20.12

15. Your purchase—$13.54;   amount given—$20.00

E. *List the pieces of money that should be given as change. Be ready to count out the change in class.*

16. Your purchase—$2.44;   amount given—$3.00

17. Your purchase—$3.65;   amount given—$10.00

18. Your purchase—$16.32;   amount given—$20.00

F. *Solve these reading problems.*

19. Mother counted the money in her purse. She had one 20-dollar bill, two 10-dollar bills, two 5-dollar bills, and six 1-dollar bills. How much money was that altogether?

20. Mother also had 7 quarters, 8 dimes, 5 nickels, and 14 pennies in her purse. How much money did she have in coins?

138. Dividing Decimals by Whole Numbers

Dividing decimals by whole numbers is much the same as dividing money. Divide as you usually do, and remember to place the decimal point in the quotient directly above the decimal point in the dividend. Study the example below.

Indiana's total precipitation one year was 39.12 inches. What was the average precipitation each month?

To find the answer, divide 39.12 inches by 12, the number of months in a year. The problem at the right shows that the average monthly precipitation was 3.26 inches.

```
        3.26
   12)39.12
      36
       3 1
       2 4
         72
         72
```

Sometimes zeroes need to be placed after the decimal point to fill up empty places. Study the examples at the right.

The multiplication check is written for the second problem.

```
     0.062              0.081      Check:
   9)0.558          33)2.673       0.081
     54                2 64        x   33
     18                  33          243
     18                  33        2 43
      0                   0        2.673
```

A. Copy and divide as shown in the lesson. Check by multiplication if your teacher tells you to.

1. 8)5.84   6)0.588   7)4.207   9)115.2

2. 26)83.2   15)11.10   11)26.4   22)0.330

3. 17)23.97   21)8.883   13)120.9   44)3.784

4. 19)457.9   31)89.90   14)182.0   12)10.44

5. 12)19.80   18)3.960   23)12.19   16)147.2

General Review

B. Copy and solve.

6. 0.378   2.764   60.75   370.9
    x   6   x   9   x   57   x   35

7. $\frac{3}{5} \times 30$ $\frac{7}{8} \times \frac{1}{2}$ $8 \times \frac{2}{3}$ $\frac{11}{12} \times \frac{3}{4}$

8. $12 \div \frac{2}{3}$ $\frac{15}{16} \div 3$ $\frac{1}{3} \div \frac{3}{4}$ $\frac{5}{8} \div \frac{5}{16}$

C. *Tell what pieces of money should be given as change.*

9. Your purchase—$3.40;   amount given—$10.00

10. Your purchase—$9.56;   amount given—$20.00

11. Your purchase—$22.73;   amount given—$40.00

D. *Write T for true or F for false.*

12. Some prime numbers are 15 and 17.

13. The factors of 21 are 1, 3, 7, and 21.

14. Some factors of 12 are 24, 36, and 48.

15. One multiple of 3 is 9.

16. A meter is a little more than a yard.

17. A kilogram is equal to about 2.2 pounds.

18. A gram is equal to about 35 ounces.

19. A kilogram has 1,000 grams.

20. A meter has 100 centimeters.

21. A centimeter has 10 millimeters.

22. A meter is equal to 1,000 kilometers.

23. A cubit is about 9 inches.

24. A fathom measures the depth of water.

E. *Solve these reading problems.*

25. The Johnsons raised a steer for meat. The butcher said that the steer weighed 960 pounds, but 385.5 pounds of that was waste. How many pounds of meat were left?

26. The part of the steer called the round weighed 50.4 pounds. From the round, the butcher cut 14 round steaks. What was the average weight of each round steak?

139. More Division of Decimals

Study the problems in the box. The first two are based on simple division facts. But though the numbers are simple, it takes special care to place decimal points and extra zeroes correctly.

When dividing a decimal by a whole number, remember the following things.

1. Place the decimal point in the quotient directly above the decimal point in the dividend.

2. Place zeroes in any empty places between the decimal point and the rest of the quotient.

$$\begin{array}{r} 0.08 \\ 4\overline{)0.32} \\ 32 \end{array} \qquad \begin{array}{r} 0.004 \\ 3\overline{)0.012} \\ 12 \end{array} \qquad \begin{array}{r} 0.053 \\ 25\overline{)1.325} \\ 1\ 25 \\ \hline 75 \\ 75 \\ \hline \end{array}$$

A. *Copy and divide. Be especially careful with decimal points and zeroes in the quotients.*

1. $6\overline{)0.354}$ $5\overline{)0.410}$ $8\overline{)1.240}$ $4\overline{)0.036}$

2. $3\overline{)0.18}$ $9\overline{)0.486}$ $7\overline{)0.056}$ $5\overline{)0.95}$

3. $12\overline{)0.72}$ $11\overline{)0.385}$ $10\overline{)4.960}$ $12\overline{)1.008}$

4. $27\overline{)1.35}$ $25\overline{)385.0}$ $14\overline{)26.88}$ $18\overline{)261.0}$

B. *Divide, and check by multiplication.*

5. $37\overline{)53.28}$ $42\overline{)67.20}$ $26\overline{)1.690}$ $14\overline{)284.2}$

C. *Answer as briefly as possible.*

6. How many meters are in a kilometer?

7. How many millimeters are in a centimeter?

8. Could a person have a birthday on June 31?

9. How many days are in a leap year?

10. What are the factors of 18?

11. Name three multiples of 8.

12. Which is more: a quart or three cups?

13. What are the freezing and boiling points on the Celsius scale?

Reading Problems

D. *Solve these reading problems. You may need to do some hidden steps before you can find the final answer.*

14. The price of tropicana rosebushes is $7.99 each or three for $21.99. How much is saved per bush if you buy three for $21.99? To solve this two-step problem, think:

   a. At three for $21.99, what is the price of one rosebush?

   b. How much less is that price than $7.99?

15. Mr. Hudson bought his wife 6 rosebushes at the price of 3 for $21.99. What did Mr. Hudson pay for the rosebushes?

16. Mrs. Fulton bought 3 red rosebushes at 3 for $21.99 and two pink rosebushes at $8.99 each. What was her bill?

17. Sister Ruth has a square flower bed that measures 6.5 feet along each side. What is the distance around the flower bed? (Hint: How many equal sides does a square have?)

18. Sister Ruth planted a row of tall zinnias, which divided her flower bed in half. If the length of her flower bed is 6.50 feet, how many feet are on each side of the row of zinnias?

19. The normal yearly rainfall in Philadelphia, Pennsylvania, is 41 inches. In 1990, Philadelphia received only 0.87 of the normal amount of rainfall. How many inches of rainfall did Philadelphia receive in 1990? (Remember that **of** means "times.")

20. Mother bought a 25-pound bag of flour. She used 2.25 pounds to make cookies, 1.5 pounds to make a cake, and 6.5 pounds to make bread. How many pounds of flour are left?

21. Grandfather is planning to order $47.50 worth of books from Camdon Bible Publishers. The company charges $\frac{1}{10}$ of the total amount of an order to pay for mailing costs. What is Grandfather's total bill? (Remember that you can divide to find $\frac{1}{10}$ of a number.)

22. Brother Vincent built a house and sold it for $75,000. His expenses were $34,842 for materials and $33,950 for labor. If Brother Vincent gives the Lord one-eighth of the profit he makes, how much of the money from the house will he give to the Lord? (Hint: Figure the profit first.)

140. Chapter 14 Review

A. *Write the answers only.*

1. 6)54   7)42   9)72   7)56   11)121   12)84

2. 8)64   5)45   7)49   8)96   10)110   11)132

3. 8)32   9)81   6)48   9)36   12)108   10)120

B. *Do these exercises.*

4. Write as decimals and as common fractions or mixed numbers.
    a. sixteen and thirty-nine thousands
    b. four and eight hundredths
    c. seventy-two and nine tenths
    d. one and three hundred sixty-five thousandths

5. Write each set in the order of size, from smallest to largest.
    a. 0.17   0.71   0.7   d. 0.03   0.1   0.002
    b. 0.25   2.5   0.025   e. 0.05   0.025   0.052
    c. 4.16   4.016 4.061   f. 0.4   0.25   0.433

C. *Write the missing words or numbers.*

6. On the Celsius scale, the freezing point is _____° and the boiling point is _____°.

7. On the Fahrenheit scale, the freezing point is _____° and the boiling point is _____°.

8. One thousand meters equals one _____.

9. Ten millimeters equals one _____.

10. One hundred centimeters equals one _____.

11. There are _____ grams in a kilogram.

12. The metric unit a little larger than a quart is the _____.

13. The basic metric unit of length is the _____.

14. A centimeter is a little less than a half (inch, foot, meter).

15. A fifth grader would be most likely to weigh (35 grams, 35 kilograms, 35 pounds).

D. *Find the change by subtraction.*

16. Your purchase—$5.36;   amount given—$10.00

17. Your purchase—$12.17;   amount given—$20.17

18. Your purchase—$7.62;   amount given—$20.00

E. *List the pieces of money that should be given as change. Start with the smallest pieces, and use as few pieces as possible.*

19. Your purchase—$3.28;   amount given—$5.00

20. Your purchase—$6.76;   amount given—$10.00

21. Your purchase—$4.35;   amount given—$20.00

Computation Review

F. *Copy and solve.*

22.
$$\begin{array}{r} \$43.50 \\ \times\ \ \ \ 12 \\ \hline \end{array} \qquad \begin{array}{r} \$30.96 \\ \times\ \ \ \ 63 \\ \hline \end{array} \qquad \begin{array}{r} \$2.78 \\ \times\ 350 \\ \hline \end{array} \qquad \begin{array}{r} \$6.29 \\ \times\ 481 \\ \hline \end{array}$$

23.
$$\begin{array}{r} 4.8 \\ \times\ 7 \\ \hline \end{array} \qquad \begin{array}{r} 0.57 \\ \times\ \ 8 \\ \hline \end{array} \qquad \begin{array}{r} 3.962 \\ \times\ \ \ \ 4 \\ \hline \end{array} \qquad \begin{array}{r} 471.6 \\ \times\ \ \ \ 7 \\ \hline \end{array}$$

24.
$$\begin{array}{r} 0.76 \\ \times\ 25 \\ \hline \end{array} \qquad \begin{array}{r} 9.3 \\ \times\ 57 \\ \hline \end{array} \qquad \begin{array}{r} 34.07 \\ \times\ \ 82 \\ \hline \end{array} \qquad \begin{array}{r} 8.160 \\ \times\ \ 89 \\ \hline \end{array}$$

25.
$$\begin{array}{r} 530 \\ \times\ 5.6 \\ \hline \end{array} \qquad \begin{array}{r} 728 \\ \times\ 0.39 \\ \hline \end{array} \qquad \begin{array}{r} 914 \\ \times\ 19.4 \\ \hline \end{array} \qquad \begin{array}{r} 607 \\ \times\ 0.749 \\ \hline \end{array}$$

26. $6\overline{)\$143.46}$ $9\overline{)\$965.16}$ $17\overline{)\$59.50}$ $35\overline{)\$23.45}$

27. $7\overline{)0.168}$ $8\overline{)0.064}$ $5\overline{)0.085}$ $4\overline{)0.252}$

28. $10\overline{)35.40}$ $11\overline{)13.2}$ $12\overline{)0.156}$ $11\overline{)2.354}$

29. $12\overline{)19.2}$ $18\overline{)10.98}$ $12\overline{)3.612}$ $22\overline{)31.02}$

30. $38\overline{)4.56}$ $26\overline{)1.378}$ $17\overline{)613.7}$ $44\overline{)118.8}$

(continued on next page)

Reading Problem Review

G. *Solve these problems.*

31. Four bars of soap cost $3.00. What is the price for one bar of soap?

32. Nectarines are 3 pounds for $1.89. What is the price for 6 pounds of nectarines?

33. If you buy a Bible for $6.55, a box of crayons for $1.69, and 3 coloring books at $1.45 each, what is your total bill?

34. The price of corn flakes is $1.98 for an 18-ounce box and $1.43 for an 11-ounce box. How much would you save per ounce by buying the larger box? (This is a three-step problem.)

35. Mr. Richardson's monthly income is $1,260. He spends $\frac{1}{4}$ of his income on rent for his house. How much does he spend each month for rent?

36. Mother and Father bought some Gospel tracts in Spanish to hand out on their trip to Mexico. They bought 8 dozen tracts at $0.60 per dozen and 6 dozen tracts at $0.65 per dozen. How much did they pay for all the tracts?

37. Father and Mother drove 623.7 miles the first day. If they keep traveling at that rate, how far will they drive in three days?

38. Father figured that he used 21 gallons of gasoline to drive 623.7 miles. At that rate, how many miles per gallon did he drive?

39. The yearly rainfall at Cleveland, Ohio, is 35.40 inches. What is the average monthly rainfall?

141. Chapter 14 Test

Chapter 15

Geometry and Square Measure

Let all things be done decently and in order.
(1 Corinthians 14:40)

142. Introduction to Geometry

Geometry (jē·om′i·trē) is a branch of mathematics that deals with shapes and their measurements. With this lesson you will begin meeting some geometric (jē·ə·met′rik) words and ideas. Study carefully the geometric terms, meanings, and symbols in the box.

Term	Meaning	Symbol
1. **point**	a location usually illustrated with a dot	•
2. **line**	a straight line extending without end in two directions	←———→
3. **line segment**	a part of a line with two end points	•———•
4. **intersecting lines**	two lines that cross each other at a point	✕
5. **parallel lines**	two lines that are always the same distance apart	═══
6. **perpendicular lines**	two lines that meet to form square corners	⌐

A. *Do these exercises.*

1. Write the geometric term for each symbol.

  a. ═══   b. ✕   c. •———•   d. •   e. ←——→   f. ⌐

2. Write **T** for true or **F** for false.

  a. Lines on a music staff are parallel lines.
  b. A line segment is a part of a line.
  c. A line has no end points.
  d. The top and bottom edges of the chalkboard are perpendicular.
  e. The two lines in the letter **X** are intersecting lines.
  f. The two lines in a capital **T** are perpendicular.

3. Write the measurements to which the arrows point. Sample answer: 1.3 cm

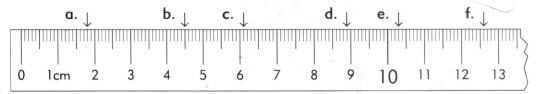

General Review

B. *Write the meanings of these metric prefixes.*

  4. a. deka-   **b.** milli-   **c.** centi-   **d.** kilo-   **e.** deci-   **f.** hecto-

C. *Write the numbers that belong in the blanks.*

5. 6 ft. = _____ yd.   6 yd. = _____ ft.   6 in. = _____ ft.

6. 2 mi. = _____ ft.   2 oz. = _____ lb.   2 cups = _____ pt.

7. 14 wk. = _____ days   14 cups = _____ qt.   14 qt. = _____ pt.

8. 1 km = _____ m   1 m = _____ cm   1 cm = _____ mm

9. 70 mm = _____ cm   70 cm = _____ mm   1 kg = _____ g

D. *Write what you would say as you count out the change. The first answer is started for you.*

10. Amount of purchase—$3.78;   amount given—$10.00

         Answer: $3.78, $3.79 . . .

11. Amount of purchase—$1.42;   amount given—$5.00

12. Amount of purchase—$7.60;   amount given—$20.00

E. *Copy and solve.*

13.
$$\begin{array}{r} 45.7 \\ \times\ 46 \\ \hline \end{array} \qquad \begin{array}{r} 0.936 \\ \times\ 308 \\ \hline \end{array} \qquad \begin{array}{r} 7.30 \\ \times\ 295 \\ \hline \end{array} \qquad \begin{array}{r} 809 \\ \times\ 7.4 \\ \hline \end{array} \qquad \begin{array}{r} 524 \\ \times\ 0.806 \\ \hline \end{array}$$

14.   7)0.133   16)0.48   35)157.5   29)4.147

F. *Solve these reading problems.*

15. One cold day the thermometer at the bank in town showed 0° C. What was the temperature on the Fahrenheit scale?

16. Water boils at 212° F. What is that temperature on the Celsius scale?

17. Lavern weighed 8 pounds when he was born. Now he weighs 88 pounds. How many pounds did he gain since he was born?

18. How many times as heavy is Lavern now than when he was born? (See number 17.)

19. On February 4 Brother Jesse and Brother Richard flew to Paraguay to visit the churches there. They drove to the airport and parked their car there at a cost of $6.00 a day. They returned from Paraguay on February 19. How much did they need to pay to park the car?

143. Introduction to Angles

An **angle** is formed wherever two line segments meet. Angles have different names depending on the position of the two line segments. Study the information in the box below, and notice how the hands of a clock illustrate the various types of angles.

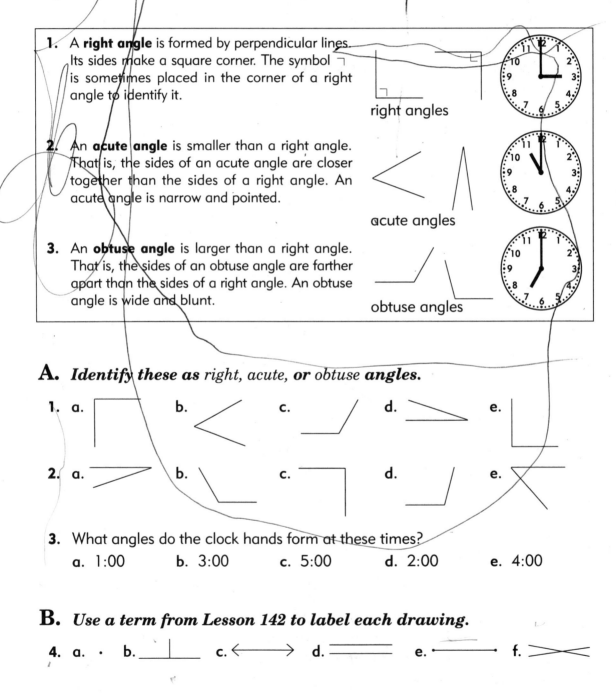

1. A **right angle** is formed by perpendicular lines. Its sides make a square corner. The symbol ⌐ is sometimes placed in the corner of a right angle to identify it.

   right angles

2. An **acute angle** is smaller than a right angle. That is, the sides of an acute angle are closer together than the sides of a right angle. An acute angle is narrow and pointed.

   acute angles

3. An **obtuse angle** is larger than a right angle. That is, the sides of an obtuse angle are farther apart than the sides of a right angle. An obtuse angle is wide and blunt.

   obtuse angles

A. *Identify these as* right, acute, *or* obtuse **angles.**

1. a.   b.   c.   d.   e.

2. a.   b.   c.   d.   e.

3. What angles do the clock hands form at these times?
   a. 1:00   b. 3:00   c. 5:00   d. 2:00   e. 4:00

B. *Use a term from Lesson 142 to label each drawing.*

4. a. •   b. ___|___   c. ⟵⟶   d. ══   e. •——•   f. ⤫

Computation Review

C. *Write the answers only. Watch the signs!*

5.
8	4	9	11	10	3	12	7	6
+ 5	× 8	× 7	− 6	× 10	× 9	− 8	+ 9	× 8

6.
14	11	8	7	12	17	5	8	10
− 9	× 12	+ 7	× 9	× 8	− 8	+ 6	− 7	− 4

7.
9	6	12	10	15	8	9	4	0
× 6	+ 8	× 6	− 7	− 9	× 8	+ 4	× 7	+ 8

8. 3)24   7)49   5)40   9)18   10)120   12)132

9. 5)30   8)72   6)48   2)10   11)110   12)108

D. *Copy and solve these problems. Check your work as indicated.*

10. Check by going over your work.

6,830	97,836	18,428	45,713
7,427	36,509	24,783	69,824
3,185	28,472	68,965	13,657
+ 4,574	+ 18,428	+ 36,509	+ 57,266

11. Check by addition.

9,010	31,280	64,000	73,025
− 4,563	− 29,458	− 37,999	− 28,174

12. Check by going over your work.

859	907	7,290	6,814
× 43	× 98	× 59	× 87

13. Check by exchanging the factors.

a. 467	b. 950	c. 708	d. 639
× 600	× 476	× 934	× 163

14. Check by multiplication.

18)3,426   35)7,350   13)4,000   29)1,218

144. Introduction to Geometric Shapes

A geometric shape is often called a **geometric figure**. Study the list of geometric figures and other terms in the box below.

1. A **triangle** is a three-sided figure.

2. A **rectangle** is a four-sided figure with four right angles.

3. A **square** is a rectangle with four equal sides.

4. A **parallelogram** is a four-sided figure whose opposite sides are parallel.

5. A **pentagon** is a five-sided figure.

6. A **hexagon** is a six-sided figure.

7. An **octagon** is an eight-sided figure.

8. A **circle** is a closed curve with all points an equal distance from the center.

9. A line drawn from the outside edge of a circle to the center is a **radius**.

10. A line drawn from the outside edge of a circle through the center to the other side is a **diameter**.

11. **Similar** figures have the same shape but not the same size.

12. **Congruent** (kən·grōo′ənt) figures have the same size and shape.

A. *Do these exercises.*

1. Write the number of sides that each figure has.
    a. square   c. hexagon   e. parallelogram
    b. octagon   d. pentagon   f. triangle

2. Write the name of each geometric figure.

    a.   b.   c.   d.   e.   f.

3. Write whether each pair of figures is **similar** or **congruent**.
    a.   b.   c.   d.

4. Write whether each angle is right, acute, or obtuse.

a.   b.   c.   d.

Review of Fractions and Reading Problems

B. *Copy and solve.*

5.

$$\begin{array}{r} \frac{3}{4} \\ \frac{1}{2} \\ + \frac{5}{8} \\ \hline \end{array} \qquad \begin{array}{r} \frac{4}{5} \\ \frac{7}{10} \\ + \frac{1}{2} \\ \hline \end{array} \qquad \begin{array}{r} \frac{4}{9} \\ \frac{1}{6} \\ + \frac{2}{3} \\ \hline \end{array} \qquad \begin{array}{r} 9\frac{1}{3} \\ + 5\frac{7}{9} \\ \hline \end{array} \qquad \begin{array}{r} 14\frac{1}{2} \\ + 11\frac{4}{5} \\ \hline \end{array}$$

6.

$$\begin{array}{r} \frac{11}{16} \\ - \frac{3}{8} \\ \hline \end{array} \qquad \begin{array}{r} 12 \\ - 4\frac{5}{9} \\ \hline \end{array} \qquad \begin{array}{r} 9\frac{11}{12} \\ - 6\frac{2}{3} \\ \hline \end{array} \qquad \begin{array}{r} 7\frac{5}{8} \\ - 2\frac{7}{8} \\ \hline \end{array} \qquad \begin{array}{r} 10\frac{1}{3} \\ - 6\frac{7}{9} \\ \hline \end{array}$$

7. $\frac{4}{5} \times \frac{1}{2}$ $5 \times \frac{2}{3}$ $\frac{7}{8} \times 4$ $\frac{3}{4} \times \frac{4}{9}$ $\frac{5}{16} \times \frac{3}{5}$

8. $\frac{5}{8} \div 5$ $\frac{1}{4} \div 6$ $8 \div \frac{2}{3}$ $\frac{7}{12} \div \frac{3}{4}$ $\frac{4}{5} \div \frac{3}{10}$

C. *Solve these reading problems.*

9. During a sale at Danner's Fabrics, material that usually sold for $3.79 was marked 50¢ a yard off. How much did Mother pay for 6 yards of material at the sale price?

10. When the Franklins left on their trip to visit the mission outpost in Colorado, the odometer on the car showed 47,635.6 miles. When they stopped the first night, the odometer read 48,275.1. How far did they drive the first day?

11. Father bought a gallon of milk for $2.35, 2 loaves of bread for $1.19 each, and a box of cereal for $2.49. Find his total bill.

12. At the hardware store, Father's bill was $17.22. What was his change from a twenty-dollar bill? Tell what pieces of money he received if the clerk gave as few pieces as possible.

13. When the children of Israel left Egypt, all the men 20 years old and older were counted except the tribe of Levi. Six hundred three thousand, five hundred fifty men were counted. Write this number as an Arabic numeral.

145. Introduction to Perimeter

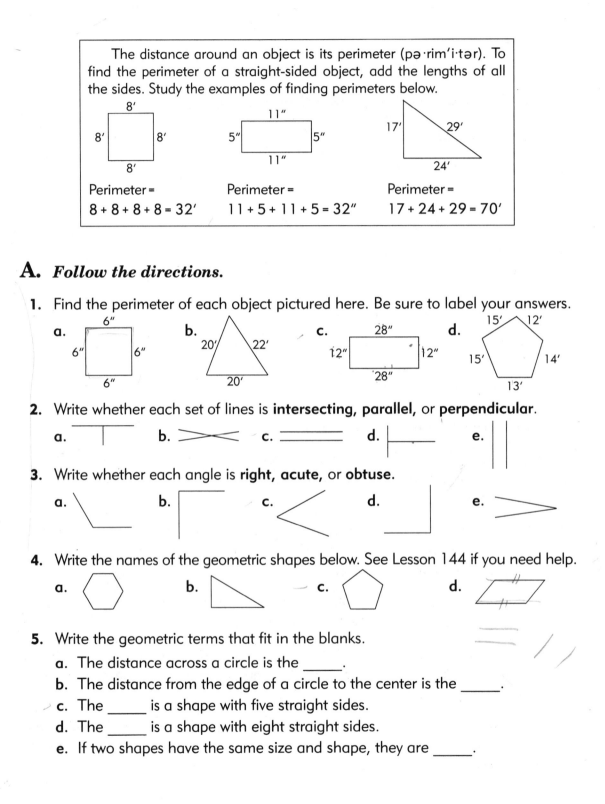

The distance around an object is its perimeter (pə·rim′i·tər). To find the perimeter of a straight-sided object, add the lengths of all the sides. Study the examples of finding perimeters below.

Perimeter =
8 + 8 + 8 + 8 = 32′

Perimeter =
11 + 5 + 11 + 5 = 32″

Perimeter =
17 + 24 + 29 = 70′

A. Follow the directions.

1. Find the perimeter of each object pictured here. Be sure to label your answers.

   a.   b.   c.   d.

2. Write whether each set of lines is **intersecting, parallel,** or **perpendicular.**

   a.   b.   c.   d.   e.

3. Write whether each angle is **right, acute,** or **obtuse.**

   a.   b.   c.   d.   e.

4. Write the names of the geometric shapes below. See Lesson 144 if you need help.

   a.   b.   c.   d.

5. Write the geometric terms that fit in the blanks.
   a. The distance across a circle is the _____.
   b. The distance from the edge of a circle to the center is the _____.
   c. The _____ is a shape with five straight sides.
   d. The _____ is a shape with eight straight sides.
   e. If two shapes have the same size and shape, they are _____.

General Review

B. *Do these exercises.*

6. Reduce these fractions to lowest terms.

  a. $\frac{18}{48}$ **b.** $\frac{16}{40}$ **c.** $\frac{20}{60}$ **d.** $\frac{45}{60}$ **e.** $\frac{8}{36}$ **f.** $\frac{20}{24}$

7. Find the missing numbers in these proportions.

  a. $\frac{3}{5}=\frac{?}{30}$ **b.** $\frac{?}{30}=\frac{1}{2}$ **c.** $\frac{25}{?}=\frac{5}{6}$ **d.** $\frac{7}{10}=\frac{?}{30}$ **e.** $\frac{27}{30}=\frac{?}{10}$

8. Write these decimals as percents.

  a. 0.03   **b.** 0.19   **c.** 0.98   **d.** 0.40   **e.** 0.76

9. Change these fractions to percents by first changing them to hundredths.

  a. $\frac{1}{4}$ **b.** $\frac{14}{25}$ **c.** $\frac{3}{5}$ **d.** $\frac{1}{2}$ **e.** $\frac{37}{50}$ **f.** $\frac{9}{10}$ **g.** $\frac{19}{20}$

10. Copy and divide. Check by multiplication.

  $8\overline{)0.344}$ $6\overline{)58.14}$ $14\overline{)49.0}$ $37\overline{)2.294}$

11. Copy the name of the larger unit in each pair.

  a. mile, kilometer   **e.** meter, yard
  b. quart, liter   **f.** centimeter, inch
  c. pound, kilogram   **g.** centimeter, millimeter
  d. ounce, gram   **h.** milligram, kilogram

12. Copy and solve these measure problems.

  3 days 16 hours   8 years 4 months   4 quarts 2 cups
  + 2 days 10 hours   − 4 years 8 months   × 4

C. *Solve these reading problems.*

13. The Yoders have a triangular wood lot at the back of their property. The three sides measure 320 yards, 275 yards, and 150 yards. What is the perimeter of the wood lot?

14. Susanna and Sylvia are collecting stamps. Susanna has 272 stamps, and Sylvia has 68. Susanna has _____ times as many stamps as Sylvia has.

146. Perimeter of Squares and Rectangles

Special rules can help us find perimeters of squares and rectangles more easily than adding all the sides together. These rules are given below.

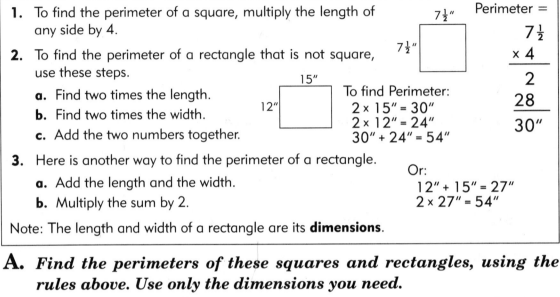

1. To find the perimeter of a square, multiply the length of any side by 4.

2. To find the perimeter of a rectangle that is not square, use these steps.

   a. Find two times the length.
   b. Find two times the width.
   c. Add the two numbers together.

   To find Perimeter:
   2 × 15" = 30"
   2 × 12" = 24"
   30" + 24" = 54"

   Perimeter =

   $7\frac{1}{2}$
   × 4
   $\overline{2}$
   28
   $\overline{30"}$

3. Here is another way to find the perimeter of a rectangle.

   a. Add the length and the width.
   b. Multiply the sum by 2.

   Or:
   12" + 15" = 27"
   2 × 27" = 54"

Note: The length and width of a rectangle are its **dimensions**.

A. Find the perimeters of these squares and rectangles, using the rules above. Use only the dimensions you need.

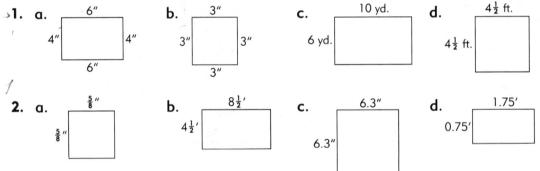

1. a. 6" 4" 4" 6"
   b. 3" 3" 3" 3"
   c. 10 yd. 6 yd.
   d. $4\frac{1}{2}$ ft. $4\frac{1}{2}$ ft.

2. a. $\frac{5}{8}$" $\frac{5}{8}$"
   b. $8\frac{1}{2}$' $4\frac{1}{2}$'
   c. 6.3" 6.3"
   d. 1.75' 0.75'

B. Write the words or numbers that fit in the blanks.

3. An octagon has _____ sides; a hexagon has _____ sides.

4. A pentagon has _____ sides; a triangle has _____ sides.

5. A parallelogram has four sides, and the opposite sides are _____.

6. A rectangle has four sides, and the corners are _____ angles.

7. A square has four _____ sides.

8. A diameter is the distance across a _____.

9. At 2:00 and at 11:00, the hands of a clock form _____ angles.

10. Figures with the same shape but not the same size are _____.

Practice With Mental Arithmetic

To add 18 + 15 mentally,
    think: 18 + 10 = 28
              28 + 5 = 33
	Or think: 10 + 10 = 20
	              8 + 5 = 13
	              20 + 13 = 33

To subtract 33 − 18 mentally,
    think: 33 − 10 = 23
              23 − 8 = 15
	Or think: 33 − 8 = 25
	              25 − 10 = 15

To multiply 4 × 16 mentally,
    think: 4 × 10 = 40
              4 × 6 = 24
              40 + 24 = 64
	Or think: 4 × 6 = 24
	              4 × 10 = 40
	              24 + 40 = 64

C. *Find the answers mentally, and write the answers only.*

11. 15 + 17   19 + 12   15 + 24   27 + 13   36 + 18
12. 16 + 14   27 + 18   19 + 14   17 + 24   35 + 20
13. 20 − 6   24 − 8   26 − 9   31 − 7   35 − 5
14. 26 − 8   32 − 7   30 − 8   24 − 6   33 − 9
15. 27 − 10   28 − 18   35 − 22   29 − 16   33 − 12
16. 31 − 17   36 − 18   42 − 17   32 − 26   40 − 16
17. 4 × 17   5 × 16   4 × 24   6 × 13   8 × 23
18. 6 × 14   7 × 13   9 × 17   4 × 18   5 × 24

General Review

D. *Review the rules of divisibility in Lesson 68. Then answer* yes *or* no *to each question below.*

19. Is 8,320 divisible by: a. 2?   b. 3?   c. 4?   d. 5?   e. 6?   f. 9?   g. 10?
20. Is 7,632 divisible by: a. 2?   b. 3?   c. 4?   d. 5?   e. 6?   f. 9?   g. 10?
21. Is 5,895 divisible by: a. 2?   b. 3?   c. 4?   d. 5?   e. 6?   f. 9?   g. 10?

E. *Write each set in the order of size, from smallest to largest.*

22. a. 0.018 0.081 0.08   b. 0.4   0.09   0.006
23. a. 0.2   0.27   0.17   b. 3.4   0.34   0.034
24. a. 6.005 6.05   6.5   b. 0.013 0.031 0.03

F. *Write these as Roman numerals.*

25. a. 784   b. 1,290   c. 975   d. 2,047   e. 428   f. 1,819

147. Introduction to Area and Square Units

Inches, feet, yards, centimeters, and meters measure one dimension: length. Perimeter has one dimension; it is the length or distance around a straight-sided figure.

Squares and rectangles do not have only length or only width; they have both. Since they have two dimensions, they contain a certain amount of **surface**. The amount of surface in a figure is its **area**.

Area is measured with units of square measure, or **square units**. Instead of using inches, feet, or centimeters, we use square inches, square feet, or square centimeters to measure area.

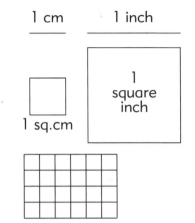

One way to find the area of a figure is to divide it into square units. The rectangle above has been divided into blocks each representing one square inch. By counting the blocks, you can tell that the rectangle has an area of 24 square inches.

The easiest way to find the number of square units in a square or rectangle is to multiply the length and the width. The rectangle above is 6 inches long and 4 inches wide. Its area is 6 × 4, or 24, square inches.

A. Do these exercises.

1. Find the area of each figure by counting. Each square represents 1 square inch (sq. in.).

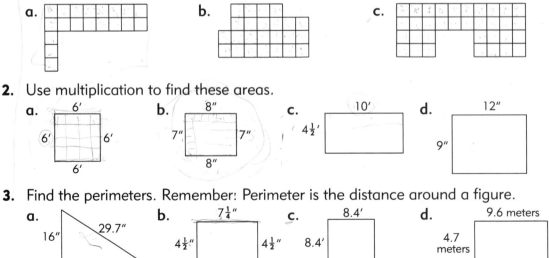

2. Use multiplication to find these areas.

a. 6' × 6' × 6'

b. 8" × 7" × 7" × 8"

c. 10' × 4½'

d. 12" × 9"

3. Find the perimeters. Remember: Perimeter is the distance around a figure.

a. 16", 29.7", 25"

b. 7¼", 4½", 7¼"

c. 8.4', 4½', 8.4'

d. 9.6 meters, 4.7 meters

B. *Write the answers.*

4. Do clock hands at these times form **right, acute,** or **obtuse** angles?

   a. 5:00   b. 11:00   c. 2:00   d. 9:00   e. 8:00

5. Write the name of each geometric shape.

   a.   b.   c.   d.   e.

6. Is 1,824 divisible by: a. 2? b. 3? c. 4? d. 5? e. 6? f. 9? g. 10?

7. Is 7,425 divisible by: a. 2? b. 3? c. 4? d. 5? e. 6? f. 9? g. 10?

Using Sketches to Solve Reading Problems

Some reading problems are easier to solve if a sketch is made. Study the example below.

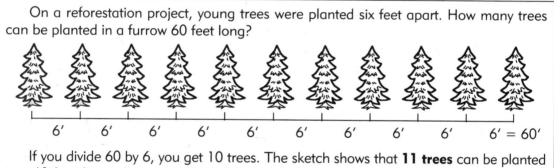

On a reforestation project, young trees were planted six feet apart. How many trees can be planted in a furrow 60 feet long?

6'   6'   6'   6'   6'   6'   6'   6'   6'   6' = 60'

If you divide 60 by 6, you get 10 trees. The sketch shows that **11 trees** can be planted in a 60-foot furrow because a tree is planted at each end.

C. *Draw a simple sketch for each problem. Then find the answer.*

8. Edwin lives 3.7 kilometers south of James's home. James lives 5.5 kilometers south of Nelson's home. How far is Edwin's home from Nelson's home?

9. The veil of the tabernacle was a beautifully embroidered linen curtain separating the two rooms in the tabernacle that Israel built for God. The veil was 15 feet long and 15 feet high. What was the area of the veil?

10. The court of the tabernacle was 100 cubits long and 50 cubits wide. What was the perimeter of the court in cubits? What was its perimeter in feet?

11. Six posts are in a row, with 12 feet between each post and the next. What is the distance between the first and last posts?

12. Mr. Freed had a rough board $\frac{15}{16}$ inch thick. When he planed the board, he removed $\frac{1}{16}$ inch from the bottom side of the board and $\frac{1}{8}$ inch from the top side. What was the thickness of the board after it was planed?

148. Working With Area

Study these facts about area and square units. Only the last one is new for you.

---

1. Area is a measurement of the surface of a two-dimensional figure.

2. Area is measured in square units. Some square units are the square inch, square foot, square yard, and square centimeter. One square inch is equal to a square measuring 1 inch along each side. One square foot is equal to a square with dimensions of one foot.

3. To find the area of a square or rectangle, multiply the length and width to find the number of square units.

$$\text{inches times inches} = \text{square inches}$$

$$\text{feet times feet} = \text{square feet}$$

4. Learn these square measure equivalents.

1 square yard (sq. yd.) = 9 square feet (sq. ft.)

1 square foot = 144 square inches (sq. in.)

A. *Write the numbers that belong in the blanks. (Multiply to change to a smaller unit of measure. Divide to change to a larger unit.)*

1. 27 sq. ft. = _____ sq. yd.   4 sq. ft. = _____ sq. in.

2. 9 sq. yd. = _____ sq. ft.   9 sq. ft. = _____ sq. yd.

3. 3 sq. ft. = _____ sq. in.   3 sq. ft. = _____ sq. yd.

B. *Find the areas of these squares and rectangles.*

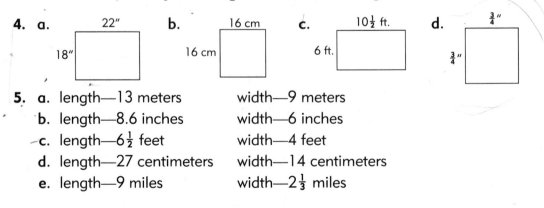

4. a. 22″ 18″   **b.** 16 cm 16 cm   **c.** 10½ ft. 6 ft.   **d.** ¾″ ¾″

5. a. length—13 meters   width—9 meters
   b. length—8.6 inches   width—6 inches
   c. length—6½ feet   width—4 feet
   d. length—27 centimeters   width—14 centimeters
   e. length—9 miles   width—2⅓ miles

General Review

C. *Do these exercises.*

6. Find the perimeter of each figure.

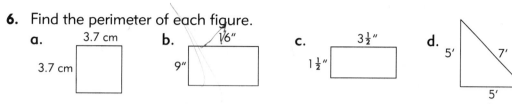

a.   3.7 cm

3.7 cm

b.   ⅙"

9"

c.   3½"

1½"

d.   5'   7'

5'

7. Draw a shape or symbol to illustrate each geometric term.

a. line
b. point
c. perpendicular lines
d. parallel lines
e. intersecting lines

f. right angle
g. obtuse angle
h. acute angle
I. square
j. congruent circles

D. *Copy and multiply.*

8.

$$27 \times 1.3 \qquad 0.256 \times 37 \qquad 4.85 \times 350 \qquad 607 \times .75 \qquad 41.9 \times 673$$

9.

$$14 \times 5\frac{3}{7} \qquad 24 \times 4\frac{2}{3} \qquad 18 \times 5\frac{4}{9} \qquad 30 \times 8\frac{5}{6} \qquad 28 \times 3\frac{3}{4}$$

10.

$$18\frac{1}{2} \times 4 \qquad 11\frac{2}{3} \times 6 \qquad 19\frac{1}{3} \times 9 \qquad 13\frac{3}{4} \times 8 \qquad 16\frac{1}{2} \times 6$$

11. $\frac{2}{3} \times \frac{7}{12} \qquad 8 \times \frac{3}{4} \qquad \frac{2}{5} \times \frac{1}{5} \qquad \frac{7}{9} \times 3 \qquad \frac{9}{16} \times \frac{2}{9}$

E. *Draw a simple sketch for each problem, and then find the answer.*

12. Aunt Lois wants to plant 16 tomato plants in a row, with 2 feet between each plant and the next. How long will the row be?

13. Wilmer and Ethan live along the same road. Wilmer lives 7.8 miles **west** of the church and 6.5 miles **east** of Ethan's home. How far is Ethan's home from the church?

14. If a car is traveling at a rate of 75 kilometers per hour, how far will it travel in 3 hours?

149. Acres and Square Miles

A **square mile** is equal to a very large square that measures a mile along each side. The number of square feet in a square mile is 5,280 × 5,280—a very large number!

The **acre** is a unit of square measure that is smaller than a square mile but much larger than a square foot or square yard. The acre is used to measure the area of land.

Learn this measure equivalent: 1 square mile = 640 acres

A. *Find the numbers that fit in the blanks. You will probably need to do the work on paper.*

1. 3 sq. mi. = _____ acres   54 sq. ft. = _____ sq. yd.

2. 6 sq. yd. = _____ sq. ft.   6 sq. ft. = _____ sq. yd.

3. 2 square miles = _____ acres   4 sq. ft. = _____ sq. in.

4. 2 square feet = _____ sq. in.   18 sq. yd. = _____ sq. ft.

B. *Do these exercises.*

5. Find the area of each shape.

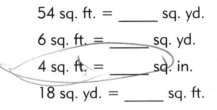

   a. 7″   7″   **b.** 8 ft.   5 ft.   **c.** 18″   6″   **d.** 13 yd.   13 yd.

6. Now find the perimeters of the shapes in number 5.

7. Find the areas of rectangles with the following dimensions.

   a. length—14 inches   width—$10\frac{1}{2}$ inches

   b. length—8.5 centimeters   width—5 centimeters

   c. length—27 feet   width—12 feet

   d. length—150 yards   width—75 yards

8. How many acres are in a square mile?

General Review

C. *Write T for true or F for false.*

9. These lines are parallel lines. _____
10. The diameter of a circle is the distance across the circle.
11. A pentagon has six sides.
12. A rectangle has four right angles.
13. Intersecting lines cross each other.
14. This is an acute angle. _____
15. The radius of a circle is half the diameter.
16. This is a square. ☐
17. These are congruent triangles. △ △
18. There are 12 square inches in a square foot.

D. *Find the answers mentally, as shown in Lesson 146. Write the answers only.*

19. 18 + 12	16 + 19	14 + 17	25 + 23	28 + 40
20. 29 + 11	18 + 15	27 + 18	19 + 24	36 + 16
21. 28 − 7	31 − 5	23 − 8	40 − 7	33 − 6
22. 36 − 20	42 − 12	37 − 15	30 − 13	23 − 14
23. 31 − 18	35 − 17	27 − 18	32 − 19	34 − 17
24. 5 × 15	4 × 19	6 × 16	4 × 15	8 × 13
25. 7 × 24	9 × 13	5 × 18	6 × 35	3 × 37

E. *Write these numbers as Roman numerals.*

26. a. 1,992   b. 2,086   c. 3,457   d. 1,649   e. 3,214

F. *Solve these reading problems.*

27. Adam was 130 years old when his son Seth was born, and Seth was 105 years old when his son Enos was born. How old was Adam when Enos was born?

28. Nancy wants to make $\frac{2}{3}$ of a batch of sugar cookies. The recipe calls for 3 eggs. How many eggs should Nancy use?

29. Nancy's cookie recipe calls for $\frac{3}{4}$ cup of margarine. If Nancy makes $\frac{2}{3}$ batch, how much margarine should she use?

30. Grandpa Miller is planting grass seed in his front yard. The yard measures 35 feet by 50 feet. One pound of grass seed will plant 750 square feet. Will 3 pounds of grass seed be enough to seed Grandpa Miller's yard?

150. Chapter 15 Review

A. *Do these exercises.*

1. Write the names of the geometric symbols shown here. Choose terms from Lesson 142.

   a. ←——→   b.   c. •   d.   e. •——•   f.

2. Write whether each angle is **right, acute,** or **obtuse.**

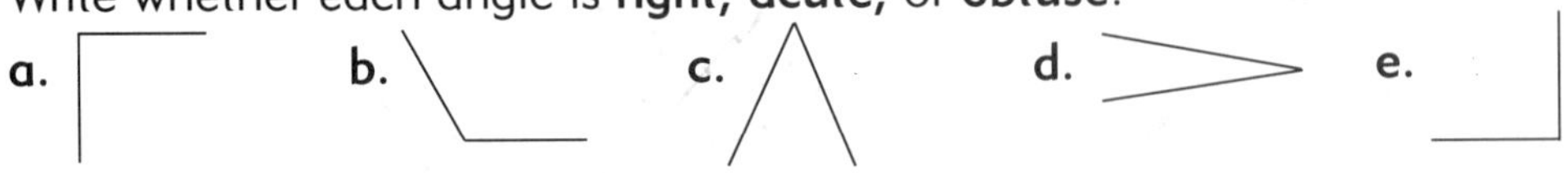

   a.   b.   c.   d.   e.

3. Write the names of the geometric figures shown here. Choose terms from Lesson 144.

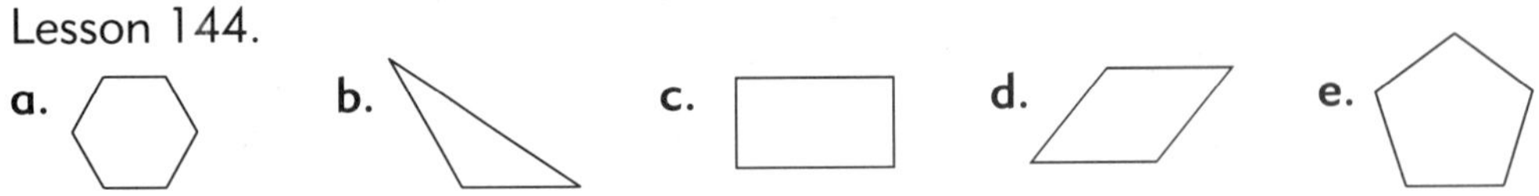

   a.   b.   c.   d.   e.

4. Write whether the figures in each pair are **similar** or **congruent.**

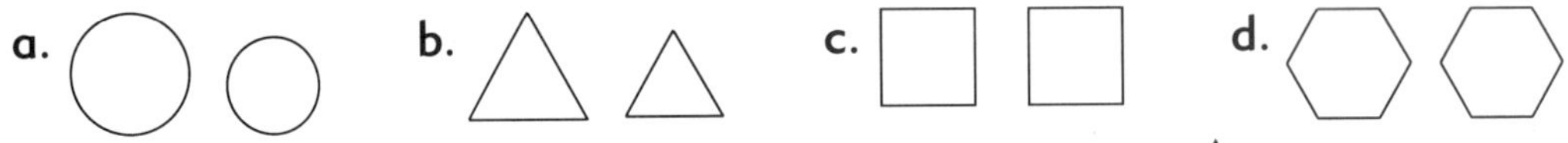

   a.   b.   c.   d.

5. In this circle, line segment AO is the _____, and line segment BC is the _____.

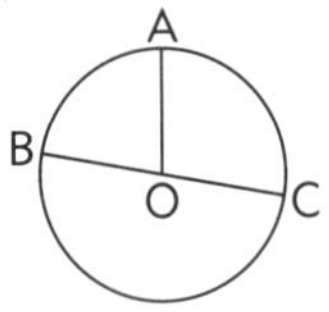

B. *Write the words that fit in the blanks.*

6. To find area, you need to _____ the length and the width.

7. An octagon has _____ sides.

8. The _____ of a shape is the distance around it.

9. The _____ of a shape is the amount of surface in it.

10. Figures of the same size and shape are _____ figures.

11. Lines that meet at a right angle are _____ lines.

12. To measure land, the _____ _____ is used for very large amounts, and the _____ is used for smaller amounts.

13. Lines that are always the same distance apart are _____ lines.

14. The _____ of a circle is half of the diameter.

15. Inches times inches equals _____ inches.

C. *Follow the directions.*

16. Find the perimeter of each figure shown here.

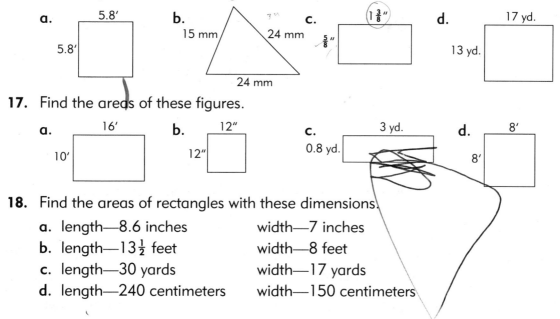

a. 5.8′ 5.8′

b. 15 mm 24 mm 24 mm

c. $1\frac{3}{8}''$ $\frac{5}{8}''$

d. 17 yd. 13 yd.

17. Find the areas of these figures.

a. 16′ 10′

b. 12″ 12″

c. 3 yd. 0.8 yd.

d. 8′ 8′

18. Find the areas of rectangles with these dimensions.
   a. length—8.6 inches   width—7 inches
   b. length—$13\frac{1}{2}$ feet   width—8 feet
   c. length—30 yards   width—17 yards
   d. length—240 centimeters   width—150 centimeters

D. *Copy these problems, and follow the signs.*

19.

$$7.5 \times 4 \qquad 16\frac{3}{4} \times 4 \qquad 160 \times 125 \qquad 12.5 \times 18 \qquad 12 \times 8\frac{2}{3}$$

20.

$$4 \times \tfrac{3}{4} \qquad 8 \times \tfrac{1}{4} \qquad 4 \times \tfrac{2}{3} \qquad \tfrac{7}{8} \times \tfrac{1}{2}$$

21.

$$1\tfrac{3}{4} + 1\tfrac{3}{4} + \tfrac{3}{4} \qquad \tfrac{7}{8} + \tfrac{9}{16} \qquad 3\tfrac{1}{2} + 4\tfrac{7}{8} \qquad 9\tfrac{2}{3} + 5\tfrac{1}{2} \qquad \tfrac{7}{16} + \tfrac{3}{4} + \tfrac{5}{8}$$

E. *Write the missing numbers.*

22. 1 square yard = _____ square feet   1 square mile = _____ acres

23. 1 square foot = _____ square inches   2 square miles = _____ acres

24. 9 sq. yd. = _____ sq. ft.   9 sq. ft. = _____ sq. yd.

(continued on next page)

Horizontal Computation

F. *Add or subtract mentally. Write only the answers.*

25.	19 + 27	16 + 18	25 + 28	37 + 14	23 + 18
26.	26 – 10	28 – 18	35 – 13	24 – 8	21 – 6
27.	32 – 14	27 – 19	40 – 16	31 – 17	44 – 19
28.	5 × 14	8 × 16	3 × 17	7 × 15	4 × 26

Reading Problems

G. *Draw a sketch for each problem, and then find the answer.*

29. The brazen altar in the tabernacle was $7\frac{1}{2}$ feet square. What was the perimeter?

30. Years later, Solomon built a larger brazen altar for the temple. His altar was 30 feet square. What was its perimeter?

31. What was the area of the top of Solomon's brazen altar? (Use the sketch for number 30 to solve this problem too.)

32. How many trees planted 20 feet apart can be placed in a 100-foot row?

33. William sawed a 12-foot board into 2-foot pieces. How many pieces did he have?

34. How many cuts did William make when he sawed the 12-foot board into 2-foot pieces?

35. The Homestead Act of 1862 allowed a settler to own a quarter square mile of land if he lived on the land and improved it for five years. How many acres are in a quarter square mile?

36. In early America, a **township** was a unit of land six miles long and six miles wide. What was the area of a township?

37. The Jonestown Christian School is on a property measuring 125 yards long and 80 yards wide. How many yards do the school children walk if they walk along all four edges of the school property? (Be careful! You are finding perimeter.)

- -

151. Chapter 15 Test

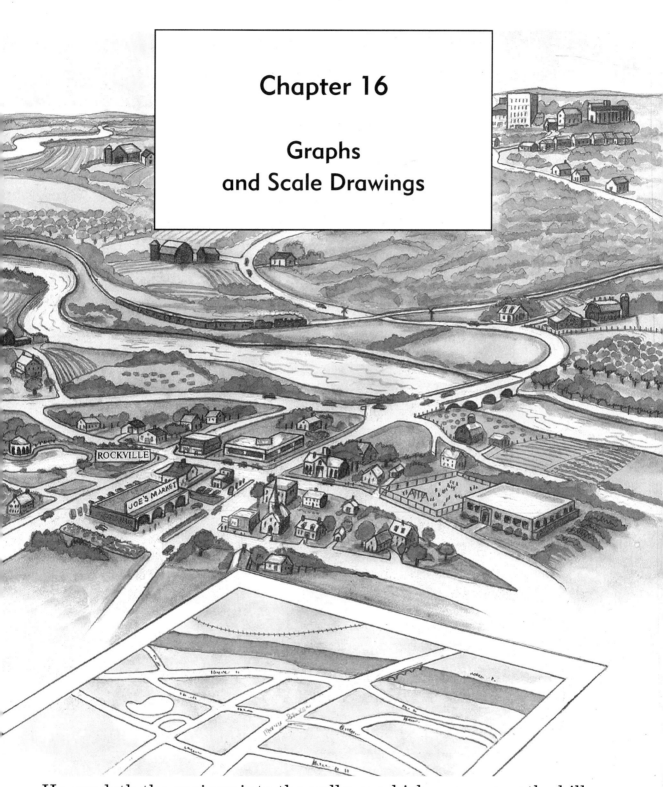

Chapter 16

Graphs and Scale Drawings

ROCKVILLE

JOE'S MARKET

He sendeth the springs into the valleys, which run among the hills.
(Psalm 104:10)

152. Working With Scale Drawings

A scale drawing is used to show large distances in a small amount of space. Maps are
good examples of scale drawings. A road
map of Pennsylvania might have a scale of
1 inch = 10 miles. That means that each
inch on the map stands for 10 actual miles
on land. A map of the whole United States
may have a scale of 1 inch = 200 miles.

The diagram below is a simple map with the scale of 1 inch = 4 miles. To find the
actual distance from one place to another, multiply the number of inches by 4 and
change the label to miles. For example, $1\frac{1}{2}$ inches on the map means $1\frac{1}{2} \times 4 = 6$ miles.

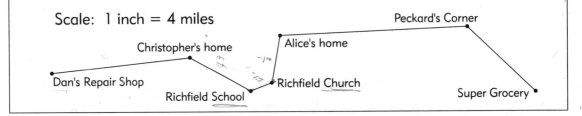

A. *Use your ruler and the map above to answer the following questions.*
Measure along the lines unless you are told otherwise.

1. How far is it from the Richfield Church to the school?

2. How far does Christopher travel to Richfield School?

3. What is the distance from Christopher's home to Dan's Repair?

4. What is the distance from Alice's home to the grocery store?

5. How far is it from Alice's home to Christopher's home by the roads? (The lines
    of the map indicate roads.)

6. What is the distance across the field between Alice's home and Christopher's home?

General Review

B. *Do these exercises.*

7. Measure these lines in inches.

    a. _____

    b. _____

    c. _____

    d. _____

    e. _____

8. Measure these lines in centimeters. Sample answer: 7.4 cm

a. _____

b. _____

c. _____

d. _____

9. Find the perimeters of the shapes below.

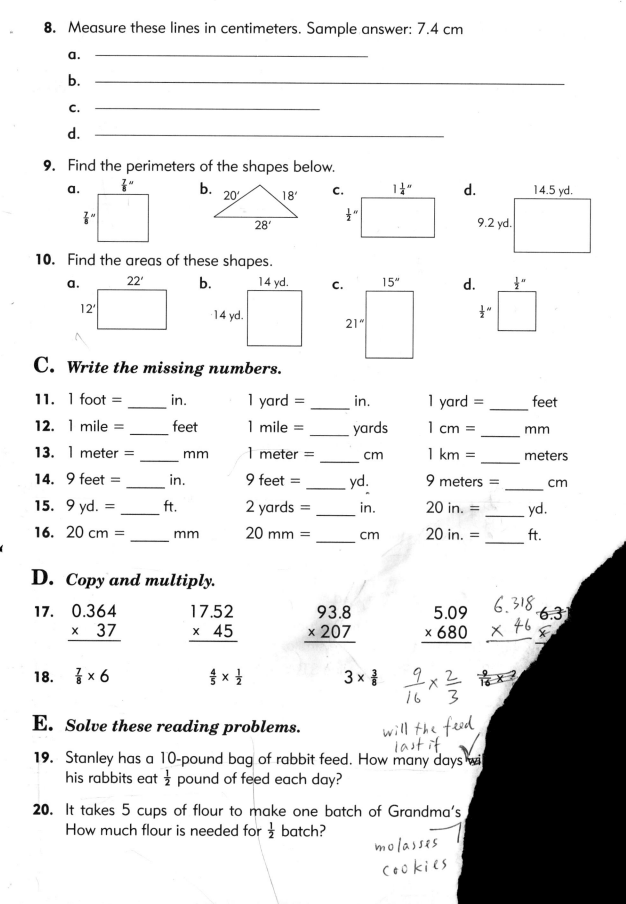

a. $\frac{7}{8}''$ $\frac{7}{8}''$

b. 20' 18' 28'

c. $1\frac{1}{4}''$ $\frac{1}{2}''$

d. 14.5 yd. 9.2 yd.

10. Find the areas of these shapes.

a. 22' 12'

b. 14 yd. 14 yd.

c. 15" 21"

d. $\frac{1}{2}''$ $\frac{1}{2}''$

C. Write the missing numbers.

11. 1 foot = _____ in.   1 yard = _____ in.   1 yard = _____ feet

12. 1 mile = _____ feet   1 mile = _____ yards   1 cm = _____ mm

13. 1 meter = _____ mm   1 meter = _____ cm   1 km = _____ meters

14. 9 feet = _____ in.   9 feet = _____ yd.   9 meters = _____ cm

15. 9 yd. = _____ ft.   2 yards = _____ in.   20 in. = _____ yd.

16. 20 cm = _____ mm   20 mm = _____ cm   20 in. = _____ ft.

D. Copy and multiply.

17.
$$\begin{array}{r} 0.364 \\ \times\ \ 37 \\ \hline \end{array} \qquad \begin{array}{r} 17.52 \\ \times\ \ 45 \\ \hline \end{array} \qquad \begin{array}{r} 93.8 \\ \times\ 207 \\ \hline \end{array} \qquad \begin{array}{r} 5.09 \\ \times\ 680 \\ \hline \end{array}$$

6.318
6.3
× 46
×

18. $\frac{7}{8} \times 6$ $\frac{4}{5} \times \frac{1}{2}$ $3 \times \frac{3}{8}$ $\frac{9}{16} \times \frac{2}{3}$ $\frac{9}{16} \times$

E. Solve these reading problems.

will the feed
last if

19. Stanley has a 10-pound bag of rabbit feed. How many days will his rabbits eat $\frac{1}{2}$ pound of feed each day?

20. It takes 5 cups of flour to make one batch of Grandma's How much flour is needed for $\frac{1}{2}$ batch?

molasses
cookies

153. More Practice With Scale Drawings

The scale drawings in this lesson are geometric shapes rather than maps. The scales on the various drawings are not the same, but they are similar. Each scale is something like this: $\frac{1}{8}'' = 1$ foot.

Follow the steps below to find the number of feet represented by a line on the scale drawing with a scale of $\frac{1}{8}'' = 1$ foot.

1. Measure the line with your ruler.

2. Decide how many times the scale unit ($\frac{1}{8}$ inch) is contained in your measurement. (Change the measurement to eighths.) This number is the number of feet represented on the drawing.

Examples: Line AB is $\frac{3}{4}$ inch long.
There are 6 eighths in $\frac{3}{4}$.
Line AB represents 6 feet.

Line AD is $1\frac{5}{8}$ inches long.
There are 13 eighths in $1\frac{5}{8}$.
Line AD represents 13 feet.

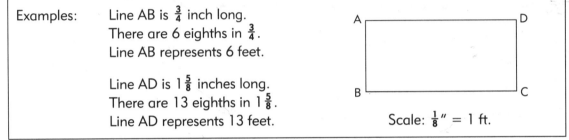

Scale: $\frac{1}{8}'' = 1$ ft.

A. Do these exercises.

1. Find the actual dimensions represented by the scale drawings below, using your ruler and the steps in this lesson.

   a. line AB
   b. line AD
   c. line EF
   d. line EG
   e. line FG
   f. line JK
   g. line KL

Scale: $\frac{1}{2}'' = 1$ yd.   Scale: $\frac{1}{8}'' = 1$ ft.   Scale: $\frac{1}{4}'' = 1$ mi.

Use your metric ruler to find the actual dimensions represented by these scale drawings. This time the scales are similar to the one in Lesson 152.

OR   b. line RQ   c. line ST   d. line TU   e. line WX   f. line WZ

line
10m = 2 km

Scale: 1 cm = 5 m

Scale: 1 cm = 4 km

this is a square and

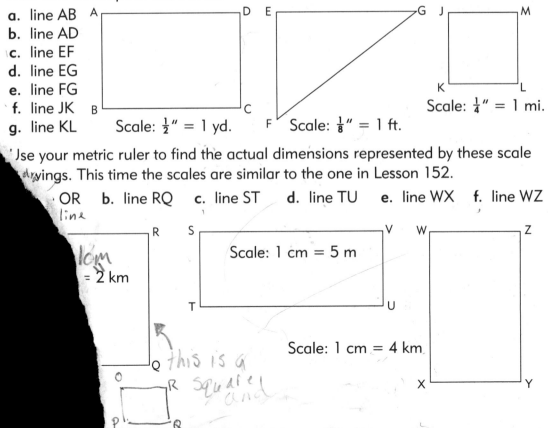

General Review

B. *Change these mixed numbers to improper fractions. Multiply the whole number times the denominator of the fraction. Then add on the numerator. Follow the example.*

How many $\frac{1}{4}$'s in $2\frac{1}{4}$? Think:
$2 \times 4 + 1 = 9$
$2\frac{1}{4} = \frac{9}{4}$

3. a. $4\frac{1}{2}$ b. $2\frac{1}{8}$ c. $7\frac{3}{4}$ d. $5\frac{1}{4}$ e. $3\frac{2}{3}$

4. a. $1\frac{13}{16}$ b. $4\frac{2}{5}$ c. $3\frac{7}{8}$ d. $6\frac{1}{2}$ e. $2\frac{11}{12}$

C. *Follow the directions.*

5. Write Arabic numerals for these number words.

   a. one hundred twenty-five billion, two hundred five
   b. one hundred twenty-five million
   c. one billion, two hundred fifty million, fifty-two
   d. one hundred two billion, one hundred twenty-five thousand
   e. twelve million, five hundred thousand
   f. five billion, twelve million, one hundred twenty thousand, twenty-five

6. What digit is in ten million's place?   45,032,098,174

7. How many thousands are in a million?

8. <u>5</u>,555,555   In this number, the underlined 5 is how many times as much as the **boldface** 5?

9. Write the number that means $400,000 + 70,000 + 2,000 + 500 + 90$.

10. Write $63,159$ in expanded form (like number 9).

11. Round these numbers to the nearest hundred.
   a. 895   b. 3,720   c. 4,283   d. 782,449

12. Round to the nearest thousand.
   a. 3,720   b. 4,283   c. 71,562   d. 782,449

13. Round to the nearest hundred thousand.
   a. 782,449   b. 354,100   c. 1,495,720   d. 28,736,825

14. Find the area of each shape.
   a. 14" × 14"   b. 6 cm × 3.4 cm   c. $\frac{3}{4}$ yd. × $\frac{1}{2}$ yd.   d. 18' × 18'

15. Now find the perimeters of the shapes above.

154. Working With Scale of Miles

A scale of miles looks a little like a ruler, but the markings on it represent miles. The scale of miles shows distances on a map. Notice the scale of miles on the map below.

To use the scale of miles, get a piece of paper with a straight edge. Follow the directions below for measuring the distance from Memphis to Houston. The same directions apply to measuring other distances.

1. Lay the straight edge of the paper on the map so that it passes through Memphis and Houston.

2. Make a mark on the paper at both Memphis and Houston.

3. Lay the paper on the scale of miles. Place one mark at 0. Read the distance at the other mark.

You need to estimate the actual distance. In this case the distance is between 500 and 600 miles, or about 550 miles.

If the distance were greater than what the scale shows, you would need to mark off 800 miles on your paper, measure what is left, and then add.

A. *Using a piece of paper and the map on the opposite page, find the distances between these cities to the nearest 100 miles.*

1. a. Dallas to Houston
   b. Milwaukee to Chicago
   c. Chicago to Pittsburgh
   d. Phoenix to Denver

   e. Washington, D.C. to Boston
   f. San Francisco to Portland
   g. San Francisco to Los Angeles
   h. Philadelphia to Washington, D.C.

General Review

B. *Copy the problems and work carefully. Check over your work.*

2.
```
  984,532        493,109        478,396         67,450
   79,467        621,893        155,728        854,317
  127,833         57,854        253,493        429,825
+ 342,157      + 673,452       + 32,646       + 76,417
```

3.
```
   80,000         76,705         37,210         90,603
 - 27,851       - 38,609        - 6,853       - 75,496
```

4. 27)999   42)6,559   15)9,580   38)10,298

C. *Solve these reading problems.*

5. At the beginning of April, the mission board had $13,920.83 in their fund. During the month they received $48,126.94 in church offerings. How much was in the fund after the offerings were added on?

6. During the month, the mission board gave $11,110.25 to their mission in the Bahamas, $27,457.35 to the mission in Guatemala, and $3,400.00 to the mission in Paraguay. What was the total amount given to the missions in the three countries?

7. The mission board had a total of $63,527.68 to work with one month. In addition to expenses of $39,445.25, they had other expenses which amounted to $6,325.00. How much money was left after all these expenses were paid? (This is a two-step problem.)

8. Brother Harold made 15 trips to Guatemala in 11 years' time, to help in the mission work there. He estimated the airline distance from his home to Guatemala at 2,100 miles. How far did Brother Harold fly on each trip from his home to Guatemala and back?

9. How many miles did Brother Harold fly on 15 trips to and from Guatemala?

155. Vertical Bar Graphs

The bar graph in this lesson has the numbers along the side, and the bars are vertical instead of horizontal. Notice that the smallest number is at the bottom.

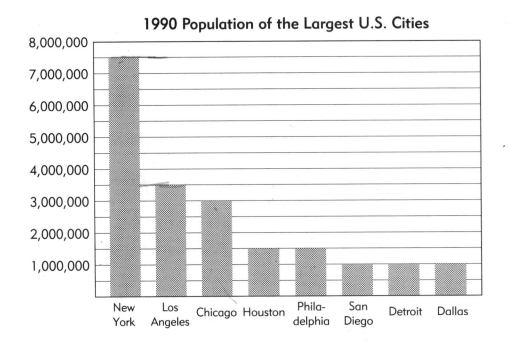

1990 Population of the Largest U.S. Cities

Populations on the graph have been rounded to half millions. The space from one line to the next is one-half million.

A. *Answer these questions.*

1. What number is one-half million? (Divide to find the answer.)

2. Which two cities have a population of about one and one-half million?

3. What is the population of New York as shown on the graph?

4. How many more people live in New York than in Los Angeles?

5. What is the total population of New York, Los Angeles, and Chicago?

6. Which is more: the population of New York, or the combined populations of Houston, Philadelphia, San Diego, Detroit, and Dallas?

Reading a Number Chart

This chart shows the same information as the graph on the opposite page. Compare the graph and the chart to answer the questions.

1990 Population of the Largest U.S. Cities

City	Population
New York	7,322,564
Los Angeles	3,485,398
Chicago	2,783,726
Houston	1,630,553
Philadelphia	1,585,577
San Diego	1,110,549
Detroit	1,027,974
Dallas	1,006,877

B. *Write the answers.*

7. Which shows rounded numbers, the graph or the chart?

8. Which shows more accurate information, the graph or the chart?

9. According to the graph, which other cities have the same population as San Diego?

10. According to the chart, how many more people live in San Diego than in Dallas?

11. What is the population of Chicago: a. according to the graph?
                                         b. according to the chart?

12. How much smaller is the actual population of Chicago than what is shown on the graph?

13. List the eight cities. After each one write **up** or **down** to tell if the actual populations were rounded up or down for the graph.

General Review

C. *Do these exercises.*

14. A map has a scale of $\frac{1}{4}$ inch = 1 mile. What actual distances are represented by the following measurements?

    a. 1"   b. $\frac{1}{2}$"   c. $\frac{3}{4}$"   d. $1\frac{1}{4}$"   e. $1\frac{3}{4}$"   f. $2\frac{1}{2}$"

15. Change these improper fractions to mixed numbers.

    a. $\frac{16}{6}$ b. $\frac{18}{4}$ c. $\frac{21}{5}$ d. $\frac{35}{8}$ e. $\frac{30}{9}$ f. $\frac{25}{7}$

16. Change these mixed numbers to improper fractions.

    a. $3\frac{1}{2}$ b. $4\frac{1}{3}$ c. $2\frac{3}{4}$ d. $5\frac{1}{7}$ e. $1\frac{7}{8}$ f. $3\frac{2}{3}$

17. Round to the nearest hundred thousand.   a. 2,397,165   b. 45,826,530

156. Line Graphs

Line graphs can be used to show the same information that bar graphs show. Points are **plotted** (placed at specific locations) on a graph, and the points are connected with lines to form a line graph. A line graph is simpler to make than a bar graph.

Study the bar graph and the line graph below. The letters at the bottom are the first letters of the months, starting with January. Both graphs show the same information, but the line graph emphasizes the **changes** in monthly precipitation.

Normal Monthly Precipitation at Tampa, Florida

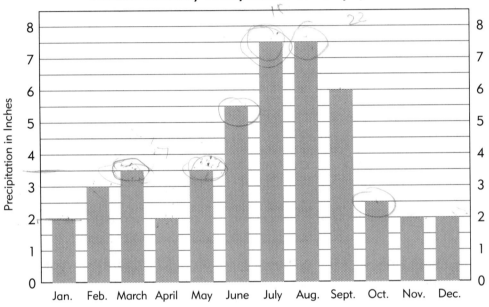

Normal Monthly Precipitation at Tampa, Florida

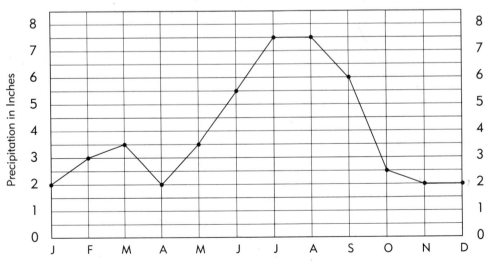

A. *Use the graphs to answer these questions.*

1. During which two months does Tampa have the most rainfall?

2. Does Tampa have more precipitation in summer or in winter?

3. According to the graph, which four months bring the same amount of rain in Tampa?

4. How much more rainfall does Tampa normally have in July than in January?

5. How much less rain does Tampa have in April than in September?

6. What is the total amount of rain that Tampa usually receives in the winter months (December, January, February)?

7. What is the average amount of rainfall that Tampa receives each month in spring (March, April, May)?

*8. What is the total amount of rainfall that Tampa receives in an average year?

General Review

B. *Do these exercises.*

9. Round to the nearest ten thousand: a. 15,844   b. 387,429

10. Round to the nearest million: a. 5,475,392   b. 26,740,599

11. Write as Arabic numerals: a. CDXI   b. MMDCLXXXIV   c. MCMXXVII

12. Write as Roman numerals: a. 735   b. 1,466   c. 2,940   d. 3,059

13. $8 \times \frac{3}{4}$ $\frac{2}{9} \times 3$ $\frac{2}{3} \times \frac{7}{16}$ $\frac{5}{12} \times \frac{3}{5}$

14. $8 \div \frac{3}{4}$ $\frac{8}{15} \div 4$ $\frac{7}{9} \div \frac{1}{3}$ $\frac{5}{8} \div \frac{5}{16}$

15. 7×15 8×13 4×17 3×29 5×24

16. $20 - 6$ $25 - 8$ $31 - 14$ $33 - 27$ $36 - 18$

17. What are the freezing and boiling points on the Fahrenheit scale?

18. Find the lengths represented by these scale drawings.

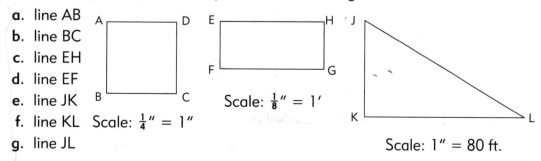

   a. line AB
   b. line BC
   c. line EH
   d. line EF
   e. line JK
   f. line KL   Scale: $\frac{1}{4}'' = 1''$
   g. line JL

Scale: $\frac{1}{8}'' = 1'$

Scale: $1'' = 80$ ft.

157. More Line Graphs

On the line graph below, you can compare the average monthly temperatures in two American cities. Temperatures are shown in degrees, with 2 degrees between the horizontal lines. Notice that the degree numbers start with 30 instead of 0.

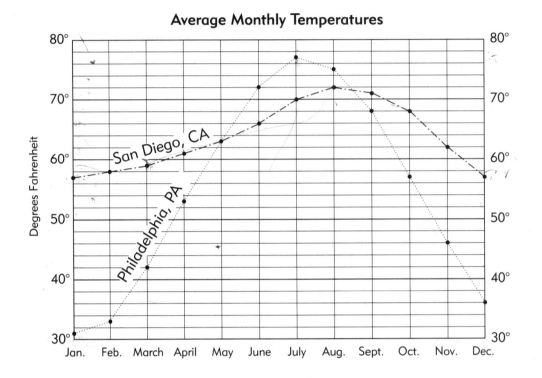

Average Monthly Temperatures

A. *Use the graph to find these facts about the average temperatures in San Diego, California, and in Philadelphia, Pennsylvania.*

1. Temperature in March: a. San Diego   b. Philadelphia

2. Temperature in November: a. San Diego   b. Philadelphia

3. Temperature in June: a. San Diego   b. Philadelphia

4. Lowest monthly temperature: a. San Diego   b. Philadelphia

5. Months of lowest temperature: a. San Diego (2)   b. Philadelphia

6. Highest monthly temperature: a. San Diego   b. Philadelphia

7. Month of highest temperature: a. San Diego   b. Philadelphia

8. Difference between highest and lowest temperatures:

       a. San Diego   b. Philadelphia

Review of Decimals

B. *Write numerals for these number words.*

9. a. thirty-nine and forty-five hundredths
   b. seventeen and twelve thousandths
   c. five hundred twenty and six tenths
   d. ninety-eight and four hundredths

C. *Write each set in the order of size, from smallest to largest.*

10. a. 3.5   3.007   3.02   b. 0.017   0.071   0.17
11. a. 0.08   0.04   0.14   b. 5.428   5.248   5.42
12. a. 1.08   1.8   1.008   b. 8.101   8.11   8.011

D. *Write the missing numbers.*

13. 1.5, 1.6, _____, _____, 1.9, _____, _____, 2.2, 2.3, _____
14. 3.07, 3.08, _____, _____, _____, 3.12, _____, 3.14
15. 5.146, 5.147, 5.148, _____, _____, 5.151, _____

E. *Copy and work carefully. Remember the decimal points in your answers.*

16. 63.8 + 3.679 + 175.63 + 24.165   300 – 65.19
17. 195.72 + 45.6 + 832.48 + 7.583   58.13 – 14.577

18. 7)0.399   6)35.82   24)1.512   38)775.2

19. 3.85   7.6   0.468   627
    × 9   × 64   × 37   × 39.2

F. *Solve these reading problems.*

20. Philadelphia received 3.5 inches of rain in April, 3.2 inches in May, 3.9 inches in June, 4.1 inches in July, and 3.3 inches in August. What was the average rainfall per month?

21. One inch represents 75 miles on a map. How many miles are represented by 3.6 inches on the map?

22. One side of a square is 3.6 feet long. What is the perimeter of the square?

23. One Sunday the offering was $875.35. The next Sunday the offering was $683.29. How much more was the first offering?

158. Location Symbols on Maps

Some maps are similar to graphs. These maps have **location symbols** (letters and numbers) along the edges. A place is located by using a letter and a number.

Perhaps you are trying to find Bethlehem on a map of Palestine. The map index says that Bethlehem is located at **G14**. Find **G** at the bottom (or top) of the map, and move one finger straight up (or down). Find **14** along one side, and move another finger straight across. Bethlehem is close to the point where your two fingers meet.

Graphical Map of Palestine

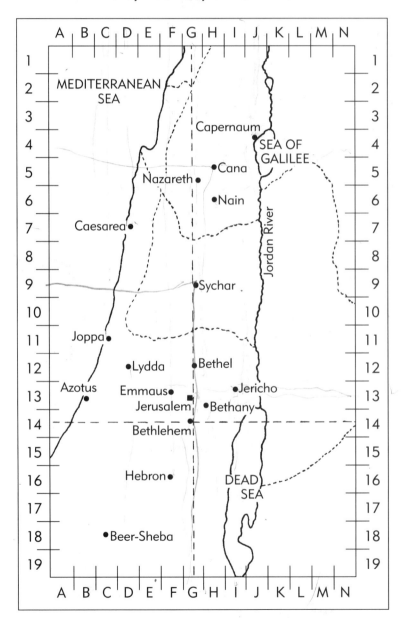

A. *Use the map on the opposite page to do these exercises.*

1. Write the name of the city located near each point.
   a. F16   b. C18   c. C11   d. I13   e. G9   f. D7   g. G12   h. J4

2. Write the letter and number that locates each place on the map.
   a. Nain   b. Lydda   c. Cana   d. Jericho   e. Jerusalem

General Review

B. *Do these exercises with money.*

3. Write the total value of each set.
   a. 4 quarters, 6 dimes, 3 nickels
   b. 7 quarters, 4 dimes, 6 pennies
   c. 3 ten-dollar bills, 5 five-dollar bills, 8 one-dollar bills
   d. 2 twenty-dollar bills, 4 ten-dollar bills, 6 quarters
   e. 3 one-dollar bills, 5 quarters, 3 dimes, 4 nickels

4. List the pieces of money that should be given as change for the following purchases. Use as few pieces as possible.
   a. Amount of purchase—$3.27;   amount given to clerk—$5.00
   b. Amount of purchase—$1.59;   amount given to clerk—$10.00
   c. Amount of purchase—$12.77;   amount given to clerk—$20.00
   d. Amount of purchase—$9.15;   amount given to clerk—$20.00

C. *Copy and work carefully.*

5. $16.75 + $9 + $3.98 + $275.60 $489 + $2.67 + $15.27

6. $30.00 - $24.65 $50 - $15.78 $30.13 - 25.13

7.
```
  $56.73      $938.25
   45.97       456.82
  374.65        74.88     $810.00      $347.08
+ 29.68      + 342.57    - 367.59     - 155.69
```

8.
```
  $5.69        $.78       $41.90       $5.93
 ×    5       × 27       ×   76       × 309
```

9. 35)$9.80   27)$12.42   18)$58.50   43)$689.29

159. Introduction to Volume

This line segment has a **length** of one **centimeter**. You can measure it with a ruler.

1 cm

This square has an **area** of one **square centimeter**. You can measure its two dimensions with a ruler.

1 sq. cm

This cube represents one **cubic centimeter**. A cubic centimeter cannot be shown exactly on a flat piece of paper because it has **three** dimensions: length, width, and height.

1 cu. cm

A cubic centimeter has **volume** because it takes up a certain amount of space. Learn the following facts about volume.

---

1. **Volume** is another name for the amount of space within a three-dimensional object.

2. Volume is measured with units of **cubic measure**, such as cubic inches and cubic centimeters.

3. Volume is found by multiplying three dimensions—length, width, and height. The answer is given in cubic units.

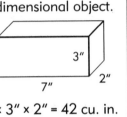
3"
7"
2"
7" x 3" x 2" = 42 cu. in.

A. *Find the volumes of boxes with these dimensions, as shown in the lesson. Give the answers in cubic inches.*

1. length—5"   width—4"   height—3"

2. length—7"   width—3"   height—3"

3. length—4"   width—2"   height—6"

4. length—9"   width—6"   height—2"

5. length—6"   width—7"   height—3"

B. *Find the areas of squares or rectangles with these dimensions. Give the answers in square units.*

6. length—8 ft.   width—8 ft.

7. length—13 yd.   width—11 yd.

8. length—15 in.   width—$10\frac{1}{3}$ in.

C. *Find the perimeters of these squares and rectangles.*

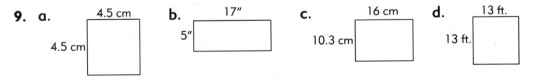

9. a.   4.5 cm / 4.5 cm   **b.**   17" / 5"   **c.**   16 cm / 10.3 cm   **d.**   13 ft. / 13 ft.

D. *Do these exercises.*

10. Write the measurements to which the arrows point.

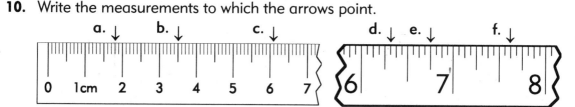

11. Name the cities located at or near these points.

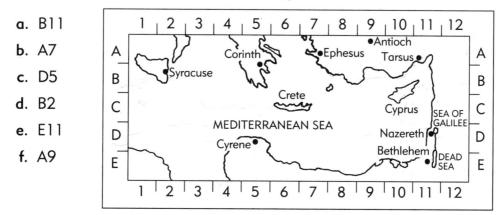

a. B11

b. A7

c. D5

d. B2

e. E11

f. A9

E. *These reading problems cannot be solved. For each one, write answers to the following two questions.*
a. What information is missing?
b. How would you solve the problem if you had that information?

12. The trustees at Garrett Church plan to lay carpet in the auditorium. The room is 21 yards long. How many square yards of carpet are needed to cover the floor?

13. Father bought 16 feet of pipe to make some plumbing repairs. What was the total cost of the pipe?

14. One map at school has a scale of 1 inch = 200 miles. How many miles apart are Miami (Florida) and Asuncion (Paraguay)?

F. *Solve these reading problems.*

15. One bag of seed corn is enough to plant 3 acres of corn. How many acres of corn can Mr. Tice plant with 18 bags of seed?

16. Mr. Floyd plans to plant 110 acres of corn. If a bag of seed corn plants 3 acres, how many bags of seed corn should Mr. Floyd buy? (Hint: He cannot buy part bags.)

17. Mr. Floyd planted 20 pounds of seed corn per acre. He harvested 115 bushels of shelled corn per acre. If one bushel weighs 56 pounds, Mr. Floyd harvested _____ times as much corn per acre as what he planted.

160. Chapter 16 Review

A. *Round these numbers as indicated.*

1. Round to the nearest hundred: a. 785   b. 4,562   c. 37,849

2. Round to the nearest thousand: a. 4,562   b. 37,849   c. 723,486

3. Round to the nearest hundred thousand: a. 723,486   b. 4,856,308

B. *Write the missing numbers.*

4. a. 3 feet = _____ in.   b. 3 yd. = _____ ft.   c. 3 ft. = _____ yd.

5. a. 3 inches = _____ ft.   b. 3 cm = _____ mm   c. 3 meters = _____ cm

6. a. 1 sq. ft. = _____ sq. in.   b. 1 sq. yd. = _____ sq. ft.

C. *Write the numerals for these number words.*

7. a. sixteen billion, forty-eight thousand
     b. one hundred seventy-five million
     c. twenty-one and thirty-three hundredths
     d. nine and four thousandths

D. *Copy the pairs of decimals. Write =, <, or > between them.*

8. a. 0.042 _____ 0.069   b. 1.23 _____ 1.023   c. 4.5 _____ 4.50

9. a. 3.7 _____ 3.582   b. 0.145 _____ 0.62   c. 3.75 _____ 3.7

E. *Do these exercises.*

10. Find the perimeter of each shape.

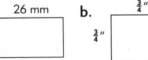
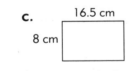
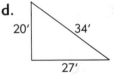

a. 26 mm 15 mm   b. ¾" ¾"   c. 16.5 cm 8 cm   d. 20' 34' 27'

11. Now find the areas of shapes **a, b,** and **c** above.

12. Find the volumes below by multiplying the three dimensions.

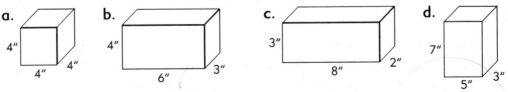

a. 4" 4" 4"   b. 4" 6" 3"   c. 3" 8" 2"   d. 7" 5" 3"

13. Find the actual measurements for these scale drawings.

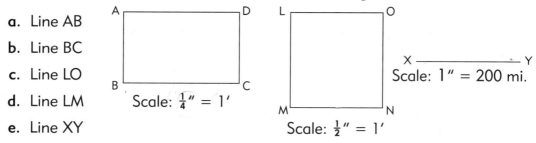

a. Line AB
b. Line BC
c. Line LO
d. Line LM
e. Line XY

Scale: $\frac{1}{4}'' = 1'$

Scale: $\frac{1}{2}'' = 1'$

Scale: $1'' = 200$ mi.

F. *This line graph shows the temperature each hour for 12 hours. Use it to answer the questions below.*

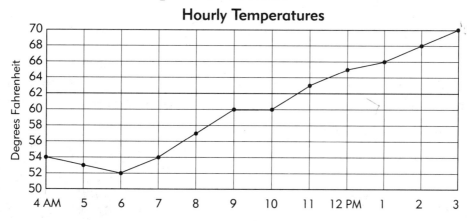

14. What is the highest temperature recorded?

15. At what hour of the day was the highest temperature recorded?

16. What is the lowest temperature recorded?

17. What is the difference between the highest and lowest temperatures?

18. What was the temperature at 8 A.M.?

19. How much did the temperature rise from 4:00 A.M. to 12:00 noon?

G. *Use the map on the second page of Lesson 159 to answer these questions.*

20. What island is located at C6 and C7?

21. What island is located at C10?

22. What small body of water is located at D11?

H. *Do these exercises with money.*

23. Count the money.

(continued on next page)

24. List the pieces of money that should be given as change. Start with the smallest pieces.

    a. Amount of purchase—$6.87; amount given to clerk—$10.00

    b. Amount of purchase—$4.65; amount given to clerk—$20.00

    c. Amount of purchase—$11.22; amount given to clerk—$20.00

I. *Solve these reading problems.*

25. The most dangerous electricity-producing fish is the Brazilian electric eel, which is two meters long. How much longer is this eel than a 30-centimeter fish? (Hint: First change two meters to centimeters.)

26. What is the price of 24 bags of seed corn at $63.75 per bag?

27. Warren read the label on a bag of seed corn and found out that the bag contained 1 bushel, or 56 pounds, or 75,000 kernels of corn. At that rate, how many kernels are in one pound of corn? (Hint: Drop the remainder this time.)

28. Aunt Ruth bought $5\frac{1}{3}$ pounds of bananas at 33¢ a pound. What was the cost of the bananas?

29. In addition to the $5\frac{1}{3}$ pounds of bananas, Aunt Ruth bought $2\frac{1}{2}$ pounds of grapes and $4\frac{1}{4}$ pounds of apples. How many pounds of fruit did Aunt Ruth buy altogether?

30. If 4 oranges cost 75¢, what is the cost of one dozen oranges? (Hint: Find how many groups of 4 oranges are in a dozen.)

31. Leon's grandfather is 60 years old. Adam lived to be 930 years old, or _____ times as old as Leon's grandfather.

32. Tomato plants are priced at $0.55 each, or a flat of 24 plants for $8.00. How much is saved by buying 24 plants on a flat rather than buying 24 plants individually?

33. On one map, the distance from New York to Moscow is $9\frac{1}{2}$ inches. The scale is 1 inch = 500 miles. What is the actual distance from New York to Moscow?

- -

161. Chapter 16 Test

Chapter 17

Reinforcement and Enrichment

I have fought a good fight, I have finished my course,
I have kept the faith.
(2 Timothy 4:7)

162. Reviewing Fractions

A. *Do these exercises.*

1. Write a fraction with a numerator of 3.

2. Does the **numerator** or the **denominator** tell how many parts the whole thing is divided into?

3. Write a pair of like fractions.

4. Write the fraction that means 2 parts out of 5.

5. Write the fraction that means 1 divided by 4.

6. How many eighths are in 2 whole pies?

7. How many fifths are in 4 wholes?

8. Write **P** for proper, **I** for improper, or **M** for mixed number.

   a. $2\frac{2}{3}$ b. $\frac{15}{16}$ c. $\frac{7}{2}$ d. $\frac{4}{4}$ e. $4\frac{3}{10}$ f. $\frac{11}{12}$

9. Find the missing numbers in these proportions.

   a. $\frac{15}{30} = \frac{?}{10}$ b. $\frac{6}{7} = \frac{12}{?}$ c. $\frac{18}{24} = \frac{?}{8}$ d. $\frac{4}{?} = \frac{2}{8}$ e. $\frac{?}{27} = \frac{1}{3}$

10. Reduce to lowest terms.

    a. $\frac{18}{30}$ b. $\frac{20}{40}$ c. $\frac{15}{24}$ d. $\frac{24}{40}$ e. $\frac{12}{18}$ f. $\frac{16}{28}$

11. Copy each pair of fractions, and write $<$ or $>$ between them. Change them to like fractions if you are not sure.

    a. $\frac{3}{8}$ $\frac{1}{2}$ b. $\frac{5}{6}$ $\frac{3}{4}$ c. $\frac{7}{8}$ $\frac{9}{16}$ d. $\frac{1}{3}$ $\frac{2}{5}$ e. $\frac{7}{10}$ $\frac{1}{2}$

12. Change these to whole or mixed numbers in simplest form.

    a. $\frac{12}{8}$ b. $\frac{7}{3}$ c. $\frac{14}{4}$ d. $\frac{9}{2}$ e. $\frac{12}{3}$ f. $\frac{30}{12}$

13. Change these to improper fractions.

    a. $3\frac{1}{2}$ b. $6 = \frac{?}{4}$ c. $1\frac{7}{8}$ d. $4\frac{1}{5}$ e. $1\frac{11}{16}$ f. $2\frac{5}{6}$

B. *Solve these problems carefully. Watch the signs!*

14.
$\frac{2}{3}$
$\frac{3}{4}$
$+\frac{1}{2}$

$\frac{9}{10}$
$\frac{1}{2}$
$+\frac{4}{5}$

$\frac{3}{8}$
$\frac{1}{4}$
$+\frac{11}{16}$

$\frac{2}{3}$
$\frac{1}{8}$
$+\frac{1}{2}$

15.
$5\frac{3}{4}$
$+2\frac{1}{2}$

$4\frac{3}{8}$
$+8\frac{5}{8}$

$1\frac{11}{16}$
$+3\frac{13}{16}$

$7\frac{7}{8}$
$+3\frac{3}{16}$

16.
$6\frac{1}{3}$
$+4\frac{1}{2}$

$13\frac{2}{5}$
$+17\frac{1}{3}$

$10\frac{3}{4}$
$+6\frac{2}{3}$

$8\frac{1}{2}$
$+9\frac{7}{10}$

17.
$12\frac{7}{8}$
$-4\frac{1}{2}$

$14\frac{3}{4}$
$-11\frac{7}{12}$

$9\frac{9}{10}$
$-3\frac{4}{5}$

$6\frac{5}{6}$
$-5\frac{4}{9}$

18.
7
$-\frac{13}{16}$

5
$-2\frac{5}{8}$

11
$-6\frac{7}{12}$

13
$-4\frac{1}{4}$

19.
$6\frac{1}{2}$
$-4\frac{2}{3}$

$8\frac{3}{10}$
$-1\frac{3}{5}$

$9\frac{1}{4}$
$-3\frac{11}{12}$

$10\frac{1}{3}$
$-3\frac{1}{2}$

20. The shop class at Highland Christian Day School is making small benches. The top is $1\frac{1}{2}$ feet long, and each of the two sides is $\frac{2}{3}$ foot long. If the top and two side pieces are cut from the same board, how long a board is needed for all three pieces?

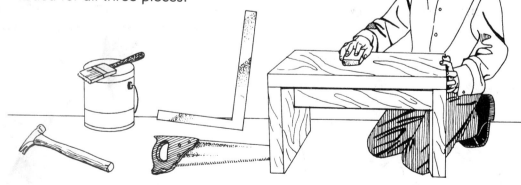

163. Review of Multiplying and Dividing Fractions

Multiplying fractions is easier than adding fractions. Simply multiply the numerators and multiply the denominators.

Canceling helps make multiplying fractions easy. Do you always cancel when you can? Cancel whenever a numerator and denominator can both be divided by the same factor. Below are several illustrations to refresh your memory.

$$\frac{3}{\cancel{10}_2} \times \cancel{5}^1 = \frac{3}{2} = \boxed{1\frac{1}{2}} \qquad \frac{\cancel{7}^1}{\cancel{8}_4} \times \frac{\cancel{6}^3}{\cancel{7}_1} = \boxed{\frac{3}{4}}$$

$$\cancel{12}^4 \times \frac{1}{\cancel{9}_3} = \frac{4}{3} = \boxed{1\frac{1}{3}} \qquad \frac{\cancel{2}^1}{3} \times \frac{7}{\cancel{16}_8} = \boxed{\frac{7}{24}}$$

A. Copy and multiply. Cancel when you can.

1. $\frac{2}{3} \times 9$ $\frac{1}{4} \times \frac{5}{8}$ $\frac{4}{5} \times \frac{3}{4}$ $9 \times \frac{1}{6}$

2. $\frac{5}{6} \times \frac{3}{10}$ $6 \times \frac{7}{9}$ $\frac{1}{2} \times \frac{8}{9}$ $\frac{5}{6} \times 3$

3. $\frac{3}{5}$ of 5 $\frac{11}{12}$ of $\frac{2}{3}$ $\frac{9}{16}$ of $\frac{4}{9}$ $\frac{1}{3}$ of 8

B. Copy and divide. Remember to invert the divisor and multiply.

4. $\frac{7}{16} \div \frac{3}{4}$ $\frac{4}{5} \div 4$ $\frac{5}{12} \div \frac{7}{8}$ $9 \div \frac{1}{3}$

5. $\frac{2}{3} \div 4$ $\frac{1}{3} \div \frac{1}{6}$ $10 \div \frac{2}{5}$ $\frac{5}{8} \div \frac{2}{3}$

C. Copy and multiply. First multiply the fraction part, then multiply the whole number part, and finally add the two partial products.

6.
$$\begin{array}{r} 20 \\ \times\, 4\frac{3}{5} \\ \hline \end{array} \qquad \begin{array}{r} 16 \\ \times\, 3\frac{1}{4} \\ \hline \end{array} \qquad \begin{array}{r} 21 \\ \times\, 9\frac{2}{3} \\ \hline \end{array} \qquad \begin{array}{r} 36 \\ \times\, 4\frac{3}{4} \\ \hline \end{array}$$

7.
$$\begin{array}{r} 13\frac{1}{2} \\ \times\, 4 \\ \hline \end{array} \qquad \begin{array}{r} 25\frac{2}{3} \\ \times\, 6 \\ \hline \end{array} \qquad \begin{array}{r} 33\frac{3}{4} \\ \times\, 8 \\ \hline \end{array} \qquad \begin{array}{r} 17\frac{1}{3} \\ \times\, 9 \\ \hline \end{array}$$

Reading Problems

Many of the problems on this page require more than one step. Think carefully and do one step at a time. Always ask yourself: "Does my answer make sense?"

D. *Solve these reading problems.*

8. Marlin has directions for making a bench that is 18 inches long and 8 inches wide. He wants to make a bench with dimensions $\frac{3}{4}$ as large as the original bench. How long and wide should Marlin make his bench? (You should have two answers.)

9. Titus helps his father feed the cows. He gives $\frac{1}{4}$ bale of hay to each one. How many bales of hay does Titus need to feed 36 cows?

10. If a cow gives 65 pounds of milk a day, how much milk will it give in two weeks?

11. Aunt Hilda bought a roast that weighed $6\frac{1}{4}$ pounds. At $2.24 per pound, what was the price of the roast?

12. A trenching machine can dig 6 feet of ditch every minute in soft soil. It can dig only half as fast in hard soil. How much time will it take for the machine to dig a ditch 990 feet long in hard soil? (Express your answer in hours.)

13. The trenching machine (number 12) dug 156 feet through soft soil and then 282 feet through hard soil. How many hours did it take to do the job?

14. Last year Philip was $46\frac{3}{4}$ inches tall. This year he is $49\frac{1}{4}$ inches tall. How much has Philip grown during the past year?

15. Mother and the girls canned $4\frac{1}{2}$ bushels of peaches one day. If each bushel yielded 24 quarts of canned peaches, how many quarts of peaches did they can?

16. Sister Faith has $\frac{3}{4}$ of a cherry pie. If she serves $\frac{1}{8}$ of a pie to each person, how many people can have cherry pie?

17. Father had several bags of old seed corn with 75,000 kernels in a bag. In a test plot, Father discovered that about $\frac{1}{10}$ of the old seed failed to germinate. At that rate, how many of the 75,000 kernels in a bag could be expected to germinate?

164. Review of Measures

A. *Write the numbers that fit in the blanks.*

1. 1 minute = _____ seconds   1 year = _____ weeks   1 year = _____ days
2. 1 mile = _____ feet   1 mile = _____ yards   1 yard = _____ inches
3. 1 bushel = _____ pecks   1 peck = _____ quarts   1 quart = _____ pints
4. 1 ton = _____ pounds   1 pound = _____ ounces   1 decade = _____ years
5. 1 day = _____ hours   1 gallon = _____ quarts   1 yard = _____ feet

6. 1 sq. ft. = _____ sq. in.   1 sq. yd. = _____ sq. ft.
7. 1 meter = _____ centimeters   1 centimeter = _____ millimeter
8. 1 gram = _____ milligrams   1 kilogram = _____ grams
9. 1 cubit = _____ spans   1 cubit = _____ feet
10. 1 fathom = _____ feet   1 furlong = _____ mile
11. 1 handbreadth = _____ inches   1 span = _____ inches

B. *Write the metric prefixes with these meanings.*

12. a. 1,000   b. 0.1   c. 10   d. 100   e. 0.001   f. 0.01

C. *Which is the larger unit in each pair?*

13. yard, meter   inch, centimeter   liter, quart
14. mile, kilometer   acre, square mile   pound, kilogram
15. dekameter, decimeter   gram, ounce   cubit, foot

D. *Use the measure rules to find the missing numbers. Express any remainders as fractions.*

16. 8 ft. = _____ yd.   8 ft. = _____ in.   8 in. = _____ ft.
17. 45 min. = _____ hr.   3 days = _____ hr.   2 yr. = _____ days
18. 15 mo. = _____ yr.   4 yd. = _____ ft.   18 in. = _____ yd.
19. 6 qt. = _____ cups   6 pt. = _____ qt.   3 sq. yd. = _____ sq. ft.
20. 70 cm = _____ mm   12 pk. = _____ bu.   2 sq. mi. = _____ acres
21. 70 mm = _____ cm   7 m = _____ cm   7 km = _____ m

E. *Copy and solve.*

22.

4 bushels 3 pecks	6 years 180 days	17 hours 35 minutes
+ 5 bushels 2 pecks	+ 7 years 200 days	+ 14 hours 25 minutes

23.

16 years 8 months	9 yards 20 inches	5 pecks 2 quarts
− 12 years 10 months	− 7 yards 27 inches	− 4 pecks 6 quarts

24.

4 yards 2 feet	6 quarts 1 pint	3 pounds 8 ounces
× 4	× 5	× 3

F. *Write the measurements to which the arrows point.*

25.

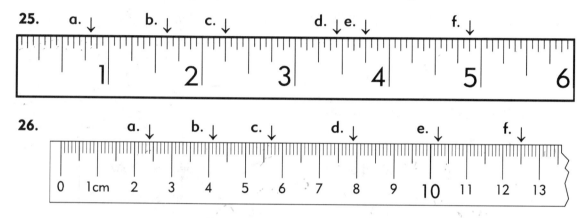

26.

G. *Do these exercises with scale.*

27. Write the actual lengths represented by these scale drawings.

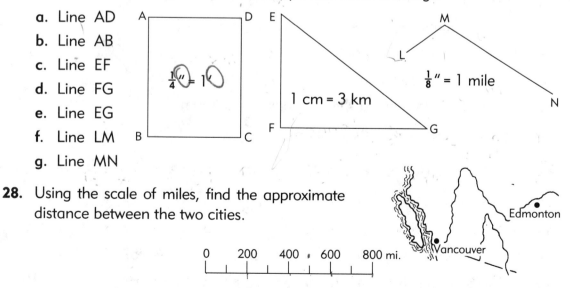

a. Line AD
b. Line AB
c. Line EF
d. Line FG
e. Line EG
f. Line LM
g. Line MN

28. Using the scale of miles, find the approximate distance between the two cities.

165. Miscellaneous Review

A. *Do these exercises.*

1. Is 2 a multiple of 6?

2. Write six multiples of 8.

3. All multiples of 10 end with _____.

4. All even numbers are multiples of _____.

5. Write the factor pairs for 20.

6. Write all the factors of 24 in order.

7. Draw factor trees for 30 and for 63.

Study the box below to review ratio.

> 1. **Ratio** is a comparison of two numbers by division.
>
> 2. A ratio is expressed as a fraction or as one number "to" the other.
>
> Example: The comparison of 6 chickens to 4 ducks can be expressed as 6 to 4, or $\frac{6}{4}$. This ratio can be reduced to 3 to 2, or $\frac{3}{2}$. It means that there are 3 chickens for every 2 ducks.

B. *Express these ratios as fractions in lowest terms. Do not change improper fractions to mixed numbers.*

8. 4 girls compared with 5 boys

9. 2 boys compared with 4 girls

10. 8 brown-haired boys compared with 3 blond-haired boys

11. 4 fifth graders compared with 16 pupils in the room

12. 4 guppies compared with 3 goldfish

C. *Apply the rules of divisibility to these numbers. Write* yes *or* no.

13. Is 316 divisible by: a. 2? b. 3? c. 4? d. 5? e. 6? f. 9? g. 10?

14. Is 4,713 divisible by: a. 2? b. 3? c. 4? d. 5? e. 6? f. 9? g. 10?

15. Is 47,130 divisible by: a. 2? b. 3? c. 4? d. 5? e. 6? f. 9? g. 10?

16. Is 2,475 divisible by: a. 2? b. 3? c. 4? d. 5? e. 6? f. 9? g. 10?

D. *Write the answers.*

17. What time is shown on each clock?

      **c.**

a.   b.   c.   d.

18. Melissa began hoeing potatoes at 8:45 A.M. She hoed potatoes for 2 hours and 15 minutes. What time did she stop hoeing? (Use your classroom clock to find the answer if you need help.)

E. *Draw sketches to illustrate these geometric terms.*

19. a. right angle   **b.** rectangle

20. a. obtuse angle   **b.** parallelogram

21. a. perpendicular lines   **b.** pentagon

22. a. line segment   **b.** diameter of a circle

23. a. parallel lines   **b.** congruent squares

F. *Follow the directions.*

24. Find the perimeter of each shape.

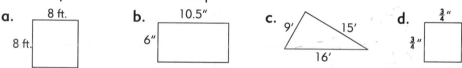

a. 8 ft. / 8 ft.   **b.** 10.5″ / 6″   **c.** 9′, 15′, 16′   **d.** $\frac{3}{4}$″, $\frac{3}{4}$″

25. Find the areas of **a** and **b** in number 24. Use the correct labels!

26. Find the volumes of boxes with these dimensions.
   a. length—7″   width—4″   height—3″
   b. length—10″   width—6″   height—5″

G. *Use the line graph to answer these questions.*

27. In which month did San Francisco receive the most precipitation?

28. How many inches fell that month (number 27)?

29. In which months did the least precipitation fall?

30. Which season (spring, summer, fall, winter) is the wettest season for San Francisco?

31. Which season is the driest?

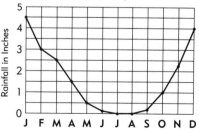

Monthly Precipitation
at San Francisco, California

166.   Review of Computation

A.   *Write the answers only.*

1.
$$\begin{array}{r} 8 \\ \times 7 \\ \hline \end{array} \quad \begin{array}{r} 10 \\ -8 \\ \hline \end{array} \quad \begin{array}{r} 12 \\ \times 9 \\ \hline \end{array} \quad \begin{array}{r} 8 \\ +6 \\ \hline \end{array} \quad \begin{array}{r} 9 \\ \times 7 \\ \hline \end{array} \quad \begin{array}{r} 7 \\ +9 \\ \hline \end{array} \quad \begin{array}{r} 11 \\ \times 11 \\ \hline \end{array} \quad \begin{array}{r} 12 \\ -7 \\ \hline \end{array} \quad \begin{array}{r} 9 \\ \times 9 \\ \hline \end{array}$$

2.
$$\begin{array}{r} 6 \\ \times 9 \\ \hline \end{array} \quad \begin{array}{r} 11 \\ -6 \\ \hline \end{array} \quad \begin{array}{r} 7 \\ \times 6 \\ \hline \end{array} \quad \begin{array}{r} 10 \\ \times 10 \\ \hline \end{array} \quad \begin{array}{r} 13 \\ -9 \\ \hline \end{array} \quad \begin{array}{r} 5 \\ +8 \\ \hline \end{array} \quad \begin{array}{r} 15 \\ -7 \\ \hline \end{array} \quad \begin{array}{r} 12 \\ \times 5 \\ \hline \end{array} \quad \begin{array}{r} 8 \\ \times 8 \\ \hline \end{array}$$

3. $4\overline{)28}$ $6\overline{)48}$ $9\overline{)72}$ $5\overline{)35}$ $10\overline{)120}$ $12\overline{)132}$

4. $12+16$ $19+15$ $26+15$ $28+26$ $31+19$

5. $43+20$ $38+10$ $25+30$ $36+16$ $44+13$

6. $27-5$ $23-10$ $30-7$ $31-4$ $27-9$

7. $29-14$ $34-17$ $31-18$ $25-15$ $40-16$

8. 10×78 10×359 10×800 100×17 $1,000\times950$

9. 7×40 8×80 3×90 6×60 9×50

10. 5×13 8×15 4×18 3×28 6×26

11.
$$\begin{array}{r} 7 \\ 8 \\ 5 \\ 6 \\ 4 \\ +9 \\ \hline \end{array} \quad \begin{array}{r} 5 \\ 5 \\ 6 \\ 2 \\ 3 \\ +7 \\ \hline \end{array} \quad \begin{array}{r} 9 \\ 8 \\ 4 \\ 5 \\ 2 \\ +6 \\ \hline \end{array} \quad \begin{array}{r} 4 \\ 7 \\ 6 \\ 1 \\ 7 \\ +2 \\ \hline \end{array} \quad \begin{array}{r} 6 \\ 8 \\ 9 \\ 4 \\ 5 \\ +6 \\ \hline \end{array} \quad \begin{array}{r} 3 \\ 6 \\ 8 \\ 0 \\ 8 \\ +9 \\ \hline \end{array}$$

B.   *Copy and work carefully.*

12.
$$\begin{array}{r} 75 \\ 84 \\ 26 \\ 57 \\ +13 \\ \hline \end{array} \quad \begin{array}{r} 852 \\ 367 \\ 47 \\ 216 \\ +84 \\ \hline \end{array} \quad \begin{array}{r} 4,908 \\ 5,364 \\ 827 \\ +6,355 \\ \hline \end{array} \quad \begin{array}{r} 3,671 \\ 268 \\ 6,346 \\ 8,924 \\ +\ \ \ 416 \\ \hline \end{array} \quad \begin{array}{r} 54,295 \\ 27,845 \\ 90,512 \\ +78,369 \\ \hline \end{array}$$

13.

6,070	5,402	90,000	72,045
− 4,635	− 2,497	− 35,906	− 6,828

14.

5,708	960	324	819	752
× 67	× 356	× 790	× 804	× 900

15.   8)55,728   14)9,380   53)2,096   19)85,424

16. $567.92 + $320 + $488.15 $780 − $87.39

17.

$36.50	$8.75		
× 75	× 403	21)$483.84	49)$760.48

Checking by Casting Out Nines

Casting out nines is an interesting way to check computations. By casting out nines, each number in a problem is reduced to one digit. The single digits are used to check the problem.

Study the example below to learn how to cast out nines.

1. Cross out all the 9's in a number.   4̶9,562

2. Add the remaining digits. If the sum has two digits, add those digits together until you get a one-digit number.   For 4̶9,562: 4 + 5 + 6 + 2 = 17 → 1 + 7 = 8.

3. To check an addition problem, cast out nines for each addend and for the sum. Then add the one-digit addends. If the sum has two digits, add those digits together until you have a one-digit answer. That one digit should equal the one digit for the sum.

   Example:
   $$49,562 \rightarrow 8$$
   $$27,841 \rightarrow 4$$
   $$+ 35,678 \rightarrow + 2$$
   $$113,081 \rightarrow 5 \leftarrow 14$$

4. Casting out nines can also be used to check subtraction, multiplication, and division. Ask your teacher if you want to learn how to check multiplication and division.

   $$70,000 \rightarrow 7$$
   $$- 37,291 \rightarrow - 4$$
   $$32,709 \rightarrow 3$$

C. *Solve these addition problems. Check by casting out nines.*

18.

298	5,634	6,098	28,743	82,961
345	2,815	3,674	9,842	16,729
+ 827	+ 4,396	+ 5,487	+ 37,298	+46,235

167. Review of Decimals, Roman Numerals, and Percents

A. *Use this number to answer the following questions: 461,038,926,450*

1. What is the place value of the 3?
2. What is the place value of the 9?
3. What is the value of the underlined 6?
4. What number is 10,000 more than this number?
5. What number is 1,000,000 more than this number?

B. *Use this number to do the following exercises: 76.045*

6. What is the place value of the 4?
7. What is the place value of the 5?
8. Write the number with words.
9. Write the number as a mixed number with a common fraction.
10. If the 0 were dropped, would the number become larger or smaller?

C. *Write numerals for these number words.*

11. three hundred sixty billion, twenty-one million
12. eight hundred ninety million
13. thirty-four billion, five million, seventeen
14. fifteen and seven tenths
15. two and forty-nine hundredths

D. *Write the answers.*

16. What is the value of 700,000 + 40,000 + 9,000 + 200 + 10 + 8?
17. Write 64,391 in expanded form.
18. Round to the nearest thousand: a. 6,529   b. 19,468   c. 368,760
19. Round to the nearest hundred thousand: a. 368,760   b. 4,529,064

E. *Copy these decimals, and place <, >, or = between each pair.*

20. 1.03 _____ 1.30   0.069 _____ 0.69   4.23 _____ 4.203
21. 7.6 _____ 7.60   5.1 _____ 5.13   9.648 _____ 9.6
22. 6.05 _____ 6.005   0.080 _____ 0.08   7.43 _____ 7.8

F. *Follow the directions.*

23. Copy the prime numbers: 3   6   8   11   15   19   22   27   29   33

24. Write as Roman numerals.
    a. 568   **b.** 2,450   **c.** 1,084   **d.** 3,919   **e.** 1,735

25. Write as Arabic numerals.
    a. CCLXXVI   **b.** MDCXII   **c.** MMCCCIX **d.** MCMXCII **e.** MMMXLV

26. **Percent** means "per _____."

27. Write these decimals as percents.
    a. 0.45   **b.** 0.97   **c.** 0.62   **d.** 0.06   **e.** 0.18

28. Change these common fractions to percents by first changing them to hundredths.
    a. $\frac{17}{20}$ **b.** $\frac{13}{50}$ **c.** $\frac{1}{2}$ **d.** $\frac{1}{4}$ **e.** $\frac{4}{5}$ **f.** $\frac{7}{10}$ **g.** $\frac{21}{25}$

G. *Answer these questions about percents.*

29. If your family ate a whole pie, what percent of the pie was eaten?

30. If 55 percent of a class are girls, what percent are boys?

31. If 89 percent of a class are present, what percent are absent?

H. *Copy and work carefully. Annex zeroes to fill in empty places. Remember the decimal points in the answers.*

32.

125.6	37.892	620.5		
47.85	5.34	8.592		
567.49	568.206	72.74	80	329.613
+ 26.458	+ 62.7	+ 284.376	− 31.92	− 47.83

33. 67.13 + 2.897 + 324.6 + 5.72   14.379 + 783.62 + 589.3

34. 5.296 + 34.71 + 25 + 864.9   736.4 + 280.769 + 53.72

35. 760 − 425.89   82.603 − 14.78   93.6 − 26.381

36.

6.2	0.468	5.07	740	163
× 37	× 54	× 839	× 6.7	× 4.89

37. 7$\overline{)0.042}$ 6$\overline{)0.372}$ 8$\overline{)321.6}$ 13$\overline{)3.38}$ 35$\overline{)1.295}$

168. Review of Reading Problems

A. *Write whether you would* add, subtract multiply, *or divide* **to solve each problem.**

1. What is the perimeter of a rectangle?

2. What is the area of a rectangle?

3. How far will a car go in 3 hours at 60 m.p.h.?

4. Four light bulbs cost $1.96. What is the price of one bulb?

5. How much older was Adam than Seth?

6. How many 3's are in 18?

7. Room 1 has 19 pupils, Room 2 has 26 pupils, and Room 3 has 23. How many pupils is that in all?

8. Each of 3 rooms has 18 people. What is the total number of people?

9. A plane traveled 1,860 miles in 3 hours. What was the speed of the plane?

10. Wrenches usually priced at $6.29 are on sale for $4.79. How much is saved by buying a wrench on sale?

B. *Write what other information is needed to solve each problem.*

11. Aunt Martha bought $4\frac{1}{2}$ pounds of bananas. How much did she pay for them?

12. The price of a used combine is $65,000. What will each man pay if they share the cost equally?

13. During the month of December, one congregation passed out 3,475 tracts. Of those, 853 were *The Meaning of the Manger*. How many more copies of that tract were distributed than of *Peace and Pardon*?

14. Sister Marie bought puzzles for her pupils at the end of the school year. What was the total cost of puzzles for 23 pupils?

15. Rebecca lives 13 miles from her Grandpa Millers. How much closer does she live to Grandpa Millers than to Grandpa Benders?

16. A train traveled 450 miles. How many hours did it take to travel that distance?

17. Mother bought a case of oranges for $13.95. What was the price of one orange at that rate?

18. Brother Myer raises hogs on his farm. If each sow has 3 litters of pigs per year and raises an average of 9.6 pigs per litter, how many pigs does Brother Myer raise per year?

C. *Solve these reading problems. Some have more than one step.*

19. When the Israelites were in the wilderness, God said that three tribes should camp on each side of the tabernacle. There were 186,400 men and their families on the east side, 151,450 men on the south side, 108,100 men on the west side, and 157,600 men on the north side. What was the total number of men counted in Israel?

20. How many more men camped east of the tabernacle than west of the tabernacle?

21. The tribe of Reuben had 46,500 men, the tribe of Simeon 59,300, and the tribe of Gad 45,650. These three tribes formed the group camped on one side of the tabernacle. According to the figures in number 19, on which side of the tabernacle were the tribes of Reuben, Simeon, and Gad?

22. Aunt Rachel bought 3 grapefruits for $1.19. At that rate, what was the price of a dozen grapefruits?

23. In the same store, Mother bought a case of 48 grapefruits for $12.00. What was the price of a dozen grapefruits?

24. The difference in price per dozen grapefruits bought by Aunt Rachel and Mother was $1.76. How much did Mother save on a whole case?

25. Aunt Rachel lives alone. She eats $\frac{1}{2}$ grapefruit at a time. How many servings will Aunt Rachel have from 3 grapefruits?

26. There are eight people in Mother's family, and each of them eats $\frac{1}{2}$ grapefruit at a meal. For how many meals will a case of 48 grapefruits last?

27. Father bought $7\frac{1}{2}$ feet of large chain at 86¢ per foot and 24 feet of small chain at 45¢ per foot. How much did he pay in all?

28. Doris is making $\frac{3}{4}$ batch of molasses cookies. The recipe calls for 2 cups of sugar. How much sugar should Doris use?

29. Mother wants to paint 4 walls each 13 feet long and 9 feet high. A quart of paint will cover 100 square feet of surface. How much paint does Mother need?

30. A good cow produced 25,740 pounds of milk in 11 months. What was the average amount of milk the cow produced each month?

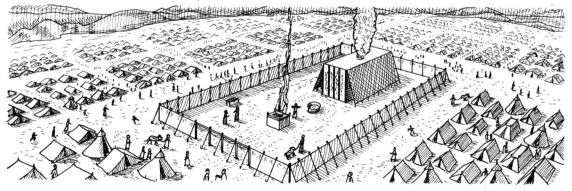

169. Year-End Review

A. *Write the answers only.*

1. 26 + 10	34 + 20	45 – 10	37 – 20
2. 18 + 19	15 + 27	26 + 18	34 + 16
3. 21 – 7	33 – 19	30 – 16	36 – 28
4. 7 × 80	5 × 16	8 × 23	4 × 29
5. 10 × 46	10 × 580	100 × 25	1,000 × 80
6. 120 ÷ 10	300 ÷ 10	4,500 ÷ 10	500 ÷ 100

B. *Write the correct words to complete these sentences.*

7. The bottom number of a fraction is the (numerator, denominator).

8. If a fraction is (proper, improper), its value is less than 1.

9. The top number in a subtraction problem is the (subtrahend, minuend, difference).

10. The answer to a multiplication problem is the (difference, multiplier, product, quotient).

11. The number being divided in a division problem is the (divisor, dividend, denominator).

12. A five-sided shape is (a pentagon, a hexagon, an octagon).

13. Lines that never meet are (intersecting, parallel, perpendicular) lines.

14. Triangles that are the same size and shape are (similar, congruent).

15. The distance across a circle is the (diameter, radius).

16. The basic metric unit of length is the (meter, liter, gram).

17. The (meter, liter, gram) is the basic unit of weight.

18. A (millimeter, centimeter, kilometer) is equal to 1,000 meters.

19. A (handbreadth, span, cubit) is equal to about 18 inches.

20. A (cubit, fathom, furlong) was used to measure long distances on land.

21. To change from a smaller unit of measure to a larger unit, we (multiply, divide).

22. A number that cannot be divided by any other numbers except itself and 1 is a (prime number, common factor, multiple).

C. *Give the answers.*

23. Write the meanings of these metric prefixes.

   a. deka-   b. milli-   c. kilo-   d. centi-   e. deci-   f. hecto-

24. Write all the factors of 18.

25. Write six multiples of 6.

26. Write the prime numbers between 10 and 20.

27. Write a common factor of 8 and 4.

28. Write a common multiple of 8 and 4.

29. Is 3,510 divisible by: **a.** 2?   **b.** 3?   **c.** 4?   **d.** 5?   **e.** 6?   **f.** 9?

30. In 783,451,028,640, which digit is in ten millions' place?

31. Copy this number, and place commas correctly: 5903720148

32. Round to the nearest ten thousand: **a.** 78,459   **b.** 3,294,610

33. Arrange these decimals in order of size from smallest to largest.
a. 4.6   4.67   4.07   **b.** 3.018   0.318   3.18

D. *Write the numbers that fit in the blanks.*

34. 1 century = _____ yr.   1 qt. = _____ cups   1 bu. = _____ pk.

35. 1 leap year = ____ days   1 hr. = _____ min.   1 qt. = _____ pt.

36. 1 sq. yd. = _____ sq. ft.   1 ton = _____ lb.   1 lb. = _____ oz.

37. 1 sq. mi. = _____ acres   1 yr. = _____ wk.   1 yd. = _____ in.

38. 1 sq. ft. = _____ sq. in.   1 day = _____ hr.   1 mi. = _____ ft.

39. 1 decade = _____ yr.   1 kg = _____ g   1 m = _____ cm

40. 3 m = _____ mm   9 yd. = _____ ft.   9 in. = _____ ft.

41. 18 ft. = _____ yd.   18 in. = _____ ft.   18 sq. ft. = ____ sq. yd.

42. 6 pt. = _____ cups   6 pt. = _____ qt.   2 sq. ft. = _____ sq. in.

43. 36 mo. = _____ yr.   3 hr. = _____ min.   12 hr. = _____ day

44. 6 cm = _____ mm   2 lb. = _____ oz.   4 liters = _____ mL

E. *Do these exercises.*

45. Reduce to lowest terms: **a.** $\frac{12}{30}$ **b.** $\frac{24}{40}$ **c.** $\frac{16}{64}$ **d.** $\frac{20}{36}$ **e.** $\frac{30}{40}$

46. Change to whole numbers or mixed numbers in simplest form.
a. $\frac{12}{3}$ **b.** $\frac{14}{4}$ **c.** $\frac{21}{8}$ **d.** $\frac{20}{16}$

47. Change to percents: **a.** $\frac{1}{5}$ **b.** $\frac{3}{4}$ **c.** $\frac{9}{10}$ **d.** $\frac{37}{50}$ **e.** $\frac{7}{20}$ **f.** $\frac{21}{25}$

48. Write as Roman numerals: **a.** 728   **b.** 1,469   **c.** 2,940   **d.** 3,094

(continued on next page)

49. Write the measurements to which the arrows point.

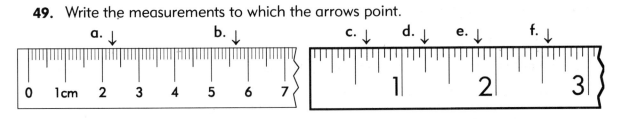

50. The school day begins at 8:30 and ends at 2:45. How long is the school day? Use a clock if you need help.

51. Turn to the map on the second page of Lesson 159. What town is located at D11?

52. Using the scales given below the drawings, find what actual lengths are represented by the lines.

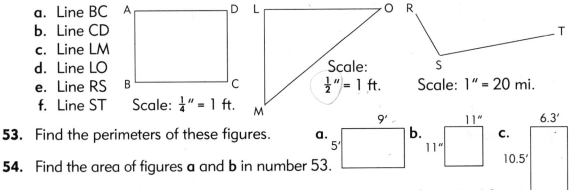

    a. Line BC
    b. Line CD
    c. Line LM
    d. Line LO
    e. Line RS
    f. Line ST   Scale: $\frac{1}{4}$" = 1 ft.

Scale: $\frac{1}{2}$" = 1 ft.   Scale: 1" = 20 mi.

53. Find the perimeters of these figures.

    a. 9′, 5′
    b. 11″, 11″
    c. 6.3′, 10.5′

54. Find the area of figures **a** and **b** in number 53.

55. What is the volume of a box 4 feet long, 3 feet wide, and 2 feet high?

56. Mr. Boyer had the following money in his wallet: one $50-bill, three $20-bills, two $10-bills, three $5-bills, and six $1-bills. What was the value of the money in Mr. Boyer's wallet?

F. *List the coins and bills that should be given as change. Start with the smallest pieces.*

57. Amount of purchase—$6.33;   amount given—$10.00

58. Amount of purchase—$3.69;   amount given—$20.00

G. *Copy and work carefully.*

59. $\frac{7}{8} \times \frac{1}{3}$ $\frac{3}{4} \times 12$ $5 \times \frac{7}{10}$ $\frac{2}{5} \times \frac{5}{8}$

60. $8 \div \frac{2}{3}$ $\frac{1}{4} \div 3$ $\frac{3}{5} \div \frac{1}{10}$ $\frac{3}{8} \div \frac{9}{16}$

61.

$$\begin{array}{r} \frac{3}{4} \\ \frac{5}{8} \\ + \frac{1}{2} \\ \hline \end{array} \qquad \begin{array}{r} 9\frac{2}{3} \\ + 7\frac{5}{6} \\ \hline \end{array} \qquad \begin{array}{r} 12 \\ - 5\frac{11}{16} \\ \hline \end{array} \qquad \begin{array}{r} 8\frac{3}{4} \\ - 6\frac{2}{3} \\ \hline \end{array} \qquad \begin{array}{r} 7\frac{1}{3} \\ - 3\frac{1}{2} \\ \hline \end{array}$$

62. $78,290 + 3,874 + 95,318$ $45.8 + 239.76 + 87.5 + 3.485$

63. $\$592.14 + \$37.50 + \$625$ $98 + 32 + 57 + 14 + 29 + 63$

64.
```
   80,000        $139.52         375          520.031
 - 62,580       - 38.75       - 198.35       - 49.69
```

65.
```
    609           285           64.7          0.819
  × 753         × 450         × 600          × 209
```

66.
```
   7 lb.   8 oz.        10 yd.  12 in.           5 bu.  2 pk.
 + 6 lb.  10 oz.       - 8 yd.  24 in.              × 4
```

67. $7\overline{)45,696}$ $24\overline{)14,520}$ $13\overline{)0.494}$ $37\overline{)\$99.90}$

H. *Solve these reading problems.*

68. David is paid 25¢ for every quart of strawberries he picks for Brother Metzler. David can pick 10 quarts in one hour if he works diligently. How much will he earn in 4 hours?

69. For a science project, Ethan bought 6 small light bulbs for $0.35 each, 20 feet of insulated wire at $0.12 a foot, and a battery for $4.39. What was the total cost of Ethan's science project?

70. Mr. Young found that his car travels 450 miles on a 10-gallon tank of fuel. At that rate, how many gallons of fuel will Mr. Young need on a trip of 2,700 miles?

71. Usually Mother uses 18 cups of flour when she bakes bread. This week the three young people in the family are away at Bible fellowship meetings, so Mother is making only $\frac{2}{3}$ of the usual amount of bread. How many cups of flour will Mother use?

72. The Nolt family sells eggs for $0.75 a dozen. Mr. Nolt figures that the expense of feed is $14.50 to produce 25 dozen eggs. What is the profit on the eggs after the feed expense is paid?

---

170. Chapter 17 Test

Interesting Number Facts

More Number Patterns

At the end of Chapter 4, you saw some interesting number patterns that are formed when the digits of two-digit numbers are added together. You saw the patterns for counting by ones, eights, twos, and sevens. This page shows the patterns for the threes and sixes, and the fours and fives.

Counting by Threes												
Numbers:	3	6	9	12	15	18	21	24	27	30	33	36
Pattern:	3	6	9	3	6	9	3	6	9	3	6	9

Counting by Sixes												
Numbers:	6	12	18	24	30	36	42	48	54	60	66	72
Pattern:	6	3	9	6	3	9	6	3	9	6	3	9

The patterns for the fours and fives are arranged so that you can recognize them easily. Notice how the number pattern is woven together. Also notice that the number pattern in these two boxes are exact opposites, like the threes and sixes.

Counting by Fours												
Numbers:	4	8	12	16	20	24	28	32	36	40	44	48
Pattern:	4		3		2		1		9		8	
		8		7		6		5		4		3

Counting by Fives												
Numbers:	5	10	15	20	25	30	35	40	45	50	55	60
Pattern:	5		6		7		8		9		1	
		1		2		3		4		5		6

All these patterns come in opposite pairs because there is something special about the number 9. The twos and sevens form an opposite pair because $2 + 7 = 9$. The threes and sixes, the ones and eights, and the fours and fives each form other opposite pairs.

Here is the pattern for counting by nines. If you know the rule of divisibility for 9, this pattern is not surprising. It also shows that there is something special about the number 9.

Counting by Nines												
Numbers:	9	18	27	36	45	54	63	72	81	90	99	108
Pattern:	9	9	9	9	9	9	9	9	9	9	9	9

Supplementary Drills

Set I: Fact Drills

Drill 1   *100 Addition Facts*

	a.	b.	c.	d.	e.	f.	g.	h.	i.	j.
1.	2 +1	5 +0	8 +6	0 +1	1 +0	2 +2	3 +6	4 +1	2 +0	1 +9
2.	1 +1	4 +6	9 +4	1 +6	2 +5	3 +2	4 +0	8 +0	6 +5	7 +2
3.	3 +0	2 +6	1 +5	9 +1	6 +0	5 +4	1 +3	1 +2	2 +7	6 +6
4.	1 +4	2 +3	7 +3	0 +0	1 +8	4 +2	4 +4	3 +1	1 +7	2 +8
5.	2 +4	8 +2	0 +9	3 +4	6 +1	5 +5	9 +0	8 +1	7 +0	6 +4
6.	4 +5	2 +9	9 +2	6 +2	3 +3	6 +3	5 +1	0 +2	5 +6	7 +4
7.	3 +5	7 +1	7 +6	5 +2	3 +8	3 +7	8 +8	5 +3	6 +7	4 +8
8.	4 +3	3 +9	6 +8	0 +6	4 +7	5 +8	8 +7	7 +5	0 +4	5 +7
9.	8 +4	9 +8	0 +5	7 +7	4 +9	6 +9	7 +8	5 +9	9 +9	0 +3
10.	8 +5	8 +9	9 +7	0 +8	9 +3	7 +9	0 +7	9 +6	9 +5	8 +3

Drill 2   *100 Addition Facts*

	a.	b.	c.	d.	e.	f.	g.	h.	i.	j.
1.	8 +9	1 +4	2 +9	0 +7	2 +0	5 +5	5 +7	3 +6	3 +8	0 +5
2.	1 +0	7 +2	8 +0	5 +9	8 +3	1 +3	3 +4	5 +4	3 +5	7 +4
3.	9 +7	4 +1	6 +6	9 +2	2 +1	5 +3	9 +9	0 +0	8 +2	9 +0
4.	1 +1	5 +1	4 +3	2 +8	3 +1	4 +4	2 +5	5 +6	4 +7	6 +8
5.	7 +3	0 +3	8 +4	6 +5	9 +8	0 +1	6 +2	2 +7	9 +4	0 +6
6.	1 +5	4 +9	3 +2	1 +2	7 +7	1 +8	6 +0	5 +8	7 +1	7 +8
7.	8 +8	6 +1	2 +2	1 +7	2 +3	3 +7	6 +3	4 +6	9 +5	7 +5
8.	0 +2	4 +8	6 +4	4 +5	9 +1	7 +0	5 +0	8 +1	7 +9	3 +0
9.	1 +9	2 +4	1 +6	8 +6	6 +9	4 +2	2 +6	9 +3	0 +8	0 +4
10.	3 +9	5 +2	8 +5	3 +3	0 +9	8 +7	7 +6	4 +0	6 +7	9 +6

Drill 3   *100 Subtraction Facts*

	a.	b.	c.	d.	e.	f.	g.	h.	i.	j.
1.	11 −9	9 −6	7 −5	6 −3	4 −1	10 −6	6 −6	8 −3	2 −0	4 −3
2.	8 −8	6 −5	4 −0	5 −5	0 −0	1 −1	8 −6	7 −1	3 −0	6 −4
3.	3 −3	1 −0	8 −7	6 −0	4 −2	5 −4	7 −0	2 −1	5 −3	7 −6
4.	7 −7	3 −2	6 −1	7 −4	4 −4	5 −1	2 −2	6 −2	5 −2	3 −1
5.	17 −8	10 −9	14 −7	15 −8	18 −9	16 −7	15 −9	9 −2	13 −8	12 −3
6.	12 −4	9 −0	16 −8	17 −9	10 −1	13 −5	14 −8	10 −3	11 −2	15 −7
7.	16 −9	12 −5	10 −4	14 −5	9 −1	11 −3	15 −6	14 −9	12 −6	13 −6
8.	14 −6	10 −8	11 −4	9 −3	9 −5	8 −1	10 −7	12 −9	13 −7	9 −9
9.	13 −9	8 −5	10 −2	12 −8	11 −5	10 −5	11 −6	13 −4	7 −3	9 −8
10.	8 −0	12 −7	11 −8	9 −4	8 −2	5 −0	7 −2	11 −7	8 −4	9 −7

Drill 4   *100 Subtraction Facts*

	a.	b.	c.	d.	e.	f.	g.	h.	i.	j.
1.	10 − 9	9 − 0	12 − 5	10 − 8	8 − 5	12 − 7	9 − 6	6 − 5	1 − 1	3 − 3
2.	15 − 9	17 − 8	14 − 5	9 − 3	12 − 6	9 − 4	6 − 3	5 − 5	6 − 0	7 − 4
3.	16 − 7	13 − 5	11 − 8	8 − 1	10 − 5	5 − 4	10 − 6	1 − 0	5 − 1	5 − 3
4.	9 − 2	10 − 3	14 − 6	12 − 8	13 − 4	11 − 3	8 − 3	7 − 1	2 − 0	6 − 1
5.	12 − 9	15 − 7	13 − 6	9 − 9	9 − 7	4 − 1	9 − 8	6 − 4	7 − 6	3 − 1
6.	7 − 7	8 − 8	8 − 0	14 − 8	12 − 3	3 − 2	11 − 6	13 − 7	16 − 9	17 − 9
7.	14 − 9	16 − 8	10 − 4	11 − 9	10 − 2	11 − 5	7 − 5	7 − 2	8 − 7	6 − 2
8.	18 − 9	10 − 1	4 − 3	9 − 5	11 − 7	8 − 2	4 − 4	0 − 0	4 − 0	9 − 1
9.	2 − 2	7 − 0	8 − 6	6 − 6	4 − 2	11 − 4	10 − 7	15 − 8	14 − 7	15 − 6
10.	13 − 9	11 − 2	12 − 4	7 − 3	13 − 8	8 − 4	2 − 1	5 − 2	3 − 0	5 − 0

Drill 5   *Multiplication Facts: 0's–6's*

	a.	b.	c.	d.	e.	f.	g.	h.	i.	j.
1.	3 ×2	5 ×3	1 ×1	3 ×3	2 ×6	4 ×5	5 ×0	8 ×2	9 ×3	6 ×2
2.	2 ×3	0 ×6	5 ×4	6 ×5	8 ×3	2 ×7	3 ×6	10 ×1	4 ×2	7 ×5
3.	7 ×4	5 ×5	8 ×4	7 ×6	3 ×0	10 ×2	4 ×3	9 ×5	6 ×3	10 ×6
4.	12 ×3	6 ×4	9 ×4	11 ×5	12 ×2	9 ×2	5 ×6	10 ×3	12 ×5	9 ×6
5.	6 ×6	2 ×5	2 ×2	12 ×4	3 ×5	10 ×5	11 ×3	4 ×6	12 ×6	7 ×3
6.	8 ×5	8 ×6	9 ×4	3 ×3	9 ×2	9 ×6	7 ×5	3 ×6	4 ×4	6 ×6

Drill 6   *Multiplication Facts: 3's–7's*

	a.	b.	c.	d.	e.	f.	g.	h.	i.	j.
1.	3 ×7	10 ×7	9 ×5	4 ×4	2 ×5	7 ×4	7 ×6	2 ×3	4 ×3	6 ×6
2.	5 ×5	7 ×5	3 ×6	6 ×4	8 ×5	1 ×3	7 ×3	12 ×4	9 ×3	5 ×6
3.	10 ×6	8 ×4	5 ×3	11 ×3	8 ×7	2 ×6	4 ×6	3 ×3	7 ×7	5 ×4
4.	2 ×4	6 ×7	9 ×7	3 ×5	6 ×3	9 ×4	5 ×7	2 ×7	12 ×6	11 ×5
5.	3 ×4	4 ×7	12 ×5	6 ×5	12 ×7	12 ×3	8 ×3	4 ×5	8 ×6	9 ×6

Drill 7   *Multiplication Facts: 3's–8's*

	a.	b.	c.	d.	e.	f.	g.	h.	i.	j.
1.	6 ×6	5 ×5	8 ×8	3 ×3	4 ×4	6 ×5	7 ×3	3 ×8	8 ×4	2 ×5
2.	7 ×8	5 ×7	12 ×4	10 ×3	1 ×8	8 ×6	6 ×4	9 ×5	6 ×3	3 ×4
3.	4 ×5	11 ×8	3 ×7	5 ×4	1 ×6	4 ×7	8 ×7	12 ×3	9 ×6	4 ×8
4.	2 ×3	7 ×4	12 ×5	7 ×6	8 ×3	2 ×4	9 ×7	4 ×6	5 ×8	9 ×8
5.	12 ×6	3 ×6	12 ×7	2 ×8	6 ×8	7 ×7	9 ×4	3 ×5	12 ×8	9 ×3

Drill 8   *Multiplication Facts: 3's–9's*

	a.	b.	c.	d.	e.	f.	g.	h.	i.	j.
1.	3 ×7	12 ×8	4 ×4	9 ×8	5 ×3	2 ×7	6 ×8	9 ×9	12 ×3	10 ×6
2.	8 ×7	5 ×5	7 ×4	9 ×3	4 ×8	11 ×7	8 ×8	3 ×4	6 ×7	4 ×6
3.	5 ×9	9 ×9	3 ×8	5 ×7	7 ×8	6 ×6	8 ×5	9 ×4	2 ×5	12 ×4
4.	12 ×9	6 ×3	4 ×9	8 ×4	9 ×6	3 ×3	0 ×5	8 ×3	7 ×6	7 ×9
5.	4 ×5	2 ×9	12 ×5	7 ×7	12 ×6	5 ×6	8 ×6	12 ×7	9 ×7	11 ×4

Drill 9   *Multiplication Facts: 6's–9's*

	a.	b.	c.	d.	e.	f.	g.	h.	i.	j.
1.	3 ×6	7 ×8	9 ×7	4 ×8	5 ×7	6 ×7	3 ×9	12 ×9	6 ×9	4 ×7
2.	1 ×9	8 ×8	5 ×6	2 ×7	8 ×6	10 ×7	3 ×8	5 ×9	9 ×9	7 ×7
3.	8 ×9	7 ×6	1 ×8	2 ×6	6 ×8	6 ×6	9 ×6	5 ×8	3 ×7	7 ×9
4.	4 ×6	2 ×8	4 ×9	9 ×8	8 ×7	2 ×9	12 ×6	7 ×8	8 ×8	12 ×7
5.	12 ×8	9 ×9	10 ×8	7 ×6	6 ×8	7 ×7	6 ×9	8 ×9	3 ×7	5 ×6

Drill 10   *Multiplication Facts: 6's–9's*

	a.	b.	c.	d.
1.	6 × 5	8 × 12	9 × 5	8 × 7
2.	6 × 9	7 × 5	9 × 8	7 × 6
3.	8 × 2	7 × 4	6 × 8	6 × 2
4.	9 × 7	9 × 3	6 × 3	6 × 7
5.	8 × 9	7 × 8	9 × 6	8 × 4
6.	8 × 3	7 × 7	9 × 9	6 × 12
7.	7 × 11	9 × 4	6 × 6	8 × 5
8.	7 × 2	6 × 4	8 × 6	8 × 8
9.	9 × 11	7 × 3	9 × 2	7 × 9
10.	7 × 1	6 × 10	8 × 7	6 × 9
11.	7 × 5	8 × 11	9 × 4	9 × 8
12.	8 × 10	8 × 6	6 × 3	9 × 9

Drill 11

Multiplication Facts: 1's–9's

	a.	b.	c.	d.	e.	f.	g.	h.	i.	j.
1.	5 ×7	6 ×9	8 ×4	2 ×1	10 ×3	4 ×5	1 ×8	7 ×6	12 ×9	4 ×7
2.	3 ×3	5 ×4	7 ×2	2 ×5	2 ×9	9 ×6	12 ×7	11 ×5	3 ×8	1 ×6
3.	6 ×6	10 ×7	9 ×3	8 ×9	4 ×9	4 ×2	1 ×3	7 ×8	8 ×8	11 ×2
4.	10 ×1	5 ×9	3 ×6	9 ×8	10 ×9	2 ×7	4 ×4	1 ×5	10 ×2	6 ×8
5.	12 ×4	3 ×7	1 ×9	7 ×9	5 ×8	5 ×6	9 ×4	8 ×7	4 ×6	1 ×4
6.	8 ×5	2 ×6	2 ×4	11 ×4	12 ×6	8 ×3	1 ×7	12 ×8	11 ×6	7 ×4
7.	12 ×3	6 ×4	8 ×1	3 ×5	11 ×1	8 ×6	10 ×5	5 ×5	2 ×8	4 ×8
8.	10 ×8	3 ×9	2 ×3	5 ×3	7 ×5	6 ×7	9 ×7	6 ×5	11 ×7	3 ×4
9.	6 ×1	2 ×2	12 ×5	7 ×7	11 ×8	10 ×4	3 ×1	9 ×9	5 ×1	7 ×3
10.	1 ×1	12 ×2	6 ×3	5 ×2	7 ×1	11 ×9	12 ×1	6 ×2	9 ×5	4 ×3

Drill 12   *Multiplication Facts: 1's–9's*

	a.	b.	c.	d.	e.	f.	g.	h.	i.	j.
1.	9 × 2	3 × 6	5 × 9	2 × 7	4 × 8	7 × 4	9 × 8	6 × 5	1 × 4	10 × 6
2.	12 × 8	1 × 6	8 × 2	4 × 5	3 × 9	5 × 3	7 × 8	6 × 7	8 × 6	8 × 9
3.	2 × 9	5 × 7	8 × 3	5 × 5	7 × 9	2 × 3	1 × 3	3 × 4	9 × 5	12 × 4
4.	1 × 9	4 × 7	7 × 6	9 × 6	2 × 5	6 × 3	7 × 5	9 × 4	9 × 1	4 × 4
5.	7 × 2	4 × 3	11 × 9	12 × 2	3 × 2	7 × 7	8 × 4	9 × 3	11 × 6	8 × 5
6.	12 × 6	3 × 7	1 × 7	12 × 2	10 × 4	6 × 4	2 × 6	8 × 7	9 × 9	10 × 2
7.	6 × 8	12 × 1	10 × 8	3 × 5	6 × 6	7 × 3	5 × 4	2 × 8	5 × 8	8 × 8
8.	12 × 3	5 × 2	6 × 9	1 × 5	10 × 3	5 × 6	2 × 4	4 × 6	9 × 7	3 × 8
9.	11 × 8	12 × 5	3 × 3	11 × 7	6 × 2	4 × 9	1 × 4	11 × 3	4 × 2	1 × 8
10.	10 × 9	10 × 5	2 × 2	10 × 1	9 × 9	7 × 5	12 × 9	8 × 7	5 × 4	6 × 9

Drill 13   *Multiplication Facts: 9's–12's*

	a.	b.	c.	d.	e.	f.	g.	h.	i.	j.
1.	10 ×5	12 ×9	11 ×2	9 ×7	11 ×8	12 ×4	10 ×9	9 ×3	11 ×6	12 ×11
2.	10 ×12	10 ×6	12 ×7	11 ×11	9 ×5	10 ×4	10 ×11	12 ×1	11 ×4	9 ×1
3.	12 ×9	10 ×9	11 ×1	11 ×9	11 ×12	10 ×1	9 ×4	10 ×8	12 ×5	10 ×2
4.	9 ×8	12 ×12	10 ×7	9 ×9	12 ×2	11 ×7	10 ×10	12 ×10	9 ×6	11 ×3
5.	10 ×11	11 ×9	12 ×6	12 ×8	11 ×5	9 ×2	12 ×3	10 ×3	9 ×8	12 ×12

Drill 14   *Multiplication Facts: 10's–12's*

	a.	b.	c.	d.
1.	12 × 1	10 × 12	11 × 2	11 × 11
2.	10 × 3	12 × 10	10 × 1	11 × 6
3.	12 × 12	10 × 9	10 × 5	12 × 4
4.	11 × 8	12 × 7	11 × 3	10 × 6
5.	11 × 12	10 × 8	11 × 4	12 × 5
6.	12 × 2	10 × 7	11 × 7	10 × 11
7.	10 × 3	12 × 6	12 × 12	11 × 10
8.	10 × 4	12 × 8	11 × 5	10 × 10
9.	12 × 11	11 × 9	12 × 9	11 × 2
10.	12 × 3	10 × 11	11 × 4	12 × 6
11.	10 × 9	11 × 12	12 × 7	10 × 4
12.	11 × 11	12 × 8	11 × 7	12 × 9

Drill 15   *Multiplication Facts: 1's–12's*

	a.	b.	c.	d.	e.	f.	g.	h.	i.	j.
1.	4 × 3	9 × 5	12 × 3	6 × 7	5 × 4	11 × 8	12 × 1	2 × 9	7 × 6	10 × 10
2.	1 × 1	11 × 8	10 × 6	10 × 4	12 × 6	10 × 2	5 × 8	3 × 6	1 × 8	2 × 5
3.	8 × 4	12 × 1	9 × 9	4 × 7	12 × 5	7 × 2	8 × 7	10 × 7	12 × 9	6 × 1
4.	11 × 12	1 × 4	5 × 6	6 × 3	10 × 7	4 × 5	10 × 5	7 × 8	10 × 1	3 × 4
5.	12 × 3	11 × 4	3 × 8	12 × 2	9 × 1	12 × 4	8 × 9	10 × 5	3 × 9	3 × 2
6.	12 × 9	7 × 4	12 × 7	11 × 1	4 × 4	8 × 3	10 × 2	1 × 6	2 × 7	5 × 7
7.	9 × 3	10 × 9	12 × 12	5 × 1	8 × 5	11 × 6	3 × 7	2 × 8	12 × 4	6 × 9
8.	1 × 9	12 × 7	9 × 7	7 × 7	2 × 2	1 × 7	12 × 6	10 × 9	12 × 10	7 × 9
9.	4 × 8	5 × 5	12 × 8	8 × 6	6 × 4	5 × 9	2 × 6	6 × 8	9 × 4	12 × 5
10.	12 × 8	12 × 11	9 × 6	8 × 8	6 × 6	4 × 6	6 × 5	7 × 5	9 × 8	3 × 5

Drill 16   *Multiplication Facts: 1's–12's*

	a.	b.	c.	d.	e.	f.	g.	h.	i.	j.
1.	11 × 11	9 × 2	7 × 7	5 × 9	11 × 3	3 × 5	12 × 12	4 × 4	12 × 1	6 × 3
2.	6 × 6	2 × 7	12 × 8	5 × 7	10 × 8	1 × 5	3 × 3	8 × 4	9 × 8	10 × 5
3.	12 × 5	7 × 9	2 × 1	11 × 4	5 × 2	4 × 8	7 × 4	2 × 3	8 × 6	9 × 4
4.	2 × 8	9 × 6	12 × 6	11 × 9	1 × 9	10 × 3	11 × 7	10 × 10	11 × 12	3 × 9
5.	5 × 5	11 × 6	4 × 6	7 × 2	8 × 1	12 × 3	8 × 3	8 × 8	5 × 4	6 × 9
6.	12 × 5	6 × 8	3 × 7	12 × 2	8 × 7	9 × 3	12 × 7	3 × 1	6 × 7	12 × 9
7.	11 × 3	3 × 8	9 × 5	6 × 4	5 × 6	7 × 5	9 × 7	10 × 11	12 × 11	10 × 1
8.	4 × 7	4 × 9	2 × 9	6 × 5	12 × 7	4 × 3	7 × 6	8 × 5	4 × 5	3 × 6
9.	10 × 7	5 × 8	6 × 2	1 × 7	11 × 5	12 × 4	7 × 3	5 × 3	2 × 5	7 × 8
10.	12 × 10	8 × 9	9 × 9	2 × 4	10 × 3	4 × 2	1 × 6	3 × 4	2 × 6	11 × 10

Drill 17   *Multiplication Facts: 1's–12's*

	a.	b.	c.	d.
1.	12 × 12	11 × 2	10 × 11	9 × 3
2.	8 × 10	7 × 4	6 × 9	5 × 5
3.	4 × 8	3 × 6	2 × 7	1 × 1
4.	11 × 11	2 × 3	10 × 4	3 × 8
5.	9 × 7	4 × 4	8 × 5	5 × 7
6.	7 × 8	6 × 3	1 × 9	12 × 5
7.	7 × 5	5 × 9	3 × 4	2 × 5
8.	8 × 7	4 × 6	1 × 6	6 × 6
9.	9 × 9	12 × 7	11 × 6	6 × 8
10.	2 × 9	4 × 10	2 × 8	7 × 7
11.	11 × 8	12 × 9	3 × 7	4 × 7
12.	6 × 5	5 × 6	7 × 6	9 × 6
13.	5 × 8	7 × 9	10 × 8	8 × 8
14.	6 × 4	4 × 5	8 × 6	9 × 5
15.	5 × 4	6 × 7	3 × 5	3 × 9
16.	11 × 9	12 × 6	2 × 6	8 × 9
17.	12 × 11	9 × 8	4 × 9	5 × 2
18.	10 × 6	7 × 12	2 × 12	3 × 10
19.	11 × 12	11 × 4	3 × 3	2 × 4
20.	1 × 7	2 × 10	6 × 10	8 × 4
21.	10 × 9	12 × 3	1 × 8	4 × 3
22.	3 × 12	5 × 10	8 × 12	5 × 12
23.	12 × 10	9 × 4	11 × 3	1 × 5
24.	9 × 10	7 × 10	6 × 12	12 × 8
25.	9 × 9	7 × 8	12 × 12	7 × 6

Drill 18   *Multiplication Facts: 1's–12's*

	a.	b.	c.	d.
1.	1 × 4	2 × 9	3 × 6	4 × 8
2.	5 × 3	6 × 12	7 × 5	8 × 7
3.	9 × 10	10 × 11	11 × 2	12 × 9
4.	2 × 3	4 × 5	6 × 4	8 × 12
5.	10 × 5	12 × 6	1 × 8	3 × 10
6.	5 × 6	7 × 8	9 × 12	11 × 8
7.	12 × 3	10 × 7	8 × 3	6 × 7
8.	4 × 11	2 × 6	11 × 4	9 × 4
9.	7 × 11	5 × 9	3 × 4	1 × 10
10.	2 × 12	3 × 8	4 × 7	5 × 11
11.	6 × 9	7 × 3	8 × 9	9 × 6
12.	10 × 9	11 × 6	12 × 11	1 × 6
13.	3 × 12	5 × 8	7 × 6	9 × 2
14.	11 × 10	1 × 12	2 × 8	4 × 9
15.	6 × 6	8 × 5	12 × 5	3 × 9
16.	4 × 6	6 × 8	7 × 9	8 × 6
17.	7 × 7	7 × 12	3 × 7	4 × 4
18.	7 × 4	6 × 10	3 × 5	12 × 8
19.	9 × 7	2 × 7	5 × 5	5 × 12
20.	10 × 12	8 × 8	6 × 5	2 × 5
21.	4 × 10	9 × 8	12 × 7	4 × 12
22.	8 × 4	4 × 3	5 × 7	6 × 3
23.	7 × 2	11 × 12	9 × 5	9 × 9
24.	10 × 8	12 × 12	12 × 4	11 × 5
25.	5 × 4	3 × 3	1 × 5	12 × 10

Drill 19   *Division Facts: 1's–6's*

	a.	b.	c.	d.	e.	f.
1.	4)36	5)10	5)60	4)48	3)12	5)15
2.	6)24	3)18	3)21	2)12	4)24	4)40
3.	6)36	6)42	5)25	3)24	2)16	4)20
4.	4)32	5)55	2)10	6)12	1)4	6)60
5.	6)72	6)54	2)14	1)6	6)48	4)44
6.	3)9	2)6	3)15	5)20	6)30	6)66
7.	4)12	2)8	1)11	4)28	3)27	3)33
8.	3)36	5)30	5)35	5)40	6)24	5)15

Drill 20   *Division Facts: 3's–7's*

	a.	b.	c.	d.	e.	f.
1.	7)42	3)9	4)12	5)10	6)36	6)42
2.	3)12	3)27	7)28	7)84	3)15	5)30
3.	7)77	6)48	5)60	6)18	4)24	4)32
4.	5)55	4)8	3)6	5)25	7)49	5)50
5.	3)18	4)28	4)36	3)36	4)20	6)72
6.	4)16	6)54	7)70	6)66	3)24	4)44
7.	7)35	5)30	5)20	7)56	3)21	5)15
8.	6)24	6)60	4)40	7)63	6)72	4)48

Drill 21   *Division Facts: 3's–8's*

	a.	b.	c.	d.
1.	$40 \div 5$	$36 \div 3$	$66 \div 6$	$96 \div 8$
2.	$8 \div 4$	$15 \div 5$	$18 \div 3$	$21 \div 7$
3.	$84 \div 7$	$36 \div 4$	$24 \div 6$	$35 \div 5$
4.	$24 \div 3$	$25 \div 5$	$88 \div 8$	$56 \div 7$
5.	$64 \div 8$	$32 \div 4$	$40 \div 8$	$12 \div 3$
6.	$6 \div 3$	$28 \div 4$	$77 \div 7$	$36 \div 6$
7.	$20 \div 4$	$30 \div 5$	$28 \div 4$	$50 \div 5$
8.	$42 \div 6$	$9 \div 3$	$12 \div 4$	$14 \div 7$
9.	$54 \div 6$	$32 \div 8$	$80 \div 8$	$72 \div 8$
10.	$24 \div 8$	$28 \div 7$	$72 \div 6$	$70 \div 7$
11.	$15 \div 3$	$18 \div 6$	$21 \div 3$	$12 \div 6$
12.	$48 \div 6$	$30 \div 6$	$84 \div 7$	$36 \div 3$

Drill 22   *Division Facts: 3's–9's*

	a.	b.	c.	d.
1.	$56 \div 8$	$21 \div 3$	$40 \div 4$	$72 \div 6$
2.	$48 \div 6$	$108 \div 9$	$32 \div 4$	$40 \div 5$
3.	$35 \div 7$	$63 \div 9$	$24 \div 6$	$27 \div 3$
4.	$16 \div 4$	$55 \div 5$	$84 \div 7$	$96 \div 8$
5.	$5 \div 5$	$12 \div 4$	$32 \div 8$	$49 \div 7$
6.	$54 \div 9$	$36 \div 6$	$3 \div 3$	$45 \div 5$
7.	$54 \div 6$	$88 \div 8$	$6 \div 3$	$30 \div 6$
8.	$48 \div 8$	$81 \div 9$	$72 \div 8$	$24 \div 4$
9.	$9 \div 3$	$14 \div 7$	$36 \div 9$	$72 \div 9$
10.	$18 \div 6$	$20 \div 4$	$15 \div 3$	$35 \div 5$
11.	$60 \div 5$	$42 \div 7$	$28 \div 4$	$63 \div 7$
12.	$25 \div 5$	$36 \div 4$	$8 \div 4$	$33 \div 3$

Drill 23   Division Facts: 6's–9's

	a.	b.	c.	d.	e.	f.
1.	7)77	7)21	9)90	6)24	6)36	6)60
2.	8)40	8)80	6)42	7)28	6)72	8)88
3.	7)70	6)48	8)24	8)64	9)81	7)35
4.	6)54	6)30	6)12	9)54	8)48	8)32
5.	7)56	9)108	7)84	6)66	6)6	8)72
6.	9)99	9)27	8)56	7)42	7)49	8)16
7.	8)96	6)18	9)63	9)45	9)72	9)18
8.	7)7	7)14	8)64	9)54	6)42	9)90

Drill 24   Division Facts: 6's–9's

	a.	b.	c.	d.
1.	$42 \div 7$	$90 \div 9$	$30 \div 6$	$84 \div 7$
2.	$56 \div 8$	$72 \div 8$	$12 \div 6$	$45 \div 9$
3.	$28 \div 7$	$60 \div 6$	$63 \div 9$	$14 \div 7$
4.	$8 \div 8$	$81 \div 9$	$54 \div 6$	$35 \div 7$
5.	$64 \div 8$	$49 \div 7$	$42 \div 6$	$108 \div 9$
6.	$9 \div 9$	$36 \div 6$	$56 \div 7$	$88 \div 8$
7.	$70 \div 7$	$27 \div 9$	$63 \div 7$	$48 \div 6$
8.	$21 \div 7$	$24 \div 6$	$72 \div 9$	$36 \div 9$
9.	$18 \div 6$	$7 \div 7$	$80 \div 8$	$72 \div 6$
10.	$96 \div 8$	$6 \div 6$	$48 \div 8$	$77 \div 7$
11.	$66 \div 6$	$54 \div 9$	$16 \div 8$	$40 \div 8$
12.	$99 \div 9$	$18 \div 9$	$32 \div 8$	$24 \div 8$

Drill 25   *Division Facts: 1's–9's*

	a.	b.	c.	d.	e.	f.
1.	9)9	4)8	7)21	4)44	8)48	5)15
2.	2)4	6)18	8)40	3)9	9)72	7)14
3.	6)60	7)63	1)5	7)84	4)12	6)6
4.	8)80	3)24	9)18	3)6	6)36	8)56
5.	2)16	7)77	6)54	7)49	2)6	3)12
6.	6)42	8)32	5)30	1)2	5)45	9)63
7.	7)28	4)16	6)12	5)20	8)88	4)48
8.	1)8	6)48	3)15	9)81	6)72	5)10
9.	9)90	5)5	8)64	2)12	2)2	9)99
10.	3)30	7)35	2)18	7)7	5)25	6)30
11.	1)7	9)27	6)24	5)50	3)27	4)16
12.	7)49	1)10	3)18	1)12	9)36	3)3
13.	5)25	5)55	9)108	4)28	2)14	8)72
14.	8)64	6)36	2)22	2)8	8)24	7)42
15.	2)24	5)40	4)20	9)54	3)33	4)32
16.	9)45	8)96	4)36	7)56	2)10	4)24
17.	5)60	3)21	8)16	3)36	5)35	9)81

Drill 26   *Division Facts: 1's–9's*

	a.	b.	c.	d.
1.	24 ÷ 3	48 ÷ 6	56 ÷ 8	108 ÷ 9
2.	12 ÷ 6	6 ÷ 2	8 ÷ 1	42 ÷ 6
3.	30 ÷ 6	16 ÷ 4	18 ÷ 3	84 ÷ 7
4.	21 ÷ 3	63 ÷ 9	36 ÷ 6	25 ÷ 5
5.	8 ÷ 2	44 ÷ 4	35 ÷ 5	60 ÷ 6
6.	48 ÷ 8	9 ÷ 3	55 ÷ 5	72 ÷ 6
7.	90 ÷ 9	24 ÷ 6	45 ÷ 5	49 ÷ 7
8.	10 ÷ 5	6 ÷ 3	30 ÷ 5	28 ÷ 7
9.	27 ÷ 9	20 ÷ 5	35 ÷ 7	5 ÷ 1
10.	27 ÷ 3	50 ÷ 5	18 ÷ 6	42 ÷ 7
11.	80 ÷ 8	96 ÷ 8	99 ÷ 9	56 ÷ 7
12.	32 ÷ 8	54 ÷ 9	40 ÷ 8	36 ÷ 9
13.	64 ÷ 8	24 ÷ 8	14 ÷ 7	15 ÷ 5
14.	12 ÷ 3	14 ÷ 2	9 ÷ 1	60 ÷ 5
15.	66 ÷ 6	21 ÷ 7	77 ÷ 7	81 ÷ 9
16.	16 ÷ 8	11 ÷ 1	20 ÷ 2	48 ÷ 4
17.	40 ÷ 5	12 ÷ 2	18 ÷ 2	36 ÷ 3
18.	20 ÷ 4	72 ÷ 8	18 ÷ 9	12 ÷ 4
19.	15 ÷ 3	24 ÷ 2	6 ÷ 1	10 ÷ 2
20.	32 ÷ 4	70 ÷ 7	88 ÷ 8	72 ÷ 9
21.	8 ÷ 4	3 ÷ 3	16 ÷ 2	22 ÷ 2
22.	4 ÷ 1	30 ÷ 3	40 ÷ 4	24 ÷ 4
23.	63 ÷ 7	45 ÷ 9	12 ÷ 1	33 ÷ 3
24.	4 ÷ 2	35 ÷ 7	81 ÷ 9	7 ÷ 1
25.	36 ÷ 4	28 ÷ 4	56 ÷ 7	108 ÷ 9

Drill 27   *Division Facts: 9's–12's*

	a.	b.	c.	d.	e.	f.
1.	10)60	11)121	12)48	9)81	9)36	11)99
2.	12)120	10)110	11)77	9)63	10)120	12)132
3.	11)66	10)90	9)54	11)88	12)72	10)40
4.	12)144	10)100	9)45	12)84	11)55	10)30
5.	12)60	12)108	9)72	11)110	10)80	9)99
6.	12)96	10)70	11)33	9)27	10)50	12)36
7.	9)108	9)18	10)10	12)24	11)44	9)90
8.	11)11	11)132	10)20	11)22	12)12	9)9

Drill 28   *Division Facts: 10's–12's*

	a.	b.	c.	d.	e.	f.
1.	12)120	11)88	10)50	12)60	11)33	10)10
2.	11)132	11)77	10)90	12)12	11)66	12)84
3.	11)110	10)60	11)55	10)70	12)48	11)11
4.	12)132	11)44	10)100	11)99	12)144	10)80
5.	12)108	10)110	11)22	12)96	10)120	12)24
6.	11)121	10)20	11)132	12)72	10)40	12)36
7.	12)144	10)30	12)48	10)80	12)108	11)99
8.	10)120	11)88	10)100	12)60	12)96	11)77

Drill 29   *Division Facts: 1's–12's*

	a.	b.	c.	d.	e.	f.
1.	11)88	9)45	2)18	10)10	6)36	1)1
2.	8)16	7)49	8)72	1)9	4)48	12)108
3.	6)48	5)40	9)9	2)24	3)33	4)28
4.	10)40	10)60	7)21	8)40	11)132	9)54
5.	4)32	1)6	8)56	5)20	2)14	3)36
6.	10)80	12)60	6)6	2)20	11)66	10)30
7.	9)27	11)22	10)50	1)10	6)54	8)32
8.	12)144	5)55	6)48	9)72	8)64	6)60
9.	3)21	10)100	5)35	2)16	4)44	11)99
10.	6)30	7)14	9)63	8)8	12)132	12)24
11.	6)12	5)25	2)22	3)27	4)16	4)36
12.	11)44	7)42	7)70	5)45	8)24	9)36
13.	12)120	3)30	12)48	7)35	6)18	7)84
14.	1)12	4)40	4)20	5)15	6)72	7)56
15.	9)81	9)108	11)99	12)36	12)12	5)10
16.	6)42	7)28	10)70	1)5	3)24	4)4
17.	12)96	11)33	3)3	6)66	6)24	5)5

Drill 30   *Division Facts: 1's–12's*

	a.	b.	c.	d.	e.	f.
1.	1)7	9)90	2)12	5)55	10)110	12)72
2.	11)11	11)121	5)50	10)20	1)8	3)15
3.	3)36	8)88	5)60	7)63	9)18	10)90
4.	12)84	11)110	5)30	1)11	2)10	3)18
5.	10)120	8)96	7)77	12)144	4)12	2)8
6.	9)27	6)42	6)24	8)56	10)30	12)48
7.	2)4	6)54	8)16	10)60	5)40	6)36
8.	7)49	9)36	8)40	2)20	11)55	12)60
9.	1)9	3)12	10)80	7)42	8)64	8)32
10.	5)45	7)35	7)84	12)36	7)7	3)27
11.	2)22	2)24	3)30	12)132	7)56	5)25
12.	9)45	2)16	3)9	4)8	11)44	7)70
13.	9)99	12)24	6)30	5)35	5)20	7)28
14.	7)21	8)48	9)63	11)66	11)132	9)108
15.	7)14	6)60	1)10	2)6	4)24	4)48
16.	1)12	6)18	9)81	8)72	9)54	10)100
17.	11)88	6)48	5)15	2)18	4)20	4)40

Drill 31   *Division Facts: 1's–12's*

	a.	b.	c.	d.
1.	$120 \div 12$	$24 \div 3$	$88 \div 11$	$48 \div 6$
2.	$50 \div 10$	$56 \div 8$	$60 \div 12$	$108 \div 9$
3.	$12 \div 6$	$33 \div 11$	$10 \div 10$	$6 \div 2$
4.	$42 \div 6$	$132 \div 11$	$30 \div 6$	$16 \div 4$
5.	$77 \div 11$	$21 \div 3$	$63 \div 9$	$36 \div 6$
6.	$60 \div 10$	$8 \div 2$	$44 \div 4$	$48 \div 12$
7.	$90 \div 9$	$24 \div 6$	$72 \div 12$	$14 \div 7$
8.	$48 \div 12$	$40 \div 8$	$20 \div 2$	$36 \div 12$
9.	$9 \div 1$	$99 \div 11$	$48 \div 4$	$10 \div 2$
10.	$30 \div 10$	$36 \div 12$	$81 \div 9$	$18 \div 2$
11.	$96 \div 12$	$24 \div 4$	$33 \div 3$	$16 \div 2$
12.	$72 \div 8$	$72 \div 12$	$144 \div 12$	$72 \div 9$
13.	$80 \div 10$	$100 \div 10$	$56 \div 7$	$24 \div 8$
14.	$63 \div 7$	$45 \div 9$	$12 \div 1$	$33 \div 3$
15.	$15 \div 5$	$88 \div 8$	$132 \div 11$	$32 \div 4$
16.	$12 \div 3$	$96 \div 12$	$14 \div 2$	$50 \div 5$
17.	$64 \div 8$	$27 \div 9$	$66 \div 6$	$40 \div 5$
18.	$63 \div 7$	$4 \div 1$	$0 \div 4$	$12 \div 1$
19.	$16 \div 2$	$96 \div 8$	$54 \div 9$	$55 \div 5$
20.	$10 \div 5$	$90 \div 9$	$8 \div 4$	$72 \div 8$
21.	$6 \div 1$	$3 \div 3$	$30 \div 3$	$45 \div 9$
22.	$80 \div 10$	$48 \div 12$	$121 \div 11$	$132 \div 12$
23.	$55 \div 11$	$24 \div 12$	$28 \div 7$	$12 \div 2$
24.	$40 \div 4$	$24 \div 4$	$63 \div 7$	$28 \div 4$
25.	$108 \div 9$	$36 \div 4$	$35 \div 7$	$4 \div 2$

Drill 32   *Division Facts: 1's–12's*

	a.	b.	c.	d.
1.	$8 \div 2$	$66 \div 6$	$16 \div 2$	$24 \div 4$
2.	$77 \div 11$	$20 \div 10$	$18 \div 9$	$22 \div 2$
3.	$12 \div 4$	$15 \div 3$	$96 \div 12$	$12 \div 12$
4.	$60 \div 5$	$84 \div 12$	$24 \div 8$	$20 \div 5$
5.	$18 \div 6$	$110 \div 11$	$21 \div 7$	$9 \div 1$
6.	$81 \div 9$	$6 \div 1$	$80 \div 10$	$45 \div 5$
7.	$42 \div 7$	$100 \div 10$	$12 \div 12$	$80 \div 8$
8.	$35 \div 7$	$108 \div 12$	$12 \div 2$	$36 \div 3$
9.	$24 \div 12$	$10 \div 10$	$132 \div 12$	$10 \div 2$
10.	$72 \div 9$	$21 \div 7$	$144 \div 12$	$32 \div 8$
11.	$10 \div 5$	$50 \div 5$	$20 \div 5$	$84 \div 12$
12.	$20 \div 4$	$4 \div 1$	$63 \div 7$	$45 \div 9$
13.	$6 \div 1$	$70 \div 7$	$16 \div 8$	$64 \div 8$
14.	$54 \div 9$	$18 \div 9$	$48 \div 4$	$9 \div 1$
15.	$66 \div 6$	$32 \div 8$	$27 \div 9$	$30 \div 6$
16.	$20 \div 10$	$108 \div 12$	$72 \div 12$	$14 \div 7$
17.	$36 \div 9$	$18 \div 2$	$11 \div 1$	$6 \div 3$
18.	$40 \div 10$	$66 \div 11$	$48 \div 8$	$132 \div 12$
19.	$12 \div 2$	$30 \div 3$	$35 \div 7$	$56 \div 8$
20.	$32 \div 4$	$48 \div 12$	$12 \div 3$	$96 \div 8$
21.	$15 \div 5$	$6 \div 1$	$24 \div 2$	$144 \div 12$
22.	$121 \div 11$	$50 \div 5$	$36 \div 6$	$99 \div 11$
23.	$120 \div 10$	$100 \div 10$	$42 \div 6$	$16 \div 4$
24.	$132 \div 11$	$18 \div 3$	$6 \div 6$	$24 \div 3$
25.	$72 \div 8$	$64 \div 8$	$5 \div 1$	$28 \div 7$

Set II: Mixed Computation Drills

Drill 33   *Mixed Computation*

	a.	b.
1.	$2 + 2 \times 8 \div 4 - 1$	$144 \div 12 \times 3 \div 4 + 10$
2.	$3 \times 8 - 4 \div 5 \times 9$	$7 \times 7 + 5 \div 9 \times 4$
3.	$2 \times 8 + 4 - 5 \div 3$	$10 + 4 - 6 \div 2 \times 8$
4.	$20 \div 2 \times 5 - 10 \div 5$	$6 \times 7 + 3 \div 9 \times 3$
5.	$15 - 7 \times 8 - 1 \div 7$	$21 \div 3 \times 2 + 8 - 22$

Drill 34   *Mixed Computation*

	a.	b.
1.	$8 \times 6 + 2 \div 5 - 6$	$3 \times 2 - 4 + 8 \div 5$
2.	$6 + 5 \times 11 + 11 \div 12$	$9 \times 9 + 3 \div 7 - 8$
3.	$8 \times 3 - 2 \div 2 \times 3$	$8 \times 5 \div 10 \times 8 + 3$
4.	$16 \div 4 \times 9 \div 12 \times 9$	$17 - 8 \times 7 - 3 \div 5$
5.	$15 \div 3 \times 9 + 4 \div 7$	$4 \times 7 + 7 \div 5 + 6$
6.	$9 + 4 - 6 \times 3 - 4$	$9 \times 6 + 2 \div 8 \times 12$

Drill 35   *Mixed Computation*

	a.	b.
1.	$8 \times 7 + 4 \div 12 + 9$	$18 \div 6 \times 12 \div 4 + 7$
2.	$36 \div 6 + 4 \times 5 - 5$	$6 \times 12 \div 8 + 6 - 4$
3.	$12 - 8 \times 3 \times 11 - 2$	$40 \div 8 + 7 - 6 \times 7$
4.	$4 \times 12 \div 6 \times 3 \div 6$	$67 - 1 \div 11 + 2 \times 8$
5.	$20 \div 4 \times 3 - 7 + 5$	$16 - 8 \div 2 + 6 \times 10$
6.	$10 + 8 \div 3 \times 5 - 3$	$5 + 9 \div 2 \times 7 - 6$

Drill 36   Mixed Computation

	a.	b.
1.	$17 + 8 \div 5 + 7 \times 7 - 3$	$7 + 7 - 2 \times 6 \div 8 - 9$
2.	$2 \times 11 + 8 \div 3 - 5 + 6$	$21 \div 7 \times 9 - 5 \div 2 - 7$
3.	$81 \div 9 + 5 - 8 \times 8 \div 4$	$32 \div 8 \times 9 + 3 - 6 \div 11$
4.	$42 \div 7 - 6 + 7 \times 8 - 5$	$18 \div 3 + 7 - 8 \times 9 - 5$
5.	$12 \times 5 \div 6 - 4 \times 6 \div 12$	$9 \times 4 + 8 \div 11 + 2 \div 6$

Drill 37   Mixed Computation

	a.	b.
1.	$6 + 6 - 4 \times 3 \div 4 - 6$	$56 \div 7 \times 2 + 6 - 2 \div 4$
2.	$3 \times 6 - 5 - 3 \div 2 + 7$	$25 + 3 \div 4 \times 3 - 4 + 2$
3.	$50 \div 5 \times 2 + 4 - 3 \div 7$	$8 \times 12 - 6 \div 10 \times 6 + 4$
4.	$5 + 3 \times 8 - 4 \div 5 \times 11$	$108 \div 9 \times 4 \div 6 \times 9 \div 12$
5.	$9 \times 9 + 3 \div 12 \times 2 - 6$	$12 + 4 \div 2 \times 7 - 1 \div 5$

Drill 38   Mixed Computation

	a.	b.
1.	$10 \times 12 + 1 \div 11 + 7 \div 3$	$9 \div 3 \times 7 - 1 \div 4 + 10$
2.	$15 \div 3 \times 6 - 2 \div 4 + 6$	$12 + 6 \div 2 \times 5 - 3 \div 7$
3.	$35 \div 5 \times 3 - 5 \div 4 \times 11$	$17 - 8 + 3 \times 5 \div 10 \div 3$
4.	$12 \times 2 \div 3 \times 2 - 9 \times 5$	$70 \div 7 \times 3 \div 6 + 8 + 7$
5.	$25 + 3 \div 7 + 8 \times 9 + 2$	$132 \div 11 - 5 \times 3 - 4 + 6$

Drill 39   Mixed Computation

	a.	b.
1.	$9 \times 4 + 4 \div 5 \times 7 + 6$	$9 \times 3 - 6 \div 7 \times 6 - 9$
2.	$10 \div 2 \times 5 + 3 \div 7 - 4$	$12 \times 8 - 6 \div 9 - 4 \times 9$
3.	$8 \times 4 + 3 \div 5 - 7 \times 6$	$32 \div 4 + 7 + 6 \div 3 \times 9$
4.	$22 \div 2 \times 6 - 2 \div 8 + 10$	$70 + 2 \div 9 \times 7 - 7 \div 7$
5.	$21 \div 3 \times 2 - 8 + 6 \times 9$	$10 \times 7 - 7 \div 7 + 8 - 10$
6.	$4 \times 3 \div 6 + 9 \times 10 + 10$	$9 \times 10 + 6 \div 12 \times 4 - 6$

Drill 40   *Mixed Computation*

	a.	b.
1.	$132 \div 12 \times 5 - 1 \div 9 + 8$	$6 \times 4 - 4 \div 10 + 5 - 4$
2.	$3 \times 7 + 7 \div 4 + 4 \times 11$	$15 - 6 \times 9 + 7 \div 11 \times 12$
3.	$7 \times 4 + 9 - 2 \div 5 + 3$	$42 \div 6 \times 7 + 5 \div 6 + 7$
4.	$6 \div 3 \times 12 - 6 \div 6 \times 11$	$3 \times 12 - 4 \div 8 + 8 \times 10$
5.	$20 \div 4 \times 3 + 7 \div 2 - 6$	$4 \times 4 \div 2 \times 4 + 4 \div 6$
6.	$13 - 8 \times 9 - 1 \div 4 + 11$	$11 \times 4 - 40 + 5 \div 3 + 8$

Drill 41   *Mixed Computation*

	a.	b.
1.	$9 + 4 - 7 \times 4 \div 8 + 9 \div 2$	$90 + 9 \div 11 \times 3 - 2 \div 5 + 7$
2.	$33 \div 3 \times 4 - 2 \div 7 \times 6 + 7$	$7 \times 12 + 4 \div 8 - 5 + 9 \div 5$
3.	$6 \times 8 + 6 \div 6 \times 8 \div 6 \times 8$	$11 \times 11 - 1 \div 10 + 4 \div 8 \times 10$
4.	$21 \div 3 \times 4 - 4 \div 6 + 8 \times 12$	$63 \div 7 - 5 \times 8 + 4 \div 6 + 5$
5.	$5 + 8 - 2 \times 4 - 4 \div 5 + 10$	$18 \div 6 \times 3 - 2 + 5 \times 9 - 8$

Drill 42   *Mixed Computation*

	a.	b.
1.	$9 \times 5 + 4 \div 7 - 3 + 7 \times 4$	$8 \times 7 - 2 \div 6 \times 7 + 1 \div 8$
2.	$45 \div 5 \div 3 \times 7 + 5 - 10 \div 2$	$10 \div 2 + 9 \div 7 \times 12 - 6 \div 6$
3.	$7 \times 9 - 3 \div 5 + 8 \div 4 \times 11$	$7 \times 12 + 6 \div 9 - 4 \times 9 + 2$
4.	$2 \times 9 + 4 - 7 \div 3 + 6 \times 11$	$8 + 3 + 4 - 6 \times 4 \div 12 + 9$
5.	$3 \times 2 + 8 \div 7 - 2 \times 9 + 6$	$10 \times 8 + 1 \div 9 \times 3 - 6 \div 3$

Set III: Addition Drills

Drill 43   *Column Addition*

	a.	b.	c.	d.	e.	f.	g.
1.	4 6 9 + 8	5 8 9 + 7	8 9 2 + 3	7 3 2 + 6	9 8 4 + 5	6 7 5 + 3	7 8 5 + 4
2.	2 6 6 8 + 1	8 2 5 7 + 9	8 5 8 0 + 3	4 7 9 7 + 6	6 9 2 5 + 8	8 1 8 4 + 7	4 9 9 5 + 7

Drill 44   *Column Addition*

	a.	b.	c.	d.	e.	f.	g.
1.	5 3 1 9 + 7	6 8 5 4 + 7	7 3 2 6 + 9	4 8 8 3 + 5	5 5 6 7 + 9	8 4 8 9 + 0	7 5 6 2 + 6
2.	3 5 7 9 2 + 4	6 8 9 5 7 + 4	5 8 2 8 5 + 4	7 9 6 6 4 + 2	2 6 7 7 9 + 3	7 1 3 8 9 + 6	9 6 8 1 5 + 4

Drill 45   *Horizontal Addition*

	a.	b.	c.	d.
1.	24 + 17	42 + 26	27 + 18	23 + 37
2.	14 + 16	39 + 20	39 + 37	40 + 55
3.	30 + 47	44 + 39	35 + 47	24 + 18
4.	22 + 64	79 + 19	33 + 48	32 + 47
5.	18 + 67	37 + 47	21 + 49	22 + 33
6.	42 + 39	11 + 84	32 + 58	63 + 19

Drill 46   *Horizontal Addition*

	a.	b.	c.	d.
1.	31 + 39	27 + 46	18 + 55	20 + 69
2.	54 + 52	66 + 28	73 + 19	34 + 47
3.	18 + 59	27 + 47	49 + 34	54 + 16
4.	24 + 94	38 + 84	35 + 46	28 + 38
5.	22 + 19	35 + 27	19 + 66	57 + 29
6.	19 + 19	25 + 29	48 + 37	43 + 27

Drill 47   *Addition*

	a.	b.	c.	d.	e.	f.
1.	87 23 + 49	53 20 + 56	94 25 + 38	64 15 + 86	69 26 + 35	36 28 + 97
2.	15 24 87 + 48	57 61 74 + 89	97 13 29 + 34	42 58 67 + 72	84 96 15 + 25	37 43 54 + 62
3.	$0.75 0.82 0.96 + 0.10	$0.25 0.32 0.45 + 0.58	$0.67 0.77 0.85 + 0.90	$0.96 0.28 0.36 + 0.43	$0.54 0.63 0.77 + 0.89	$0.95 0.69 0.22 + 0.35

Drill 48   Addition

	a.	b.	c.	d.	e.
1.	121 342 + 575	792 901 + 478	246 492 + 675	888 326 + 594	707 944 + 155
2.	1,056 2,400 + 3,948	4,675 5,794 + 6,244	7,944 8,429 + 9,054	2,977 4,835 + 6,221	8,829 1,025 + 3,549
3.	$55.25 74.32 + 91.25	$25.00 47.86 + 68.92	$84.56 95.72 + 15.23	$34.98 57.82 + 76.49	$26.33 43.17 + 19.50

Drill 49   Addition

	a.	b.	c.	d.	e.
1.	7,824 1,029 + 2,436	4,817 6,420 + 8,974	3,547 5,982 + 7,416	1,491 2,349 + 4,115	6,782 8,920 + 9,464
2.	19,753 26,847 + 96,312	34,532 57,641 + 74,286	92,027 26,308 + 45,796	67,345 89,362 + 35,791	72,190 12,054 + 94,798
3.	$789.10 237.54 + 489.36	$521.05 768.94 + 923.49	$140.72 394.59 + 223.46	$589.29 743.50 + 914.25	$294.35 478.98 + 613.42

Drill 50   Addition

	a.	b.	c.	d.	e.
1.	246 455 689 + 895	135 357 579 + 792	924 267 472 + 653	875 922 143 + 376	576 721 957 + 200
2.	473 691 825 + 141	375 563 721 + 928	222 475 609 + 856	153 347 562 + 799	920 215 422 + 689

Drill 51   Addition

	a.	b.	c.	d.	e.
1.	1,544 3,269 5,748 + 7,292	9,768 2,604 4,503 + 9,714	6,534 7,586 1,098 + 3,720	5,324 7,465 9,687 + 2,109	4,132 3,965 8,567 + 1,987
2.	$54.23 72.91 49.35 + 14.52	$25.57 43.25 67.98 + 84.72	$45.97 59.84 75.42 + 13.25	$24.64 49.89 68.75 + 82.94	$37.84 58.92 75.30 + 19.20

Drill 52   Addition

	a.	b.	c.	d.	e.
1.	10,432 95,786 29,832 + 47,925	67,891 82,346 14,572 + 39,012	59,413 78,625 92,561 + 23,640	49,052 67,941 80,405 + 58,435	37,908 55,672 71,025 + 94,862
2.	29,046 47,921 68,324 + 81,689	17,643 35,420 58,614 79,028	94,531 28,642 49,751 + 60,586	84,623 17,435 34,927 + 58,345	77,921 90,572 29,347 + 41,922

Set IV: Subtraction Drills

Drill 53   *Horizontal Subtraction*

	a.	b.	c.	d.
1.	46 – 5	32 – 9	75 – 4	81 – 8
2.	22 – 3	30 – 7	15 – 2	24 – 7
3.	59 – 8	42 – 4	61 – 7	50 – 6
4.	72 – 10	66 – 12	25 – 11	52 – 22
5.	65 – 47	84 – 26	33 – 15	42 – 18
6.	92 – 35	76 – 28	50 – 14	65 – 39

Drill 54   *Horizontal Subtraction*

	a.	b.	c.	d.
1.	51 – 14	43 – 17	32 – 15	89 – 78
2.	62 – 14	75 – 25	91 – 18	83 – 35
3.	70 – 61	34 – 15	67 – 29	62 – 51
4.	74 – 69	61 – 45	55 – 38	41 – 19
5.	56 – 27	45 – 38	78 – 59	99 – 84
6.	37 – 16	21 – 13	54 – 28	73 – 49

Drill 55   *Three-Digit Subtraction*

	a.	b.	c.	d.	e.	f.
1.	124 – 29	792 – 378	924 – 57	358 – 179	524 – 205	746 – 183
2.	407 – 228	625 – 199	800 – 325	421 – 76	370 – 222	501 – 68
3.	$7.05 – .72	$9.00 – 5.21	$5.13 – 1.57	$4.76 – .99	$8.01 – 4.39	$6.90 – 5.59

Drill 56   *Four-Digit Subtraction*

	a.	b.	c.	d.	e.
1.	7,592 - 4,896	4,000 - 1,999	5,034 - 3,129	1,574 - 575	9,040 - 6,583
2.	5,742 - 2,595	7,020 - 6,964	9,450 - 875	6,341 - 3,952	5,094 - 3,186
3.	$70.00 - 8.05	$56.14 - 34.75	$68.95 - 29.29	$42.30 - .72	$90.30 - 70.98

Drill 57   *Four-Digit Subtraction*

	a.	b.	c.	d.	e.
1.	7,503 - 986	9,045 - 4,787	5,000 - 4,930	8,040 - 3,509	5,921 - 3,923
2.	8,280 - 2,685	7,543 - 1,498	6,532 - 694	3,049 - 2,862	5,102 - 79
3.	5,742 - 1,655	4,009 - 2,986	7,243 - 3,273	2,400 - 1,702	1,053 - 625

Drill 58   *Four-Digit Subtraction*

	a.	b.	c.	d.	e.
1.	4,982 - 2,366	3,207 - 589	2,452 - 1,459	9,784 - 3,825	8,000 - 2,406
2.	7,010 - 5,835	6,241 - 3,795	5,802 - 4,967	7,043 - 2,048	9,563 - 6,884
3.	$72.00 - 37.98	$98.75 - 27.88	$15.74 - 6.82	$83.12 - 57.54	$40.50 - 26.42

Drill 59   *Five-Digit Subtraction*

	a.	b.	c.	d.	e.
1.	80,000 − 37,489	72,145 − 49,856	64,052 − 59,875	97,100 − 5,781	84,000 − 67,570
2.	59,600 − 892	75,230 − 43,865	60,403 − 27,492	52,006 − 29,087	41,090 − 26,809

Drill 60   *Five-Digit Subtraction*

	a.	b.	c.	d.	e.
1.	52,007 − 24,898	42,062 − 7,984	70,504 − 59,625	64,352 − 795	73,010 − 59,845
2.	$329.48 − 158.64	$950.00 − 392.84	$604.00 − 275.97	$843.10 − 750.80	$800.00 − 295.13

Drill 61   *Five-Digit Subtraction*

	a.	b.	c.	d.	e.
1.	70,000 − 28,324	52,009 − 29,846	70,204 − 67,844	51,840 − 8,857	60,020 − 18,456
2.	85,502 − 47,960	62,045 − 48,937	50,940 − 14,852	56,073 − 998	78,031 − 42,872

Drill 62   *Five-Digit Subtraction*

	a.	b.	c.	d.	e.
1.	29,084 − 9,868	50,000 − 37,905	57,820 − 18,957	70,024 − 36,187	50,402 − 24,982
2.	$221.90 − 133.45	$538.02 − 298.94	$432.01 − 57.79	$720.49 − 489.64	$840.00 − 553.04

Set V: Multiplication Drills

Drill 63   ***One-Digit Multipliers***

	a.	b.	c.	d.	e.	f.
1.	683 × 6	519 × 3	479 × 8	324 × 9	291 × 7	478 × 4
2.	724 × 3	895 × 9	948 × 6	425 × 8	756 × 7	548 × 5
3.	329 × 4	843 × 7	725 × 6	495 × 2	672 × 5	318 × 8

Drill 64   ***One-Digit Multipliers***

	a.	b.	c.	d.	e.
1.	3,419 × 8	6,370 × 7	2,509 × 9	5,429 × 6	4,892 × 7
2.	6,098 × 4	8,475 × 5	2,635 × 3	7,802 × 8	4,879 × 3

Drill 65   ***One-Digit Multipliers***

	a.	b.	c.	d.	e.
1.	36,087 × 7	72,984 × 9	84,603 × 3	35,724 × 5	28,607 × 4
2.	48,009 × 2	68,090 × 6	36,005 × 9	83,526 × 8	75,934 × 4

Drill 66   ***Two-Digit Multipliers***

	a.	b.	c.	d.	e.	f.
1.	53 × 38	24 × 94	39 × 71	85 × 40	63 × 82	50 × 79
2.	46 × 19	92 × 52	67 × 64	98 × 36	87 × 57	34 × 68

Drill 67   ***Two-Digit Multipliers***

	a.	b.	c.	d.	e.	f.
1.	37 × 58	85 × 24	92 × 65	78 × 94	95 × 89	67 × 38
2.	$0.58 × 65	$0.97 × 46	$0.95 × 32	$0.80 × 87	$0.36 × 40	$0.29 × 98

Drill 68   ***Two-Digit Multipliers***

	a.	b.	c.	d.	e.	f.
1.	872 × 36	698 × 57	429 × 75	804 × 94	198 × 26	345 × 49
2.	527 × 19	790 × 34	956 × 58	864 × 72	798 × 60	614 × 96

Drill 69   ***Two-Digit Multipliers***

	a.	b.	c.	d.	e.	f.
1.	759 × 84	956 × 60	145 × 49	395 × 72	574 × 67	708 × 98
2.	$5.47 × 91	$2.29 × 39	$3.04 × 58	$7.85 × 43	$4.63 × 94	$6.30 × 62

Drill 70   *Two-Digit Multipliers*

	a.	b.	c.	d.	e.
1.	6,098 × 53	4,253 × 78	2,675 × 49	9,864 × 19	7,405 × 78
2.	3,457 × 29	5,894 × 45	7,860 × 57	2,948 × 98	6,419 × 50

Drill 71   *Two-Digit Multipliers*

	a.	b.	c.	d.	e.
1.	7,045 × 29	9,256 × 38	5,409 × 47	7,908 × 81	2,387 × 59
2.	$48.50 × 67	$68.45 × 83	$80.09 × 79	$94.78 × 50	$14.56 × 78

Drill 72   *Three-Digit Multipliers*

	a.	b.	c.	d.	e.
1.	741 ×825	243 ×549	722 ×345	482 ×231	578 ×324
2.	429 ×234	528 ×412	679 ×124	756 ×643	927 ×342

Drill 73   *Three-Digit Multipliers*

	a.	b.	c.	d.	e.
1.	865 ×472	928 ×673	746 ×475	672 ×894	429 ×376
2.	$5.78 ×743	$9.28 ×479	$2.49 ×786	$4.75 ×394	$9.56 ×892

Drill 74 — Three-Digit Multipliers

	a.	b.	c.	d.	e.
1.	408 × 275	702 × 564	609 × 324	909 × 876	506 × 496
2.	420 × 978	560 × 492	780 × 329	840 × 362	350 × 472

Drill 75 — Three-Digit Multipliers

	a.	b.	c.	d.	e.
1.	346 × 705	429 × 680	572 × 908	756 × 340	819 × 405
2.	654 × 980	721 × 409	325 × 760	579 × 104	896 × 390

Drill 76 — Three-Digit Multipliers

	a.	b.	c.	d.	e.
1.	159 × 308	345 × 917	824 × 780	697 × 904	829 × 426
2.	$7.12 × 980	$4.25 × 609	$5.74 × 750	$9.56 × 425	$4.35 × 918

Drill 77 — Three-Digit Multipliers

	a.	b.	c.	d.	e.
1.	926 × 407	472 × 680	958 × 362	475 × 921	683 × 499
2.	789 × 264	695 × 148	753 × 705	845 × 369	973 × 426

Set VI: Division Drills

Drill 78   *One-Digit Divisors*

	a.	b.	c.	d.	e.
1.	5)340	4)296	6)994	8)744	6)444
2.	3)855	9)858	7)994	8)992	7)488
3.	6)534	4)949	5)985	7)609	9)432

Drill 79   *One-Digit Divisors*

	a.	b.	c.	d.
1.	6)2,376	3)9,825	8)4,960	6)8,448
2.	9)7,209	7)5,495	2)9,612	9)4,284
3.	4)9,948	8)4,784	5)4,525	7)9,142

Drill 80   *One-Digit Divisors*

	a.	b.	c.	d.
1.	5)8,745	8)5,984	5)4,303	9)5,280
2.	9)9,846	6)4,241	4)9,586	7)3,401
3.	7)$67.34	8)$48.24	6)$95.64	3)$87.09

Drill 81   *Two-Digit Divisors*

	a.	b.	c.	d.	e.
1.	40)84	30)90	20)84	20)69	30)62
2.	30)96	20)88	40)86	20)96	10)39

Drill 82   Two-Digit Divisors

	a.	b.	c.	d.	e.
1.	24)79	22)96	41)90	13)29	24)79
2.	32)81	11)58	34)76	31)81	42)93

Drill 83   Two-Digit Divisors

	a.	b.	c.	d.
1.	35)875	52)936	64)448	93)558
2.	42)924	75)600	94)658	73)803
3.	84)756	45)630	65)845	54)378

Drill 84   Two-Digit Divisors

	a.	b.	c.	d.
1.	49)451	18)801	77)332	57)448
2.	27)905	89)562	48)932	37)866
3.	78)655	69)407	39)940	59)391

Drill 85   Two-Digit Divisors

	a.	b.	c.	d.
1.	58)1,450	29)2,262	78)8,268	59)5,310
2.	47)9,541	77)5,313	68)5,712	37)7,585
3.	67)1,206	19)8,170	89)4,183	38)7,942

Drill 86   Two-Digit Divisors

	a.	b.	c.	d.
1.	94)2,869	62)6,703	27)8,343	83)4,814
2.	67)3,129	48)9,648	36)9,825	59)2,968
3.	85)$67.15	31)$94.55	78)$84.24	19)$77.14

Drill 87   Two-Digit Divisors

	a.	b.	c.	d.
1.	75)27,023	89)40,851	33)22,453	17)14,637
2.	48)25,491	56)50,587	69)51,267	25)18,750
3.	88)75,856	59)16,419	36)22,968	82)17,056

Drill 88   Two-Digit Divisors

	a.	b.	c.	d.
1.	83)59,220	25)19,850	43)13,287	88)82,950
2.	96)57,893	57)25,650	36)19,836	65)41,615
3.	78)$316.68	54)$283.50	47)$404.67	38)$139.84

Set VII: Fraction Drills

Drill 89   *Reducing Fractions*

Reduce these fractions to lowest terms.

	a.	b.	c.	d.	e.	f.
1.	$\frac{5}{15}$	$\frac{4}{16}$	$\frac{12}{24}$	$\frac{15}{20}$	$\frac{6}{18}$	$\frac{16}{36}$
2.	$\frac{20}{25}$	$\frac{12}{18}$	$\frac{8}{12}$	$\frac{35}{40}$	$\frac{9}{24}$	$\frac{10}{25}$
3.	$\frac{10}{12}$	$\frac{18}{21}$	$\frac{12}{16}$	$\frac{12}{14}$	$\frac{16}{24}$	$\frac{3}{30}$
4.	$\frac{20}{36}$	$\frac{9}{12}$	$\frac{5}{20}$	$\frac{4}{10}$	$\frac{10}{15}$	$\frac{8}{32}$

Drill 90   *Improper Fractions*

Change these improper fractions to whole or mixed numbers.

	a.	b.	c.	d.	e.	f.
1.	$\frac{41}{5}$	$\frac{18}{12}$	$\frac{60}{10}$	$\frac{16}{10}$	$\frac{20}{8}$	$\frac{28}{7}$
2.	$\frac{15}{3}$	$\frac{16}{6}$	$\frac{30}{4}$	$\frac{63}{9}$	$\frac{15}{6}$	$\frac{42}{5}$
3.	$\frac{20}{16}$	$\frac{15}{8}$	$\frac{12}{8}$	$\frac{50}{12}$	$\frac{24}{3}$	$\frac{25}{4}$
4.	$\frac{39}{9}$	$\frac{34}{6}$	$\frac{20}{3}$	$\frac{18}{8}$	$\frac{16}{14}$	$\frac{21}{16}$

Drill 91   *Improper Fractions*

Change these mixed numbers to improper fractions.

	a.	b.	c.	d.	e.	f.
1.	$2\frac{2}{3}$	$1\frac{2}{5}$	$8\frac{3}{4}$	$3\frac{5}{6}$	$8\frac{1}{2}$	$6\frac{1}{9}$
2.	$5\frac{5}{6}$	$3\frac{7}{10}$	$4\frac{7}{12}$	$7\frac{1}{3}$	$5\frac{5}{7}$	$3\frac{3}{4}$
3.	$9\frac{3}{5}$	$1\frac{7}{8}$	$7\frac{1}{7}$	$10\frac{3}{8}$	$2\frac{1}{12}$	$2\frac{5}{8}$
4.	$6\frac{3}{10}$	$4\frac{1}{3}$	$6\frac{7}{8}$	$10\frac{2}{5}$	$4\frac{2}{9}$	$9\frac{7}{9}$

Drill 92   Improper Fractions

Change these mixed numbers to improper fractions.

	a.	b.	c.	d.	e.	f.
1.	$3\frac{5}{8}$	$9\frac{1}{3}$	$8\frac{3}{4}$	$5\frac{3}{5}$	$3\frac{3}{7}$	$1\frac{3}{4}$
2.	$8\frac{3}{8}$	$4\frac{7}{10}$	$2\frac{8}{9}$	$1\frac{9}{11}$	$2\frac{11}{16}$	$17\frac{1}{2}$
3.	$1\frac{13}{16}$	$2\frac{4}{17}$	$10\frac{7}{10}$	$12\frac{2}{3}$	$16\frac{1}{4}$	$4\frac{3}{10}$
4.	$20\frac{3}{4}$	$3\frac{7}{16}$	$9\frac{5}{6}$	$4\frac{4}{15}$	$6\frac{1}{6}$	$13\frac{3}{5}$

Drill 93   Adding Like Fractions

	a.	b.	c.	d.	e.
1.	$\frac{3}{12}$ $+\frac{7}{12}$	$\frac{5}{6}$ $+\frac{1}{6}$	$\frac{5}{8}$ $+\frac{7}{8}$	$\frac{7}{10}$ $+\frac{9}{10}$	$\frac{11}{16}$ $+\frac{7}{16}$
2.	$6\frac{2}{5}$ $+3\frac{3}{5}$	$4\frac{3}{10}$ $+3\frac{3}{10}$	$2\frac{1}{12}$ $+3\frac{7}{12}$	$2\frac{3}{4}$ $+8\frac{3}{4}$	$4\frac{3}{8}$ $+2\frac{7}{8}$
3.	$5\frac{7}{16}$ $+3\frac{5}{16}$	$2\frac{7}{10}$ $+3\frac{3}{10}$	$1\frac{1}{12}$ $+\frac{5}{12}$	$5\frac{3}{8}$ $+2\frac{3}{8}$	$4\frac{7}{12}$ $+4\frac{9}{12}$

Drill 94   Subtracting Like Fractions

	a.	b.	c.	d.	e.
1.	$\frac{11}{12}$ $-\frac{1}{12}$	$\frac{15}{16}$ $-\frac{7}{16}$	$\frac{7}{8}$ $-\frac{1}{8}$	$\frac{13}{15}$ $-\frac{8}{15}$	$\frac{7}{10}$ $-\frac{3}{10}$
2.	$4\frac{7}{8}$ $-2\frac{3}{8}$	$5\frac{9}{10}$ $-\frac{3}{10}$	$2\frac{4}{5}$ $-1\frac{1}{5}$	$10\frac{5}{16}$ $-2\frac{3}{16}$	$9\frac{11}{12}$ $-4\frac{5}{12}$
3.	$8\frac{5}{6}$ $-2\frac{1}{6}$	$1\frac{8}{9}$ $-1\frac{4}{9}$	$5\frac{5}{8}$ $-2\frac{3}{8}$	$2\frac{7}{12}$ $-\frac{5}{12}$	$7\frac{9}{16}$ $-2\frac{5}{16}$

Drill 95 — Adding Unlike Fractions

	a.	b.	c.	d.	e.
1.	$\frac{1}{2}+\frac{11}{12}$	$\frac{7}{8}+\frac{5}{16}$	$\frac{1}{2}+\frac{2}{3}$	$\frac{3}{4}+\frac{1}{3}$	$\frac{1}{2}+\frac{9}{10}$
2.	$\frac{1}{2}+\frac{5}{8}$	$\frac{3}{4}+\frac{2}{3}$	$\frac{7}{10}+\frac{1}{2}$	$\frac{2}{3}+\frac{3}{5}$	$\frac{3}{4}+\frac{7}{12}$
3.	$\frac{1}{4}+\frac{5}{16}$	$\frac{2}{3}+\frac{1}{6}$	$\frac{3}{4}+\frac{1}{12}$	$\frac{3}{8}+\frac{3}{16}$	$\frac{1}{5}+\frac{3}{10}$

Drill 96 — Adding Mixed Numbers With Unlike Fractions

	a.	b.	c.	d.	e.
1.	$6\frac{1}{2}+1\frac{1}{5}$	$4\frac{5}{9}+4\frac{1}{3}$	$4\frac{1}{3}+3\frac{7}{15}$	$1\frac{2}{3}+5\frac{1}{5}$	$2\frac{3}{8}+3\frac{1}{2}$
2.	$3\frac{1}{4}+5\frac{13}{16}$	$5\frac{5}{6}+1\frac{3}{8}$	$6\frac{2}{3}+4\frac{7}{12}$	$2\frac{4}{5}+2\frac{3}{10}$	$5\frac{1}{2}+\frac{2}{3}$
3.	$4\frac{1}{2}+\frac{4}{5}$	$3\frac{5}{8}+1\frac{11}{16}$	$2\frac{7}{12}+4\frac{5}{6}$	$1\frac{1}{4}+5\frac{2}{3}$	$3\frac{5}{6}+8\frac{1}{2}$

Drill 97 — Adding Unlike Fractions

	a.	b.	c.	d.	e.
1.	$\frac{5}{8}+\frac{1}{2}+\frac{3}{4}$	$\frac{1}{2}+\frac{5}{6}+\frac{3}{4}$	$\frac{1}{6}+\frac{2}{5}+\frac{2}{3}$	$\frac{1}{2}+\frac{4}{5}+\frac{3}{10}$	$\frac{3}{4}+\frac{1}{2}+\frac{2}{3}$
2.	$\frac{2}{3}+\frac{3}{8}+\frac{1}{4}$	$\frac{5}{6}+\frac{1}{2}+\frac{2}{3}$	$\frac{2}{3}+\frac{5}{6}+\frac{3}{4}$	$\frac{3}{5}+\frac{2}{3}+\frac{1}{2}$	$\frac{2}{5}+\frac{1}{2}+\frac{3}{4}$

Drill 98 — Subtracting Unlike Fractions

	a.	b.	c.	d.	e.
1.	$\frac{5}{8}$ $-\frac{7}{16}$	$\frac{11}{15}$ $-\frac{1}{3}$	$\frac{1}{2}$ $-\frac{1}{16}$	$\frac{3}{4}$ $-\frac{2}{3}$	$\frac{4}{5}$ $-\frac{1}{2}$
2.	$7\frac{3}{4}$ $-5\frac{5}{12}$	$9\frac{11}{12}$ $-4\frac{1}{6}$	$8\frac{1}{4}$ $-3\frac{1}{8}$	$9\frac{17}{20}$ $-6\frac{3}{5}$	$8\frac{5}{6}$ $-2\frac{3}{8}$

Drill 99   Subtracting Fractions From Whole Numbers

	a.	b.	c.	d.	e.
1.	3 $-\frac{3}{8}$	4 $-\frac{2}{3}$	6 $-\frac{3}{4}$	5 $-\frac{1}{6}$	8 $-\frac{3}{5}$
2.	4 $-1\frac{7}{12}$	2 $-1\frac{3}{10}$	7 $-3\frac{1}{4}$	9 $-3\frac{5}{8}$	8 $-5\frac{1}{6}$
3.	6 $-4\frac{3}{5}$	5 $-2\frac{9}{16}$	7 $-4\frac{5}{12}$	8 $-6\frac{7}{10}$	4 $-3\frac{11}{16}$

Drill 100   Borrowing to Subtract Like Fractions

	a.	b.	c.	d.	e.
1.	$3\frac{3}{8}$ $-\frac{5}{8}$	$8\frac{1}{6}$ $-\frac{5}{6}$	$7\frac{3}{5}$ $-\frac{4}{5}$	$5\frac{1}{4}$ $-\frac{3}{4}$	$4\frac{3}{10}$ $-\frac{5}{10}$
2.	$8\frac{1}{12}$ $-4\frac{5}{12}$	$9\frac{7}{10}$ $-6\frac{9}{10}$	$9\frac{5}{12}$ $-4\frac{11}{12}$	$7\frac{5}{16}$ $-3\frac{9}{16}$	$5\frac{1}{8}$ $-4\frac{7}{8}$
3.	$6\frac{3}{7}$ $-1\frac{6}{7}$	$4\frac{11}{16}$ $-2\frac{15}{16}$	$5\frac{5}{8}$ $-2\frac{7}{8}$	$8\frac{1}{12}$ $-4\frac{11}{12}$	$9\frac{2}{9}$ $-3\frac{8}{9}$

Drill 101   **Borrowing to Subtract Unlike Fractions**

	a.	b.	c.	d.	e.
1.	$10\frac{1}{3}$ $-\,4\frac{7}{12}$	$7\frac{1}{2}$ $-\,5\frac{2}{3}$	$3\frac{1}{15}$ $-\,1\frac{2}{3}$	$5\frac{1}{5}$ $-\,1\frac{1}{2}$	$12\frac{5}{16}$ $-\,7\frac{5}{8}$
2.	$9\frac{3}{8}$ $-\,5\frac{3}{4}$	$10\frac{3}{16}$ $-\,9\frac{1}{2}$	$9\frac{2}{3}$ $-\,7\frac{5}{6}$	$11\frac{2}{3}$ $-\,4\frac{3}{4}$	$4\frac{1}{2}$ $-\,2\frac{5}{8}$

Drill 102   **Borrowing to Subtract Unlike Fractions**

	a.	b.	c.	d.	e.
1.	$8\frac{3}{4}$ $-\,7\frac{7}{8}$	$5\frac{2}{5}$ $-\,2\frac{3}{4}$	$9\frac{1}{12}$ $-\,6\frac{3}{4}$	$8\frac{1}{3}$ $-\,4\frac{3}{4}$	$13\frac{1}{6}$ $-\,8\frac{7}{12}$
2.	$12\frac{1}{2}$ $-\,7\frac{7}{10}$	$11\frac{5}{12}$ $-\,4\frac{1}{2}$	$4\frac{3}{8}$ $-\,1\frac{5}{6}$	$16\frac{3}{16}$ $-\,7\frac{3}{4}$	$6\frac{1}{3}$ $-\,5\frac{1}{2}$

Drill 103   **Multiplying Whole Numbers and Fractions**

	a.	b.	c.	d.	e.
1.	$\frac{1}{4} \times 11$	$\frac{5}{6} \times 3$	$\frac{3}{8} \times 4$	$5 \times \frac{5}{8}$	$7 \times \frac{2}{9}$
2.	$\frac{5}{9} \times 2$	$\frac{7}{10} \times 4$	$\frac{1}{10} \times 12$	$7 \times \frac{3}{5}$	$18 \times \frac{1}{6}$
3.	$\frac{2}{7} \times 9$	$\frac{3}{10} \times 6$	$\frac{4}{9} \times 4$	$5 \times \frac{7}{8}$	$8 \times \frac{4}{5}$
4.	$\frac{7}{9} \times 3$	$\frac{2}{5} \times 5$	$\frac{3}{4} \times 8$	$17 \times \frac{1}{8}$	$6 \times \frac{3}{4}$
5.	$\frac{9}{10} \times 5$	$\frac{5}{7} \times 6$	$\frac{5}{8} \times 3$	$9 \times \frac{3}{8}$	$11 \times \frac{4}{7}$

Drill 104   Multiplying Whole Numbers by Mixed Numbers

	a.	b.	c.	d.	e.
1.	$1\frac{1}{5} \times 25$	$2\frac{1}{3} \times 6$	$3\frac{1}{4} \times 8$	$1\frac{1}{6} \times 12$	$1\frac{1}{3} \times 9$
2.	$4\frac{1}{2} \times 10$	$1\frac{1}{4} \times 12$	$2\frac{1}{3} \times 9$	$1\frac{1}{4} \times 16$	$4\frac{1}{2} \times 4$
3.	$1\frac{1}{7} \times 21$	$2\frac{1}{4} \times 4$	$2\frac{1}{4} \times 20$	$5\frac{1}{3} \times 6$	$3\frac{1}{2} \times 12$
4.	$1\frac{1}{3} \times 15$	$2\frac{1}{5} \times 10$	$1\frac{1}{6} \times 18$	$1\frac{1}{8} \times 24$	$9\frac{1}{2} \times 2$

Drill 105   Multiplying Whole Numbers and Mixed Numbers

	a.	b.	c.	d.
1.	$12 \times 4\frac{2}{3}$	$24 \times 5\frac{3}{8}$	$36 \times 8\frac{1}{6}$	$45 \times 4\frac{4}{5}$
2.	$32 \times 5\frac{5}{8}$	$50 \times 7\frac{1}{2}$	$36 \times 3\frac{3}{4}$	$80 \times 6\frac{7}{10}$
3.	$13\frac{1}{4} \times 8$	$30\frac{2}{5} \times 5$	$84\frac{2}{3} \times 9$	$67\frac{1}{2} \times 6$
4.	$81\frac{7}{8} \times 8$	$38\frac{3}{4} \times 4$	$25\frac{3}{4} \times 8$	$93\frac{1}{3} \times 9$

Drill 106   Multiplying Fractions

	a.	b.	c.	d.
1.	$\frac{3}{4} \times \frac{8}{9}$	$\frac{4}{5} \times \frac{15}{22}$	$\frac{2}{3} \times \frac{6}{7}$	$\frac{1}{2} \times \frac{2}{9}$
2.	$\frac{5}{8} \times \frac{16}{25}$	$\frac{8}{9} \times \frac{7}{8}$	$\frac{3}{8} \times \frac{2}{3}$	$\frac{7}{8} \times \frac{20}{21}$
3.	$\frac{4}{15} \times \frac{3}{4}$	$\frac{5}{24} \times \frac{3}{10}$	$\frac{9}{16} \times \frac{4}{5}$	$\frac{5}{12} \times \frac{8}{25}$
4.	$\frac{2}{3} \times \frac{4}{5}$	$\frac{8}{9} \times \frac{27}{28}$	$\frac{10}{13} \times \frac{14}{15}$	$\frac{1}{4} \times \frac{4}{7}$
5.	$\frac{4}{5} \times \frac{15}{29}$	$\frac{11}{12} \times \frac{3}{4}$	$\frac{7}{8} \times \frac{3}{5}$	$\frac{3}{7} \times \frac{7}{9}$

Drill 107 — Multiplying Fractions

	a.	b.	c.	d.
1.	$\frac{5}{6} \times \frac{9}{10}$	$\frac{3}{8} \times \frac{7}{12}$	$\frac{5}{12} \times \frac{12}{25}$	$\frac{5}{8} \times \frac{12}{13}$
2.	$\frac{2}{3} \times \frac{3}{8}$	$\frac{11}{12} \times \frac{9}{22}$	$\frac{4}{7} \times \frac{5}{6}$	$\frac{7}{16} \times \frac{6}{7}$
3.	$\frac{4}{5} \times \frac{23}{24}$	$\frac{2}{3} \times \frac{3}{5}$	$\frac{2}{3} \times \frac{9}{20}$	$\frac{9}{10} \times \frac{3}{7}$
4.	$\frac{1}{4} \times \frac{8}{9}$	$\frac{10}{21} \times \frac{3}{4}$	$\frac{5}{16} \times \frac{4}{5}$	$\frac{6}{25} \times \frac{5}{9}$
5.	$\frac{5}{8} \times \frac{4}{15}$	$\frac{9}{10} \times \frac{4}{9}$	$\frac{7}{8} \times \frac{6}{11}$	$\frac{15}{16} \times \frac{2}{5}$

Drill 108 — Dividing Whole Numbers by Fractions

	a.	b.	c.	d.
1.	$9 \div \frac{1}{3}$	$2 \div \frac{1}{5}$	$4 \div \frac{1}{8}$	$5 \div \frac{1}{3}$
2.	$12 \div \frac{1}{4}$	$7 \div \frac{1}{8}$	$9 \div \frac{1}{7}$	$8 \div \frac{1}{6}$
3.	$10 \div \frac{1}{3}$	$12 \div \frac{1}{10}$	$6 \div \frac{1}{6}$	$8 \div \frac{1}{5}$
4.	$20 \div \frac{1}{2}$	$14 \div \frac{1}{3}$	$18 \div \frac{1}{2}$	$9 \div \frac{1}{4}$

Drill 109 — Dividing Fractions by Whole Numbers

	a.	b.	c.	d.
1.	$\frac{1}{2} \div 5$	$\frac{3}{4} \div 2$	$\frac{9}{16} \div 3$	$\frac{7}{8} \div 7$
2.	$\frac{5}{8} \div 10$	$\frac{6}{7} \div 4$	$\frac{7}{8} \div 5$	$\frac{3}{4} \div 12$
3.	$\frac{4}{5} \div 16$	$\frac{7}{10} \div 14$	$\frac{2}{3} \div 6$	$\frac{5}{16} \div 5$
4.	$\frac{2}{3} \div 10$	$\frac{9}{10} \div 6$	$\frac{6}{11} \div 4$	$\frac{7}{12} \div 7$

Drill 110   *Dividing Fractions by Fractions*

	a.	b.	c.	d.
1.	$\frac{4}{5} \div \frac{1}{2}$	$\frac{3}{5} \div \frac{4}{5}$	$\frac{7}{8} \div \frac{3}{10}$	$\frac{3}{4} \div \frac{1}{12}$
2.	$\frac{7}{8} \div \frac{3}{4}$	$\frac{1}{5} \div \frac{1}{2}$	$\frac{3}{4} \div \frac{3}{10}$	$\frac{5}{6} \div \frac{1}{4}$
3.	$\frac{3}{4} \div \frac{5}{16}$	$\frac{7}{10} \div \frac{1}{7}$	$\frac{3}{5} \div \frac{4}{15}$	$\frac{5}{9} \div \frac{5}{6}$
4.	$\frac{7}{12} \div \frac{1}{4}$	$\frac{5}{12} \div \frac{5}{8}$	$\frac{3}{4} \div \frac{3}{16}$	$\frac{5}{16} \div \frac{3}{8}$
5.	$\frac{3}{4} \div \frac{5}{6}$	$\frac{2}{3} \div \frac{8}{9}$	$\frac{3}{10} \div \frac{9}{16}$	$\frac{11}{16} \div \frac{1}{6}$

Drill 111   *Dividing Fractions*

	a.	b.	c.	d.
1.	$\frac{4}{5} \div \frac{4}{9}$	$\frac{3}{4} \div \frac{3}{4}$	$6 \div \frac{3}{4}$	$\frac{5}{6} \div \frac{3}{8}$
2.	$\frac{2}{3} \div 4$	$\frac{5}{16} \div \frac{5}{8}$	$\frac{11}{12} \div \frac{2}{3}$	$8 \div \frac{2}{3}$
3.	$\frac{7}{12} \div 7$	$\frac{1}{6} \div \frac{1}{4}$	$\frac{2}{3} \div 6$	$8 \div \frac{6}{7}$
4.	$\frac{13}{15} \div \frac{1}{10}$	$\frac{5}{6} \div 3$	$\frac{5}{16} \div 2$	$\frac{1}{3} \div \frac{11}{12}$
5.	$9 \div \frac{3}{5}$	$\frac{3}{10} \div \frac{1}{4}$	$\frac{7}{12} \div \frac{7}{10}$	$\frac{9}{16} \div 3$

Drill 112   *Dividing Fractions*

	a.	b.	c.	d.
1.	$\frac{2}{5} \div \frac{4}{5}$	$6 \div \frac{4}{9}$	$\frac{7}{16} \div \frac{7}{10}$	$\frac{2}{3} \div 3$
2.	$\frac{5}{8} \div \frac{5}{8}$	$\frac{11}{12} \div 2$	$\frac{3}{10} \div \frac{3}{8}$	$\frac{3}{4} \div \frac{1}{4}$
3.	$\frac{7}{8} \div \frac{5}{16}$	$10 \div \frac{2}{5}$	$\frac{7}{10} \div 14$	$\frac{3}{5} \div \frac{4}{5}$
4.	$\frac{3}{4} \div 6$	$\frac{8}{15} \div \frac{2}{3}$	$9 \div \frac{3}{5}$	$\frac{1}{12} \div \frac{3}{4}$
5.	$\frac{1}{2} \div 4$	$5 \div \frac{15}{16}$	$\frac{5}{12} \div \frac{1}{3}$	$\frac{1}{4} \div \frac{13}{20}$

Set VIII: Secondary Skills Drills

Drill 113   *Understanding Decimals*

Write these words and mixed numbers as decimals.

1. six and twenty-five hundredths
2. eighty-seven and four thousandths
3. two hundred fifteen and three tenths
4. seven hundred four and twelve thousandths
5. ninety-one and fourteen hundredths
6. eight hundred eleven and two hundredths
7. a. $18\frac{16}{1,000}$ b. $4\frac{4}{10}$ c. $72\frac{325}{1,000}$ d. $5\frac{5}{100}$ e. $65\frac{39}{100}$ f. $8\frac{1}{1,000}$

Drill 114   *Understanding Decimals*

A. Write these words as decimals.

1. nineteen and five thousandths
2. three hundred thirteen and thirty-five hundredths
3. twelve and six tenths
4. eight hundred seven and forty-five thousandths
5. sixteen and nine hundredths
6. one hundred fifty-eight and six hundred seventy thousandths

B. Copy. Write <, >, or = between the numbers in each pair.

	a.	b.	c.
7.	0.3 ____ 0.03	1.2 ____ 1.200	4.50 ____ 4.5
8.	7.24 ____ 7.42	6.5 ____ 6.279	8.2 ____ 9.20
9.	3.19 ____ 3.2	8.600 ____ 8.60	5.009 ____ 5.01
10.	6.7 ____ 6.73	5.25 ____ 5.5	2.64 ____ 2.599

Drill 115   **Adding and Subtracting Decimals**

	a.	b.	c.	d.	e.
1.	35.2 14.8 45.7 + 72.7	62.85 74.65 12.76 + 25.05	8.519 6.722 3.409 + 0.655	746.4 839.7 125.5 + 57.8	0.621 5.096 3.750 + 4.629
2.	346.0 - 277.5	7.685 - 3.769	143.05 - 75.98	5,270.4 - 2,695.6	375.10 - 266.35

Drill 116   **Adding and Subtracting Decimals**

Copy in columns with the decimal points lined properly. If you need them, annex zeroes at the right. Then add or subtract.

1.   89.4 + 236.25 + 64.356 + 5.8
2.   450 + 27.8 + 365.59 + 27
3.   48.753 + 625 + 38.6 + 450.82
4.   98.512 + 863.27 + 44 + 211.9
5.   825.62 + 344.6 + 28.679 + 5.78
6.   410.5 - 36.78
7.   65 - 48.475
8.   723.26 - 47
9.   32.19 - 18.367
10.   780 - 329.96

Drill 117   **Multiplying Decimals**

	a.	b.	c.	d.	e.
1.	87.3 × 26	9.36 × 465	129.8 × 83	0.375 × 274	6.804 × 47
2.	209 × 4.7	780 × 8.65	6.359 × 0.43	4.285 × 0.287	9.036 × 16.9

Drill 118   *Dividing Decimals*

	a.	b.	c.	d.
1.	8)30.32	7)340.2	6)8.754	9)93.42
2.	6)1.062	4)0.16	5)162.5	8)0.784
3.	32)27.52	12)4.608	24)367.2	19)1.083
4.	17)0.051	51)234.6	63)27.09	28)1.288

Drill 119   *Understanding Large Numbers*

A. Write these number words with digits.

1. eighty-five million
2. two hundred fifty billion
3. six hundred four million, twenty-nine thousand, seven hundred
4. eleven billion, two hundred ninety million, six hundred forty
5. seven billion, seven million, seven thousand, seven
6. one hundred one billion, one million, one hundred thousand, ten
7. five hundred twenty-five million, three hundred sixty thousand
8. fourteen billion, eight hundred twelve
9. nine hundred forty-one billion, two hundred ninety-six million
10. seven hundred nineteen billion, fifty-eight million, three hundred two thousand, four hundred twenty-six

B. Write these numbers with words.

11. 78,003,110,064
12. 9,000,000,000
13. 821,000,027
14. 945,123,700,000
15. 12,210,021,102

Drill 120   *Understanding Large Numbers*

A.   Study this number: **362,450,289,175.** Then answer the following questions about it.

1.   Which digit is in hundred millions' place?
2.   Which digit tells the number of ten billions?
3.   What is the **place value** of the 3 in this number?
4.   What is the **total value** of the 8?
5.   What number is 1,000,000,000 more than 362,450,289,175?
6.   What number is 10,000,000 less than 362,450,289,175?

B.   Write these number words with digits.

7.   thirteen billion
8.   eight hundred million
9.   seventy-four billion, six hundred ninety-seven million
10.   two hundred thirty-one billion, four hundred eighteen million, fifty-two thousand, six
11.   one hundred forty-eight billion, twelve
12.   sixteen billion, six million, six hundred thousand
13.   three hundred seventy-three million, seven hundred two thousand, one hundred fifty
14.   four hundred billion, forty million, four hundred four

C.   Write these numbers with words.

15.   22,000,200,012
16.   110,001,010,100
17.   478,203,000,000

Drill 121   *Rounding Numbers*

1.   Round these numbers to the nearest 10.
     a. 6,913   b. 2,567   c. 75,694   d. 145,852   e. 754,378

2.   Round these numbers to the nearest 100.
     a. 6,913   b. 2,567   c. 75,694   d. 145,852   e. 754,378

3.   Round these numbers to the nearest 1,000.
     a. 6,913   b. 2,567   c. 75,694   d. 145,852   e. 754,378

Drill 122   *Rounding Numbers*

1. Round these numbers to the nearest 1,000.
   a. 285,379   b. 462,546   c. 1,239,482   d. 5,075,920   e. 84,326,713

2. Round these numbers to the nearest 10,000.
   a. 285,379   b. 462,546   c. 1,239,482   d. 5,075,920   e. 84,326,713

3. Round these numbers to the nearest 100,000.
   a. 285,379   b. 462,546   c. 1,239,482   d. 5,075,920   e. 84,326,713

Drill 123   *Roman Numerals*

1. Write these Arabic numerals as Roman numerals.
   a. 367   b. 824   c. 589   d. 238   e. 195   f. 642   g. 456

2. Write these Roman numerals as Arabic numerals.
   a. DCCXLVIII   b. CDXXXIX   c. XCIV   d. CCCLXXVI   e. DCCCXV

Drill 124   *Roman Numerals*

Write as Roman numerals.

1. a. 1,965   b. 878   c. 2,514   d. 3,429   e. 1,642   f. 736

2. a. 2,457   b. 3,500   c. 1,090   d. 983   e. 2,000   f. 3,145

3. a. 491   b. 1,813   c. 2,609   d. 274   e. 3,926   f. 1,760

Drill 125   *Roman Numerals*

Write as Arabic numerals.

1. a. MMM   b. MCMLXIX   c. MMCDLXXX   d. DCCCXIV

2. a. ML   b. MMD   c. DCXCVIII   d. XXXVI

3. a. MDCXII   b. MCDXVII   c. MMMCCLIX   d. XCI

4. a. MMXLIX   b. CMLXXV   c. MMDCCLXXXIII   d. DCX

5. a. MCMXCIV   b. MMMCCXX   c. MMDCCCXXVI   d. MCD

Drill 126   *Using Measure Equivalents*

Find the missing numbers. You will need to decide whether to multiply or divide.

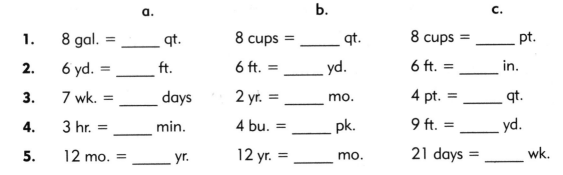

	a.	b.	c.
1.	8 gal. = _____ qt.	8 cups = _____ qt.	8 cups = _____ pt.
2.	6 yd. = _____ ft.	6 ft. = _____ yd.	6 ft. = _____ in.
3.	7 wk. = _____ days	2 yr. = _____ mo.	4 pt. = _____ qt.
4.	3 hr. = _____ min.	4 bu. = _____ pk.	9 ft. = _____ yd.
5.	12 mo. = _____ yr.	12 yr. = _____ mo.	21 days = _____ wk.

Drill 127   *Using Measure Equivalents*

Find the missing numbers. Some answers will be fractions.

	a.	b.	c.
1.	9 cups = _____ qt.	12 hr. = _____ day	3 bu. = _____ pk.
2.	2 yd. = _____ in.	4 tons = _____ lb.	4 oz. = _____ lb.
3.	6 pt. = _____ qt.	6 qt. = _____ pt.	6 qt. = _____ gal.
4.	35 days = _____ wk.	5 pk. = _____ qt.	2 min. = _____ sec.
5.	30 min. = _____ hr.	24 in. = _____ yd.	3 centuries = _____ yr.

Drill 128   *Using Measure Equivalents*

Find the missing numbers. Some answers will be fractions.

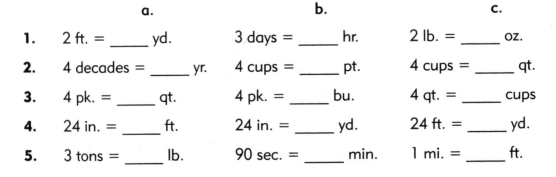

	a.	b.	c.
1.	2 ft. = _____ yd.	3 days = _____ hr.	2 lb. = _____ oz.
2.	4 decades = _____ yr.	4 cups = _____ pt.	4 cups = _____ qt.
3.	4 pk. = _____ qt.	4 pk. = _____ bu.	4 qt. = _____ cups
4.	24 in. = _____ ft.	24 in. = _____ yd.	24 ft. = _____ yd.
5.	3 tons = _____ lb.	90 sec. = _____ min.	1 mi. = _____ ft.

Drill 129   ***Ruler Practice***

Use your ruler to measure these lines to the nearest $\frac{1}{16}$ inch.

1. _____

2. _____

3. _____

4. _____

5. _____

6. _____

7. _____

8. _____

Drill 130   ***Metric Measures***

1. Write the meanings of the following metric prefixes.
   a. deka-   b. hecto-   c. milli-   d. deci-   e. centi-   f. kilo-
2. The metric system is based on the number _____.
3. What is the basic metric unit of length?
4. Which metric unit is a little less than a half inch?
5. Which metric unit is about the same length as a yard?
6. Which metric unit is used instead of English miles?
7. Which metric unit means $\frac{1}{1,000}$ of a meter?
8. How many millimeters are in a centimeter?
9. How many centimeters are in a meter?
10. How many meters are in a kilometer?

Drill 131   ***Metric Measures***

1. Write the metric prefixes that have these meanings.
   a. 0.01   b. 10   c. 0.1   d. 1,000   e. 0.001   f. 100
2. What is the basic metric unit of length?
3. What is the basic metric unit of capacity?
4. What is the basic metric unit of weight?
5. Which metric unit is about the same measure as a quart?
6. Which metric unit is used instead of English pounds?
7. Write the larger unit in each pair.
   a. meter, yard   d. millimeter, centimeter   g. pound, kilogram
   b. ounce, gram   e. mile, kilometer   h. quart, liter
   c. gram, kilogram   f. inch, centimeter   i. ton, kilogram

Drill 132   *Ratios*

A. Compare the following items by dividing, or finding **ratios**. Express the ratios as fractions or mixed numbers in simplest form.

1.   8 boys compared to 10 girls

2.   10 girls compared to 8 boys

3.   15 boys compared to 24 pupils

4.   9 girls compared to 24 pupils

5.   9 girls compared to 15 boys

6.   15 boys compared to 9 girls

7.   7 oranges compared to 12 apples

8.   2 heifer calves compared to 6 bull calves

9.   21 jars of pears compared to 28 jars of peaches

10.   6 miles compared to 4 miles

B. Compare the following measures by expressing them as ratios in simplest form.

11.   a foot and a yard

12.   an inch and a foot

13.   an hour and a day

14.   an ounce and a pound

15.   6 inches and a yard

16.   8 inches and a foot

17.   15 minutes and an hour

18.   4 days and a week

19.   9 months and a year

20.   8 ounces and a pound

Drill 133   *Ratios*

A. Do the following ratios form proportions? Write **yes** or **no**.

1.   a. $\frac{3}{5}$ $\frac{10}{15}$ b. $\frac{6}{8}$ $\frac{18}{24}$ c. $\frac{10}{12}$ $\frac{5}{6}$ d. $\frac{3}{4}$ $\frac{8}{12}$ e. $\frac{12}{20}$ $\frac{3}{5}$

B. Use division to find the parts of these measures. Write your answers as ratios, or fractions, in simplest form.

2.   What part of a pound is
      a. 1 ounce   b. 6 ounces   c. 12 ounces   d. 13 ounces   e. 4 ounces

3.   What part of a yard is
      a. 4 inches   b. 12 inches   c. 30 inches   d. 18 inches   e. 24 inches

4.   What part of a minute is
      a. 15 seconds   b. 30 seconds   c. 50 seconds   d. 24 seconds   e. 45 seconds.

Drill 134   *Percents*

1.   Write these decimals as percents.
      a. 0.27   b. 0.15   c. 0.08   d. 0.98   e. 0.67   f. 0.84

2.   Write these fractions as percents.
      a. $\frac{5}{100}$ b. $\frac{79}{100}$ c. $\frac{35}{100}$ d. $\frac{3}{100}$ e. $\frac{94}{100}$ f. $\frac{50}{100}$

3.   Subtract these percents from 100%
      a. 18%   b. 25%   c. 10%   d. 80%   e. 49%   f. 7%

Drill 135   *Percents*

First express these fractions with denominators of 100. Then write the fractions as percents.

1.   a. $\frac{1}{4}$ b. $\frac{2}{5}$ c. $\frac{3}{10}$ d. $\frac{19}{20}$ e. $\frac{3}{4}$ f. $\frac{13}{25}$

2.   a. $\frac{9}{10}$ b. $\frac{21}{25}$ c. $\frac{1}{2}$ d. $\frac{43}{50}$ e. $\frac{4}{5}$ f. $\frac{11}{20}$

Handbook

of Terms and Rules

Page numbers in parentheses tell where additional information is found.

Addition   (14)

1. The **sum** is the answer to an addition problem.
2. An **addend** is one of the numbers added together to make a sum.
3. Addends can be grouped in any order and the sum will be the same.
   Example: $3 + 4 + 5 = 3 + 5 + 4 = 5 + 4 + 3$

Adding and subtracting fractions

1. Only like fractions can be added or subtracted. Add or subtract the numerators and keep the same denominator.   (61)
2. To add or subtract unlike fractions, first express the fractions with common denominators. Always express answers in simplest form.   (146, 160, 162, 164, 198)
3. See pages 166, 168, and 170 for help to subtract fractions when borrowing is necessary.

Acre   (318)

A unit for measuring land. There are 640 acres in a square mile.

A.M.   (13)

Before noon (from Latin *ante meridiem*).

Angles   (See *Geometry.*)

Arabic numerals

Numerals written the way we usually write them, using the figures 0, 1, 2, 3, 4, 5, 6, 7, 8, and 9.

Area   (314, 316)

The measure of surface space. The area of a square or rectangle is found by multiplying the length times the width. Area is expressed in square units.

Average   (148)

A balance between smallest and greatest in a group of numbers. To find the average of a group of numbers,

1. Add all the numbers;
2. Divide the sum by the number of addends.

Bar graph   (220, 330)

A graph using bars of different lengths to represent the things being compared.

Bible measures   (See page 268.)

Change, finding

1. To find the amount of change, subtract the amount of the purchase from the amount paid.   (46)
2. To count change to the customer, start with the amount of the purchase. Give the smallest denominations first. Use pennies to reach the next higher 5 or 10; use dimes and/or a nickel to reach the next 25; use quarters to reach the next dollar; and then use bills.   (48)

Common factor   (142, See also *Factor.*)

A number that is a factor of two or more numbers. The **greatest common factor** is the largest number that is a factor of two numbers.

Example: 2 and 4 are common factors of 8 and 12.
The greatest common factor is 4.

Common denominator   (See *Lowest common denominator.*)

Common multiple   (138, See also *Multiple.*)

A multiple of more than one smaller number. A common multiple of 4 and 8 is 24.

The **lowest common multiple** of a pair of numbers is the smallest number that is a multiple of both. The lowest common multiple of 4 and 8 is 8.

Decimals   (204)

1. A **decimal** is a number with a decimal point and digits on both sides of the decimal point. The first three places to the right of the decimal point are tenths, hundredths, and thousandths.

Examples: 7.5   18.26   0.3   9.045

2. A **decimal fraction** is a decimal less than one. A zero is usually written in the ones' place.

Examples: 0.7   0.18   0.375

3. When adding or subtracting decimals, the decimal points must all be lined up one under the other.   (208, 212)
4. The size of decimals can be compared more easily by **annexing** zeroes to the right of the number.   (210)

Digit

One of the characters used to write numerals. The digits used in our number system are 0, 1, 2, 3, 4, 5, 6, 7, 8, 9.

Digital value

The value of a written character, regardless of its place value.

Distance, rate, time   (202)
1. To find the distance, multiply the rate and the time.
2. To find the rate, divide the distance by the time.
3. To find the time, divide the distance by the rate.

Dividing fractions   (252, 254, 256)

To divide fractions,
1. Invert the divisor in the problem;
2. Multiply the dividend and the inverted divisor;
3. Reduce the answer to simplest form.

Division   (26, 30)
1. Parts of a division problem
   a. The answer to a division question is called the **quotient**.
   b. The **dividend** is the number that is divided into parts. Six is the dividend in both of these examples: $2\overline{)6}$ $6 \div 3$
   c. A **partial dividend** is part of the dividend used in division problems with more than one digit in the quotient. In this problem $8\overline{)125}$, the first partial dividend is 12.
   d. The **divisor** tells into how many parts the dividend is divided. Four is the divisor in both of these examples: $4\overline{)12}$ $8 \div 4$
   e. A **remainder** is the part of a division answer that shows how many are left after the dividend is divided into groups.
2. The steps for solving division problems are Divide, Multiply, Compare, Subtract, Compare, Bring down.   (28)
3. To check the answer to a division problem, multiply the quotient by the divisor. If there is a remainder, add it on. The answer is the dividend.   (26, 30)
4. Remainders can be expressed as fractions by using the remainder as the numerator of the fraction and the divisor as the denominator. Then the fraction should be reduced.   (66)

Divisibility rules   (See *Rules of divisibility.*)

Estimate

An answer that is not exact but gives us an idea what the exact answer is.

Expanded form of numbers   (See page 37.)

Factor   (140, See also *Multiplication*.)

A number that is multiplied to form a product. The multiplier and the multiplicand are both factors.

The factors of a number are all the numbers by which the number can be divided evenly.

Examples: $3 \times 7 = 21$ 3 and 7 are factors of 21;

1, 2, 3, 4, 6, and 12 are all factors of 12.

Fractions

Fraction words

1. The **denominator** is the bottom number of a fraction. It tells into how many parts a whole thing is divided. The **numerator** is the top number of a fraction. It tells how many of the parts are included. The numerator and denominator are called the **terms** of the fraction.   (54)

2. **Like fractions** have the same denominator.   (54)

Example: $\frac{3}{5}$ and $\frac{1}{5}$ are like fractions.

3. **Equivalent fractions** are equal in value. The fraction with the smallest numbers possible is in simplest form, or **lowest terms**.   (58, 60)

Examples: $\frac{6}{12}$, $\frac{2}{4}$, and $\frac{1}{2}$ are equivalent fractions.

$\frac{1}{2}$ is in lowest terms.

4. A **proper fraction** is less than one whole unit. The numerator is less than the denominator.   (56)

Example: $\frac{4}{7}$

5. An **improper fraction** has enough parts to make one whole unit or more. The numerator is equal to or greater than the denominator. (56)

Examples: $\frac{5}{5}$ and $\frac{4}{3}$

6. A **mixed number** is the combination of a whole number and a fraction.   (56)

Example: $2\frac{1}{4}$

Working with fractions

1. To change an improper fraction to a whole or mixed number, divide the numerator by the denominator.   (56, 68)

2. To find an equivalent fraction, multiply or divide both the numerator and the denominator by the same number.   (58)

3. To **reduce** a fraction to lowest terms, divide the numerator and the denominator by the greatest common factor.   (60)

Example: $\frac{6}{12}$ reduced is $\frac{1}{2}$

4. To find how many fractional parts are in a whole number, multiply the number by the number of parts in one whole.

Example: How many thirds are in 5? $3 \times 5 = 15$

5. To add or subtract fractions, the denominators must be the same. Unlike fractions must be changed to like fractions by using the lowest common denominators.   (61, See also *Adding and subtracting fractions.*)

6. To find a fractional part of a number, divide by the denominator of the fraction. If the numerator is more than one, also multiply by the numerator.   (62)

Examples: $\frac{1}{5}$ of 25 = 25 ÷ 5 = 5;

$\frac{3}{4}$ of 12 = 12 ÷ 4 = 3, then 3 × 3 = 9.

7. To change a mixed number to an improper fraction, multiply the whole number by the denominator and add the numerator   (156)

8. To multiply fractions, multiply the numerators and multiply the denominators. (See also *Multiplying fractions.*)

9. To divide fractions, invert the divisor and multiply. (See also *Dividing fractions.*)

Geometry   (304, 306, 308)

Points and lines   (304)

1. A **point** is a location usually illustrated with a dot.

2. A **line** is straight and extends without end in two directions.

3. A **line segment** is a part of a line with two endpoints.

4. **Intersecting lines** cross each other at a point.

5. **Parallel lines** are always the same distance apart.

6. **Perpendicular lines** are lines that meet to form right angles.

Angles   (306)

1. A **right angle** forms a square corner. A right angle is formed when one line is perpendicular to another.

2. An **acute angle** is less than a right angle.

3. An **obtuse angle** is greater than a right angle.

Geometric shapes   (308)

1. A **triangle** is a three-sided figure.

2. A **rectangle** is a four-sided figure with four right angles.

3. A **square** is a rectangle with four equal sides.

4. A **parallelogram** is a four-sided figure with opposite sides parallel.

5. A **pentagon** is a five-sided figure.

6. A **hexagon** is a six-sided figure.

7. An **octagon** is an eight-sided figure.

8. A **circle** is a curve with all points an equal distance from the center.

9. A **radius** is the distance from the outside edge of a circle to its center.

10. A **diameter** is the distance across a circle through its center.

11. **Similar figures** have the same shape but not the same size.

12. **Congruent figures** have the same size and shape.

Indefinite units   (268)

Units of measure that are not all exactly the same. The **span** and **cubit** are indefinite units.

Invert   (254)

To exchange the numerator and the denominator in a fraction.

Line graph   (332, 334)

A graph using points connected with lines to compare items.

Lowest common denominator   (146)

The **lowest common multiple** of two or more denominators. Lowest common denominators are used to add or subtract unlike fractions.

Example: 12 is the lowest common denominator for $\frac{1}{3}$ and $\frac{7}{12}$.

Measures

Units of measure (See tables inside back cover.)

Working with measures

1. Know your **key numbers**. When a measure is stated like this: 1 yard = 3 feet, 3 is the key number for yards and feet. Because 1 hour = 60 minutes, 60 is the key number for hours and minutes.

2. To change larger units of measure to smaller units, **multiply** by the key number. (74)

3. To change smaller units of measure to larger units, **divide** by the key number. (74)

4. To add measures, see page 86.

5. To subtract measures, see page 88.
6. To multiply measures, see page 188.

Metric measure system   (270, 272, 274, 276, 278)

A measure system based on tens. The basic metric unit of length is the **meter,** the basic unit of weight is the **gram,** and the basic unit of capacity is the **liter.** Prefixes used with the basic units form new units.

Following are the six most commonly used prefixes and their meanings:

milli-	$\frac{1}{1,000}$ or 0.001
centi-	$\frac{1}{100}$ or 0.01
deci-	$\frac{1}{10}$ or 0.1
BASIC UNIT	1 (meter, gram, or liter)
deka-	10
hecto-	100
kilo-	1,000

Mixed number   (56, See also *Fractions.*)

The combination of a whole number and a fraction.

Money

See pages 106 and 107 to identify money.

Multiple   (136, See also *Common multiple.*)

A number that is the product of another one.

Examples: 10 is a multiple of 2 and 5;
6, 12, 18, 24, 30 are all multiples of 5.

Multiplication

Parts of a multiplication problem   (22)

1. The answer to a multiplication problem is the **product.**
2. The **multiplicand** tells the value of one group. Five is the multiplicand in both of these examples: 2×5 $\begin{array}{r} 5 \\ \times 4 \\ \hline \end{array}$
3. The **multiplier** tells how many times a group is repeated. Three is the multiplier in both of these examples: 3×8 $\begin{array}{r} 6 \\ \times 3 \\ \hline \end{array}$
4. The multiplier and multiplicand are also called **factors.**
5. A **partial product** is the answer from multiplying by one digit in a problem that has more than one digit in the multiplier.

$$\begin{array}{r} 632 \\ \times 24 \\ \hline 2,528 \\ 1,264 \\ \hline \end{array}$$ partial products

6. To check the answer to a multiplication problem, reverse the factors.   (126)

Multiplication shortcuts   (118)
   To multiply a number by 10, write 0 after it.
   To multiply a number by 100, write 00 after it.
   To multiply a number by 1,000, write 000 after it.

Multiplying fractions

1. To multiply a mixed number times a whole number,
   a. First multiply by the whole number;
   b. Then multiply by the fraction;
   c. Then add the two together.   (64)
   (See pages 240 and 244 to multiply larger mixed numbers and whole numbers.)
2. To multiply a fraction by a whole number or a whole number by a fraction, multiply the whole number and the numerator of the fraction. Keep the same denominator. Then reduce the fraction.   (242, 246)
3. To multiply two proper fractions, multiply the numerators and multiply the denominators. Then reduce the fraction.   (248)
   Canceling is a shortcut that can be used to multiply some fractions.   (250)

Multiplying measures   (See page 188.)

Number family

The related facts that are made with the same numbers.
This is a number family of addition and subtraction facts:
$$8 + 7 = 15; \quad 7 + 8 = 15; \quad 15 - 7 = 8; \quad 15 - 8 = 7$$
This is a number family of multiplication and division facts:
$$6 \times 9 = 54; \quad 9 \times 6 = 54; \quad 54 \div 6 = 9; \quad 54 \div 9 = 6$$

Percent   (230, 232)

Per hundred, or one hundredth.
80 percent, usually written 80% means $\frac{80}{100}$ of the whole.

Perimeter   (310, 312)

The distance around a straight-sided figure.
   To find the perimeter of a shape add the lengths of all the sides.

6" + 4" + 6" + 4" = 20"

Period   (20, 38)

A group of three digits for ones, tens, and hundreds. A period can represent units, thousands, millions, or greater values. Periods are separated by commas.

Picture graph   (218)

A simple graph using pictures to represent the objects being compared.

Place value   (20, 38)

The position of a digit which indicates its value as ones, tens, hundreds, thousands, and so forth.

P.M.   (13)

After noon (from the Latin *post meridiem*).

Prime number   (140)

A number which has no factors except itself and 1.
Example: 7 is a prime number.

Proportion   (226)

A pair of equivalent fractions, or ratios, such as $\frac{2}{3} = \frac{6}{9}$.

Ratio   (224)

A comparison of two numbers by division. A ratio shows what part one number is of a larger one, or how many times as much a larger number is compared to a smaller one.

Roman numerals   (27, 44)

A number system used by the Romans in the past. In this system I, V, X, L, C and other letters are used to represent numbers.
These rules will help you read Roman numerals:
1. If a letter is followed by an equal or smaller value, add the two values.
2. If a smaller letter comes before a larger letter, subtract the smaller value from the larger.
3. If a smaller letter comes between two larger letters, first subtract the small value from the one after it. Then add.
4. Never repeat or subtract V or L.
5. Subtract I only from V or X. Use X before L or C.

Round numbers   (40, 42)

Numbers that are not exact and usually end with one or more zeroes. Follow these rules to round numbers correctly:
1. Find the place to which you are rounding off.
2. If the digit to the right of that place is less than 5, round down.
3. If the digit to the right of that place is 5 or more, round up.

Rules of divisibility   (150)

Rule for   2: A number is divisible by 2 if it ends with 0, 2, 4, 6, or 8.
Rule for   3: A number is divisible by 3 if the sum of its digits is divisible by 3.
Rule for   4: A number is divisible by 4 if the last two digits are zeroes or if they are divisible by 4.
Rule for   5: A number is divisible by 5 if it ends with 5 or 0.
Rule for   6: A number is divisible by 6 if it is an even number and the sum of its digits is divisible by 3.
Rule for   9: A number is divisible by 9 if the sum of its digits is divisible by 9.
Rule for 10: A number is divisible by 10 if it ends with 0.

Scale drawing   (324, 326)

A drawing in which a small measure represents a larger unit of measure.

Scale of miles   (328)

A scale used on a map to show actual distances.

Subtraction

1. The **difference** is the answer to a subtraction problem.
2. The **minuend** is the top, or larger, number.
3. The **subtrahend** is the bottom, or smaller, number.

Unit

1. The number one, as in "units, tens, hundreds."
2. One whole thing, such as "a whole unit has three thirds."
3. One of a type of measure. Feet, minutes, bushels, and pounds are all units of measure.

Volume   (338)

A measurement of the amount of space within a three-dimensional object. Volume is found by multiplying the length times the width times the height and is measured in cubic units.

Whole number

A number that does not include a fraction. (See also *Fractions*.)

Index

Multiplication Tables

0	1	2	3	4	5	6	7	8	9	10	11	12
×1	×1	×1	×1	×1	×1	×1	×1	×1	×1	×1	×1	×1
0	1	2	3	4	5	6	7	8	9	10	11	12

0	1	2	3	4	5	6	7	8	9	10	11	12
×2	×2	×2	×2	×2	×2	×2	×2	×2	×2	×2	×2	×2
0	2	4	6	8	10	12	14	16	18	20	22	24

0	1	2	3	4	5	6	7	8	9	10	11	12
×3	×3	×3	×3	×3	×3	×3	×3	×3	×3	×3	×3	×3
0	3	6	9	12	15	18	21	24	27	30	33	36

0	1	2	3	4	5	6	7	8	9	10	11	12
×4	×4	×4	×4	×4	×4	×4	×4	×4	×4	×4	×4	×4
0	4	8	12	16	20	24	28	32	36	40	44	48

0	1	2	3	4	5	6	7	8	9	10	11	12
×5	×5	×5	×5	×5	×5	×5	×5	×5	×5	×5	×5	×5
0	5	10	15	20	25	30	35	40	45	50	55	60

0	1	2	3	4	5	6	7	8	9	10	11	12
×6	×6	×6	×6	×6	×6	×6	×6	×6	×6	×6	×6	×6
0	6	12	18	24	30	36	42	48	54	60	66	72

0	1	2	3	4	5	6	7	8	9	10	11	12
×7	×7	×7	×7	×7	×7	×7	×7	×7	×7	×7	×7	×7
0	7	14	21	28	35	42	49	56	63	70	77	84

0	1	2	3	4	5	6	7	8	9	10	11	12
×8	×8	×8	×8	×8	×8	×8	×8	×8	×8	×8	×8	×8
0	8	16	24	32	40	48	56	64	72	80	88	96

0	1	2	3	4	5	6	7	8	9	10	11	12
×9	×9	×9	×9	×9	×9	×9	×9	×9	×9	×9	×9	×9
0	9	18	27	36	45	54	63	72	81	90	99	108

0	1	2	3	4	5	6	7	8	9	10	11	12
×10	×10	×10	×10	×10	×10	×10	×10	×10	×10	×10	×10	×10
0	10	20	30	40	50	60	70	80	90	100	110	120

0	1	2	3	4	5	6	7	8	9	10	11	12
×11	×11	×11	×11	×11	×11	×11	×11	×11	×11	×11	×11	×11
0	11	22	33	44	55	66	77	88	99	110	121	132

0	1	2	3	4	5	6	7	8	9	10	11	12
×12	×12	×12	×12	×12	×12	×12	×12	×12	×12	×12	×12	×12
0	12	24	36	48	60	72	84	96	108	120	132	144

Division Tables

Quotient	0	1	2	3	4	5	6	7	8	9	10	11	12
÷1	1)0	1)1	1)2	1)3	1)4	1)5	1)6	1)7	1)8	1)9	1)10	1)11	1)12
÷2	2)0	2)2	2)4	2)6	2)8	2)10	2)12	2)14	2)16	2)18	2)20	2)22	2)24
÷3	3)0	3)3	3)6	3)9	3)12	3)15	3)18	3)21	3)24	3)27	3)30	3)33	3)36
÷4	4)0	4)4	4)8	4)12	4)16	4)20	4)24	4)28	4)32	4)36	4)40	4)44	4)48
÷5	5)0	5)5	5)10	5)15	5)20	5)25	5)30	5)35	5)40	5)45	5)50	5)55	5)60
÷6	6)0	6)6	6)12	6)18	6)24	6)30	6)36	6)42	6)48	6)54	6)60	6)66	6)72
÷7	7)0	7)7	7)14	7)21	7)28	7)35	7)42	7)49	7)56	7)63	7)70	7)77	7)84
÷8	8)0	8)8	8)16	8)24	8)32	8)40	8)48	8)56	8)64	8)72	8)80	8)88	8)96
÷9	9)0	9)9	9)18	9)27	9)36	9)45	9)54	9)63	9)72	9)81	9)90	9)99	9)108
÷10	10)0	10)10	10)20	10)30	10)40	10)50	10)60	10)70	10)80	10)90	10)100	10)110	10)120
÷11	11)0	11)11	11)22	11)33	11)44	11)55	11)66	11)77	11)88	11)99	11)110	11)121	11)132
÷12	12)0	12)12	12)24	12)36	12)48	12)60	12)72	12)84	12)96	12)108	12)120	12)132	12)144